Praise for *Deuteronomy for the Church*

"The book of Deuteronomy, set in the liminal space between desert and promised land, between the leadership of Moses and that of Joshua, offers many of Scripture's foundational passages. Intriguing in its origins and complex in its genre, Deuteronomy is part sermon addressed to a generation that had never known home, part 'message in a bottle' for generations centuries hence, part updated law, part primordial poetry. In this new book, Eugene Boring plumbs Deuteronomy's—and the theological tradition's—depths, using the Shema ('Hear, O Israel') as a starting point, but traveling beyond the threshold of Canaan to early Judaism and early Christianity—and beyond them to those who hear Moses speaking today. Boring engagingly interweaves understanding of Deuteronomy itself, its New Testament echoes, and contemporary theology and cultural experience, offering a full tour for people who have no idea how all-encompassing such a journey could be."

—Patricia K. Tull, Louisville
Presbyterian Theological Seminary

"Veteran interpreter that he is, Eugene Boring has been prepping his entire life for the writing of this remarkable book. He begins with Israel's most important Scripture, the book of Deuteronomy. And then he writes an expansive, breathtaking, mind-bending, life-redefining exposition. His own wheelhouse in New Testament studies leads to important extensive linkages to the books of Romans and 1 Corinthians. The book teems with contemporaneity through an appeal to Ricoeur and Gadamer. In the end this is a winsome, accessible biblical theology that soars well beyond critical issues to what matters for lives lived faithfully. We have nothing else like this book; it merits close and sustained engagement."

—Walter Brueggemann,
author of *Old Testament Theology*

"Inviting. Informed. Provocative. Eugene Boring's new book, *Deuteronomy for the Church*, helps theologically curious readers hear again the most influential book of the Old Testament, not as a dry collection of obscure rules, but as a vibrant quest for a people's robust identity. He captures the oral nature of the book as it retells Israel's story of redemption for new generations and explores the contours of faithful life together as a people repeatedly liberated from the forces of evil. In doing so, he helps the modern church as it also reclaims its heritage as a community of grace. By leading us through Deuteronomy as it narrates stories, gives laws, and calls for decision, Boring helps his readers understand that the ancient text can be totally contemporary."

—Mark W. Hamilton,
Abilene Christian University

DEUTERONOMY FOR THE CHURCH

DEUTERONOMY FOR THE CHURCH

Who We Are, What God Requires

M. Eugene Boring

FORTRESS PRESS
MINNEAPOLIS

DEUTERONOMY FOR THE CHURCH
Who We Are, What God Requires

Cover design: Kristin Miller

Print ISBN: 978-1-5064-7475-5
eBook ISBN: 978-1-5064-7476-2

For Russell Pregeant

In gratitude for fifty-eight years of friendship

Contents

Preface

"Hear, O Israel . . ."

This book, for author and readers alike, is an exercise in improving our hearing. This means, in the first place, hearing the biblical text of Deuteronomy itself, listening for the Word of God that comes through human words. The book will explore the value of historical study of the Bible, as that facilitates coming within hearing distance of what the biblical texts want to say to us and, through us, to others. The book does not necessarily assume that we will be preaching, teaching, or discussing Deuteronomy in or out of the pulpit or classroom—though that may likely happen. The goal is to enhance our competence in hearing and understanding every biblical text we engage.

"Can you hear me?" is not a yes/no question. Every reading of Deuteronomy is a hearing test. The effort to listen with insight and understanding may call for minor adjustments in our hearing aids, paying more attention to our doctor ("doctor" means "teacher"—cf. "doctrine"), getting a second opinion, or even changing doctors.

In its canonical context in the Christian Bible, Deuteronomy addresses 'all Israel,' the whole people of God of every time and place, the already/not-yet generation living between deliverance from bondage to the pharaohs of this world and the good life in the promised land.[1] Believers in the One God of Israel need to know how to live faithfully as the people of God in the midst of a multicultural society of peoples with their own gods but who still belong to the One God who created and loves them.

'All Israel' is addressed—women and men, masters and slaves, clergy and laity, rich and poor, educated and illiterate. Israel includes those who already know the stories of Israel from ancient Abraham and Sarah to modern Moses and Zipporah, just as it includes those who have only lately been incorporated into the people of God, still thinking of the world and life in terms of the values and culture of their previous bondage. Deuteronomy is a people's book, but its sharpest focus is directed to Israel's preachers and teachers, the priests, elders, and other leaders (including parents) charged with preaching and teaching the transforming word that called Israel into being, nourishes them for the journey, and equips them for their mission.

Like Deuteronomy, this book presumes to address 'all Israel.' Like Deuteronomy, this book intends to speak more directly to preachers and teachers in the community of faith responsible for mediating and interpreting the words of Scripture to the church. In its peripheral vision, the book also welcomes both professional academic scholars as well as readers who may not consider themselves insiders but have a wholesome curiosity about the Bible and the faith. And like Deuteronomy, this book is launched into the world with the prayer that it will help the people of God achieve a deeper understanding of who we are and what God requires of us.

I am grateful for the many students, colleagues, and fellow ministers (the categories largely overlap) who over the years have shared insights, given constructive criticism, and encouraged the completion of this project. As I began to work intensively on Deuteronomy three years ago, two professors who are experts in Deuteronomic literature reviewed my initial efforts and kept me from straying too far from mainstream Old Testament scholarship: Mark Hamilton of Abilene Christian University and Raymond F. Person Jr. of Northern Ohio University. More recently, as the book neared completion, the whole manuscript was read carefully by a group of ordained ministers who made suggestions and corrections large and small: Bobby Wayne Cook, Charlotte Coyle, Russell Brammer, and Roger Mcmurry. Jerry L. Coyle read the penultimate draft with the eyes of a practicing attorney and teacher in the church who deals every day with issues of personal ethics and social justice. Carey C. Newman, executive editor of Fortress Press, has been a trustworthy source of encouragement and guidance on major items of form and content. I offer heartfelt thanks to each and all for their contribution to this book. I also express my sincere gratitude to University Christian Church of Fort Worth, Texas, and Rush Creek Christian Church of

Arlington, Texas, for invitations to present preliminary versions of some of this material as lectures and to Brite Divinity School of Fort Worth for the invitation to deliver the McFadden Lectures at Texas Christian University Minister's Week in 2019, where I was much encouraged by the response of ministers to my efforts to help preachers and teachers interpret Deuteronomy for the life of the church.

Several drafts of the manuscript were read and annotated by Russell Pregeant, to whom this book is dedicated. Russ and I happened to meet as we stood in the registration line on the first day of the 1963 fall semester at Vanderbilt Divinity School. We had come by different routes to study New Testament theology with Leander Keck, our Doktorvater (as we said in those days), who had a formative influence on each of us that endures to this day. Russ and I became immediate friends, beginning a serious theological conversation (theology includes ethics and politics) that has continued nearly sixty years and is still going strong, sometimes in the language of "Putdownese," in which we are both fluent. Our conversations, and his solid books on biblical and political ethics, have influenced me deeply. Said in straightforward English, with gratitude and respect.

I

Deuteronomy

Theology That Laughs and Sings

Chapter 1

The First Commandment and Sarah's Laughter

This book begins, and will conclude, with the question of *ethics*: How should we live our one and only life, who gets to say, and how do *they* know? With this issue always in mind, we will explore a key segment of the Bible: Deuteronomy, with side-glances at the Deuteronomistic History, Joshua–2 Kings. We will seek to sharpen the kind of binocular vision to which both Deuteronomy and Jesus call us, with the same twin focus: the church as the people of God and the life appropriate to this community of faith—who we are and what God requires of us.

There was once a Jewish teacher who inquired of a colleague, an itinerant second-career lay preacher, "Which commandment is the first of all?" (Mark 12:28). Jesus cited the Shema from Deuteronomy 6:4–6:

> The first is, "Hear, O Israel: the Lord our God, the Lord is one; you shall love the Lord your God with all your heart, and with all your soul, and with all your mind, and with all your strength." The second is this, "You shall love your neighbor as yourself." There is no other commandment greater than these.
>
> Then the scribe said to him, "You are right, Teacher; you have truly said that 'he is one, and besides him there is no other'; and 'to love him with all the heart, and with all the understanding, and with all the strength,' and 'to love one's neighbor as oneself,'—this is much more important than all whole burnt offerings and sacrifices." (Mark 12:29–33)

Jesus responded with a theological confession of faith, joining his voice with the whole Jewish community's affirmation that the One God is the Lord,[1] the God of Israel. Every ethic rests on a faith, a conviction, a coming-to-terms with the question built into every human life: Is there anything or anyone more definitive for the way I live my life than my own common sense, feelings, aspirations, conscience? Are we alone, on our own in the universe, responsible for creating our own sense of decency and worth? Or is there a command, a Commander? This is not, of course, a theoretical question, religion-as-hobby: "This is no trifling matter for you, but rather your very life" (Deut 32:47). This book will probe the theological foundations for the ethic of both Deuteronomy and Jesus.

The whole Jewish and Christian tradition follows Deuteronomy and Jesus in pointing to the double commandment of love as the most important of the Torah's 613 commands. There are numerous references to God's love for humans and human love for other human beings, but the Bible's first command to love God is found in the Shema, Deuteronomy 6:5, given to 'all Israel' on the plains of Moab as fundamental for the covenant law of the people of God, within sight of the promised land. This is rather late in the Bible's story of creation and humanity as a whole.

If one opens the Bible to the first page and begins looking for the first commandment God gives to human beings, it is already there in the first chapter: "Be fruitful and multiply, and fill the earth and subdue it" (Gen 1:28). This command was given to all humanity (*Adam* = Man, Humanity; *Eve* = Mother of All Life; Gen 2:7; 3:20; 4:25). This command was given in the garden of Eden, before anything had gone wrong, before there was an Israel or a church. God addressed it to all the human beings in the world. They were God's people, for God had created them and blessed them. The first commandment is based on the gift of life and the blessing of humanity, already given unconditionally, before any human being had heard or violated a single command. Ever after, God's command is preceded by and issues from God's grace. Adam and Eve belonged to the newly minted creation, pronounced "good" six times before the climactic "God saw everything that he had made, and indeed, it was very good" (Gen 1:31). The first commandment came directly from God; our primal parents, Humanity and Mother of All Life, didn't get it from a book or from a church or preacher. The first commandment was not a "Thou shalt not . . ."; it was not against anything but was a positive, upbeat command dealing with the most intimate of human relationships and with the ultimate purpose of God the Creator. God had created human beings because God is love; God wanted people/children he could love and who could respond to love. God wanted relationship with other loving beings; God didn't want to dwell in eternal solitude.

God not only speaks but wants to be spoken to, in prayer and praise. God didn't want to be God without us.[2]

The command to "fill the earth and subdue it" is also a promise, repeated in various contexts (Gen 1:28; 8:17; 9:1, 7; Lev 26:9; Jer 23:3; Ezek 36:11; cf. Gen 12:3; 28:14; 35:11; Acts 3:25). God's earth is to be filled with God's peoples,[3] every individual among them created in God's image, all of them commissioned to participate in God's purpose of subduing the world's chaos and bringing God's creation to fulfillment. In the tradition of the Jewish people, their own story is understood as incorporated into the Story of Everything[4] that began with Adam and Eve. The first command human beings heard was to bring children into this world, to increase the number of God's peoples until the children of God filled the earth. Part of the blessedness of being human is to participate in God's own creative work. Human beings are not cocreators but God's servants in God's world, filling the whole earth with God's peoples. *Subdue* means not to "dominate and exploit" but to subject the chaotic elements that remain in the world to the will of God the Creator, to participate in God's good rule over creation. People who participate in this original Great Commission given to all humanity laugh and sing, and they pray, "Thy kingdom come, thy will be done *on earth*. . . ." The Creator's gift of life and blessing is unconditional, and the promise knows no bounds.

The Deuteronomic teachers had no idea they were writing texts that would eventually be understood as part of the larger canonical corpus. They did know they were launching their instructions into the historical context of the people of God in which there were other and different traditions and texts that claimed to be testimonies to the saving acts of God, instructions for what Israel should be and do. These testimonies included texts, streams of tradition, and clusters of songs, stories, and laws later to be identified as J, E, and P, or embedded in Israel's histories, prophetic writings, and the Psalter. At a critical juncture in the life of Israel, Judah, and the Diaspora, the Deuteronomic preachers and teachers call for a renewed vision of who Israel is and what God calls Israel to do and be, charging Israel to realize and recover its primal identity, way of life, and mission. The story told in Deuteronomy and the Deuteronomistic History assumes it belongs to this larger story that became the mainstream of Israel's tradition. The narrative of Deuteronomy can only be understood as a segment of this grand narrative, represented for the original reading audience by the story line of what is now Genesis–2 Kings. Israelites who don't already know this story are encouraged to learn it from their parents and teachers, from the bearers of Israel's tradition (Deut 4:32; 6:6–9; 27:1, 9; 31:9–13; 32:7; 33:8–11). For Christian readers of the later canonical version, this narrative now extends from Genesis through Revelation.

The Universal Story. This Story of Everything that begins with creation proceeds through Noah, Abraham, and Moses to the plains of Moab, where Moses speaks in God's name to all Israel. This story tells us who *we* are. First, before we ever belonged to Israel or the church, we belonged to God's peoples by creation, whether we wanted to or not, whether we believed it or not. We didn't get to decide. The world didn't decide to be created; we didn't get a vote on whether to be born. God chose us before we ever chose God, or refused God, or were aware that there was a choice to be made. Listening to Moses in Deuteronomy, we become aware of our life as already underway from point A to point Z, unable to know what either end of the road is like. We are on the same road as all other human beings. This identity-question as community-en-route is encapsulated in Deuteronomy 1:28, "Where are we headed?" Note *we*. The question of identity is asked by a people on the way, a people *no longer* in the bondage of Egypt, a people *not yet* in the good life of the promised land. In a larger sense, this *we* identifies with all human beings, the human race, all God's creatures, also on a journey from creation to consummation. In Deuteronomy, there is no possibility that an individual listening to Moses's sermons on the plains of Moab might just decide to separate from the foibles of Israel and head off on their own for some gated community in Canaan to find their own bit of happiness by themselves. They cannot *not* belong to the people of God. Likewise, as a human being, I cannot *not* belong to God's peoples, the human race scattered about the earth (and other planets?). We shall see that all this is not speculative philosophical theory that may interest some people but a practical matter of Christian, and human, *ethics*, which by definition cannot be an individualistic question.

This *we* stands in contrast with the individualistic, existential *I* that focuses on "Who am *I*?" "What is the meaning of *my* life?" for in Deuteronomy and the Bible as a whole, my individual identity is bound up with a community. I do not and cannot exist as a human being by myself. We belong to humanity, and humanity belongs to God the Creator: all humanity comprises God's peoples. We are, all of us, cosmopolitans—citizens of the cosmos. Even if we have never been outside the county in which we were born, speak only our native language, and regard everyone else as "foreigners," as human beings we exist only in community. This belonging to the one human race, God's peoples created by the One God, is our identity, including our individual identity. We belong to Adam before we belong to Israel, Judah, or the United States or the synagogue, church, or *jamaat*. Being human involves learning to say "we."

That we all belong to the same universal story, that our individual and national stories are subplots of the Story of Everything, is not a matter of common sense, nor do we learn it by looking at the stars, our culture, or into our own hearts. That we belong to the human race created by God, that as human beings we belong to God's peoples, is something that must be revealed. We must be *told*, and if we believe it, it is because we have heard, in the biblical sense. "Faith comes by hearing / what is heard" is the climax and conclusion of the most extensive reference to Deuteronomy in the New Testament (Rom 10:5–17). In reading all that Deuteronomy has to say about God's choice of Israel, there is no suggestion that "other nations are . . . merely stage props in the Israelite drama of journeying into the occupied land of Canaan; those other nations are also recipients of God's ongoing care, concern, and protection."[5]

The Story Goes Awry. The story that began in Eden takes several sharp turns before it comes to Deuteronomy, Moses, and all Israel on the plains of Moab. By the fourth page of the Bible, the unimaginable catastrophe happened. Humanity had rebelled. Not just made a mistake, a misstep, as though they had trespassed, casually ignoring a "Do Not Walk on the Grass" sign on the lawns of Eden or a "Thank You for Not Picking the Fruit" sign posted on a tree. The snake got to the root of the matter: "God knows that when you eat of it . . . you will be like God" (Gen 3:5). The seed of suspicion was planted. The Creator is not on our side, wants to keep something good from us, doesn't want us to *know*, to have knowledge like adults. Humanity was not willing to be God's servants in God's world. They/we wanted to be like God, to be our own gods, did not want to have God as God. When the Bible calls this human compulsion "sin," it is not using a quaint old term for naughtiness, making a mistake, engaging in inappropriate behavior, or failing to live up to our highest ideals. It's not missing the mark, a failure to hit the target we aimed at, not even a "fall" from which we can get up, dust ourselves off, and try to do better next time. The first occurrence of the word *sin* in the Bible is in God's address to the first child born to Adam and Eve, who had just killed his younger brother: sin is a murderous power, always lurking at the door, seeking to enslave and pervert even our best efforts and highest aspirations (Gen 4:7; cf. the exposition of this image in Rom 6). In the biblical vocabulary for sin, the most formidable designation of this human compulsion is *pesha* (rebellion, rejection of constituted authority, as repeatedly mentioned in Amos 1–2). God is Creator and Lord, but humanity rebelled, worshipped itself and the creation rather than the Creator: "Ever since the creation of the world . . . though they knew God, they did not honor him as God or give thanks to him . . . [but] exchanged the truth about God for a lie and worshiped and served the creature rather than the Creator, who is blessed forever" (Rom 1:20–25). Humanity's rebellion was not just a personal matter, one in which "I'm not hurting anybody but myself":

> Earth felt the wound, and Nature from her seat
> Sighing through all her works gave signs of woe,
> That all was lost. (Milton, *Paradise Lost*, IX 780)

God expels humanity from the Garden into the world as we know it, the only world we have ever known or can know. Is this story a total disaster, or is there an upside? In the Garden, there had been no human culture, with its brutality and violence, but life in the Garden also lacked the beauty, joy, and satisfaction of human accomplishment. Eden had known neither the thrill of victory nor the agony of defeat. In Eden, there had not been, and could not have been, a Parthenon or Taj Mahal. No Homer or Shakespeare; no Milton, Goethe, or Dostoevsky; no Mozart, no Beethoven, no Handel, no Beatles. No Rembrandt, no Picasso. No cities. No money, no investment banking. No tools, no labor-saving devices, no inventions, no licensing, no patents. No education, no progress, no Industrial Revolution.

Outside the Garden, human potential and creativity are unleashed. People are no longer servants/serfs/slaves of the Deity but take responsibility for themselves and for the world. Civilization emerges. Cain's son Enoch, the first human being born outside the Garden, built a city (Gen 4:17). In cities, people are not merely individuals but divide up the work. All depend on one another—interdependent individuals who develop specialties for the sake of the community. All live on the bounty of the land, but not all are farmers or hunter-gatherers. Some plant, some cultivate, some harvest, some process and cook the food, some open and manage restaurants, some go out to eat. Community and a sense of responsible citizenship develop. A sense of ownership and pride in private property develops. Adam and Eve, freshly created, did not emerge into consciousness, look around, and say, "Wow! Who *owns* all this?" This is a postrebellion, outside-the-Garden question. The good life in the land now requires this sense of private property, ownership, pride of possession, and this requires law, economics, engineering, politics. Humanity increases, universities are founded that include not only departments of engineering and biology but departments of humanities where people learn their own history, literature, art, music—and language. Human culture increases, and so do evil and violence. Violence, or the threat of violence, is the given, simply the way the world works. No city can exist without police, no nation without military. Genesis 4–11 realistically describes things as they are, the only world *we* have ever known. Deal with it. Don't whine; you're not a victim. Get out there and get yours.

The story is not told to report the literal first stage of cultural anthropology. The Garden devoid of culture is not pictured as a situation that could have and should have lasted. The authors do not try to picture it as the "ideal" life, do not try to imagine what it could have been like ("What did Adam and Eve do all day?") nor how long it lasted. The biblical narrative theologian wants only to make a particular "point" from the post-Eden perspective, the only perspective we have or can have. The author tells the story knowing this first scene will end soon. There was no mythical golden age to which we should long to return. *God* does not want us to go back to the Garden—a flaming whirligig sword makes this impossible, and we should not dream about going back. The story moves very quickly from Eden to the post-Eden world of human culture, the world we know and live in. The Bible is a big book, its story is a long story, but by page four, the story is already outside the Garden and never looks back.

God expelled humanity from the Garden, but God did not abandon the world or humanity. Human beings, all of us, are still created in the image of God. Brother kills brother, God judges and condemns the murderer, but God also protects the murderer from lynch justice, and under God's protection, civilization flourishes. Violence also flourished, and the strong lived off the weak (Gen 6:11). Those who were good at it succeeded and "subdued the earth" in a grim perversion of God's original command. God met the world on its own terms, answered violence with violence: "God said to Noah, 'I have determined to make an end of all flesh, for the earth is filled with violence because of them; now I am going to destroy them along with the earth'" (Gen 6:13).

God started all over. But how? What kind of new beginning? God could have made a new Garden: Eden 1.1, Adam 2.0, Eve 2.0. *This* time God could have upgraded them, fixing the bugs in the first version so that the new model of humanity would be impervious to temptation and unable to rebel. The biblical author-theologians do not toy with such a fantasy. God works within the world and humanity already created, within the history of an earth and humanity already accursed (Gen 5:29). God chooses to start over with someone from the old humanity. The choice of Noah is given two explanations: God's grace (5:8) and Noah's righteousness (5:9), which are neither harmonized nor parceled out. This dialectic continues throughout the Bible (for our purposes, see especially Deut 4:32–40). Salvation is entirely by God's grace; salvation requires human response-ability in doing the will of God.

The flood came. All life was destroyed except that saved in the ark. God starts all over with one family, the only remnant of the old creation. Noah emerges from the ark, builds an altar, and worships the LORD. God makes a covenant with this saved remnant of all humanity and renews the original command to all human beings: "Be fruitful and multiply, and fill the earth" (Gen 9:1). But violence, even all-encompassing divine violence, had not solved the human problem, had not changed humanity. Noah planted a vineyard, drank its wine, got so drunk he didn't know what he was doing, and did something so evil, the biblical authors do not describe it—readers are left to imagine what brings the renewed curse on humanity. Slavery becomes part of the human scene. Humankind (*'adam*, Gen 11:5) rejected God's command to scatter, fill the earth, and subdue it as God's servants. Instead, they settled down and said to each other, "Come, let us build ourselves a city, and a tower with its top in the heavens, and let us make a name for ourselves" (Gen 11:4). Even after Noah and the flood, the rebellion continued. They still had the command to fill the earth with God's peoples. But they built a tower to make a name for themselves. God's judgment was to garble their language. A fractured humanity, a planet of human beings divided into groups that no longer speak the same language, do not understand one another, is the judgment of God.

Overkill, the divine violence of the flood, did not change humanity. But human violence and the divine violence of the flood had worked a change in God. The biblical authors, of course, have no interest in speculative philosophical discussions of the immutability and aseity of God and are not bothered by portraying God as one who can change his mind. This is what persons do, as a matter of their dependability and faithfulness. Israel's theological teachers who wrote the biblical texts are wholehearted in their commitment to represent God in personal terms, as affected by and responsive to the actions of others. God the faithful

Creator responds to human violence with sorrow and grief: "And the Lord was sorry ['repented,' KJV, ASV] that he had made humankind on the earth, and it grieved him to his heart" (Gen 6:6). After the horrific story of the flood, God hangs up his warrior's bow, like a repentant gunslinger hanging up his revolver, and places the bow in the clouds as the sign of hope and pledge of God's faithfulness to all humanity with the words "never again" (Gen 8:21). So what is God going to do? Start all over *again*? The story continues.

Within the *universal* story, there is a *particular* story. Within the grand narrative, there is a separate story-within-the-story, the key that opens up the whole. Within the story of *God's peoples*, there is the story of the *people of God*. God had made a covenant with the world and all the peoples within it. When they failed to respond in gratitude and obedience to their Creator, God made a covenant with a particular people for the sake of all people. The Creator has a plan for the creation and universal history. This is an essential dimension of the character of the Lord, a constituent element of belief in the personal God with a particular name, the Lord (Yhwh), not God in general. The One Eternal God, who is Author, Producer, Director, and Leading Actor in the Story of Everything, reveals that this grand narrative has an unlikely subplot. This means not that the Creator abandons the original story but that the Lord of all history now reveals his purpose at work within the story of one people for the sake of all.

What is God's plan? That the Lord could once again wipe everything out and start over is a possibility the Deuteronomic teachers have pondered and rejected (cf. Deut 9:8–29). God has already destroyed the rebellious people once and started over with Noah. It didn't work, and God has renounced violence. Nor does God say anything like "Don't worry; I'll send a Messiah, and whoever accepts him as their personal savior will go to heaven." Deuteronomy has an eschatology, but no explicit Christology—though the perspective and content of Deuteronomy provide imagery and vocabulary that Christian teachers of the New Testament period will use to formulate the meaning of Jesus Christ and eschatological salvation. So what's God's plan for the salvation of a lost world?

The narrative makes a dramatic, unpredictable turn at Genesis 12, designated by Walter Brueggemann as "perhaps the most important structural break in the Old Testament."[6] In Genesis 12:1–3, the Lord called Abraham and Sarah, an elderly, childless couple, and promised them a child. God's saving act to restore creation and bless all nations was to call a new community into being, to create a covenant people who would be God's witnesses and agents through whom God would bless the whole world. They were not Israelites or Jews. If the Jew/gentile distinction had existed then, they would have been gentiles. The LORD's unilateral gift of the covenant to Abraham and his descendants represented a shift

- from Genesis 1–11's focus on universal history and all humanity, with its culture of grandeur and horror, to the ups and downs of a particular, somewhat dysfunctional family.
- from a humanity living on God's *'eretz* (the earth, as in Gen 1:1) to a covenant community oriented to God's promise of a particular *'eretz* (the land, as in Gen 12:1).
- from a literary saga in which people live hundreds of years and a flood covers the whole earth to a more history-like narrative. This story within the Story utilizes traditional legendary materials and now names historical and history-like individuals, events, and places. Adam and his descendants lived for nine centuries and more, corresponding to other sagas of the ancient Near East; Abraham and Sarah, in their nineties, are considered old.
- from God's unilateral covenant with the world and all humanity to a particular covenant with one people for the sake of all God's peoples.

The covenant (*berith*) was not a contract or treaty negotiated between peers but a gift from a superior to subjects. Peoples of the ancient Near East were familiar with this scene: A powerful king sends an army during the night to surround a town some distance away. In the morning, the king's messenger speaks to the surprised townspeople: "I am your new king. You are my people. This is my covenant with you. I will protect you from your enemies and guarantee your peace and prosperity. From now on, you must obey the following laws." The people had no voice, no vote, in the decision to become part of the realm. They do have a choice in how they will respond.

Though the comprehensive biblical story shifts its focus after Genesis 12, it is still the same narrative, the story of the One God who is Lord of all creation and all history. The One who called the universe into being by his powerful Word now calls a new people into being by the same powerful Word (Deut 32:6–15). This community-creating Word was addressed not to the chaotic void but to persons created in God's own image. In contrast to God's unilateral, unconditional care for all creation in Genesis 1–11, there is a new focus on the human response of *faith*. In the previous epoch of the universal story, in and out of the Garden, the LORD God speaks, and the world and (some) people obey, but it is never said that anyone believed. Faith emerges in response to God's Word, God's promise.

In Genesis 12:1–3, God calls Abraham from his native land and promises to show him a new land and make a great nation from him, to bless all the families of the earth through him. It is not yet said that Abraham believes, but he obeys, and in a later dramatic scene, the narrator reveals that Abraham's response to God's *command* was his *faith* in God's *promise* of a people so numerous it could not be imagined (Gen 15:1–6). This story contains the first instance of the word for "faith" in the Bible, as Abraham "believed the LORD; and the LORD reckoned it to him as righteousness" (Gen 15:6). Abraham's faith is not merely that a particular biological miracle would happen as the fulfillment for the old couple's frustrated and abandoned hopes for a family. God promises uncountable "descendants of Abraham." This scene, this text, becomes paradigmatic for later Christian theology (e.g., Gal 3:6–9; Heb 11:8–12); the scene is not complete until Genesis 22, when, in obedience to God's command, Abraham is willing to sacrifice the promised son who is finally born as the sole bearer of the fulfillment of God's mysterious purpose. A reminder: The Deuteronomic teachers presuppose familiarity with this larger story as the precondition for hearing, believing, and obeying the Word of God that comes through Deuteronomy.

But "faith" was not a once-and-for-all event that could be checked off the list of God's requirements. Faith was neither a condition for God's acceptance, a "step" in the plan of salvation, nor "Abraham's response to the challenge." The message is not "We, too, should believe, just as Abraham did." It's not about Abraham. The whole story is about what God has done, is doing, and will do and the unlikely role that human beings will play in God's plan. The stories that follow God's personal and effective call of Abraham reveal the mixed human motives always involved in the response of faith. In the next episode following Abraham's call, he takes Sarah and his clan to Egypt, passes Sarah off as his sister to save his own skin, increases his property holdings, and is expelled by the pharaoh when his duplicity is exposed—hardly an exemplary model of the "life of faith." Yet it's not about Abraham; it's about God, the same God who did not abandon the murderer Cain when his parents had been expelled from the Garden, the faithful God who both judged and saved him, the God who did not start all over with someone else (Gen 4:1–16; cf. the Deuteronomic passage in Exod 32:7–14). The promise remained valid.

Time passes. No child is born. Abraham and Sarah decide that the fulfillment of God's promise requires them to take some initiative themselves, "just in case." With the help of a surrogate mother at their disposal, the household slave girl Hagar, a child is born when Abraham is eighty-six (Gen 16:1–15). This breach of trust does not cause God to negate the promise (think Adam and Eve; think Cain; think Noah!). God in fact gives the new baby a significant name, Ishmael, or "God hears"—but it was Hagar, not Abraham, whom God heard (Gen 16:11). Even for "heroes of the faith," sincere prayer is always "I do believe, help my unbelief!" (Mark 9:24 NAB).

All this is the backstory of the episode that begins when the aged nomadic chieftain shows hospitality to three weary travelers who promise that he and his wife will soon have a child (Gen 18:1–15). Readers whose minds have not been dulled by familiarity may find this story disappointing, fantastic, weird, or simply laughable: the primal command had been to be fruitful, multiply, and fill the earth with God's children. The original promise had been incredible enough. Now it is specifically reaffirmed to people who have lied and tried to manipulate God's plan according to their own common sense, and anyway, they are *way* too old to be starting a family. *This* is the way God's promise will be fulfilled? The pensive reader might also think of the beginning of the Gospel story in Mark 1:1–20. God's promised Messiah finally appears. Jesus prepares for the task. He is baptized, tested by Satan, preaches the advent of the promised kingdom of God. It's about time. The time of preparation is over. What will Jesus do to confirm the faithfulness of God's promise and initiate the fulfillment of God's plan? He calls four fishermen, then others—twelve (!) people as pledges and agents of the present-and-coming kingdom, the embodiment of a renewed Israel. One will betray him. Their leader will deny that he ever knew him. They all abandon him and flee. *This* is the beginning of God's plan for the salvation of the world? Should we just laugh it off with a knowing smile?

Sarah of the dead womb, Abraham of the numb genitals, receive an impossible promise. Without applying for the job, and way past the time when their biological clocks had stopped ticking, they are hospitable to some strangers who announce that they will be participants in fulfilling the ultimate plan of God to fill the earth and bless all its peoples:

> The LORD appeared to Abraham by the oaks of Mamre. As he sat at the entrance of his tent in the heat of the day, he looked up and focused his eyes, and there they were, three men standing nearby. When he saw them, he ran to meet them, bowed his face to the ground, and said:
>
> "My lords, if I find favor with you, do not pass by your servant. Let a little water be brought, and wash your feet, and rest yourselves under the tree. Let me bring a little bread, so you may refresh yourselves, and then you may go on your way—after all, you've come to your servant."
>
> "Do as you have said," they responded.
>
> So Abraham rushed into the tent to Sarah and said, "Hurry up and prepare five gallons of fine flour, knead it, and make cakes." Abraham ran to the herd and took a calf, tender and good, and gave it to the servant, who prepared it quickly. Then he took butter, milk, and the veal he had prepared and set it before them. He stood by them under the tree while they ate.
>
> They said to him, "Where's your wife Sarah?"
>
> "She's right here, in the tent," he said.
>
> Then one said, "I will surely be back here about this time next year, and by then your wife Sarah will have a son." (author's translation)

How will they respond? They could follow a typical, respected, decent human pattern: "No, thanks, I'll just live my own life, have my own brand of spirituality, mind my own business. I don't try to impose my religion on anyone else, and I ask them to show me the same respect. Anyway, this saving-the-world business is not really my thing. Sure, I try to live a decent life, be nice to other people, go to church sometimes, but I just want to live a happy life; have good health, a nice family and a few friends, a pleasant home and job; and live my own life." This would be an honest response. We could hardly blame them.

An aside for preachers and teachers on this Genesis text, a "Bible story" about Abraham and Sarah: We all need to be wary of the "life application" approach to every Bible story of the sort that looks for a "lesson for today" in every text, the moral-of-the-story perspective. This story has no intention of "teaching us" anything like "If we have faith, God will do impossible things for us too." Especially childless couples longing for a baby to love must not be burdened with guilt or falsely encouraged that if they had faith like Abraham and Sarah, God would bless them with a baby too. Every newborn child is a gift from God, but receiving this blessing is not a matter of our believing hard enough. Abraham and Sarah are not asked to believe or do anything else. There is nothing to join, no pledge card to sign. It's not about them but an announcement of incredible good news of what God will do, what will happen nine months in the future, in the ultimate future of God's plan for all people. Scary.

> Sarah had been listening at the tent entrance behind him. Now Abraham and Sarah were elderly, in their old age. Sarah was long past menopause. So Sarah laughed, thinking to herself, "After I've gotten old, and my husband is old too, we're going to have another honeymoon?"
>
> The LORD said to Abraham, "Why did Sarah laugh, and say, 'What, me have a baby? At my age?'
>
> "Is anything impossible for the LORD? I will be back at the appointed time next year, and by then Sarah will have a son."
>
> But Sarah denied it and said, "I didn't laugh," for she was afraid. But the LORD said, "*Oh yes, you laughed alright.*" (Gen 18:1–15; author's translation; cf. 17:15–21; 21:1–7)

Well, she *did* laugh. And the biblical authors and editors must have considered the story important, for they include three versions of it. Nonetheless, it may seem strange to begin a book about Deuteronomy with a story that features the laughter of Abraham and Sarah. But if we were to simply begin with Deuteronomy 1:1, we soon learn that the Deuteronomic teacher presupposes that 'all Israel' knows that their own story is included in the comprehensive story of Genesis–2 Kings and that the Deuteronomic School sees themselves as writing the interpretative key to the larger story. In this story, the election of Abraham and Sarah and their descendants is definitive, pivotal. Much of the meaning of this story is focused in Genesis 18. Laughter is an indispensable element in the grand narrative.

But why in the world did she respond to God's announcement with laughter? If we could see the expression on her face and hear her tone of voice, we would know how to understand this curious biblical text. "Biblical" movies that include this scene solve the problem for us—in fact, they don't even let us raise the question. A part of the problem with the genre shift in going from biblical words to wide screen, from the verbal medium of the Bible to the visual media of the stage drama and the movies, is that the audience becomes accustomed to being spectators with no hermeneutical responsibility, and such interpretive questions are not allowed to arise. Ready-made answers are already there on the stage or screen, without the audience ever being aware that what they see is already an interpretation. Sarah's facial expression, tone of voice, and body language are already determined by the screenwriter and director and can only convey their interpretation. But we cannot be spectators when reading the Bible, merely observing the interpretations others have already imposed on it. Holy Scripture insists that we participate in the tough questions of how it is to be interpreted (see "Biblical 'Hearing' versus Cultural 'Seeing'" in ch. 3). Why is a scene like this included three times in the Bible? How should we understand Sarah's laughter?

Is it the *spontaneous, happy laughter* with one's partner, anticipating the joy of sex? Should we imagine the aged Sarah and Abraham laughing together as they envision the restoration of youth and sexual intimacy? Abraham is a hundred, Sarah ninety. It's been a while. This interpretation is quite possible. The Bible is hardly prudish about such things, and the noun *'edna* ("sexual pleasure" in Gen 18:12) might point us to this interpretation.

Or is it *sitcom laughter*? Abraham gives Sarah the bedroom look, and she laughs—but in a different tone: "Yeah, right. *You wish!*" She laughs, and we, the audience, laugh along with her and suppose we've dealt with an interesting Bible story. Jesus and Moses had a sense of humor, maybe even God does, so it's OK to have a few chuckles in church and Sunday school—after all, this Christianity stuff is not all gloom and doom, and "Bible study" can be *fun*, and we can all have a good laugh and go home.

Or is it "*nervous laughter*?" In a stressful situation where we might be embarrassed by our ignorance or some other perceived threat to our self-esteem, we might laugh because we want to make ourselves or others think what we are encountering is not really to be taken seriously. Politicians can laugh when a reporter raises a question that might lose votes no matter how it is answered, and preachers and professors can dismiss honest questions with a laugh without risking either an answer or an "I don't know."

There is a more serious version of such laughter, used as a cover for what is really going on. Such laughter can be a way of dealing with the holy, the presence and claim of God, when the most personal and intimate experiences of my life start being part of a conversation that deals with the purpose of God and the meaning of our life, of history, of the universe. God is not necessarily a fun person to be with, and in the presence of the holy, one can make a joke, get off the hook, and appear to have everything under control and be relieved that they have dealt with it. When things get too serious, just laugh, and everyone is more comfortable. Someone dies. *Dies*. It may be a twelve-year-old girl, just about to bud into womanhood. At the funeral, people cry. That's what one does at funerals. In biblical times, there were professional mourners who wailed at funerals. It's too bad, but things like this happen. We can deal with it. Then an itinerant preacher shows up and speaks about waking her up from the world of the dead. They *laugh* (Mark 5:40). In the last several years, it has become customary in much of the United States to tell funny stories about the deceased as part of the funeral service. This can be an appropriate aspect of celebrating an essential dimension of the person's life, a sincere tribute, even a way of not letting death and the grave have the last laugh. It can also be a way of not facing up to the reality of death, a way of dealing with the claim that there is One who raises the dead. At least twice, the early Christian preachers and teachers who composed our New Testament texts bring this story of Abraham and Sarah into the context of faith in the resurrection (Rom 4:13–25; Heb 11:8–19).

All these overtones may have been present in Sarah's laughter, but when she denies she laughed at all, God will not let her off the hook. God took her laughter seriously. Sarah and Abraham needed to deal with something so big and serious that it is *too good to be true*. They are addressed not by God in general but by YHWH, the LORD, the God of Israel, the Creator who has a purpose for the whole of creation, the God who promises and commands, the God who calls them to be involved in his plan for the whole world. "By this time next year you will have a baby" announces not only the fulfillment of an impossible hope and dream for their personal lives but that it somehow fits into the eternal purpose of the One True God for the whole universe. Jesus calls four guys away from their everyday lives where they're working hard to make a living for their families. His two-word "follow me" calls them to participate in the kingdom of God that was no longer a distant hope but had already come near. What would it mean to take the gospel seriously? Better to just laugh it off?

There is another kind of laughter. The impossible happens. The child is born (Gen 21:1–6). They name him "Isaac," a little one-word Hebrew sentence that means "He laughs / laughed / will laugh." (The Hebrew verb form does not specify the time to which the action refers, which must often be determined by the broader context.) It is a strange name and unique. There is only one person in the Bible named Isaac. The biblical narrative has several "Marys" and "Simeons," and four different people named "Jesus." There are even other "Ishmaels." But only one Isaac. The Ishmael story ("God hears") in Genesis 16–17 is paired with the Isaac story ("He laughs") that evokes Sarah's laughter in Genesis 18 and raises the same two questions: "*Who* laughs?" and "What *kind* of laughter?"

Who laughs? Who is the "he" of "He laughs"? The grammatical gender of the verb form is masculine, so Sarah can't be the subject. Perhaps "he laughs" refers to Abraham, the happy father. The subject could be Isaac himself. He may well have been a happy baby. We know stories about his later life that feature his laughter. As a grown man, he is observed fondling Rebekah as the happily married couple play and laugh together (Gen 26:6–11). The "he" could be generalizing, "one," "whoever," which would fit Genesis 21:6: "Everyone who hears will laugh with me." Any of these interpretations are possible. The text does not explain. The hearer must ponder and decide. The most challenging possibility, also the most probable, seems to be signaled by verse 6: "God has brought laughter for me; everyone who hears will laugh with me." The phrase can have the pedestrian meaning "Everybody who hears about Abraham and Sarah's new baby will celebrate the happy event along with us." "Laugh and the world laughs with you." However, two features of the text and its wider context point toward a more theological meaning. Deuteronomic teachers would resonate with the story at this theological level. *Everyone* and *hear* are loaded words in their theology. That everyone will finally hear, that all people will finally join in the eschatological joy of the triumph of God's kingdom, that the descendants of Abraham and Sarah will finally be an uncountable, joyful multitude filling the earth, is the eschatological vision of the Deuteronomists. Most interpreters agree that *God* is the subject of the little sentence-name "He laughs." In the parallel story of Ishmael's birth, after Abraham, Sarah, and Hagar had attempted to get God's promise fulfilled in their own way, the new baby had been named Ishmael (*yishmaᶜel*, "God hears," 16:11), a linguistic counterpart to Isaac (*yiṣḥḥāq*, "He laughs"). It seems best to read "Ishmael" in Genesis 16:11 as "God has heard" and "Isaac" in 21:3 as "God will laugh," readings supported by both grammar and context. It is not laughing-at, which excludes and hurts but God's ultimately inclusive laughing-with. Thus Abraham and Sarah are listed in the Believers' Hall of Fame of Hebrews 11 not only because of the birth of Isaac but because they "considered him faithful who had promised," whose descendants would be "as many as the stars of heaven and as the innumerable grains of sand by the seashore" (Heb 11:11–12). Unlimited. Innumerable. The laughter that includes Abraham and Sarah is God's own laughter that finally includes everyone.

The laughter of God rings through the Old Testament. Especially the Psalter, filled with the tears and lamentations of a people often subjected to the world's injustice, includes the laughter of God. To be sure,

God, too, grieves at human sinfulness (Gen 6:5–6), and Jesus himself joins the weeping of humanity and laments the sins of the beloved city Jerusalem (John 11:35; cf. Matt 23:37–38). Nonetheless, God's eschatological laughter is not mockery but the joyful laughter when everything finally turns out all right, the laughter God initiates and shares. Israel's worship book repeatedly reverberates with God's eschatological laughter of what is / ought to be / will be shared with all God's peoples (Pss 2:4; 37:12–13; 52:6; 59:8; 126:2). The editors of the Psalter seem to have placed the combination of Psalms 1 and 2 as the introduction to the collection of Israel's prayers and praises that celebrate the rule of God over the whole creation. Israel's worship was filled not only with anguished lamentations that God's kingdom has not yet eliminated the suffering and tragedies of human life but with joyful confidence in God's final triumph. The Psalter was influential in the formation of Deuteronomic theology (see ch. 7). Its introit presents a key text:

> The one enthroned in the heavens is already laughing;
> the LORD has them in derision. (Ps 2:4; author's translation)

The scene is the enthronement of the new Judean king (or perhaps the annual reenactment of the enthronement ceremony). The nations and their kings mutter and plot, "Now is our chance, now we'll reassert our own rule over the world." But the real ruler of the world, not only of Israel and Judah but of all the nations, is already and always enthroned in the heavens. The psalm celebrates God's promise to the newly anointed Messiah, "I will make the nations your heritage, and the ends of the earth your possession" (Ps 2:8). These words may not be dismissed as mere hyperbole, typical royal hype at the inauguration. They echo the promise of the faithful God in Genesis 12:1–3, and anticipate the prayer of the people of God, "Thy kingdom come, thy will be done on earth. . . ." This God has a plan for the world.

The inauguration of the new Israelite king represents the rule of God that is / ought to be / will be the ultimate reality of God's good creation. When God laughs, this is the opposite of that nervous laughter trying to cover up its lack of confidence, nor is it merely divine scornful laughter at the pomposity of human beings who build their own towers and strut around the earth trying to convince themselves and others of their own importance. It is the relaxed, confident laughter of One who knows that neither human pride nor human suffering is the last word about the reality of life in God's good creation. It is anticipated in the capable, strong, virtuous woman of Proverbs 31:25: "Strength and dignity are her clothing, and she laughs at the time to come." It is anticipated in the laughter of trusting, carefree children, but it is not childish. It is the laughter of a big family—*big* family—family of God, all together. It is the laughter of the one who taught us to call God Father, to regard one another as brother and sister, the one who said we would never enter the kingdom of God unless we become like little children—not glorifying immaturity and childishness, but encouraging us to grow up into the inheritance of the children of God, not an entrance qualification, but a description, prediction, and promise of life together in the kingdom. It is not a Freudian projection for those who need a father figure but means finally being delivered from the nervous laughter of anxious self-concern, when "the creation itself will be set free from its bondage to decay and will obtain the freedom of the glory of the children of God" (Rom 8:21, which goes on to cite Deuteronomy). Psalm 2 already projects this grand vision of God's future, instructing those who (suppose they) now rule the earth, "Serve the Lord with reverent, worshipful awe, and rejoice in him with trembling" (Ps 2:10–11, as the LXX rightly translates; author's translation). This laughter resounds in the voice from heaven at Jesus's baptism, celebrating the reality that one has been anointed who will finally represent God's rule that will include all people and stretch to the ends of the earth (Ps 2:2, 4, 7–8; cf. Matt 3:17; Mark 1:11; Luke 3:22; John 1:33–34; Acts 13:33; Heb 1:2; Rev 11:15; 12:5; 19:15). This is God's laughter in which all will join when the prayer Jesus taught his disciples is fully answered, when his kingdom comes and his will is done on earth, when the promise made to Abraham and Sarah is completely fulfilled and the peace of God prevails on this earth. It is the Father's laughter, when all the children are safely home, the laughter around the table at the ultimate thanksgiving dinner.

Jesus's imagery for the present and coming kingdom of God explicitly pictured God's eschatological laughter, already anticipating the time when lamentation becomes laughter and the whole creation will join in the joyful good times of the messianic banquet:

> "Blessed are you who are hungry now,
> for you will be filled.
> "Blessed are you who weep now,
> for you will laugh." (Luke 6:21; cf. John 16:20–22)

In the story, Abraham and Sarah don't understand the meaning of their own nervous laughter. But the narrator does, and the biblical author lets us readers anticipate this final reality, foreshadowed by all human joy and laughter. Think of the best dinner party you've ever been to, the best family Thanksgiving celebration, multiply it by infinity, the Ultimate Homecoming, good things to eat and drink, everybody is there, good stories all around, back from Jericho and Megiddo, back from Waterloo, Little Big Horn, Gettysburg, Dunkirk, Pork Chop Hill, back from Vietnam, back from Afghanistan, back from Dachau, Auschwitz, My Lai, and Abu Ghraib—victims and perpetrators, all together. Around one table. Lamentation not repressed, it's over, behind us now. Not innocence, not blame. *Laughter.*

This is the story the Deuteronomic teachers understood to be the story of the world and of our individual lives, the story "that knows laughter, delight, healing, transformation and life are at the bottom of things."[7] This is the story of God's creation, of all God's peoples, the story of 'all Israel,' the covenant people of God, the story of where we came from, where we are, and where we are finally going, the story of who we are and what God requires of us. It is a strange but true story.

Chapter 2

Deuteronomy

A Strange but True Story

When the narrative curtain on the Deuteronomic drama opens, all the Israelites in the world are gathered on the plains of Moab just east of the Jordan. In its present biblical context, Deuteronomy's opening scene already looks back on the creation and human rebellion, the formation of Israel and their deliverance from Egypt, their wanderings and escapades in the wilderness as told in Exodus and Numbers. 'All Israel,' their journey to the promised land almost over, wait on the East Bank of the Jordan for Moses to appear and speak to them.

The Lord, the God of Israel's ancestors, had delivered the Israelite slaves from Egypt, had brought them to Sinai—called "Horeb" in Deuteronomy—had given them the Ten Commandments, and had promised to lead them to a land of their own. They moved closer and were camped at Kadesh Barnea, southwest of their goal, almost in sight of the promised land. But they were afraid and looked back at the security and dependability of the only life they had ever known, the life of slavery. It was hard to look ahead, to trust God's promise, to venture into a life they had never known. They played it safe and turned down the opportunity and threat presented by the promised land. The God who had saved them from Egypt and granted them his covenant and promises now judged their disobedience and withdrew his presence. The Israelites then made an abortive attempt to take the land on their own. Catastrophic results. When God saw their refusal to hear, he was wrathful and swore, "Not one of these—not one of this evil generation—shall see the good land that I swore to give to your ancestors" (Deut 1:35). Not even Moses, who was excluded along with the others. The only exceptions were Joshua and Caleb, who had heard, trusted, and acted in obedience to God's promise.

A new generation grew up in the wilderness between Egypt and Canaan—an in-between generation that had *never been* in Egypt and were *not yet* in Canaan.[1] They had known neither the life of slavery in Egypt nor the splendor of Egyptian civilization and its religions, and they do not yet know the cultural religion of Canaan. Their future is to move into the land of Canaan, where they will be surrounded by an impressive, advanced culture with a vigorous spiritual and religious life. They had all been born as Israelites, belonged to the people of God, were heirs to God's promises, but they had not personally come through the Reed Sea or heard the thunder of God's voice from Mount Sinai. They must now learn how to believe, think, and live as the people of God. They are formatted but blank hard drives, ready to be filled with new content.

Their teacher is to be Moses, now 120 years old (40 years as an adopted son in the palace of the pharaoh, 40 years as an expatriate shepherd in the Sinai desert, 40 years in the wilderness from Egypt and Sinai to the plains of Moab). Now, in one long speech (or lecture series),[2] this third-career preacher-teacher, called late in life, will instruct 'all Israel' on what it means to be the covenant people of God. Readers of the final form of Deuteronomy as the conclusion of the Pentateuch or in its present canonical location will envision the scene in terms of the statistics given in the immediately preceding book of Numbers, in which approximately 2.5 million Israelites journey through the desert and encamp on the plains of Moab. Deuteronomy itself gives no numbers but pictures enormous crowds that God has already multiplied "so that today you are as numerous as the stars of heaven" (Deut 1:10; 10:22; cf. Gen 15:5). Even allowing that this is to be understood more as theology than as statistics—the promise to Abraham and Sarah is already being fulfilled—Moses is pictured as speaking to a vast multitude seated on the plains of Moab, without reference to crying babies, food and drink, or sanitation arrangements. Since, we are assured, his "vigor had not abated" at 120, he seems to have managed well without microphone, amplifier, or loudspeakers—contrast the mere five hundred thousand at Woodstock or the one hundred thousand at the Rose Bowl, unimaginable without electricity and amplification. A spectacular drama indeed!

The subject of the speech is instruction on how to live as the covenant people of God in the promised land. Israel is promised blessings if they obey, threatened with terrible curses if they are not faithful: siege that eventuates in cannibalism, physical and mental sickness, and ultimately the loss of the land and exile among the gentiles (chs. 28–29). The speech concludes with a long song to be memorized by the whole nation and sung in the future as a testimony against their disobedience (ch. 32) and a final blessing on each of the twelve tribes (ch. 33).

We are not told how the crowds responded. Whatever they thought, we know how we might respond: Why dally here for long speeches? Why hold a class when we've already been delivered from slavery and the promised land stands before us. The *promised* land! God has promised to be with us. Let's get on with it. It's time for action, not thirty-four chapters of words. It is a good question, not to be easily dismissed. Shouldn't the Bible go straight from Numbers to Joshua, from liberation to conquest, personal fulfillment for ourselves, and setting things right in the real world?

They sat still and listened. Moses then explained that he could not go with them into the promised land. Henceforth, for all time to come, those who hear the Word of God that came through Moses's preaching and teaching will get it through this book. Moses ordained Joshua as his successor and then went to the top of Mount Pisgah, from which he could survey the land oozing with milk and honey that he had sweated, pleaded, and bargained with God to help them attain but in which he would have no inheritance. Moses died alone on Mount Pisgah, and God buried him in an unmarked grave. We still have his book, still listen to it.

This is indeed a *strange* story. In what sense is it a *true* story? As we work seriously through the text of Deuteronomy, we may need to face some difficult questions head-on. Before we launch into our efforts to get within better hearing distance of what the biblical text wants to say to us, we might get our own questions more clearly in mind. Suggestion: Reserve a couple of quiet hours to read through Deuteronomy in one sitting, without pausing too much to ponder the individual issues that leap from the page. With notepad or iPad at hand, you might just jot down questions that emerge as you read, for further reflection later. Some of these questions are our own built-in concerns, doubts, or agendas we bring to the text, consciously or without realizing it. Other issues are posed by the text itself. As a pump primer, here are a few of my own of both sorts.

1. Isn't Deuteronomy a *Law* book? The subtitle of this chapter refers to it as a "strange but true *story*." How do "law" and "story" fit together? There are, in fact, a lot of laws in Deuteronomy (better, *Torah*, meaning instruction, direction, catechesis[3]), principally in the fifteen chapters that constitute the core of the book (chs. 12–26). But this is less than half of its content and is enclosed in an extensive narrative framework—precisely like the Sermon on the Mount in the Gospel of Matthew. In both Deuteronomy and Matthew, we are interpreting a story that includes substantial sermons with sizeable lists of authoritative dos and don'ts. How should I understand and take seriously *rules* that are part of a *story*, especially if it's a story about somebody else? In any case, can morality be legislated?

2. This book claims throughout that Deuteronomy is true, ultimately true—that it mediates the truth of God. But I have already pointed out the difficulty in trying to picture Deuteronomy's story as an accurate report of a historical event (2.5 million in the audience, no loudspeakers, no snack bars, no Porta Potties). This and the preceding comments about Deuteronomy as a law book raise the question of *genre*. What kind of story is Deuteronomy? A literally true, accurate chronicle of actual events? If not, is it helpful to repeat the widespread slogan "We take the Bible seriously, but not literally"? While I would agree with what seems to be the general thrust and intention of this slogan, can we "take the Bible seriously" without probing the question of its *truth*? In the following chapters, we will explore this question as honestly as we can in some depth and detail. As preachers and teachers, we want to tell it like it is. This means we must first *hear* it like it is (Isa 50:4; Mark 7:35–37).

3. Does God care for oxen (1 Cor 9:9, citing Deut 25:4)? There are rules in Deuteronomy about how to treat animals (e.g., 5:14; 22:4, 10; 25:4). Paul cites Deuteronomy 25:4, "You shall not muzzle an ox while it is treading out the grain," but interprets it as biblical support for his argument that Christian preachers and teachers are entitled to financial support, claiming that this text is not concerned with God's care for animals, but in this text God speaks "entirely for our sake" (1 Cor 9:9–12; cf. Rom 15:4).

4. Will it preach? For most of us readers, including the present writer, the Bible is canonical Scripture, the norm and substance of the church's message. We are rightly concerned with the question of how, or even whether, Christian preachers and teachers can listen to Deuteronomy for an authentic message from God for ourselves, our congregations, our students. A time-honored approach to biblical texts is to pore over them looking for "preaching values." One's homiletic or didactic filter finds inspirational "golden nuggets" or texts amenable to "life application." Another approach mostly finds opportunities to "preach against the text" in the name of the gospel or the preacher's ideology.

5. Are not the teaching and example of Jesus the norm for interpreting the Old Testament for all who claim to follow him as Lord? Indeed, they are. But which Jesus serves as the norm, who gets to say, and how is this norm to be applied?

6. Some texts seem so alien to both the New Testament and the modern interpreter's situation that it might at first seem futile to try to find "Christian meaning" in them for contemporary followers of Jesus. For myself, I must confess that three chief aspects of Deuteronomy's Torah fall into this category:

a. Number one on my own list is the repeated, insistent command to eradicate the Canaanites and take their land, sparing the fruit trees but killing everything that breathes, showing no mercy to old or young (2:12; 7:2), and killing all men, women, and children.
b. A somewhat distant second is the command for animal sacrifice, killing animals as an act of worship to God.
c. Like much of the Bible, Old Testament and New, Deuteronomy assumes and reflects a society in which women and children are regarded as subordinate and dependent, at the disposal of their male superiors.

All three of these concerns are culturally conditioned, to some extent shaped by the assumptions of another time and place in which those who gave and repeated these commands were no more aware of their cultural assumptions than a fish is aware of water—until it is jerked out onto the riverbank. But everything we do and are is also culturally conditioned, and our cultural assumptions are often invisible, or "just the way things are." Deuteronomy causes us to think long and hard about how human culture relates to the Word of God.

7. What does it mean to "be saved," for either the individual or the world? Deuteronomy's *lack* of an explicit eschatology or clear doctrine of life beyond death seems to be too easily understood as the promise of this-worldly health and prosperity for those who do God's will. This not only is ethically problematical but flies in the face of what we see just by looking around. By Deuteronomy's criteria, why were not Jesus and his followers blessed with long, happy, and prosperous lives? At least at first reading, Deuteronomy seems to look no further than a good life in Canaan as the promised reward for a righteous life and has no need of, or hope for, a Messiah to come or eternal life beyond the grave. The word *Messiah* never appears in Deuteronomy. *Sin* is rare (three times);

forgiveness is entirely absent. Those who understand Christian faith as primarily oriented to "accepting Jesus as my personal savior so I will go to heaven when I die" may find little of value in Deuteronomy. Other Christians, those who understand following Jesus as a commitment to his concern for social justice and expressing the love of God to others in this world, may find useful texts for their purpose and celebrate Deuteronomy's this-worldly perspective and call to do justice and love mercy. Has *either* group *listened* to what this text of Scripture wants to say? Or have both groups heard, at least partially? Can we just opt for a both/and and get on with our own lives?

No, we can't. It is possible, of course, to flip through the pages of the book, finding texts that seem important, inspirational, or preachable, skipping over the hard or off-putting texts. Deuteronomy itself (and Jesus of Nazareth) calls us to *hear*, not use, reject, or defend. This is the only legitimate approach to anything in the Bible, including the "easy" texts. There are none. Finding a text "easy" typically means locating verses I already find acceptable, something that fits into my culturally conditioned view of the way things are. When we stand before a congregation or class, when we sit quietly by ourselves, we want to be honest, we want to listen before we make up our minds—or unmake them.

This will be our concern in the following chapters. It will be difficult to put aside our prior understandings and open our ears and hearts to the strange new world of the Bible. I certainly cannot claim this for myself, and readers may note examples in this book of its author's own tone deafness. With the Scripture open before us and some good secondary literature at hand (see bibliography), we will work through the text of Deuteronomy guided by the following outline:

The Command
The Story
The People
The One God: Theology That Laughs and Sings

The Command

We begin with the core theology of Deuteronomy and the Bible, the Shema of 6:4: "Hear, O Israel: The LORD is our God, the LORD alone." We ask what it means to hear, wanting to know the identity of the Israel to whom these words are addressed—does it include *us*, or do we only draw "lessons for living" from sermons preached a long time ago to other people? We are challenged to understand *hearing* as the call to open our ears and hearts and allow our own story to be engaged by the Bible's story.

The Story

The Bible's story is actually a multilayered composition of three interrelated stories: the story *in* the text (its "narrative world"), the story *behind* the text ("what really happened"), and the story *of* the text (how the words once spoken by Moses came to be part of the English Bible on our desks, computers, and lecterns—the story interpreted, preached, and taught in our sermons and lessons). The one house of Scripture is a three-storied structure. Study of each level of the text attunes the ear to hear the Voice that sounds through the whole house of God, the whole house of Israel.

The People

The Bible's story engages Israel's story. Who is this "Israel" to whom Deuteronomy claims to speak? God speaking through Moses is the center of the circle, and the people of Israel constitute its circumference. How far does this perimeter extend? To later Israelites and Jews? To Christians, who include Deuteronomy and the Deuteronomistic History in their Bible? To the Islamic community that looks back in respect to Abraham and Moses? To interested, searching "outsiders"? Does it include me? Or am I a spectator to the biblical drama, perhaps seriously interested and leaning forward from my seat in the front row? Or am I on the stage, part of the action, involved in the story? When I hear God speak through Moses to 'all Israel,' must I somehow be an Israelite for the story to be my own story and speak directly to me? Deuteronomy's (and Jesus's) answer may be surprising and may be resisted, just as it may be welcomed. These are not only questions I may (or may not) bring to the text; these are questions the text brings to me.

The One God: Theology That Laughs and Sings

Here we delve into the content of the revelation of the One God, the Torah. This is the heart of the book, what we have been preparing ourselves to hear. *Torah* means "instruction." The term is directly related to the verb for "teaching" (*yrh*) and to the term for "teacher," as in the *Moreh Tzedeq* of the Qumran community. The phrase means not "lawgiver" but "Right Teacher." God gives instruction for the life and mission of the people of God who are called and charged with a mission to all peoples. This instruction is focused not on theology, in the sense of right ideas about God, but on *ethics*, the life of the people of God. Practice, not theory; life, not thought; orthopraxy, not orthodoxy; doing and being, not thinking—that's what Deuteronomy and the Bible are about. But *what* to do and be, and *why* and *how*, all depend on who we understand God and ourselves to be. This is what Deuteronomy wants to teach us. Deuteronomy thus leads us through several chapters of theological instruction on the way to directions on how to live as the people of God. We join Tevye in *Fiddler on the Roof*, listening to Deuteronomic tradition to learn "who we are and what God requires of us."

II

The Shema

Core Theology

Chapter 3

The Shema

Confession, Testimony, Command

We now want to better attune our ears to the bedrock affirmation of Israel's and the church's faith, long designated by its first word, שְׁמַע (*Shema*)—"the pivot around which everything else in Deuteronomy revolves."[1] The following is the standard English translation of Deuteronomy 6:4–5 in the Tanakh of the Jewish Publication Society (JPS), which agrees verbatim with the NRSV. Notes in each translation give other possibilities for translating *ekhad*, the final word of the first line:

> Hear, O Israel! The Lord is our God, the Lord alone.
> You shall love the Lord your God
>   with all your heart
>   and with all your soul
>   and with all your strength.

We may be sure that Jesus, Paul, and thousands of other first-century Jews and Christians recited the Shema not only in synagogue and church worship but every morning and evening in their personal prayers. While there is no magic in the words themselves, we may find it meaningful to pronounce the words as a personal confession and prayer, allowing our lips and ears to express and our ears to resonate with the very sounds of this ancient biblical confession, echoing the twice-daily prayer and praise of Judaism, Jesus, and the earliest church (Hebrew word order is right to left):

שְׁמַע יִשְׂרָאֵל יְהוָה אֱלֹהֵינוּ יְהוָה אֶחָד׃

Sheh-MA Yis-rah-EL Ah-do-NAI El-lo-HEY-noo Ah-do-NAI eh-KHAD.

Hear O Israel the LORD [is] our God the LORD [is] one.

Strictly speaking, the Shema comprises only six words (6:4), as indicated by the enlarged final letters of the first and last words in printed editions of the Hebrew text, but the Great Commandment of the following verse is so closely related, it is often included in translations and discussions of the Shema. This corresponds to the essential nature of the Shema, which is confession, testimony, and command.

The Shema Is Israel's Confession

The question is not "Who is YHWH?" but "Who is God?" The confession assumes the reality of God. Atheism, agnosticism, and materialism are not considered live options. The world of gods and spiritual beings is presupposed. The Shema confesses not only faith in the being and reality of God—"There is a god, however you may think of him, her, or it"—but that YHWH, the Deity as a particular, personal, named reality, the one who has revealed himself in Israel's history, is *our* God, and this God is confessed to be *one*.

The Hebrew text is a compact noun clause of six words, none of which are verbs. There is nothing unusual about this Hebrew syntax, but for nonnative speakers in later contexts, the syntax allows several valid translations. The confession was doubtless sometimes understood in slightly different ways over the generations and centuries, but the meaning of the canonical form intended by the Deuteronomy teachers seems to be clear:

1. "The LORD our God" is the subject. The confession does not assert "The LORD is our God," which is assumed. "The LORD our God" occurs twenty-one times elsewhere in Deuteronomy, always as a unified phrase, and never with "the LORD" as subject and "our God" as predicate. The Shema is not addressed to the issue "Who is the God of Israel?" but intends to say something crucial about this God—"The LORD our God is *one*."
2. The final word, *ekhad* (one), proclaims the LORD as a singularity, but this can be understood not only as unity ("the LORD is one") but in an exclusive sense ("the LORD alone"). "The *LORD alone*" can be understood in a henotheistic sense: "We, Israel,

> have only one God," without affirming a strict monotheism—other nations have their gods, but as for us, we worship only the Lord. This is certainly not the way the confession has been understood in the Jewish tradition and probably not the meaning originally intended. The Shema is not directed to the theoretical question, "How many beings are there that can be called 'God'?" but to the issue of loyalty and commitment. In the biblical literary context and in Jewish and Christian tradition and liturgy, verse 4 (*one* God) has always been understood as fused with verse 5 (love with *whole* heart). Loyalty to the One God may not be portioned out among several wannabe deities. God wants my whole self, my whole being, and will not settle for being one loyalty on a list, even if in first place. While the exclusive sense was always present, the monotheistic sense may have sometimes been only implicit in Israel's confession. In the context of the sophisticated, cultured polytheism of Babylon, the monotheistic sense became clear and insistent, as in Deutero-Isaiah (e.g., Isa 43:10, 12; 44:8; cf. Deut 4:35, 39). The modern slogan of a liberalism wanting to be tolerant can tend to be a minimalist, lowest-common-denominator statement, such as "Well, after all, we all worship the same God," which can actually function as a sophisticated polytheism. Israel's theologians, chastened by the experience of exile, oppose precisely this kind of "tolerance."

This is the way the Shema was understood by the LXX (Septuagint), the Greek translation used by New Testament authors (Mark 12:29; cf. the discerning Jewish scribe's elaboration and Jesus's response in 12:32–34): *"Hear, O Israel: the Lord our God, the Lord is one."* The confession communicates that the Lord, the God of Israel, is the only God, neither one of many nor one in many manifestations but unique, exclusive—God the one and only. In the whole cultural and religious spectrum of the ancient Near East, Israel was the only people to worship God as one who demanded exclusive loyalty. When Israel calls the Lord a jealous God, this is meant not in the emotional sense of envious, suspicious feelings involved in petty competition but as a confession that the One God calls for total, uncompromising devotion that tolerates no hedging of bets, no self-made idols as rivals. The elaboration of the first of the Ten Commandments in Deuteronomy 5:6–10, like the Shema that immediately follows, declares that Israel will be devoted totally, exclusively, and without reservation to the One God. This is the meaning of "perfect" in Deuteronomy 18:13, where Israel is commanded to be "perfect" (*tamim*; KJV and CEB translate it as "perfect," and NRSV as "completely loyal").

In the rhetorical situation posited by Deuteronomy's narrative world, Israel is about to enter the multicultural, polytheistic religious context of Canaan, where *Baal* is the standard term for God. Moses is instructing Israel on how to understand, confess, and live out their faith in the new situation. Since the Shema is formulated with this rhetorical situation in view, it is crucial to understand the key vocabulary involved—that is, to clarify the relation of "the LORD" to the terms *God*, *Lord*, and *Baal*, if we would be clear about how these words function theologically in the Shema and in Deuteronomy as a whole.

In narrative compositions such as the Deuteronomistic History, Israel's worship of "the LORD" is contrasted with the Canaanites' devotion to Baal. Typical is Elijah's challenge to Israel in the famous confrontation on Mount Carmel: "If the LORD is God, follow him; but if Baal, then follow him" (1 Kgs 18:21; cf., e.g., Judg 2:13; 2 Kgs 10:13; Jer 11:17). The monotheistic reader of the English Bible can easily and understandably get the impression that in such expressions, including in the Shema, "the Lord" is a generic term for the Deity used by the worshippers to refer to the One True God, and Baal is the personal name of a particular (false) god worshipped by the Canaanites. *The reality is exactly the reverse:* "the LORD" in English Bibles is the standard way of representing the Hebrew Tetragrammaton יהוה (the *LORD*, pronounced "Adonai"), while *Baal* is not the personal name of a particular god but simply the Hebrew and Canaanite word for "lord."

In the Hebrew of Israel and Canaan, *baal* is a generic term for rulers and authorities, human or divine, while יהוה (the LORD) is the personal name of a particular deity, like Zeus or Jupiter. The word בעל (*baal*) means simply "one who is in charge" and is commonly used to mean rulers, masters, owners, husbands, and experts, all of whom were addressed as "Baal so-and-so," as the word *Mister* is used in English (now a weakened form of the original *Master*). Deuteronomy itself uses *baal* in this general sense, for example, in 15:2, where a "creditor" is literally the "*baal* of a debt," and 21:23, where *baal* is "husband." This common title (used 229 times in the Old Testament) was used to designate leading members of the human communities addressed as "lord" (think "Lord Macbeth," "Lord Byron," and the "House of Lords" as distinguished from the "House of Commons"). *Baal* can be used in the plural, as in Isaiah 16:8, which refers to "the lords [baalim, 'baals'] of the nations." "Yhwh," "the *Lord*," is a personal name that cannot occur in the plural. No human being could be called by this name, though many human beings can be called "Baal so-and-so." "Baal / the Lord" can be used to designate a member of the Canaanite pantheon. When used in this religious sense, the Canaanite "Lord" was manifest and active in the numerous local shrines and temples, and his reality was experienced in the awesome power of the storm, in the fertilizing rain, and in the life force that generated calves, lambs, and human babies. Baal was a manifestation of "the law of nature and nature's god," echoed in the Declaration of Independence.

In the rhetorical situation of Deuteronomy, Moses is preparing Israel for their new life in Canaan. There, they will hear their new neighbors say, "At our local shrines, we worship the Lord who gives life, rain, and good crops. You worship your own god called *Yhwh*.'" The Canaanites have their shrines, their teachers, their prophets, their time-honored rituals. They devote themselves to the Lord even to the point of sometimes sacrificing their children to him for the good of the country. The Canaanites are city people with a powerful military and booming economy. They have ancient, impressive temples, speak of deep religious experiences in which "the Lord is very near to us," and attribute their agricultural and military success to "the Lord." This could all be very attractive to a group of ex-slaves or returning exiles coming out of the desert into a fertile, prosperous, and civilized country.

Over against the accommodation to cultural religion that had been Israel's problem their whole history and finally led to the loss of the land and exile for a significant element of the population, the teachers who gave us the book of Deuteronomy and retold the story of Israel from Joshua through 2 Kings—now known as the Deuteronomistic History—asserted their understanding of what it means to belong to the people of God. It requires thirty-four chapters of Deuteronomy and the six books of the Deuteronomistic History (Joshua–2 Kings, minus Ruth) to express this encounter between the traditional faith of Israel and the cultural religion of Canaan and how to deal with it. *This* is what is focused on and summed up in the Shema. In light of the theology of Deuteronomy as a whole, we might here venture a proleptic paraphrasing summary of the meaning of the Shema as Israel's confession:

The Lord, the God of Israel—
—who created, rules, and cares for all that is,

—who made promises to Israel's ancestors,
—who delivered Israel from slavery,
—who called them into being as his covenant people,
—who instructed them in how to live and taught them the meaning and purpose of their lives,
—who chastened and disciplined them when they were unfaithful but
—who loves them with a love that will not let them go, for they have a crucial role in God's purpose for the salvation of the world and the blessing of all people.
—*This* LORD is the one and only God.

The Shema Is Israel's Testimony

The confession cannot be made once and for all but is constantly renewed. Even when uttered as one's private prayer, as *confession*, the Shema expresses the communal declaration of Israel's faith before God and the believing, worshipping community—the declaration of who God is and therefore who Israel is. The confessional thrust is centripetal, inwardly toward the community and toward the heart of the individual believer, but confession is also centrifugal, pressing outward from the center, confession before the world. To confess Israel's faith is to become a witness, to bear *testimony*. Israel confesses its faith: "The LORD is our God." "Our" does not claim the LORD as Israel's possession but precisely the other way around—Israel is the LORD's possession, just as when we speak of "our church," we do not and cannot mean it belongs to us, but we belong to it. The "our" of the Shema belongs to the same "our" as the first word of the Lord's Prayer. God the Father does not belong to us; we belong to God, the God who is Lord and Father of all his wayward children in the whole world. And as is the case with the Lord's Prayer, the "our" of Israel's confession does not contrast those who claim the LORD in some exclusive, tribal sense with others who confess some other God to be theirs, as though Israel was content to declare, "The LORD is our God, but Baal is your God, and Marduk is the God of the Babylonians." The "our" is inclusive. It unites believers in the LORD with adherents of all other faiths and none—the LORD is their God too, God the one and only, whether or not *they* realize it and even if they deny it.

The witness-character of the Shema was inherent in the confession from the beginning and is symbolically indicated in the way the Hebrew Bible is printed—the final letter of the first and last words are printed in large, bold type and compose the Hebrew word (*'ed*), which means "witness, testimony." In its essential nature, the Shema not only has a centripetal force but is always directed outward. Israel was called into being for the blessing of all peoples (Gen 12:1–3) and was called to understand itself as a "light to the nations" (Isa 42:6; 49:6). Israel is called not only to confess the common monotheistic faith of the people of God but to be witnesses to the world of all God's peoples that the Lord is the one and only God of all the peoples of the earth (Isa 43:10, 12; 44:8).

Israel's confession of faith proclaims that there is only one God but does not claim that no one in the world except Israel worships the One True God. The faith confessed in the Shema as understood in the final form of Deuteronomy and the Deuteronomistic History continued through the prophets and wisdom sections of the Old Testament into early Judaism and was presupposed by the early church and the New Testament. This is well illustrated in Acts 17, when, at the beginning of the third generation of Christian history, the author of Luke–Acts sums up his comprehensive understanding of Jesus and early Christian faith as the Deuteronomists did for sixth-century BCE Israel in a composition strongly influenced by Deuteronomy. Acts 17:22–30 portrays Paul, missionary to the gentiles, standing in the midst of the sophisticated, multicultural religious environment of Athens:

> Athenians, I see how extremely religious you are in every way. For as I went through the city and looked carefully at the objects of your worship, I found among them an altar with the inscription, "To an unknown god." What therefore you worship as unknown, this I proclaim to you. The God who made the world and everything in it, he who is Lord of heaven and earth, does not live in shrines made by human hands, nor is he served by human hands, as though he needed anything, since he himself gives to all mortals life and breath and all things. From one ancestor he made all nations to inhabit the whole earth, and he allotted the times of their existence and the boundaries of the places where they would live, so that they would search for God and perhaps grope for him and find him—though indeed he is not far from each one of us. For "In him we live and move and have our being"; as even some of your own poets have said. . . . While God has overlooked the times of human ignorance, now he commands all people everywhere to repent.

Israel understands itself as charged with the responsibility of proclaiming that when people worship, the One they worship, whether they realize it or not, is the One True God who has revealed himself in and through the history of Israel. To witness to the faith that the Lord is the one and only God is to claim that the one, universal God of the whole world and all its peoples is YHWH, the LORD. Such affirmations about the Ultimate must necessarily bend conventional logic and are often best expressed in poetry. Deuteronomy ends with a grand poem, a hymn, the Song of Moses (Deut 32), which pictures YHWH, the one and only God, apportioning the world to subordinate beings and powers of the transcendent world:

> When the Most High
> apportioned the nations,
> when he divided humankind,
> he fixed the boundaries of the peoples
> according to the number of the gods;
> the LORD's own portion was his people,
> Jacob his allotted share. (Deut 32:8–9)

The One God is called both "Most High" (*'Elyōn*), supreme over the other transcendent beings of the heavenly court, and YHWH, the LORD God of Israel. "There is no god besides me" (Deut 32:39) is not theoretical monotheism but YHWH's own declaration that he does not belong to some sort of pantheon. Whatever gods may be are all subject to the One God. These other "divine beings" are sometimes called "gods," "sons of God," or "angels" in other biblical texts and translations. God remains in charge but delegates temporary authority over the peoples of the world to these subordinate "gods" while retaining Israel under his personal direction as his agent and witness for the divine mission to all peoples. Israel's election as the chosen people, which happened in historical times, is here conceived as God's plan from the beginning of history. This is analogous to the New Testament's affirmation that God "chose us in Christ before the foundation of the world" (Eph 1:4).

Deuteronomy often distinguishes Israel as the people of God (*'am* sg.) from God's peoples (*'amim* pl.). The plural is used twenty-five times in Deuteronomy, almost always referring to all the peoples of the world, often specifically distinguishing Israel as the chosen people from the peoples of the earth (e.g., Deut 7:6; 14:2; 28:10, 37, 64; 30:3; 32:8–9). Israel worships YHWH, the One God, the Creator; all nations and the "gods" they worship are ultimately subject to the one Creator (cf. Gen 6:2; Deut 4:19; 7:7–8; 32:21, 43; Dan 10:10–21; Ps 82:1; Job 1:6–12; 2:1–6; 38:7). The Deuteronomic teachers do not here embark on a systematic essay about interreligious dialogue, but their understanding of YHWH, the One LORD, provides a basis for such dialogue (as does, e.g., John 1:1–18 and

Acts 17:22–28). Theological monism does not exclude religious pluralism. The Shema points to a style of interreligious dialogue that maintains both faith in the One God and the responsibility to testify to the identity of this one God to all God's peoples.[2]

This double-edged confession of faith and mission proclamation reverberates in the last words of Rabbi Akiva, a great Jewish saint and teacher in the second century CE. He supported the Jewish rebellion against Rome in 132 CE. The revolution failed, and the victorious Romans arrested Akiva and burned him at the stake. The Talmud pictures Akiva as silent until the flames engulfed him. Then he died with the confession and proclamation of the Shema on his lips, sustaining the final syllable with his last breath—*ekha-a-a-d* (o-o-o-ne)—until he died.

There is only one God, the Creator of the world, sovereign over all the nations, who loves every creature he has made with a love that will not finally be frustrated. But what we religious types, of whatever religion, could never find out in all our religious searching, the One True God has definitively revealed in his mighty acts in history. For Deuteronomy, Akiva, and all faithful Jews, the being, character, and purpose of God have been revealed in the deliverance of Israel from slavery and their formation into the covenant people who, in word and deed, bear witness to God's saving purpose for the world. For the author of Luke–Acts, this same God has brought this history to a definitive climax in sending Christ as the Savior of the world. The world misunderstood, rejected, and crucified him, but God has vindicated him by raising him from the dead. The *people of God* witness to all *God's peoples*—all human beings—and the whole creation to the identity, character, and saving acts of the One True God.

The Shema Is Israel's Command

When we confess with 'all Israel' that the Lord is God, we realize that we have been placed under orders. The Shema commands love. Jesus pronounces the command to love God with all one's being as the first command, the wellspring from which all love and all obedience flow. God is not merely "loving." Love is not a quality that God has, one among other good character traits. God *is* love; love is God's essential being (1 John 4:8, 16). We love because God first loved us (1 John 4:19). Love can be commanded, but no one can love just because it is commanded. Try as we may, we cannot muster up the love of God within ourselves by trying harder to obey the command. Whether aware of its source or not, the believer's love comes as a response to the love of God. It is God's own love that generates love in us and through us to others (Rom 5:1–5). We can respond in obedience to the love command built into the Shema only if our ears and hearts are opened to the incredible good news that the one and only God loves us, has already loved us with a love that will not let us go, before we are ever given any command, including the love commandment.

There is thus a sense in which the first word of the Shema is itself the primal command: "Hear!" God speaks, we hear, love happens in us and through us. This is the significance of "Hear, O Israel," found only in Deuteronomy, where the phrase occurs six times. We resonate with the positive cultural vibes associated with the importance ascribed to "hearing" in our own social settings. We have learned that helping troubled souls in a counseling session or friendly conversation requires, above all else, listening. Some have become very good at it, having long since learned the wisdom of James, addressing especially the church's preachers and teachers: "You must understand this, my beloved: let everyone be quick to listen, slow to speak" (Jas 1:19; cf. 3:1!).

Of course, preaching and teaching require having something to say. And having something to say requires listening. Such hearing means listening to the congregation, its families and individual members, their hurts and needs. Such hearing means listening to our friends and neighbors who don't come to our churches, don't consider themselves religious, listening for the subtext beneath the fixed pleasant expressions people sometimes wear to disguise the pain, frustration, and meaninglessness experienced as life. Such pastoral care listens for the unconscious, barely audible attempts to express the gratitude and joy of living that may only emerge as superficial cultural clichés. Such hearing means listening to the TV news (not only our favorite channel), listening to society—local, national, international—and its pains built into its economic and political systems, its tribulations and sorrows that can't be pinned on some individual we don't like much anyway. Such hearing means listening to the celebrations of the world, its songs and dances and worship, celebrating the goodness of life in ways that sometimes cause us to back off and shake our heads. Such hearing means listening to the cries of the animal world and the nonhuman cosmos, all of which belong to the world created and loved by God, a world writhing in labor pains, standing on tiptoe, looking out and ahead for the dawn of the new creation in which not only death but predatory life has been overcome (Isa 11:1–9; Hos 2:16–23; Rom 8:18–25; 2 Cor 5:16–17; Rev 21:5).

And such hearing means listening to our own story—the personal story that we have and are, the story that we bring to the text, the story through which all the other stories are filtered—being aware that we not only hear things as they are; we hear them as *we* are. This is no endorsement of egocentrism and narcissism, but the call to hear and understand does include being self-aware, not only sensitive to the joys and sorrows of other people and the world, but aware of the kind of persons we ourselves are, we who dare to open our ears to the text and be addressed by voices that may be strange, off-putting, disturbing—and liberating, compelling.

In Deuteronomy, to *hear* means to submit one's whole life. Only the One God, the Creator, can ask for such obedience. We rightly resist such demands from any human tyrant, institution, or cause. Only to God can the human creature submit in absolute dependence and joyful obedience. To confess that the Lord is the *One True God* (Deut 6:4), to confess Jesus as *Lord* (Rom 10:9), means to hear and obey. The word *hear* itself, of course, can have its ordinary meaning associated with acoustics and audiology, the kind of problem that "hearing aids" can indeed alleviate to some extent. There is no theological magic in the Hebrew word *shema* or its Greek counterpart *akouō*—the biblical words themselves have approximately the same meaning in Hebrew and Greek as their English counterpart "hear." Nonetheless, biblical theology, especially Deuteronomy and the canonical literature influenced by it, uses *hear* more often, and more intensely, in a theological sense that includes "obey"—as in English, we might say, "I tried to tell you, but you wouldn't *listen* to me," or the military command that comes through the ship loudspeaker, "Now *hear* this!" (One of numerous instances in Deuteronomy is 13:18: "If you obey [Heb. *tishma*, 'hear'] the voice of the Lord your God by keeping all his commandments . . .") The NRSV and many other English translations often and rightly simply translate the Hebrew "hear" (*shema*) with the English "obey" (e.g., Deut 8:20; 11:28; 13:4, 18; 15:5; 21:20; 26:17; 27:10; 28:2, 13, 15, 45, 62; 30:2, 8, 10, 16).

The story with which Jesus concludes the Sermon on the Mount (Matt 7:24–27) contrasts the "wise man's" *hearing* with the "foolish man's" failure to *obey*. Jesus's distinction between the wise and the foolish has nothing to do with native intellectual ability or education but represents the theological sense of hearing typical of the Jewish Scriptures. Hearing and doing are not two steps that can be separated, with "doing" as an optional second step separate from "hearing." As in Deuteronomy cited by Jesus, the one who doesn't *do* has not really *heard*. The voice of God that resounds in the transfiguration story, "This is my Son, the Beloved; *listen* to him!" (Mark 9:7) is a call to obedience.

Just as hearing in the biblical sense means more than auditory perception, so the biblical meaning of understanding means more than the cognitive ability to "get it" of the sort that can be measured by IQ, SAT, or GRE scores. Biblical hearing requires *humility* but has nothing to do with low self-esteem. Humility means that in the presence of God, I acknowledge that I don't already know, that I am willing to be told, that I do not stand before God presuming that whatever God might want to say to me must fit within my own presuppositions, my own commonsense view of what's what, and that I'll be the judge of that. Humility is the acknowledgment that God is in heaven and I am on earth (Eccl 5:2), that God is the Lord and I am not.

The six words of the Shema are thus inextricably fused with the love command that immediately follows, the command that sums up all God's commands. To confess and testify to one's faith in God is at the same time to hear and accept the love command as the guiding rule for all of life. To confess faith in the God of Israel as the One True God is to be given a way of life and a commission. *The indicative is inseparable from the imperative.* But to acknowledge that believing in God involves obligations is also to recognize that ethical obligations cannot stand alone. Otherwise, the Christian minister or teacher has nothing to say to the good and honest people who respond to our preachments about love and justice by saying, "Your ideals and opinions about how to live may be fine for you, but don't impose your theories (or ideals, superstitions, values, etc.) on me." This cultural ethic, dependent on the false cultural story of the autonomous individual, is the story we must unlearn when we hear the real story of who we are and what God requires of us. Our ethical commitments are inseparable from confession and testimony. *The imperative is inseparable from the indicative.*

Hearing and Understanding

Just as hearing requires obedience, so obedience requires understanding. "Hearing" includes "understanding," as in Deuteronomy 28:49, "a nation whose language you do not understand" (literally, "hear," the same word as in the Shema). One can hear the words of another language perfectly but not understand them at all. In calling for obedience, the Shema calls for understanding. Jesus commanded his disciples; he called for obedience. He was their Lord, not just their teacher of lofty ideals or their spiritual guru. But the kind of obedience Jesus called for required understanding; he wanted disciples, or *mathētai*—a word meaning "students," in both ancient and modern Greek. In the Gospel of John, Jesus called his disciples to the obedience of loving friendship rather than the blind, fearful, unthinking obedience of slaves: "I do not call you servants [literally, 'slaves'] any longer, because the servant does not know what the master is doing; but I have called you friends, because I have made known to you everything that I have heard from my Father. You did not choose me but I chose you. And I appointed you to go and bear fruit, fruit that will last" (John 15:15–16).

Like the Johannine Jesus, the Deuteronomic teachers placed no value on blind obedience. The whole thrust of Deuteronomy is to explicate the Torah in a convincing and understandable way. The narrator's introductory preface declares that Moses did not simply promulgate a list of rules but "undertook to expound this law" (*bēʾēr*, Deut 1:5). The actual rules of personal and community conduct detailed in chapters 12–26 are prefaced with lengthy explanations and exhortations so that those who hear will not respond with robotic obedience but love God with all their heart and soul; they will understand what they are doing and why. This is the sense in which the following chapters are devoted to helping the reader come within hearing distance of the Word of God that comes through the text of the Bible.

We see that "hearing" is a crucial, multifaceted aspect of all human experience, including its religious dimensions. Hear-believe-understand-obey are not four separate acts, four rungs of a ladder. Even trying to separate them diachronically brings up such questions as "Which comes first, believing or understanding?" "Can we claim to 'believe' something when we don't understand it or can't explain to others what we mean by 'God,' 'love,' 'justice,' 'truth'?" "Can one really understand something important and personal unless one believes (is committed to it)?" "Can one believe something unless one to some extent understands it ('I believe it, whatever it means')?" We're rightly against "blind faith." But is authentic faith always contingent on complete understanding? Can I postpone believing in God until I understand what the word *God* means? These are not merely academic questions confined to the ivory tower but authentic, human questions. They also risk making our own prior understandings and commitments the filter through which the call of God must come, which is precisely what Deuteronomy wants to warn us against. The Bible offers no analytical discussions for us to ponder before we make our step-by-step commitment of faith but makes response to God a package deal—all or nothing, offering our whole self to God or not. When we are lost in the deep woods, the way out is never clear until we begin to walk. Jesus called for discipleship with two words, "Follow me," and people either did or didn't. Those who did learned along the way, perhaps a long time later, the meaning of discipleship. Paul speaks of "the obedience of faith," which inseparably fuses the human response to God's revelation: faithful obedience, obedient faith, the obedience that faith is (Rom 1:5; Gal 3:2). Later in the same letter, he distinguishes "hearing" from "believing" and "confession" from "believing" (Rom 10:9–10, 17). *In Deuteronomy, these dynamics of faith are all collapsed into the one command, "Hear!"*

Biblical "Hearing" versus Cultural "Seeing"

While one can "see" without obedience, *hearing* and obedience are a single alloy, smelted into unity in the response of faith to the Word of God. True enough, the Deuteronomic teachers can appeal to what the community of hearers has seen as an element of human experience that strengthens faith (Deut 1:30; 2:24, 31; 3:21; 4:3, 9, 34; 6:22; 7:19; 10:21; 11:7; 29:2; 30:15; 32:39), yet they nonetheless oppose Canaanite religion and culture because they had gods one could see, represented by *images* made by human minds and hands. And Moses insists that when 'all Israel' saw the reality of God at Sinai, what they saw was that there was nothing to be seen (Deut 4:9–14): "You heard the sound of words but saw no form; there was only a voice" (Deut 4:12). Israel had personally *heard* the voice of God, whose first two commands were to worship no other God and to make no images (Deut 5:7–8). Deuteronomy's horror at idolatry is that idols are constructed by humans, that they come from, belong to, and fit into our world. Leander Keck accepts the current deconstructionist, postmodernist claim that biblical language about God does not necessarily refer to anything beyond itself. There is nothing new about this. For centuries now, responsible, believing theologians have ceased to claim that human language can provide an accurate description of the Holy One, the transcendent Reality beyond all objective description: "I see no reason to bewail that this is so. To the contrary, Christian theology must insist that the God-Reality with which it is concerned is not an empirically demonstrable deity. A demonstrable god is a curiosity but not the Creator. . . . To be sure, faith is not believing what we know isn't so; but it is trusting beyond the demonstrable."[3] Keck thus rejects the whistling-in-the-dark efforts to refashion God language that supports our own ideas of truth and justice typified by Daniel Liechty's one-hundred-page *Theology in Postliberal Perspective*: "The only God who can save us from our predicament is the God whom we construct. . . . We alone may construct this image of God."[4] Deuteronomy's horror at self-made gods can be summed up by the fact that they can be *seen*. Representatives of the cultural religion were called "seers." Their gods could be seen but had nothing to say. The One True God can be heard but not seen. Deuteronomy's antitheses between the cultural religion of seeing and the Shema's call to hear the Word of God can be expressed in a series of overlapping contrasts:

- Idols are fixed, firm, solid, and available for objective observation, but the LORD is known by being addressed by the Word of God. This is explicit in the vocabulary of the LXX, which uses *eidolon* for "idol," derived from *eidon*, the common word for "see."
- Idols are manageable, but the LORD is free. The idol cannot prevent me from looking and making up my own mind, but I cannot force God to speak or to be silent. But when I am addressed by a living voice, I may be asked to decide before I can check out all the facts. In the world where God can be seen, I can look before I leap.
- Idols represent "objective," neutral data that can be inserted into the framework of our conceptual world with minimal disruption of our commonsense view of reality, but hearing the Word of the LORD seeks not only to give us new information but to transform our view of the world in which all data are processed.
- Seeing need not be personal, but the hearer perceives the tone of voice, the warmth or distance of personal address. One can see a road map, a recipe book, a sunset. But when I am spoken to, a person awaits my response. In Isaiah's account of his call to prophetic ministry, he doesn't just see a vision; he hears a voice: "Whom shall I send, and who will go for us?" (Isa 6:1–8). Isaiah's claim, "I saw the LORD, high and lifted up," need not be denied, but the vision was not the means of God's call. One need not respond to a vision. But the personal word calls for response, its joy and terror.

Much of this is memorably and cogently expressed in Martin Buber's *I and Thou*, which frames this distinction as the contrast between "I-It" and "I-Thou."[5] In I-It relations, the other is regarded as an object; in I-Thou relations, the other is a person, who speaks and can be spoken to, who listens and can be listened to, who enters into dialogue, and who can be changed by the dialogue. Objects can be seen and may even make sounds that I perceive audibly but that I do not and cannot hear in the sense of the Shema. I am in control of I-It relations. In the I-Thou relation, the other is not an object but another subject, free and unmanipulable.

Buber elsewhere argues that when Exodus 3:13–16 "explains" the unfathomable and unpronounceable name of the LORD in terms of *hyh*, the verb "to be," the explanation *ehyh asher ehyh* is best translated as "I will be what I will be." The disclosure of the divine name simultaneously reveals and conceals. It does not hand over the name of God as a magic word that can be used to maneuver the Deity for one's own benefit. The LORD is not on tap; The Name (*HaShem*) points to the God who cannot be conjured.[6] The I-It relation views the other as an object within a universe of other objects, a firm datum that fits into an objective, mechanical world of cause and effect, a world of objective reasoning in which all truths fit together into one interlocking logical sequence. In such a world, every true proposition must include all that can be inferred from it and can itself be inferred from other rational truths. But "God cannot be inferred in anything—in nature, say, as its author, or in history as its master, or in the subject as the self that is thought in it. Something else is not 'given' and God is elicited from it; but God is the Being that is directly, most nearly, and lastingly, over against us, that may properly only be addressed, not expressed."[7] The Deuteronomic teachers would say, "God can only be heard, not seen." Faith cannot be generated by such logical appeals to evidence. Faith that comes by hearing is not a matter of logical inference (Rom 10:5–17, which cites and interprets Deut 30:11–14).

Does this mean Deuteronomy wants us to abandon the "worldly, cultural" language of seeing and speak of our faith only in terms of the "biblical" language of hearing? No, it does not. In any case, we couldn't do it if we tried. Such language is a dimension of our humanity, and we are not asked to stop being human beings when we become believers. When we respond to God's call and find ourselves members of the people of God, we still belong to the human race; we are still numbered among God's peoples.

With the Hellenization of the eastern Mediterranean world in the wake of Alexander's conquests in the 330s BCE, the teachers in what was becoming the community of early Judaism were faced with a new challenge—how to express Israel's traditional core theology in the world of Greek thought and language. In a useful oversimplification, we might say that Greek thought emphasized the visual over the verbal, seeing over hearing, abstract systematic thought over the encounter of personal address. Israel's teachers, such as Jesus ben Sirach (ca. 175 BCE) and his contemporaries who translated the Pentateuch into Greek, struggled to express Israel's biblical faith in what had become the thought world of Greece and Rome, which was destined to be the intellectual basis of "Western civilization," now widespread throughout the planet. They attempted, with considerable success, to interpret the call to hear the Word of God in a world more accustomed to seeing truth in ideal and abstract forms. The visual arts, lacking in Israel, became central in Western culture. Plato's allegory of the cave featured someone chained in darkness coming into the clear light of day. The Greek *logos*, the linguistic root of "logic" and all our -ology words, was a matter not of personal speaking and hearing but of "seeing." Euclid's geometry allowed truth to be visualized. One who "got it" said, "Ah, I see." To be sure, the difference between a circle and an oval could be precisely defined in words, but clarity came when a teacher drew a circle and an oval on the moist clay, chalkboard, or PowerPoint screen and said, "See!"

Continuing in the same vein, we could say that the thought world typical of the Platonic "ideal" was vertical and otherworldly, and the mindset and worldview of Israel's prophets and teachers were horizontal and this-worldly. The Greek ideal pointed upward, away from the messy material world we live in, to the timeless, pure truth of abstract reason. Israel's prophets and teachers pointed outward and forward to the future of the world we live in, to the continuing unfolding of the creation under the lordship of the Creator. *Logos* came to be equated with rational thought that could be visualized. Jewish wisdom teachers appropriated this rational, systematic dimension of Greek thought and celebrated the regularity of nature—they saw it too—but interpreted it as the faithfulness of the personal God to creation. We creatures celebrated the beauty and awesomeness of the world not as the "world of nature," a *cosmos* that operates by its inherent *logos*/rationality, but as the creation called into being by the Word of the faithful, dependable Creator who has given us a dependable world, not an arbitrary one. The LXX, with considerable but not total success, preserved Israel's theology of the personal God oriented to hearing the Word of God when they translated it into the thought world of the emerging West.

Early Christianity emerged from the womb of Judaism, a Judaism already adapting to the Hellenistic world even in Jerusalem and

Palestine, a world whose thought patterns were already more like our own than those of Deuteronomy. The LXX that became the Bible of early Christianity had already taken major steps in expressing the ancient faith in the linguistic and conceptual world of Greco-Roman culture we have inherited. Paul, Mark, and the New Testament authors in general typically cite the Bible in Greek translation. Early Christian missionary teachers such as Paul and Mark adapted to the Hellenistic thought world without losing the biblical dynamic in which "faith comes from what is heard" (Rom 10:17) is typical—but they also expressed this conviction by using the more Greek conceptuality of *seeing*. This, of course, is more attuned to our own modern Western assumptions. When we read the New Testament's appropriation of the faith and theology of the early Christian Bible, this major hermeneutical step has already been made for us, making it possible to read our Bible, Genesis to Revelation, without breaking stride.

It is the teachers of the Johannine community who most clearly grasp the dialectical theology of the Word, all the while translating this theology into the visual categories of the Hellenistic world. In the Gospel of John, Jesus's first words are "What are you *looking* for?" (John 1:38), and he says to the woman of Samaria, "Come and *see*" (John 4:29). One of the Gospel of John's most profound summaries of the meaning of the Christ event is the dramatic healing of the eyes of a man who had been blind from birth (John 9:1–41).[8] The man had not lost his sight or refused to see. He represents the human condition that not only deafness but blindness come with the package of being human. We are not born blind but are inevitably blinded as we are conditioned by human culture, never able on our own to see the glory of God or our own lost condition. Jesus, God-in-the-flesh, does what no human being can do for others or for themselves—he who is the Light of the World heals the blind.

These and several other features of the Johannine Gospel show that the Johannine teachers had mastered the hermeneutic of translating their biblical faith into the language of the culture. Yet all of this is within the framework of a Gospel that begins with "In the beginning was the *Word*" (John 1:1) and concludes with the risen Jesus speaking to Mary Magdalene on the first Easter morning (John 20:11–28). Mary had already *seen* the empty tomb, the angels, even Jesus himself, but she only came to faith in him as the risen Lord when he *spoke* to her personally, calling her by name (20:16). As portrayed in the Johannine narrative, the disciples come to faith in the risen Lord on the testimony of Mary Magdalene, the first preacher of the gospel. The risen Jesus himself appears to the disciples on Easter evening, commissions them to their ministry, and confers the Holy Spirit (in the Fourth Gospel, Easter and Pentecost are collapsed into one day). In the sequel to this scene that occurs the next Sunday evening, Thomas, a good, model disciple throughout the Gospel (11:16; 14:5), who had been absent the previous week, becomes the key illustration of how one comes to faith. In this Gospel that has maintained a positive relationship between human seeing and God's speaking the transforming, salvific word, Jesus's concluding words are "blessed are those who have not seen and yet have come to believe" (John 20:29).

John leaves the door open to our human misunderstanding, our assumed contrast between the confident certainty of seeing for ourselves and faith as a second-best, secondhand believing, as though real knowledge rests on our own seeing. In this view, shared with human common sense in general, faith is what we do when we can't see for ourselves and so must "believe." John, like Deuteronomy, affirms the primacy of the Word, that faith is a gift generated by being spoken to by the Word of the living God that comes through the testimony of the incarnate Word. The Johannine Jesus takes up the Deuteronomic word *blessed* (fifty times in Deuteronomy!) and declares that blessed assurance rests not on our seeing but on God's speaking, the God who gives us ears to hear.

When we become believers and find ourselves among the chosen people of God, we do not cease to belong to the human race; we still share the relation to God inherent in being able to see the world of nature and respond with our own best judgment. Seeing, sight and insight, is part of our human heritage, which we continue to share with all God's peoples. Philosophy, art, music, literature, and the natural sciences remain vehicles that declare the glory of God. This translation of the incarnate Word into the visual categories of human culture was shared by other New Testament theologians so that the Gospel of Luke could picture the conversion/call of Paul as responding to the risen Christ who speaks to him and describe it as scales falling from his eyes (Acts 9:4, 18). This imagery has rightly continued in the history of the church so that millions of Christians who have heard and responded to the Word of God in the church's preaching, teaching, and action now celebrate the amazing grace of God by singing together, "I once was lost but now am found, / Was blind but now I see."

III

Hear

The Story

Chapter 4

Hearing the Story

Deuteronomy deploys the same theological literary strategy as the Bible as a whole, which contains revealed ethical instructions to God's covenant people embedded in a universal narrative. The first book in the New Testament is a clear illustration. The Gospel of Matthew is not a law book but a narrative that includes instructions on how the followers of Jesus are to live, not rejecting the Torah but radicalizing it. People become Jesus's disciples not by pondering the Sermon on the Mount as a list of commandments but by asking whether their own little stories could be included in the universal story of the Gospel. Jesus called people into the joyful and dangerous path of discipleship not by providing new information, ideals, and principles but by telling them stories to reshape their understanding of themselves, the world, and what it's all about. The framework and substance of Matthew's theology are derived from his Bible. He understands that Deuteronomy calls us to hear a story and to recognize it as the larger story that includes our own life. A story can't be ready-made and seen; it must be told and heard, even if the hearing is on the internal stage of the reader's imagination. Once told, it is not an objective, unchangeable reality to which one can return, but it must be retold and reheard.

The Deuteronomic teachers do not address us with an essay explaining the principles of the faith of Israel, which we may weigh and ponder in conjunction with our own common sense or sophisticated philosophy. They tell us a story. The Bible is a story, a true story about the real world. Each "Bible story" is heard within the framework of the one unified story that stretches from the beginning of the universe to the end of time. The story is about God, whose reality spans the whole narrative world from creation to eschaton; who is the author, producer, and director of the whole drama, mostly from behind the scenes and occasionally seen and heard on the stage; and who finally appears personally as the central and defining character. To hear the Bible's story is to hear the self-defining story of God.

The Bible's story is a true story about the real world. This means that to believe the Bible, to hear the Word of God that comes through it, we must overcome our prejudice against story-truth we have inherited from our culture. We often hear and may ourselves say, "Is that true? Or just a story?" (No one in the Bible could have said something was "just" a story!) When I was a small child, my mom, calling me to account for some mischief, would say, "Now don't you story to me"—a euphemistic way of avoiding the accusation that her son was lying. This prejudice against the story as a vehicle of truth is a mindset I cannot overcome on my own; it's part of the built-in cultural DNA I may not be aware of. I may suppose there is nothing to be "overcome," may consider my cultural view of the relationship of stories and truth to be simply common sense. "Common sense" refers not to native intelligence but to the set of assumptions we have in common with the culture, taken for granted as "what everybody knows." Without ever being aware of it, we may have been conditioned by our culture to believe that a good story may entertain or inspire, may illustrate something I already know to be true, but stories and truth operate in different worlds.

This, too, is a matter of faith: I can simply fit all stories I know into the view of truth I already have, just as I can ignore or reject them. We hear new data, new information, and fit them into the symbolic world we already live in. Our lifeworld is not a given, not just objectively "there"; it is constructed. This does not mean it is subjective or unreal or exists only in our imagination. The world we live in, our lifeworld, arranges our perceptions of the "objective" world into a meaningful whole.[1] The molecules, atoms, and subatomic particles that constitute "objective" reality are indeed "out there" in a world that exists prior to and apart from us. But these elements do not arrange themselves into the world we live in. Guided by our culture, we do that on our own, and without a second thought, we suppose that the way we perceive the world is realism, or "just the way things are." Anything that challenges that construction is not the real world. We can hear, read, and integrate new information, inspiration, and insights into our present world; we can use them as building blocks for constructing or rearranging the living room on the same old foundation or reshuffling the deck chairs on the *Titanic*. Such hearing does not change our world, does not change us. That's the way we like it.

Transformation calls for a new world, a new narrative/story/myth/framework into which we integrate our experience, a new foundation on which we construct our lifeworld from available information. Ponder Jesus's concluding story in the Sermon on the Mount, which involves constructing our lifeworld on a solid foundation (Matt 7:24–27). We resist this, cannot help resisting it, perhaps do not even know that we resist it. Taken seriously—*heard*—a story might open up a new world that subverts our self-constructed mythological world, undermines our foundation. Paul Tillich's classic series of sermons called *The Shaking of the Foundations* and *The New Being* already suggest the world-shaking, threatening aspect of the biblical message, in line with Jesus's and the New Testament's imagery of building on the right foundation and being aware of God's new creation.

We can accept new information and insights as long as we can set them within our old framework, on our old foundation. This is not threatening but "educational" or "inspirational," illuminating or reinforcing the convictions we already have. But when our world itself is threatened, we instinctively resist, more or less consciously aware that this story poses a subtle threat to our world, our life. People who heard Jesus's parables could dismiss them as "just stories," but if they took them seriously—*heard* them—they either were transformed or decided they had to get rid of him. Biblical theology does not give us new increments of inspiration packaged in quotable verse units. Biblical theology does not communicate in verses but speaks comprehensively of the whole framework of our little lives as "this world / the world to come," as this creation / new creation. This is hard to hear. We hear the new information with old ears, try to insert it into the old framework on the old foundation, and often succeed without knowing what we have missed.

Stories: False and True

A False Story Can Only Be Overcome by a True Story. We cannot, with gusto and good intentions, remodel this creation into the kingdom of God. In the Bible, our story world is confronted by a new story, which projects / communicates / brings into being a new world. In faith, fear, and trembling, I may step into this strange new world of the Bible, perhaps with only a tentative first step. Or if I can't bend it into a shape that fits into the world I already have, I must reject it and consider the one who tells it a threat. Jesus was opposed by the guardians of true religion and stable society not because he directly called for the overthrow of the present political system and cultural religion but because his message, embodied in disturbing short stories, projected a fundamental change in the comprehensive cultural story accepted as "realism." It can be dangerous to listen to a story. I must be willing to take a risk. If I am willing, and even if I am aware I have hearing difficulties, with the best of intentions, I can't just make up my mind to improve my hearing. To be sure, faulty hearing is sometimes mainly a matter of paying attention, of being interested in what the other person is saying, but that is not what the Bible is talking about. Deafness can't be cured by just trying harder. Hearing is a gift. Hearing requires a kind of transformation of the self that deaf people themselves cannot bring about. But we are responsible to hear, are commanded to hear. Preachers and teachers cannot speak until they are given the gift of hearing (Mark 7:31–37!). Even if I want to respond in obedience to the Word of God that comes through the teaching of Jesus, this willingness is something I cannot conjure up within myself. The story itself must do it to and for me.

Enter Jesus, Teller of Stories. Jesus's call to build on a new, solid foundation, his message of the present-and-coming kingdom of God, was clothed in stories that initially seemed harmless enough, but when *heard*, they turned out to be both promise and threat. His stories do not merely illustrate important points about the kingdom of God, points that can be stated on their own and incorporated into our stable world. The kingdom of God presents a new, different symbolic universe. Jesus's preaching and teaching of the kingdom of God did not describe and discuss the kingdom but actualized it, *mediated* a different world, called a new symbolic universe into being. It was a linguistic event that made something happen. He did not say, "I'm going to tell you a parable that illustrates some truths about my ideals for you to consider." He did not designate his stories as parables, did not explain how parables work, did not say, "I'm going to tell you a story that, if you listen, may mess with your mind, subvert your world, and threaten your understanding of what's real." He just did it, beginning a story with "Listen!" (Mark 4:3) and concluding with "Let anyone with ears to hear listen!" (Mark 4:9). Those who heard were transformed, never again lived in the same old world. "Let those who have ears, hear!" echoes Deuteronomy, as does Jesus's resistance to the demonic test at*tempt*ing to shape his ministry into an up-to-date cultural package that would respond to the way people already understood themselves and their world (Matt 4:1–11; Luke 4:1–13).

The New Testament's appropriation of this biblical understanding of what it means to *hear* is illustrated by the Jesus of the Gospel of Mark, who cites the Shema as the foundation of the love command (Mark 12:28–34, citing Deut 6:4) and then zeroes in on the command "Hear!" more than any other Gospel. Only Mark has two stories that focus on Jesus's giving the gift of hearing to deaf persons, stories omitted by the other Gospels, apparently because they portray Jesus too much in terms of the magicians and miracle workers of the Hellenistic world (7:31–37; 9:20–27). Hearing is the command of God; hearing is the gift of God—God heals the deaf. As the promised "prophet like Moses" (Deut 18:15–18), Jesus *gets* this from his Bible. Moses and the biblical prophets did not present Israel with some of the LORD's basic principles for living a happy life or making the world a better place. They and the Deuteronomic teachers who preserved and interpreted their teaching for us stood within the grand narrative of God the Creator, the story of the LORD's saving acts. They called Israel to be the people of God who know and live out this story in the way they live their lives and construct society, state, and nation. They called Israel to hear the good news of what the LORD had done, is doing, and will do and to understand themselves as living in this story.

In all this, to *hear* means to allow our own story world to be confronted and challenged by a different story. It is not a matter of the story world of the Bible confronting and challenging the real world of the hearer. Two story worlds confront each other. Jesus did not create this dynamic but received it from his Bible and Jewish tradition. This is the way the Bible *works*. For our purpose, I venture the following summary statement formulated in the personal "I" of the hearer:

Hearing the biblical message calls for

engagement of my story with the Bible's story,
in which I risk myself,
the transformation of my own story,
reorienting my understanding of who I am as a human being,
reshaping my understanding of what it means to belong to the people of
God and participation in its mission, and
refocusing my perspective on what is real and what matters.

Such hearing that renews and transforms the mind (Rom 12:1–2) is what Jesus and the New Testament call "repentance" (*metanoia*, change of mind and heart; cf., e.g., Mark 1:15; 6:12; Matt 11:20–21; Luke 15:7, 10; 16:30; Acts 2:38; 11:18; 17:30; Rev 3:19). This biblical challenge has the ring of truth about it because as human beings, as God's creatures bearing God's image, we all already know something about hearing and listening. Such engagement is like hearing a friend's story in a personal conversation, like listening to a troubled parishioner or fellow church member. Such listening to Scripture involves an *I-Thou* dialogue between two persons, not an *I-It* dealing with "objective reality." Whether or not the dialogue effects any change in my partner, if I am truly listening, I may never be the same again. There is a world of difference—I use *world* advisedly—between using the Bible and listening to it, the same difference between using other persons and listening to them. The biblical world posts a sign to all would-be hearers: "Enter at your own risk." In Deuteronomy, this sign is posted repeatedly, in every case with only three words: "blessing or curse," "life or death" (Deut 11:26, 29; 23:25; 30:1, 15, 19). The warning is not a matter of law but exhorts, "Choose life" (Deut 30:19), with the piercing word that expresses loving concern for the listening community: "This is no trifling matter for you, but rather your very life" (Deut 32:47).

** ** **

"Stories" and the Story

At this point, we must be clear that we are thinking of the comprehensive story of the Bible, Genesis 1 through Revelation 22, as one story, the self-defining Story of God the Creator and Redeemer. This is different not only from the way "Bible stories" are often thought of in children's Sunday school (Joseph and his Technicolor coat, David and Goliath, Jesus calling the wee little man Zacchaeus down from the tree) but also from the way serious, sincere adult preachers and teachers use "Bible stories" as illustrations of their points—*their* points—with little apparent awareness of the comprehensive biblical narrative and its holistic theology.

Both my story and The Story[2] encountered in the Bible are complex, multilayered realities. Attaining a better understanding of myself—the story I bring to the text—is a matter of psychology, becoming more aware of my personal and cultural history and the ways these unavoidably influence what and how I hear. We will explore the relation of the reader's own story to the story world of the Bible in the following chapters, but first we must pursue the interwoven layers of the Bible's own story.

We now turn to the content and substance of what is heard. Just as nourishment is a matter not of chewing but of chewing food, so saving faith comes not merely by hearing but by hearing the saving message, the good news of the gospel (Rom 10:17). This gospel is heard as a story, which has three dimensions:

1. *The story in the text*, which is far and away the most important. It is best understood when read and heard as a whole by those who approach the text with a *second naiveté* (chs. 5 and 12).
2. *The story behind the text*, "what really happened" as constructed by historical method, Ricoeur's "critical distance" (chs. 6 and 12).
3. *The story of the text*, which traces the ways in which the original preaching of Israel's prophets and teachers became a book, how the book became canonical Scripture, how the Scripture became the English translations we use, and how this Bible was and is reinterpreted into the preaching of our own time and place. This aspect of the story, often told under the heading "How We Got Our Bible" or something similar, is much more than an interesting and inspiring story—though it certainly is that. The text's own story is a hermeneutical tool that opens up the authentic dialogue between Scripture and the reading audience, facilitating a hearing of the text that mediates the words of the text as both address and meaning (chs. 7–10 and 12).

Chapter 5

The Story in the Text

Narrative World and "What the Bible Says"

In James Michener's 1965 bestseller *The Source*, Cullinane is an American archaeologist, part of a team excavating a tell in Israel. He is trying to get a better grasp of the essence of Judaism. After a tiring day on the tell, he goes into the office of a Jewish colleague on the dig:

> "Have you any new material I could read about the Jews?"
>
> "You catch me off guard," Eliav replied.
>
> "The nonsense I've been hearing today. I'm disgusted. I'd like to bite into something solid."
>
> "You've read De Vaux, Kaufmann, Albright?"
>
> Cullinane nodded.
>
> "Maimonides?"
>
> "He's the best."
>
> "There's one better."
>
> "What?"
>
> "Read Deuteronomy. Five times."
>
> "What's your thought?"
>
> "It's the great central book of the Jews and if you master it you'll understand us."
>
> "But is it worth five readings?"
>
> "Yes, because most Gentiles think of the ancient Hebrews as curious relics who reached Israel ten thousand years ago in some kind of archaic mystery."
>
> "How do you think it happened?" Cullinane asked.
>
> "Deuteronomy is so real to me that I feel as if my immediate ancestors—say my great grandfather with desert dust still on his clothes—came down that valley with goats and donkeys and stumbled onto this spot."

> "Will reading Deuteronomy give me such a feeling?"
> "Read it five times and see," Eliav countered.[1]

Now is the time to turn our attention to the content of the instruction 'all Israel,' to get our minds around the substance of Deuteronomy as a whole. The goal is to broaden and deepen our ability to think through the story line of the text in the same way we can retell the plot of a good novel or film from beginning to end.

A helpful way to get a holistic grasp of the contents of a biblical book is to construct one's own outline. The most insightful outlines attempt to discern and present the rhetorical structure of the book, the Deuteronomist's own priorities and agenda, the communication strategy built into the text. Most books about Deuteronomy will present an outline of the canonical text. I here suggest an abbreviated form of my own efforts in this regard, not as a prescription, but as a dialogue partner for readers who may be interested in working out their own understanding of the rhetorical structure of the book. The prehistory of the canonical form of the text probably included more than one edition; the outline suggested here attempts to represent the structure of the final form.[2]

A satellite view of the whole of Deuteronomy's thirty-four chapters suggests that the central core of the book comprises chapters 12 to 26, the "Deuteronomic code," the covenant stipulations for the personal, family, social, political, and religious life of the people of Israel in the promised land—"what God requires of us." *Ethics*, personal and social, is at the center of Deuteronomy. Ethics does not begin with a list of laws, nor does Deuteronomy. The central ethical code is framed on either side by Moses's speeches instructing Israel in what it means to be God's covenant people. The code is preceded by the "Great Sermon" (chs. 4–11) confirming their identity as the elect people of God and the meaning of their history and exhorting and threatening the hearers to be faithful members of the people of God. It is this section that contains the Shema, the love command, and the Ten Commandments. Such Deuteronomic sermons are the basis of many scholars' designation of the genre of Deuteronomy as *preaching* rather than *law*. The central code is followed by the covenant ceremony in which, after hearing the detailed stipulations, the people of God (re)affirm their responsibility (chs. 27–30). The surprising conclusion (to a "law" book!) includes a song all Israel is to learn (ch. 32) and God's blessing pronounced by Moses on each of the twelve tribes of Israel, the people of God (ch. 33). The whole composition is thus framed by Moses's initial speech that looks *back* on their common history that shapes their present (chs. 1–3) and a concluding section that looks *forward* to the consummation of God's purpose (chs. 31–34). Moses dies, and the people are to be led by Joshua into the promised land (ch. 34). The unified composition, to be heard and understood as a whole, is shaped as a chiastic worship service centered on ethics, the practice of justice that flows from faith in the One True God. Though composed of traditional elements that have their own history, the final, canonical edition has a chiastic overall structure: ABCBA.

A	B	C	B^1	A^1
[1–4	[5–11	[12–26]	27–30]	31–34]

A—The outer frame: Looking Backwards in Memory that Shapes the Present (1–4)

B—The inner frame: The Great Sermon/Exhortation (5–11)

C—The central core: Covenant Stipulations for Life in the Present (12–26)

B^1—The inner frame: The Covenant Ceremony (27–30)

A^1—The outer frame: Looking Forward in Hope that Shapes the Present (31–34)

Such outlines are helpful in getting our minds around the composition as a whole and hearing each segment as speaking within its encompassing framework. The outline here presents chapters 27–30 and 31–34 as integral parts of the book, not as one or more "appendixes." This perception of the book's rhetorical structure also lets us see that the legal-sounding instructions in Deuteronomy are framed by the story of the saving acts of God. Deuteronomy includes the Ten Commandments and other laws, but Deuteronomy is not a law book, just as the Gospel of Matthew contains the great Sermon on the Mount but is not a compendium of "the teachings of Jesus"; Jesus's teachings are framed and given meaning by the Gospel narrative in which they are set. So also Deuteronomy is a narrative that can be read as a complete, self-contained story, which is now a segment of the larger biblical drama that extends from Genesis to Revelation. Deuteronomy is a verbal-visual event, an audio drama enacted on the stage of our minds.

** ** **

So here we are, seated in the front row along with a great cloud of witnesses from around the world and across the centuries. It promises to be a soul-stirring presentation, with a cast of thousands. More or less aware of our fellow readers, we await the opening curtain and the beginning of the onstage action. The lights dim, the murmur around us subsides, we open our Bibles to Deuteronomy 1:1, we hear a voice. The curtain on the narrative stage remains closed. There is nothing to see. We are not here to watch a stage production in which other people act out the biblical story before our eyes. We will hear one speaker, one voice: "These are the words that Moses spoke to all Israel beyond the Jordan—in the wilderness, on the plain opposite Suph, between Paran and Tophel, Laban, Hazeroth, and Di-zahab" (Deut 1:1). We already know the story is about Moses and Israel, but this sounds like too much stage setting, perhaps more information than we care to hear. We may wonder why this is important; why begin with so much obscure geography? We want to hear what Moses has to say; we may even long to hear the Word of God—or be fearful that we might. But Moses will not begin to speak until the narrative curtain is opened in 1:6 and we hear his breathtaking first words: "The LORD our God spoke to us." To our surprise or relief, the voice we hear in these first five verses is neither Moses's nor God's. The first voice we hear is the voice of the narrator.

The Narrator

The only voice we hear throughout the whole presentation is the offstage narrator. The narrator will communicate entirely through the spoken word. There is a narrative stage on which the action takes place, but it is totally in the mind of the audience, constructed in the hearer's act of imagination, generated by the words of the narrative, not ready-made on an external stage. In contrast to dramas performed on the stage or movie screen, in verbal narratives, the audience is addressed as those who already belong in the world generated by the spoken or written word. They participate in the creation of the story, are actively involved rather than passive spectators. In the perception of the narrative truth of the Bible, imagination is not truth's enemy. The *hearer* cannot be a passive *viewer* but must respond, participate, in order to "get the picture." The narrator will warn us about making *images*. The narrator tells us what Moses says, who tells us what God says.

Biblical interpretation, including our ability to hear the Word of God that comes through the text of Scripture, has been greatly enriched in the last generation by the rediscovery of the insights of literary criticism, especially the dynamics at work in composing, reading, and hearing narratives—plot, characterization, point of view, narrator, implied and real author, and implied and real reader (see bibliography). For our purposes, here I will only briefly sketch the role and function of the narrator and related issues.

1. **The narrator of Deuteronomy is not the author but the voice created by the author to tell the story.** The author composes the words on the page. It is the narrator's voice the reader or listening audience hears speaking from the printed page.

2. **The author must choose what type of narrator will tell the actual story.** The basic decision is whether the narrator speaks from within or outside the narrative world projected by the story. The same author may employ different types of narrators in different works, as illustrated in the writings of Samuel Clemens (Mark Twain).

a. In his autobiographical writings, Clemens chose to speak through an internal narrator, mostly casting himself in the role, speaking as the principal character from within his own life story. Nonetheless, Twain illustrates that even in diaries and autobiographies, the narrator is not identical to the author, who could create any number of versions of himself, whether factually true, distorted, or intentionally false.[3]

b. In *The Adventures of Huckleberry Finn*, the author chose to tell the story in the words of Huck himself, speaking in the first person from inside the story being told. Such an internal narrator can only tell what he has observed himself, his own thoughts and opinions, which he may share with the readers. He cannot know what other characters in the story are thinking or planning unless they tell him and cannot report on the future, past, or narrate events at which he is not present. Such a narrative can have no "Meanwhile, back at the ranch" switching of scenes. Nor does the reading audience ever wonder how the narrator got his information. Every such credible narrator gets it the same way every other human being does: by personal experience, by remembering what was said or done in his presence, or by research, such as is done by investigative reporters. Biblical authors employ internal narrators only sparingly. Canonical examples are provided by Paul's autobiographical section in Galatians, by the book of Revelation narrated in the first person by "I, John," and by the Ezra and Nehemiah memoirs (Gal 1:11–2:14; Rev 1:9; 22:8; Ezra 7–10; Neh 8–9; lightly edited in Neh 1–7; 11:1–2; 12:31–43; 13:4–31). None of the canonical Gospels has an internal narrator, but the apocryphal *Gospel of Peter* is told in the voice of Simon Peter (e.g., "I, Simon Peter, and my brother Andrew, took our nets and went to the sea" [*Gos. Pet.* 14.60]).

c. The external narrator is illustrated by *The Adventures of Tom Sawyer*. We typically tend to think of such a narrator as the author himself, but there is a significant difference. The external narrator is not a participant in the story but the invisible spectator reporting the action in the narrative to the listening audience, perhaps with his own observations and interpretative comments. The hearer/reader can see and hear the story's actions and words only through the voice of the invisible narrator. Most histories are narrated by an external narrator. Even though the actual writer may have lived through some or all of the history, the author narrates the history in the voice of one who stands outside the narrative and describes it to the audience. Most of the Bible's narrative books have an external narrator.

3. The narrator of Deuteronomy is exterior to the narrative itself. To understand Deuteronomy, we must be clear that Moses, the principal character and speaker, is neither author nor narrator. Unlike Moses, who is the main character in the narrative, the narrator speaks from outside the narrative framework, refers to Moses in the third person, and refers to the Israelites as "he," "they," "them," and "the people" (e.g., Deut 1:1, 3; 5:1; 10:7; 27:1; 29:1). Though the narrator is clearly an Israelite who regards the LORD as the One True God, Moses as God's primary prophet, and Israel as the elect people of God, he never makes his Israelite identity explicit, never speaks in the first person as "I" or "we," never refers to the LORD as "our God," and never refers to what the LORD has done for "us," as does the main character Moses. We might contrast this, for example, with the narrator of Luke–Acts, who speaks overtly in the preface to each volume and emerges in the "we" sections of Acts (Luke 1:1–4; Acts 16:10–17; 20:5–15; 21:1–18; 27:1–28:16 [+11:28 in a few manuscripts]). The narrator of Deuteronomy makes no claim to have been a participant in the action he narrates or to have personally heard Moses speak. In this regard, Deuteronomy is more like the Gospel of Mark than either Luke–Acts or the apocryphal *Gospel of Peter*. In both Deuteronomy and Mark, the narrator represents the actual author's theology in form, function, and content.

4. The narrator of Deuteronomy knows and communicates information that transcends the narrative framework itself. Such narrators are sometimes described as "omniscient," since they may speak as if they have a God's-eye view of the universe and all history and know the thoughts and hearts of every character in the story. Such a narrator is the silent, invisible observer of every scene in the narrative and can report verbatim the secret conversations among the priests plotting Jesus's death or what Jesus prayed when he was alone in Gethsemane (cf. Mark 14:1–2, 10–11, 32–36). Some narrators even know what happened before the world was created and what will happen after it ends—not only the events in every corner of the world here below but the goings-on in the heavenly world above. The narrator of Genesis 1 lets the reader hear and see the drama of creation, and the narrator of Job 1–2 knows what happens in the heavenly court, sharing with the audience the verbatim report of the conversation between the Lord and the *satan*, the heavenly prosecuting attorney. The narrator of Deuteronomy has a kind of finite "omniscience" but does not parade it. His knowledge transcends the particulars of time and space. He knows, and allows the audience to know, more than the characters in the story know or can know. From the opening paragraph onward, the narrator knows that the Lord had given Moses the words he speaks to Israel (1:3), and at the narrative's conclusion, he is able to take the audience along with him as he accompanies Moses to his death on Mount Pisgah, when Moses is alone with God, to narrate the dialogue there between Moses and the Lord that is heard by the later audience of Deuteronomy but not by the Israelites in the narrative on the plain below. He knows of revelations from God that are not included in Moses's own speeches, telling us that God revealed certain things to Moses that Moses himself does not communicate either to the Israelites in the story or to Deuteronomy's later audiences (31:14b, 16b–21, 23b; 32:49–52). He does not, however, claim to know events in the transcendent world, what happened at creation or will happen in the eschatological future, or the interior thoughts and feelings of characters in the story. The audience never learns what is going on in the minds and hearts of Moses, Aaron, or the Canaanites.

5. **The narrator of Deuteronomy is a minor but controlling voice.** In the present, canonical form of Deuteronomy, the audience is addressed by a single voice throughout, which for the most part directly quotes "the words that Moses spoke to all Israel" (1:1). Moses speaks about 93 percent of the text of Deuteronomy—even though in Exodus 4:10–17, he famously claimed that he was no speaker! In about 2 percent of the text, the narrator quotes the Lord directly. Thus about 95 percent of the text of Deuteronomy is composed of quotations, so the quantity of the narrator's direct address to the reader is relatively small. Nonetheless, the 5 percent in which the narrator speaks to the listeners plays a significant role in the way the story is communicated to the audience, which has no independent access to the story but is entirely dependent on what the narrator says and how it is said. The narrator controls the way the narrative is presented to the audience, arranging the order of the narrative's content and the relative length of its sections (its "outline") and its spatial, temporal, and theological perspectives. The narrator keeps a low profile, is only a voice, heard but not seen. He wants to be invisible, to mediate the story to the audience but stay out of the way. So well has he

done his work that most readers never think about the narrator, and this is the way he wants it.

6. The narrator of Deuteronomy is located in space and time and tells the story from this temporal and geographical perspective.

a. The cosmopolitan, world-wise narrator speaks from a particular standpoint in space—namely, from within the promised land, on the West Bank between the Jordan and the Mediterranean, looking eastward as he reports the words of Moses being spoken to 'all Israel,' "beyond the Jordan," which always clearly refers to the East Bank (1:1, 5; 4:41, 46, 47). This is made explicit in 4:41 (cf. 4:49). The listening community is apparently to see themselves as exiles in Babylon or new returnees from there (see ch. 6, "The Story behind the Text"). They are to hear Deuteronomy's good news from their perceived situation outside the land. They wonder what is the way forward for the people of God who come *back* into the land that had been lost, from which they or their parents had been deported because of Israel's rebellion—a rebellion not only against Babylon but against God. Now, through the grace and power of God, they are returning or have recently returned. They have a second chance, a new beginning. They are chastened by their experience. They realize they need direction from God lest the error be repeated.

The audience addressed by Moses in the narrative world is told what they must do to retain the land; the reading audience addressed by the narrator is told what they must do to regain the land and reclaim the promises made to previous generations of Israelites. They hear themselves addressed by God through the prophet Moses, speaking to them in the words of the narrator, who is "already there" in the promised land—as are many of the readers. The narrator almost always portrays the Moses of the narrative as "in character," looking westward, toward the promised land that Israel has not yet attained and that he will never enter. "Beyond the Jordan" in Moses's speeches pictures Moses with the Israelites on the plains of Moab looking west (Deut 2:29; 3:20, 25; 4:21, 22, 26; 9:1; 11:30, 31 [explicitly identifies "beyond the Jordan" as "to the west"]; 12:10; 27:2, 4, 12; 30:18; 31:13; 32:47). Twice, however, Moses shares the narrator's and narratees' perspective and refers to the land "beyond the Jordan" as the East Bank (3:8; 11:30). This is probably best explained not as an editorial or scribal lapse but as an artful, intentional fusion of the narrator's perspective with that of Moses in the narrative world. It corresponds to the author-editor's compositional technique, which has the narrator shuttling back and forth between "that day" of the speaker's past and "this day" of his own here and now.

This standpoint is important to the author/narrator, who does not try to conceal it but actually emphasizes it in a number of ways. The narrator's initial words, the paragraph that sets the stage for the appearance of Moses addressing all Israel, begin and end with the explicit statement that "Moses spoke to all Israel beyond the Jordan—in the wilderness" (1:1) and that it was "beyond the Jordan in the land of Moab" that "Moses undertook to expound this law" (1:5). This initial emphasis is repeated four times (4:41, 46, 47, 49) in the conclusion of this opening section of Deuteronomy, forming a framework for the four chapters of narrative that prepares for the exhortation and laws that follow. This makes it unmistakably clear that Deuteronomy intends to be heard by an audience that pictures itself as already in the land, whether actually there or soon to be (re)entering the land. As they hear the text of Deuteronomy read, they picture themselves "overhearing" what Moses says to the Israelites of a former generation, listening to instructions for how the people of God are to live in this land in which they and/or their ancestors had lived for some time. The audience joins the narrator in seeing and hearing all this from within the land, already aware of its history, looking east and looking back on Moses's instructions to 'all Israel' on the plains of Moab. As we shall explore more carefully below, such a subtle communication strategy allows the audience both to listen in on ("overhear") what was directly said to someone else ("not written to us") *and* to hear the word spoken in the text as directly addressing us ("written to us").

b. The narrator also is clear about his temporal location and perspective. *Like the later narrators of the canonical Gospels*, who speak from their postresurrection point of view and tell their story of what Jesus did and said from that perspective, the narrator of Deuteronomy looks back on a lengthy history of Israel, telling it in the words of Moses, who, in the narrative world of Deuteronomy, is still looking ahead (cf., e.g., Deut 17:14–20; 28:15–68; Mark 13; Matt 24; Luke 17, 21; John 13–17). The audience hears the voice of Moses—a voice conveyed to the audience by the narrator, who stands with them in their own time, looking back on the history of Israel in the land to which the Moses in the story world of the text looks forward. The audience can choose whether they will interpret this history—in which they themselves continue to participate—from the standpoint of the narrator, who guides them and us to its proper interpretation. The narrator encourages later readers, including those in the twenty-first century, to look back on the story being told and to accept the narrator's guidance built into the text itself.

Though having the kind of finite "omniscience" described above, the narrator does not speak from a transcendent perch outside time and history but surveys and narrates the drama from a particular time and place in this world. He is not Moses's contemporary, looking out on the drama unfolding on the plains of Moab as it happens, listening to Moses's speeches and relaying them to the audience "in real time," but looks *back* on them. Indeed, he looks back on the death and burial of Moses, which are communicated not as predictions of the future but as events of the past—some considerable distance in the past, since no one knows the location of Moses's grave "to this day" (34:1–6). He speaks from a time after Israel's settlement in the land (2:12!) and after they had experienced the presence and heard the testimony of a number of prophets, none of whom could supersede Moses, who knew YHWH face-to-face (34:10). From this post-Moses point in time, he looks back even prior to Moses, viewing the previous history of the world—including Israel, the Edomites, and other nations—and looking forward to the history of Israel and the nations.

7. **The narrator of Deuteronomy utilizes a quotation format that is part of his strategy of communication.** Deuteronomy has more spoken words, reported as direct discourse, than any other book in the Bible. The author of Deuteronomy could have written most or all of the composition in his own voice, speaking directly to the audience, giving an account of God's saving acts in his own words, and summing up what God, Moses, and Israel said as indirect quotation (*diegesis*, or discursive narrative, "telling"): "Moses told us that we should not make images of the LORD, should observe the Sabbath," and so on. In direct quotation (*mimesis*, or "showing"), however—especially in extended sections of direct discourse—the audience tends to forget that they are hearing the voice of the narrator quoting someone else and readily thinks of themselves as being directly addressed by the speaker on the narrative stage: "You are there." This is the vivid mimetic "show" mode rather than the diegetic "tell" mode typical of biblical narrative. The audience directly hears the voice of the characters on the stage rather than hearing the narrator's voice describing or summarizing the action in his own words. In Deuteronomy, the narrator speaks almost entirely in the mode of direct quotation—showing, not telling, and placing virtually everything he has to say in the mouth of Moses, who is the only character to speak on the narrative stage (with the exception of the voice of the LORD that intrudes unmarked into the Song of Moses in 32:34). Even the Ten Commandments are embedded three layers deep

in Deuteronomy's quotation strategy: the narrator says (5:1a) that Moses said (5:1b–21) that God says (5:6–21; note the use of double and single quotation marks in the RSV and other modern English translations). Yet when reading the Ten Commandments, and especially when hearing them read aloud, the audience hears them as direct address, as intended by the narrator: "I am the LORD your God, who brought *you* out of the land of Egypt, out of the house of slavery; *you* shall have no other gods before me" (Exod 20:2–3).

Though the substance is the same, the rhetoric is different from the experience of reading a text that speaks in the discursive mode of "telling": "Our great prophet Moses taught Israel that God is the one who had brought them out of Egypt, and that they must not worship any other gods." Deuteronomy's narrator wants to stay out of the spotlight, to facilitate the encounter between the hearers and the living God. Here, too, preachers and teachers can learn from the form of biblical communication, not only from its content. A skillful narrator can blend mostly direct speech interspersed with some indirect quotation in a way that helps the audience bridge the gap between the there-and-then of the world of the text and the here-and-now voice of God that still speaks through the text to our own generation. Deuteronomy has such a narrator, a preacher-teacher who adroitly incorporates signals into the text to facilitate direct address to the audience.

In Deuteronomy, as often in the Jewish Scriptures, quoted speech within the narrative world is fused with the direct address of God that comes through the narrative. Early Christian authors were profoundly influenced by this fusion of horizons between the narrative world of Scripture and their own world. This is especially striking in the Fourth Gospel, where the voice of Jesus "back there" in the story modulates seamlessly into the present voice of God / the risen Christ, as in John 3:1–21. Early Christian preachers and teachers lived in the narrative world of the Bible, adopting its vocabulary and style intentionally or by osmosis. Their Bible provided them with a model of quotation and communication strategies that bridged the gap between hearing the Bible as report and being confronted by it as address. Here, the biblical mode of communicating the Word of God provides an archetype for biblical preaching and teaching. In a sermon or lesson, a biblical story safely "back there" about "somebody else" modulates into direct address to the congregation or class *without* shifting gears with a disruptive "Now, let's see if we can apply this to our own situation."

Narrative World

Every narrative projects a world, inviting the audience to enter the story world of the narrative and—at least while reading or listening—to experience that world as the real world. The following paragraphs attempt to sketch the way the Deuteronomists wanted 'all Israel' to see that world. It is a world Israel does not know (they've never been anyplace except the desert), a world they can't know by common sense, just by looking around.

Like all human beings, they already have a view of the world / a mindset about how the world works, what is real and what is not—a worldview/mindset they have constructed, mostly unconsciously, through a combination of heredity, environment, and personal experiences. Deuteronomy presents them and us with a different world, an alternative, new, nonobvious view of the way things *are*, the *real* world. Before they or we even ask how this world is related to the world we grew up in and have always assumed was the only real world, we need to get our minds around the narrative world of the biblical text—to get this world around our minds. We need to just enter the narrative world of the Bible without getting it mixed up with other information and views of the world, in the Bible and out, however true they may be. We'll get to that in due course. First, we need to listen to these words of the narrator/Moses/God and their invitation to enter "the strange new world of the Bible."[4] What is this world like?

In the narrator's own direct speech to the listening audience, he gives only a bare outline of the events, dealing almost entirely with what Moses and Israel did while encamped on the plains of Moab: Moses spoke and the people listened. By gathering up the texts in which the narrator directly addresses the listening community, the reader can easily reconstruct the world as presented by the narrator, the "Narrator's Story":

- Prior to Israel's arrival, the LORD had long since already given the East Bank to Esau and Ammon and had helped Israel dispossess the other peoples on the East Bank, the Amorite kingdoms of Sihon and Og.
- In Moab, Israel had already come out of Egypt via Horeb and Kadesh Barnea (1:1–5).
- Moses then revealed/interpreted the Torah he (but not they) had already been given at Horeb. (The narrator cites these lengthy speeches.)
- Moses, the elders, and the Levites charged the people to keep the Torah.

- Moses wrote the Torah and arranged for its communication to later generations.
- Moses wrote the song and taught it to the people as a testimony to future generations.
- Moses blessed each tribe and portrayed something of their future.
- Moses died, was buried, and was mourned.

The bulk of the text of Deuteronomy is thus composed of speeches of Moses quoted by the narrator. These speeches refer to a large number of events of the past and future in places far beyond Israel's camp by the Jordan. These words of Moses refer to a world his hearers have barely experienced for themselves, a world they can only imagine as they hear Moses speak. This is what literary critics refer to as the *narrative world.* It is not identical to the world of real events that may be behind the text; it is the world projected by the narrative itself. Later reader/hearers of the text of Deuteronomy may be aware of events not reported in the narrative (as was the author!), since every narrative represents a minuscule fraction of what could have been said (John 20:30–31!).

A close reading of Deuteronomy will disclose all the events referred to or presupposed in the narrative. By my count, there are approximately 377 events in Deuteronomy's narrative world. Such tabulations necessarily involve several types of ambiguities. These events may be listed in the order they occur in the text (the "plotted order"). They may then be rearranged into the chronological order in which they happened (the "referential order"). This exercise reveals something of the way the author thinks of the world, the way he wants the reader to think. A streamlined result of such an analysis is presented below, documented with only a few selected texts. We have noted above that the story in which both narrator and audience live is divided into three epochs of the larger story:

I. The story of the whole creation, embracing *all God's peoples*
II. The story of Israel, the *covenant people of God*
III. The future consummation of God's purpose for the *whole creation*

All the events of Deuteronomy's narrative world fit readily within this grand scheme of universal history. The narrator takes his stance with the people of Israel, looking back to the creation and forward to the consummation of God's purpose.

I. Creation

The earliest event in Deuteronomy's narrative world is the creation of human beings. The story of Israel is incorporated into the universal human story that began with Adam (4:32). The particular story of Israel begins with the call of Abraham, but it cannot be understood unless it is seen as a segment of universal history that begins at creation *but not earlier*. In contrast to some pagan and Jewish mythologies, what happens in the world we live in is not the result of goings-on in the world of the gods before creation. Deuteronomy's narrative world contains no precreation events. This is in step with biblical theology as a whole. Like the creation stories of Genesis 1–2, even the New Testament texts that affirm the preexistence of Christ (e.g., Phil 2:5–11; Col 1:15–20; John 1:1–18) have no interest in speculations about what might have happened before creation. The One God made the good world, and human history began and continues to unfold in this-worldly history, under the firm dome of heaven. Some streams of noncanonical apocalyptic Judaism developed theories of precreation fall or rebellion of angels, whose leader became the Satan of Milton's *Paradise Lost* and Goethe's *Faust*, but these mythological attempts to explain the origin of evil are not adopted in mainstream canonical Judaism and Christianity. In Deuteronomy, the story of God's peoples begins at creation but not before.

The Deuteronomic narrator skips lightly over the events we know as Genesis 1–11, from the creation of the world and humanity to the covenant with Abraham/Israel. Nonetheless, God was active in universal history, had given the Edomites and Ammonites their lands long before the arrival of Israel on the plains of Moab, and the Creator's sovereignty included even the migration of the Caphtorites (Philistines?) who dispossessed the peoples on the west coast of Canaan and took over their territory (2:5, 9, 12, 19, 22, 23).

II. Covenant

In some way that Deuteronomy does not narrate, God's good creation became perverted and alienated from its Maker. Even so, in Deuteronomy, God's response to human sin is not the promise to send a Messiah. In Deuteronomy's narrative world, God's saving act is not messianic but ecclesial, not a Christ to come but the creation of a historical community in this world.

THE ANCESTORS

The story moves quickly to God's choice of a particular people as his agents and witnesses to the whole world. As a pure act of God's love and grace, not only for the ancestors, but for the whole world, God chose Abraham and his descendants through Isaac and Jacob to be his treasured possession (Deut 4:37; 7:6). None of the troubles and triumphs of this family found in Genesis is narrated or presupposed in Deuteronomy or the Deuteronomistic History. From Deuteronomy, the reader would never know that the story of Abraham began in Ur of the Chaldees, followed by the migration through Haran to Canaan, where the wayfarer Abraham worshipped God at a number of altars he constructed along the way. Both the narrator and the actual audience know that these gaps can be filled in later by Israel's teachers after Israel is settled in the land (4:32; 32:7), but Moses does not rehearse this ancestral history to the Israelites in the story world of the text of Deuteronomy. Of sole importance is only that God has made a unilateral covenant with this people and will never forget it (4:31). Three hallmarks of this covenant are repeatedly emphasized: (1) the covenant included the promise of a *land*, a *place* (1:8; 6:10; 7:8; 19:8, 30:20); (2) the covenant people began as a small group comprising one clan of blood relatives, is already a large assembly, and is destined to be a countless multitude, "a thousand times more" than the stars (1:11; cf. 1:9; 10:22; 26:5); and (3) the covenant is not conditional or temporary but endures forever (5:29; 12:28; 28:45; 29:29).

EGYPT TO HOREB

The covenant people is not a static, fixed social body but moves through history. Israel began as a small, wandering clan (homeless, near death [see 26:5 and commentaries thereon]) and migrated to Egypt, where they were accepted as resident aliens (11:10; 23:7; 26:5; 29:16). Deuteronomy does not say how long Israel was in Egypt (no "400 years" [Gen 15:13; Acts 7:6; 13:19] or "430 years" [Exod 12:40–41; Gal 3:17]), but their residence there pictures it as long enough for a small group to become a "great nation, mighty and populous" (Deut 26:5).

All Israel became Egyptian slaves (4:34; 5:15; 26:5). God delivered all Israel from Egyptian slavery (4:20, 34; 5:15; 7:8; 29:2). God led all Israel through the wilderness to Horeb, through many trials; provided them with food, water, and clothing; tested and disciplined them; and protected them from their enemies (2:7; 6:16; 8:2–4). At Horeb, God instructed Israel through Moses to form a structured community with commanders, officials, and judges to regulate the life of the people and settle disputes (1:9–18). The crucial event at Horeb was God's speaking to the whole community in the mountain epiphany. They directly heard God's voice out of the fire, making the covenant with them and speaking the Ten Commandments, which God himself wrote on the stone tablets (4:10–13, 23, 32; 5:2). The experience was so fearsome, the people could not bear to hear God's voice and asked that Moses alone hear the details of the covenant law and tell them later (5:4). This "later" is the contemporizing "today" (*hayōm*), which occurs fifty times in Deuteronomy. In contrast to the chronology portrayed in Exodus–Numbers, 'all Israel' does not hear the detailed instructions for the life of the people of God in the promised land until Moses addresses the new generation forty years later, encamped on the plains of Moses shortly before crossing the Jordan to possess the land.

While Moses is on the mountain alone with God, Israel makes a golden calf as their way of worshipping God, already at Horeb misunderstanding and rebelling against the God who is preparing to teach them his identity and theirs. Moses intercedes, and God does not destroy them. At God's command, Israel leaves Horeb for the holy place of Kadesh Barnea (1:19).

KADESH BARNEA

At Kadesh Barnea, God commands them to enter the land (from the southwest! They are still west of the Jordan; 1:20–21). They propose to send twelve scouts to reconnoiter the land. Moses approves, and the spies investigate. Eleven of the twelve report: it is a good land but too strong for Israel to invade. The people accept the negative report and refuse to budge. God is angry and swears that none of the Israelites except Caleb and his descendants will receive their inheritance in the good land God had promised to the ancestors (1:22–36; Joshua and the young children are added in vv. 38–39). Israel repents and, against God's command, makes an abortive attempt to invade Canaan on their own. Suffering a terrible defeat by the indigenous Amorites, the warriors return to camp and raise a great lamentation, but God pays no attention (1:41–44).

In the Deuteronomist's view, Israel spent forty years in the wilderness between Egypt and the promised land (2:7; 8:2, 4; 29:4). During this time, the exodus generation died out, and a new generation of Israel emerged that had known neither Egypt nor Horeb. The story of the thirty-eight years from Kadesh to Moab is virtually empty. For the Deuteronomist, the next truly significant event after the departure from Kadesh is the command to the new generation to cross the Wadi Zered and begin the struggle to possess the promised land—this time from the east (2:13, 18). The exilic and postexilic readers recognize themselves in the story and take heart.

The Campaigns East of the Jordan

Israel encounters five nations east of the Jordan. Three are peaceful: YHWH commands Israel to pass by the Edomites, the Moabites, and the Ammonites, all of them distant ancestral kin to whom the Lord has allotted land just as he had allotted Israel's land to them (2:3–25). Edom is cooperative and respectful, but the Moabites and Ammonites do not respond to Israel's peaceful proposal. Not only do they not share their food and water with the wandering and needy Israelites; they hire the false prophet Balaam to curse Israel—but it doesn't work (23:3–5). The Lord protects Israel from their hostility, putting the fear of God into all people everywhere (2:25). Two encounters are hostile: Moses sends messengers to Sihon, king of the Amorites, offering him terms of peace, but God hardens his spirit and makes his heart defiant in order to hand him over to Israel (2:25–30). Sihon resists, God commands Israel to take possession of his land, and the Israelites invade and kill all the inhabitants, leaving no survivors—the first instance of the *herem* (2:31–36). So also in the encounter with the giant-king Og of Bashan: all the people are killed, and Israel takes their land, keeping the livestock and plunder for themselves (3:1–7). The tribes of Reuben and Gad and half the tribe of Manasseh are granted land in the conquered territories but are to join with all Israel in the conquest of Canaan (3:8–22).

Moses's Speech to All Israel

With the territories east of the Jordan pacified, the stage is set for Moses's speeches to all Israel, which compose the bulk of the book (4:1–33:29). At Horeb, God had made a covenant with all Israel on the basis of the Decalogue. These extended speeches present, update, and interpret the Torah that had been given on Horeb, which the Israelites now hear for the first time. Moses now gives the stipulations of the covenant, setting forth the way of life for those who are to be the people of God in the midst of the Canaanite culture of the promised land, and provides a preview of Israel's future. The speaker concludes with curses and threats if Israel is not faithful to the Torah and promises of life and blessing if they faithfully obey the stipulations of the covenant (28:1–68).

Covenant Confirmed, Renewed, Elaborated / Fleshed Out

After the covenant-Torah speech has ended, the covenant is instituted/confirmed/renewed with the present generation that will enter the land (Deut 29:1, 10–13). Moses renews the series of threats and promises, exhorting the people to "Choose life" (Deut 27:11–30:20; 30:19 summarizes the challenge).

Leadership Passes from Moses to Joshua

God appears at the tent of meeting in the sight of all Israel, God commissions Joshua, Moses lays his hands on him, Joshua is filled with the spirit of wisdom, and God commands all Israel to obey Joshua after Moses's death (31:14; 34:9). Joshua then has no successors in the role of sole leader of all Israel. (The Deuteronomistic Historians know that a long period of individual judges played this role, none too successfully, until the kingship was established.)

Provision Made for Later Generations

The revelation is written down and handed on. The very words that mediated the original revelation are preserved. The same day they cross the Jordan, the words are inscribed on plastered stones and available to all who can read or be read to (27:1). Moses writes down the Torah and places the document beside the ark, in the charge of the Levites.

The revealed Word of God is mediated to later generations not only by written texts available to all but by authorized teachers. Moses, the elders, and the Levites speak in unison to all Israel (27:1–10). The revelation communicated to the people through Moses will continue to be interpreted in the ongoing history by Israel's elders and Levitical teachers. Just as the voice of God is fused with that of Moses, so the voice of Moses is fused with that of the elders and Levitical teachers. Later generations who *hear* their elders and teachers hear Moses/God.

God instructs Moses to compose a poem or song and teach it to all Israel (31:19–22; 32:1–43). Like the Torah (31:26), the song is not only to instruct but to be a witness *against* Israel when they are unfaithful (31:19).

Moses blesses 'all Israel,' with a particular blessing for each of the twelve tribes (33:1–29).

Despite Moses's repeated pleas to enter the promised land with the people, God does not allow this, and Moses dies "at God's command"—not from violence, old age, or illness, though he was 120 years old—and God buries him in an unmarked grave. Israel laments him for thirty days and then moves on to cross the Jordan under Joshua's leadership (34:5–8).

Neither the story of Israel nor the narrative world of Deuteronomy ends with the death of Moses. Moses's speeches had looked ahead to many events in Israel's future, filling in the content of Deuteronomy's narrative world. Just as the authors of each of the Gospels present Jesus's Farewell Discourses as his address to his disciples in the pre-Easter situation looking ahead to the cross, resurrection, and mission of the church, so Moses's long speeches project a narrative world that is still future to 'all Israel' on the plains of Moab. And just as the authors and readers of the Gospels looked back on the tragedy and triumph of the end and new beginning of Jesus's life, so later readers of Deuteronomy hear Moses's speeches looking back at the history of Israel from their own later situations. The following sketch does not draw on the Deuteronomistic History but continues to portray the narrative world "predicted" by Deuteronomy.

THE CONQUEST AND SETTLEMENT

Just as God had led Israel out of Egypt, God will go with Israel into the land, fighting for Israel, doing to the Canaanite kingdoms as he had done to the Egyptians and the kingdoms east of the Jordan, clearing out seven nations before them, and bringing them into the land (1:30; 3:21; 7:1, 17–26; 8:20; 9:3; 11:29; 31:3). In contrast to the exodus, when God alone fought to deliver Israel and destroyed the Egyptian army, the armies of Israel itself are to fight, destroy the previous inhabitants of Canaan, and make no covenant with them but kill them and take their land, showing them no mercy (2:12; 7:2). 'All Israel,' comprising tribal units from both east and west of the Jordan, participate in the conquest.

LIFE IN THE LAND

In Deuteronomy's view, Israel's worship is not a special area of life that can be separated from their "secular" life, but all of life is of one piece, the good life lived before the LORD in community with the whole people of God. For our convenience in getting our minds around the story world of Deuteronomy, we may unravel these interwoven life strands into two main categories: Israel's good life and Israel's relation to God in worship.

The Good Life

Israel no longer comprises wandering clans of nomads or displaced immigrants. They now have their own land, their own place, their homeland, their inheritance (1:36). The Israelites will not only inherit houses they did not build, vineyards they did not plant, and cisterns they did not dig

(6:10–11); they will build new houses and plant new vineyards (20:1–9). It is a good land, a beautiful, fertile land, "a land that the LORD your God looks after. The eyes of the LORD your God are always on it, from the beginning of the year to the end of the year" (Deut 11:12). The promised land is not a land of scarcity, where life is marginal and must be eked out day by day, but a land oozing with milk and honey (paradigmatically 26:9; the phrase occurs six times in Deuteronomy and twenty times in the Old Testament, mostly under the influence of Deuteronomy's usage). The abundance will be shared by all. If Israel is faithful to the covenant and keeps God's commands, there will be no needy, no poor people (15:4). Debts will be forgiven every seventh year and mortgaged homes and property returned to their owners (15:1–9). This is the picture of the good life the LORD intends, the world projected in Deuteronomy's narrative.

Worship and Relation to God

The good life not only includes worship; it is essentially worship, all of life lived before God in gratitude and praise. The hearers of Moses's speeches in Deuteronomy have never experienced cultic worship. They (i.e., their parents) received no instructions at Horeb about building a tabernacle or ordaining priests to serve at the altar, no rules for sacrifice. During the wilderness wanderings, God set apart the tribe of Levi to carry the ark of the covenant, minister to the LORD, and bless Israel in God's name (10:6–9), but there is no reference to priests who offer sacrifice—that will come after Israel has entered the promised land. Deuteronomy's instructions are for life in the land, which already had a powerful and seductive religious tradition. How to come to terms with *that* is the issue for the hearers of Moses's message in Deuteronomy.

Other traditions included in the framework of the Deuteronomistic History report the LORD-approved worship at various shrines (e.g., Shechem [Josh 24:26]; Nob [1 Sam 14:3; 21:2–6], Shiloh [Josh 18:1; 1 Sam 1:3], Carmel [1 Kgs 18:17–40], Gilgal [Josh 5:10; 1 Sam 10:8; 11:15; 15:21]), but the narrative world projected by Deuteronomy has only two brief preliminary steps toward the establishment of the *one* central shrine. On the same day they cross the Jordan and enter the land, they are to build an altar, make sacrifices, celebrate what God has done, and write all the words of the Torah clearly on stones for all to see (27:5). They are then (on the same day? regularly?) to gather at Shechem for a ceremony in which six tribes stand on Mount Gerizim to pronounce blessings on the people, and six are to stand on the opposite mountain, Mount Ebal, to pronounce curses (11:29). Otherwise, Deuteronomy assumes and repeatedly commands that legitimate worship can only be performed at the central shrine, the one place the Lord will choose to place his name (12:1–28; 14:23–25; 15:20; 16:2, 6–7, 11; 17:8–10). All other places of worship, where the Canaanites had practiced their own religion, are to be demolished (7:5; 12:3). In the story world of Deuteronomy, faithful Israel will worship the One True God at the one place the Lord will choose and kill or drive out those who worship other Gods—including apostate Israelites (13:1–18). The only people in the land, the only people on earth (the word *eretz* means both "land" and "earth"), will be the faithful people of God, welcoming all those who worship the Lord, living happily and free in their own land God had given them, so that "Your days and the days of your children may be multiplied in the land that the Lord swore to your ancestors to give them, as long as the heavens are above the earth" (Deut 11:21; cf. 12:28, "forever"; 18:5 "for all time").

Unfaithful Israel

This grand picture of the promised glorious future for Israel was not to happen—not in Moses's time, not in the narrator's time, not in the time of the original hearers of either Moses or the authors of Deuteronomy. Moses's speeches constantly repeat that the promise of the good life in the land is conditional on obedience to the Torah (4:25–28; 7:12; 8:19; 11:13; most intensely 28:1–65). Israel was not faithful. The Lord was faithful. Even so, God's faithfulness could be pictured as conditional or unconditional. The narrative world portrays this both ways. During Israel's long history in the land, God's faithfulness is (mostly) represented as dependent on Israel's obedience. Although they already belong to the chosen people and bear the mark of the covenant people on their bodies, they are commanded, "Circumcise your hearts" (Deut 30:6). They must take the demands of the covenant upon themselves, live by its laws, love the Lord with all their hearts, accept God's love for them, and become channels of that love to others, loving the stranger and providing them food and clothing (10:13–17). The final words of Moses's sermon say, "I call heaven and earth to witness against you today that I have set before you life and death, blessings and curses. Choose life so that you and your descendants may live, loving the Lord your God, obeying him, and holding fast to him; for that means life to you and length of days, so that you may live in the land that the Lord swore to give to your ancestors, to Abraham, to Isaac, and to Jacob" (Deut 30:19–20). Israel made their choice. The result was disaster. The threat was to 'all Israel,' Israel as a whole, the people as such, not individuals within the covenant people. There is nothing in

Deuteronomy like "Those who are faithful will receive life; the unfaithful will receive death." If Israel forgets the covenant, Israel as a people will be utterly destroyed—will be driven out and scattered among the nations, where they will serve other gods of wood and stone (4:26–28). If Israel follows other gods, God will be angry and destroy Israel from the face of the earth (6:15). God will afflict unfaithful Israel with the horrors of warfare and siege, including starvation and cannibalism (28:15–68). The ultimate punishment is loss of the land itself—deportation into exile, where they will again become a landless, homeless people as they had been before the LORD delivered them from slavery and formed them into a nation. The catalog of threatened catastrophes reaches this fearsome climax:

> You shall be plucked off the land that you are entering to possess. The LORD will scatter you among all peoples, from one end of the earth to the other; and there you shall serve other gods, of wood and stone, which neither you nor your ancestors have known. Among those nations you shall find no ease, no resting place. . . . The LORD will bring you back in ships to Egypt, by a route that I promised you would never see again; and there you shall offer yourselves for sale to your enemies as male and female slaves, but there will be no buyer. (Deut 28:65, 68)

Faithful LORD, Transformer of Hearts

Israel was unfaithful; their land, cities, and *central sanctuary* were destroyed; and they were exiled (the narrative world perspective does not permit the sanctuary to be called "temple" or to be located in "Jerusalem"). But the LORD remained faithful. The covenant that was portrayed as conditional, as they looked forward to receiving the land, turns out to be unconditional after the Israelites themselves have shown themselves to be unfaithful. Without diminishing the Israelites' own responsibility, the overruling reality turns out to be that the salvation of the world is the responsibility of God the Creator. But this is to anticipate. The narrative projects a world in which the LORD is merciful, will not abandon or destroy Israel, will not forget the covenant promise made to the ancestors. The ultimate fulfillment of the promise is a matter not of Israel's efforts but of God's faithfulness (Deut 4:30–31). When the deported Israelites remember the Torah in the lands of their exile, YHWH will have mercy on them and restore them to the good life in the promised land (30:1–10). This is the real world, projected by the Deuteronomic narrative.

III. Consummation

This picture of 'all Israel,' transformed Israel, in the land, living the good life, is the final scene in Deuteronomy's narrative world, "as long as the heavens are above the earth" (Deut 11:21). The ultimate happy ending of the story is promised and guaranteed but not plotted or detailed. Like the opening scene of the story, no events are narrated. The declaration that the story had an ultimate beginning at creation and the promise that it will have an ultimate ending are both proclaimed, providing the transcendent framework for the this-worldly story that unfolds between these narrative bookends. Deuteronomy provides no details, no imagery, for either creation or consummation. Just as is the case for Deuteronomy's protology, so with its eschatology—there is no cataclysmic break between the pictures of creation and the historical world we live in; there is no apocalyptic break between the historical world we live in and the final, lived-happily-ever-after picture in which "all Israel will be saved." These words from the climactic theological passage in Paul's letter to the Romans fit perfectly as the final scene in Deuteronomy's narrative world, expressed in the Deuteronomic language 'all Israel': "And so all Israel will be saved; as it is written, 'Out of Zion will come the Deliverer; he will banish ungodliness from Jacob'" (Rom 11:26).

** ** **

The story in the text of Deuteronomy and the Deuteronomistic History is clear and powerful. The Israelite people are all one extended family, blood kin, descendants of the Abraham-Isaac-Jacob family. During a famine, the whole clan migrates to Egypt, where they become a numerous people. When the Egyptians enslave them, God rescues them all and brings them to Horeb, where he gives them the Ten Commandments and constitutes them as his own covenant people. When they are unfaithful, God raises up a new generation, leads them for forty years through the wilderness, and gives them victories and land east of the Jordan. There, on the banks of the Jordan, Moses gives them God's directions for how to live in the land as the people of God. Moses dies, and under Joshua's leadership, they cross the Jordan, and in a rapid series of battles, with the help of God, they quickly destroy or drive out the Canaanites and gain possession of the whole land. Both land and people have a rest from war, and Joshua divides the land among the twelve tribes, just as God had commanded through Moses (Deut 1–5; 7:1–2; 20:16–20; Josh 11:16–23). Yet within this grand story are occasional indications of a different version of the emergence of Israel in the land and its later history. We must now ask how this story in the text corresponds to the story of the "real world," of "what actually happened" in the historical reality that lies behind the text, and how we should best understand the relation of these two stories.

Chapter 6

The Story behind the Text

"Quest of the Historical Israel?"

As we now turn our attention from the narrative world of Deuteronomy and explore Israel's history as constructed by historians, I am by no means suggesting that the story behind the text is the true story that should replace the theological story in the text that represents the faith of Israel. Nor should we suppose we are now leaving the "imaginary" world of the Bible to enter the "real" world as constructed by scholars. Both worlds, the world presented by the biblical texts and the world presented by the history books, represent the story as composed for their respective purposes, and in *each* case an imaginary world is presented—the narrative world of the biblical authors and the objective, historical world of events as imagined by the secular historian. Both stories represent imaginary worlds constructed by their respective authors. Both are fabrications—that is, human constructions. They have different sources, methods, values, and goals. The message the preacher, teacher, congregation, and class want to hear is in the biblical text. What the Bible wants to say to us—that is, what the living God wants to say to us through the Bible—is not in the scholar's reconstruction of "what really happened" in the life of Jesus or the history of Israel but in the biblical text itself. Critical historical study of the text is an ally in this struggle, not an enemy.

Here we might pause briefly to ponder the meaning of the "historical study of the Bible." By this phrase I mean the array of historical disciplines usually subsumed under the heading "historical-critical method" or "higher criticism." These terms have become traditional, and despite their problematic nature, we may be stuck with them. In any case, most university religion students and seminary graduates know how to understand them. For many people in the congregations, however, this terminology continues to have unfortunate negative connotations. "Critical" sounds carping and negative; "higher" can give the impression of arrogance, condescension. In the field of biblical studies, *criticism*, of course, refers to informed analytical study, as in university courses in art and music appreciation. The alternative to *critical* is *uncritical*, not *believing* or *conservative*. Historical study is by definition critical—that is, not naive or superficial. In the history of biblical studies, *criticism* was sometimes modified by *higher* to distinguish the discipline from "lower" criticism—that is, textual criticism that dealt with the effort to establish, by analysis and evaluation of the variations in extant manuscripts, the original text of a composition when the original no longer exists. This "lower criticism" is the necessary foundation on which all interpretation of texts is built. So understood, "higher criticism" designates what historians do as they seek to build on this foundation and describe the actual events depicted in a narrative so far as available sources and historical methods permit. The same set of methods are used whether they are dealing with accounts of the battles of the Revolutionary War that led to the formation of the United States or the accounts of battles in Palestine that led to the formation of the kingdoms of Israel and Judah. Such historical study is neither the enemy of biblical faith nor an alternative to faithful hearing of the Word of God that comes through the biblical texts. On the contrary, historical study has positive value in facilitating hearing their message and clarifying their meaning.

The Issue: How Did There Get to Be a People of Israel, Settled in the Land of Canaan? The Main Choices

The Deuteronomic teachers and final editors of the Deuteronomistic History apparently had their reasons—theological, not necessarily historical—for combining the varied accounts of their sources into one grand story as it is now found in the Bible. We shall explore this theological perspective later. The first issue to be faced is the extent of reliable eyewitness testimony in the extant texts. For our purposes, it can be stated simply as a yes-or-no question: "Was Deuteronomy written by Moses?" Virtually all historians of every theological stripe and none, including scholars who identify themselves as conservative evangelicals, now respond with a clear no—the present form of the Pentateuch and the historical books Joshua–2 Kings were composed by authors and editors generations or even centuries after the events they narrate. They did not create their works ex nihilo but combined earlier written sources with firm oral traditions and their own perspectives and theological insights. This is the view assumed in the present book and by many of its presumed readers. Nothing like a detailed argument can be given here and need not be. University and seminary courses in biblical literature and history often deal with the evidence and arguments pro and con, as do commentaries on the relevant biblical books and monographs on specific issues (see bibliography). Since some such courses and books assume the issue was solved long ago, it is often not studied in detail in classes or commentaries but assumed as the "assured results" of historical study. "We don't need to continue to invent the wheel or give evidence that the earth orbits around the sun"—true enough, but there are enough sincere and intelligent people who presuppose that Moses wrote Deuteronomy "because the Bible says so" that the claim should be neither accepted nor denied on the basis of party line, theological stance, or traditional dogma. There is a fundamentalism of the left and middle as well as of the right. My own stance is that Deuteronomy, like the Pentateuch as a whole, is a mosaic, but is not Mosaic in the sense that Moses is the author. A mosaic is not a random assortment of pieces of stone or glass but a careful selection and artistic arrangement, held together and formed into a complete picture by the artist's vision of something beautiful, important, and true. Deuteronomy has material and perspectives that go back to Mosaic times and earlier, but the book itself, like the Deuteronomistic History, was written in stages and edited more than once, with the canonical form composed in the sixth century BCE, during or just after the exile. (See chs. 8–10 for a detailed outline of the process from Moses to our Bible.)

As a historically firm starting point, all can agree that about 1000 BCE, there existed in the land of Canaan a united nation known as Israel and led by King David. How should we think of the formation of this state of Israel? At the present, three major reconstructions command the field. Though each includes a degree of complexity, they may be labeled (1) conquest, (2) migration, and (3) revolution. Each has been supported by widely respected advocates. Acknowledging that no view can be adequately represented in a sentence or two, these three options might be described as follows.

The *conquest* model generally pictures a sudden, violent invasion from outside the land by a united Israel of twelve tribes who took over the whole land, killing or driving out the native inhabitants. This model has been defended especially by interpreters who suppose that this is "the" biblical view, sometimes arguing that the issue is simply "whether one believes the Bible or not." Some critical historians have also advocated aspects of this view, represented especially by the eminent archaeologist W. F. Albright of Johns Hopkins University and in the early works of John Bright of Union Theological Seminary (Richmond), a student of Albright's. Bright's 1959 *A History of Israel* was twice revised by the author himself and often reprinted and was a standard, widely used textbook in many university and seminary courses. Even so, Albright, sometimes cited as a defender of what is supposed as "the" biblical view, continued to adjust his judgment in the light of continuing archaeological research, argued that not all the Israelite tribes were in Egypt, and became convinced that there were two waves of invasion: one from the southwest and one from the east.

The *migration* view is represented by Martin Noth's 1960 *The History of Israel*. Noth, professor of the University of Bonn, Germany, argued the Israelite people emerged by a process of gradual settlement, mostly peaceful, as different nomadic groups migrated into Canaan and settled down to form a twelve-tribe confederation on the model of the Greek amphictyony. This model regards the settlement of Israelites in Canaan as corresponding to the peaceful wanderings of Abraham, Isaac, and Jacob/Israel through the land, living differently but peaceably alongside the native population.

The *revolution* model was represented by the liberation theologian Norman Gottwald of New York Theological Seminary, whose 1979 *The Tribes of Yahweh* adopted earlier views and argued on the basis of anthropology and sociology that Israel originated when groups of oppressed peasants in Canaan united to throw off the yoke of their masters and establish a more just social order. The Israelites came into possession of the land not by a violent assault from outside but by a peasants' revolt against their masters inside the land.

Each of these reconstructions by historians of the last century continue into the present, modified by interaction with one another and ongoing research. Each of them may incorporate facets and elements of the complex history of what actually happened. In such a situation, lacking complete consensus among competent historians, the open-minded interpreter may decide just to interpret the story in the text without reference to the story behind the text. It seems better to me to make finite judgments based on our best available data, open to revision as more evidence and insight emerges. This is the nature of all historical study and is in step with the incarnational nature of the Christian faith and biblical revelation. The following sketch of the emergence and history of Israel, from Abraham to the exile, is intended not to replace the story in the biblical text but to illuminate it and facilitate our capacity to hear and understand it better.

A (Penciled-in) Sketch of Israel's History

I have neither the competence nor the space to present here a comprehensive reconstruction of the history of Israel behind the Deuteronomic narratives, but I will attempt an impressionistic sketch of what seem to me to be the most probable results of such historical work.

Pre-1400 BCE: Memories

The Israel that became a nation-state in the land of Canaan had roots that extended back many generations, but not to the beginning of humanity—not even to the beginnings of civilization. Israel was in fact a latecomer among the nation-states of the ancient Near East. We must avoid the tendency to lump everything together as "back in Bible times." Even on the most conservative understanding, if Abraham visited the Giza pyramids when he went down to Egypt, he and the other tourists and pilgrims already regarded them as interesting monuments from the distant past. The earliest phase of pre-Israelite rootage was later remembered as beginning with Abraham, stylized in the turn from the historically dim period between the sagas of Genesis 4–11 to the fresh beginning in Genesis 12, composed of more realistic history-like stories that deal with attested places, events, and personages. Still, no person or occurrence in Genesis 12–50 can be related to any figure or event otherwise historically documented outside the biblical text.

In Israel's earliest memories, the people's origin is always associated with Abraham, Isaac, and Jacob, who lived many generations before the time of Moses and the exodus. In Israelite historiography, such names may represent individuals, clans, or both. Such notes as "Esau (that is, is Edom)" (Gen 36:1) and the personification of the tribes in Judges 1–2, where tribes are even given speaking parts in the story, remind us that even "Israel" can designate either the individual Jacob or the people later identified as descended from him (cf. Gen 32:28, 32). Our earliest traditions represent the patriarchs not only as blood relatives but as sharing a common faith in a transcendent God who had initiated a covenant with them stemming from God's covenant with Abraham (Gen 12:1–3). As a seminomadic people on the move, the "Hebrews" (*hapiru*)—a general term for the social class of such landless peoples—did not share the nature religion of their Canaanite neighbors, a settled agricultural people. The patriarchal clans called their God by several names, including the common generic terms for deity, *El* (God) and *Baal* (Lord). These sometimes were made more specific and related to a particular clan leader. Abraham was associated with *El Shaddai* (Gen 17:1, meaning unknown, often translated "God Almighty"). The deity associated specifically with Isaac was called "the *Pachad* of Isaac" (meaning "fear," "dread," "awesome one"; Gen 31:42, 53). God was known to Jacob as "the *Abir*" ("mighty one"; Gen 49:24). By the time the biblical texts were written, all these were considered appellations for YHWH, later Israel's distinctive name for God.

The biblical texts give mixed signals as to when Israel's God began to be called YHWH. Genesis 4:26 indicates that already in the time of Adam, people began to invoke the name of YHWH, and in several texts, the later narrator quotes Abraham and others as worshipping YHWH by name (e.g., Gen 24:7). Yet Exodus 6:3 insists that Israel's ancestors knew God by other names and that YHWH as the name of Israel's God was first revealed to Moses. During the patriarchal period, of course, there were no "Israelites" or "Jews." *Israel* and *Israelite* did not become the designation of a particular national group until the settlement of the tribal groups in Canaan. *Jew*, *Jewish*, and *Judaism* only became a religio-ethnic category during and after the exile, when Israel was constricted to Judah, and *Jew* meant "Judean." The Jew/gentile distinction could only come after the formation of Israel as a national state with a distinct religious understanding of its identity. Abraham and Sarah, Isaac and Rebecca, and Jacob and Rachel were not Jewish—nor was Moses. If we insist on using our own later terminology, they were all gentiles.

In sum, there is little solid historical information recoverable from this period of Israel's ancestors. What is solid is that when Israel later appears as a distinct people, they are almost unanimous in looking back to the patriarchal era for the roots of their religious and national life: no "Abraham, Isaac, and Jacob," no Israel.

1300s BCE: Tribes

By about 1250 BCE, we have the first objective evidence outside the Bible for the existence of the people of Israel. They lived in Canaan as one people within the population of Canaanite peoples. This historical situation is documented by a monument erected in Thebes by Pharaoh Merneptah in the latter part of the thirteenth century to memorialize Egyptian victories over several national and ethnic-tribal groups, including Israel in the land of Canaan. The symbol used for Israel represents a tribal group or groups, not an established nation-state. Other evidence points to groups of Semitic tribespeople living in and around Canaan on both sides of the Jordan. They were from the same ethnic background, understanding themselves to be connected by elements of common ancestry.

They shared a common culture with other Canaanites. They spoke the same language, with some variety of dialects. What later became biblical Hebrew is a minor variation of the language of Canaan commonly spoken on both sides of the Jordan. The Israelite clans had the same physical features and skin color as the surrounding Canaanite clans. There were probably minor variations from their neighbors in clothing, but one could not tell the difference between Israelites and Canaanites in the shower, not even by circumcision, which was a cultural feature of many ethnic groups in the Syro-Palestinian region. The Israelite groups shared many religious perspectives and practices with their neighbors, such as animal sacrifice and the prophetic phenomena of inspired people speaking by the power of the gods or spirits.

Several biblical texts later specifically identify Israel's Canaanite ancestry, with no reference to deliverance from slavery in Egypt. Ezekiel apparently opposes Israel's later claim that it has a single, honorable genealogy and history. While citing traditions that affirm God's choice of Israel and deliverance from Egypt, Ezekiel makes no reference to rescue from slavery. Rather, the prophet's point is that already in Egypt, Israel was a sinful people practicing pagan abominations, and God delivered them for the sake of his own name (Ezek 20:4–10, 22). Ezekiel cites other traditions that place Jerusalem and Judea's origin and history in Canaan, with Amorite and Hittite parents, without reference to Egypt and the exodus (16:3–52): "Thus says the Lord God to Jerusalem: 'Your origin and your birth were in the land of the Canaanites; your father was an Amorite, and your mother a Hittite'" (Ezek 16:3). Ezekiel preserves traditions in which the story begins when God finds (some of) Israel's ancestors destitute in the wilderness, continues with a version of Israel's history that parallels that of Sodom and Gomorrah, and emphasizes Israel's origins in the regions east of the Jordan along with Edom, Moab, and Ammon (cf. Hos 2:14–15; 9:10; Jer 2:2–3). Even Deuteronomy 32:10–33 portrays Israel's history as beginning in the wilderness, along with Edom, Moab, and Ammon in the regions east of the Jordan.

1200s BCE: Slavery, Deliverance, and Sinai

Sometime prior to the thirteenth century, one or more of these "Israelite" tribes, a relatively small group, migrated to Egypt during a period of economic or political distress. We may think of waves of migrant workers in our own time who cross national boundaries in hard times, looking for work. At first they were received as *gerim*, or resident aliens without citizenship status, but later were enslaved by the Egyptian Empire (cf. Deut 23:7, which sees Israel's previous *gerim* status in a positive light). We should not think of this in terms of the dehumanizing chattel slavery of Africans by the United States of the eighteenth and nineteenth centuries. Egyptian slavery did not involve the ownership of human beings by individuals who could buy, work, and sell them like farm animals. Neither was there a racist ingredient, though the migrating *hapiru* (Hebrews) were still looked down on as outsiders with a different language and culture, and their situation was still a terrible oppression of defenseless, landless immigrants by a state that compelled them to perform forced labor. Somewhat like the medieval serfs of Europe, the *hapiru* did not own real estate, nor were they merely employees in menial jobs who were free to resign and look elsewhere for other employment.

We do not know when this migration of some of Israel's ancestors to Egypt took place. We do not know whether there was more than one wave, whether they were a united group that entered Egypt together, or whether they were scattered groups that only later united. We do not know how long the sojourn in Egypt lasted, how long they lived in Egypt before being enslaved, or how long their enslavement lasted; later traditions blend all this together into one chapter in their corporate memory and vary in their accounts of how long it lasted. Exodus 12:40 reports that the Israelites lived in Egypt 430 years. Genesis 15:13 speaks of them being in Egypt as *gerim* and (then?) as slaves for a total of 400 years but does not indicate how long each period lasted. Genesis 15:16 speaks of Israel's return from Egyptian slavery "in the fourth generation," which would mean the great-great-grandchildren of those who migrated to Egypt would return to Canaan—not even close to a period of 400 years. However long it lasted, the "Egyptian period" of Israel's beginnings left no trace in history—not in Egypt's, not in Israel's. God's deliverance of Israel from Egyptian slavery was indelibly impressed in later Israel's corporate memory, but the memory is devoid of details. Except for the stories of Moses and his family, there is no name or event recorded for all this time—no names of pharaohs; no geographical details indicating knowledge of the locale; no indication of social conditions; no reference to what language the slaves spoke after at least three generations; no indication of whether or how they preserved and educated their children in their ancestral language, culture, and traditions; no indication as to whether they associated with other *hapiru* of non-Israelite ancestry who had been enslaved by the Egyptians. This would be like a blank period of four generations, or 400 years, in American history, from Columbus to 1900, of which we know nothing. Israel's teachers and storytellers were not interested in detailing the history of their Egyptian background, whatever it may have been, even if they had information they could have shared. That God had rescued them from being landless slaves and given them their own land is the only focus of their theological vision of their history. Historians who would tell us "what really happened" behind the story in the biblical text have little to go on prior to the settlement in Canaan and formation of the Israelite nation-state.

Moses, Miriam, and the Prophetic Interpretation of History

This period came to an end when Moses, a kinsman of the Israelites with an Egyptian name and background, emerged as their leader and deliverer. Moses was a prophetic figure who had experienced an encounter with the ancestral God of some of the Israelites. He understood himself to be God's response to the cries of the oppressed slaves for deliverance. A large number of the *hapiru* believed him, accepted his leadership, and followed him in a dramatic escape from Egypt. For the time being and for simplicity's sake, we may refer to them all simply as "Israelites," whatever they called themselves. The pursuing Egyptian army trapped the escapees at Yam Suf, a marshy body of water between northeast Egypt and the Sinai Peninsula, not to be confused with the Red Sea of Rand McNally. In an amazing event firmly lodged in Israel's collective memory, a strong wind that blew all night opened up a path through the waters that allowed the fugitives to escape. The Egyptian army, attempting to follow, was destroyed by the returning waters. Safe on the East Bank, the prophet Miriam, Moses's sister, is pictured as interpreting the breathtaking event as the saving act of the Lord and leading the Israelite women in a celebratory song of praise:

Sing to the LORD,
    for he has triumphed gloriously;
horse and rider
    he has thrown into the sea. (Exod 15:1, 21)

The song was later elaborated (vv. 2–18), but the core confessional affirmation, cited twice, is generally accepted by historians as going back to Israel's earliest times. Something extraordinary happened at Yam Suf. That it involved the saving action of God was not obvious, and the Egyptians missed it, likely thinking, "Lucky for them the wind came up at the right time. Too bad our soldiers got stuck in the mud and died." Interpreters of all stripes can agree that a remarkable event was interpreted by an Israelite prophet as the saving act of God and that this interpretation was accepted by the community and transmitted as authentic, paradigmatic testimony to Israel's later self-understanding: God acted to deliver a group of slaves and create a people to be part of God's program of blessing for all peoples. Whether this interpretation of what happened is actually *true* is a matter of faith and theology, outside the bailiwick of the historian per se. Most readers of the Bible who are interested in this story would think of themselves as in some sense believers, theologians, and historians, in some way combining the story in the text and the story behind the text. We will consider the available options below. Here we continue our sketch of the story behind the text.

MOSAIC CONTENT IN DEUTERONOMY?

The story in the framework of Deuteronomy's narrative world presents a powerful rhetorical picture. The first words of the book picture the narrator telling the readers, "These are the words that Moses spoke to all Israel beyond the Jordan—in the wilderness" (Deut 1:1). This opening statement declares that Moses gave a long speech or speeches now contained in Deuteronomy, during which he refers several times to "this book of the law" (Deut 28:61; 29:21; 30:10; 31:26) or simply "this book" (29:20, 27). Near the end of the book, the narrator states that Moses wrote the whole book and directed that it be placed beside the ark of the covenant as a witness against future generations (31:24–26). Later biblical, Jewish, and Christian traditions identified this book as Deuteronomy, written by Moses himself. However, it is difficult to picture the sequence of events involved in this claim. It can hardly mean that before, during, or after Moses delivered the speeches in Deuteronomy, he had written "this book" out in advance and holds this book in his hands as he speaks to the assembled multitudes. Also keep in mind that "this book" includes the speeches in a narrative framework about himself containing his death, burial, and funeral lamentation (34:1–8).

But the audience reading the text—Jewish and Christian readers through the ages, beginning with Deuteronomy's first hearers in exilic or postexilic times and extending to twenty-first-century readers who read or hear this text as Holy Scripture—*these* readers know what "this book" refers to. It is the book of Deuteronomy that became part of the Bible and mediates the voice of God through Moses and Israel to them and us. Virtually all historians concur that Deuteronomy does not represent anything like a verbatim speech actually given by Moses. Many Jewish and Christian interpreters, of all theological persuasions, would agree with the prominent evangelical scholar John Goldingay that "the whole of Deuteronomy" was written by teachers centuries after Moses's time who wrote with "inspired creativity as they used their imaginations to generate material. Like other ancient historians, they composed speeches that were not uttered by the people to whom they were attributed."[1] In what sense, then, does the story of the book of Deuteronomy begin with Moses? Not only is this claim difficult to accept historically, but it seems clear that the author(s) never intended the audience to imagine that Moses held in his hands a manuscript of the later book of Deuteronomy as he spoke to the assembled multitudes. This would be like claiming that Jesus held a copy of the Gospel of Matthew in his hands as he delivered the Sermon on the Mount. The rhetorical purpose is to declare that the Torah comes from Moses—that is, from the Lord through Moses—not that Moses himself wrote out a verbatim account of his speech in advance.

Historically speaking, it is in fact probable that the book does contain a historical core that goes back to the exodus period and to Moses himself. The claim to Mosaic authority is probably best understood to mean that Israel's confession and testimony to the nations rest from the beginning on a Mosaic-exodus foundation. From the time of Moses and the exodus, the conviction existed that God had delivered a group of slaves from Egypt and formed them into a covenant community called to live by the revealed will of God as testimony to God's intention for the whole world.

The Egypt-exodus group moved into Canaan, preserving the traditions that defined its identity. Authorized leaders were responsible for preserving these traditions, but they were not esoteric or the private property of particular individuals; they were public, belonging to the people as a whole and known by them.

1100s–1000s BCE: Emergence of the People of Israel in the Land

The escapees from Egypt included clans of Israelites related by genealogy along with other people of differing ethnic backgrounds, the "mixed crowd" of Exodus 12:38. The term *mixed* is a sociological term that includes Israelites related by ancestry along with other marginalized people who had been liberated from socioeconomic bondage and forced labor (Neh 13:3; Jer 25:20, 24; and 50:37). Deuteronomy 29:11 speaks of the *gerim* (resident aliens) as already a constituent element in the camp of Israel while still en route from Egypt to the promised land. In terms of blood relationship, even Caleb—who, along with Joshua, was one of the two "spies" who gave a positive report of Canaan and encouraged Israel to enter and possess it—seems not to have been of Israelite ancestry. He and his brother Othniel are elsewhere identified as "Kenizzite" and thus as Edomite (cf. Gen 36:15; Num 32:12; Josh 14:6; Judg 3:9–11). A firm twelve-tribe system, each descended from one of the sons of the patriarch Jacob/Israel, seems to be a later theological construction. The twelve, all biologically related "brothers," became theologically important, but there is considerable variation in the listing of the names of the tribes and their histories. This is seen, for instance, in the differences between Jacob's blessing of the twelve tribes in Genesis 49 (eleventh-century text?) and Moses's blessing of them in Deuteronomy 33 (eighth-century text), which is sometimes understood by historians as evidence for changes in the tribal structure of Israel in this three-century period: Simeon disappeared, Reuben almost died out, Levi was no longer a secular but a priestly tribe, and Dan moved from the southwest to Bashan in the northeast.

The settlement of the clans and tribes that were to become the nation of Israel in the land thus appears to have been a gradual process, characterized in part by episodes of military violence but mostly a piecemeal takeover or infiltration that progressed at varying speeds along different fronts. Moses had played the dominant role in the story of the exodus but died before crossing the boundary into Canaan, and the Israelites and other ex-slaves who had been in Egypt entered Canaan without him. There was no particular leader for the whole people. The transition from a loose connection of separate tribes to a united people occurred over the course of several generations, more like the situation described in Judges than the dramatic conquest portrayed in Joshua.

Not all the tribes had been in Egypt and/or Sinai. Separate tribes had their own histories, which were later combined into the united story of 'all Israel.' Some remembered entering Canaan from the west; others crossed the Jordan into the promised land from the east. Israel's earliest extant national anthem, the "Song of Moses" in Deuteronomy 32, for instance, represents an ancient tradition that presents a résumé of Israel's history intended to be learned and sung as a testimony to future generations of Israel. Yet the song has no reference to Abraham, Isaac, or Jacob, though the patriarchs are indispensable to the understanding of Israel throughout the rest of Deuteronomy, just as there is no reference to slavery, Moses, Sinai, or the Decalogue. The song's picture of early Israel emphasizes that *God discovered Israel in the desert*, as in Ezekiel 16. They had been not slaves but (semi)nomads, without a country. Israel came to Canaan from the *east*, as did some tribes that were absorbed into Israel's history (32:10–14). Even the key "creedal" recitation of Deuteronomy 26:5–11 rehearses the major events in the history of Israel from the patriarchs through Egyptian slavery, the exodus, and the return to the promised land with no reference to Sinai, the giving of the Torah, and the making of the covenant, which may have originally belonged to separate tribal traditions. Similarly, the writer of 1 Chronicles, considerably later than Deuteronomy and for his own theological purposes, pictures the Israelites as already inhabiting Canaan during the period of Egyptian slavery. Even Joseph's son Ephraim was happily settled in the land with his children and grandchildren (1 Chr 7:20–29).[2]

Some tribes not in Egypt and with different traditions of the ancestral religion joined the emerging Israelite people. In the *covenant at Shechem*, newcomers appear to enter the covenant (Josh 24). In such sacred rituals, *the acceptance of the* LORD *as "our God"* means *the acceptance of Israel's Story as "our story."* This may well have been the experience of the eastern Jordan tribes, who had never been in Egypt but were adopted into the covenant people and adopted the exodus story as their own.

The analogy is by no means exact, but we may be reminded of the transition from British colonies in North America to the United States of America. The United States did not exist until the Constitution was ratified in 1789. Its prehistory preserved the memories of different beginnings, including a variety of national backgrounds with different self-understandings and aspirations for the future. Not all Americans had come over on the *Mayflower* or fought at Valley Forge. Not all looked back to George Washington as their Founding Father. The separate stories significant to each colony had a broad unifying framework, but their many variations were fused into a selective national memory, the kind of US history now popularly celebrated on July 4 and transmitted in high school textbooks. Memory is a matter of community formation. There is a corporate memory that has a formative power on each new generation. We remember through the lens of what we have become, seeing things not as they were but as we are. Historians need not deny this as they delve through layers of community formation and the concomitant combination and interpretation of traditions in the legitimate quest for "how it really happened."

** ** **

We may now pause with 'all Israel' listening to Moses on the plains of Moab. The preceding discussion sketches and illustrates some differences in the story in the biblical text of Deuteronomy and the story behind it. Further detailed reconstructions of the story behind the text, with pro and con evidence of various events in the story, can be read in the well-documented histories of Israel listed in the bibliography. These valuable studies give preachers and teachers a sense of the degree of confidence we may place in various historical reconstructions of events in the biblical narrative. Though events are selected and narrated from their theological perspective, the Deuteronomic teachers' account of Israel after they became a nation in the land is not radically different from that reconstructed by critical historians. We will only comment on a few selected highlights important for our present purpose.

1050–950 BCE: The United Kingdom

For two centuries, Israel existed in the land as a loose confederation of clans and tribes, living more or less comfortably alongside the other Canaanites, and gradually became the dominant population in most of the hill country. They shared the language of Canaan, of which Hebrew is a dialect, and adopted and adapted much of Canaanite culture. The primary difference from other Canaanites was religious.

The Philistines were one of the groups of the "Sea Peoples" who had arrived in Canaan about the same time as Israel, settling along the southern coast in the area now known as the Gaza Strip. Unlike the Canaanites, the Philistines were true foreigners to the Israelites, speaking a different language, not practicing circumcision, and having the more high-tech culture of the dawning Iron Age. From early times, Israel engaged in the kind of border skirmishes reflected in the Samson stories of Judges 13–16. When the day came that the informal Israelite tribal coalition could not hold out against the increasing Philistine pressure, Israel needed a united front and an organized army representing 'all Israel.' They needed a king.

From the beginning, the movement toward a monarchy was supported by some groups in Israel and opposed by others (1 Sam 1–13). Saul, a Benjamite identified with Israel in the north, was chosen as king and drew his support mainly from the northern tribes. His leadership was erratic; he may have been troubled with mental illness. Under his leadership, Israel was unable to restrain the Philistine advance. Saul and his son Jonathan were killed in battle, and his army was dispersed.

David was from Bethlehem in the southern tribe of Judea, which had absorbed Simeon and thus was virtually the only southern tribe. David had been an effective and popular leader in Saul's army. Saul's instability, combined with David's popularity, political cunning, and cruel disregard for others, allowed David to become king of Judea. He ruled from his own city, Jerusalem, captured by his personal army. After seven years, he incorporated the northern kingdom of Israel into Judea. He brought the ark of the covenant, the symbol of the ancestral traditions, from Israel to Jerusalem. "David's city" became both the political and religious capital of 'all Israel.'

At David's death, through a series of palace intrigues, his son Solomon inherited the united, prosperous kingdom. The fragile and somewhat artificial political unity imposed by David did not endure, nor did the attempted religious unification of worshipping only the Lord at the central Jerusalem shrine. Virtually the first comment about Solomon's kingdom is that the people continued to sacrifice on the high places and that the king himself went to Gibeon to sacrifice at the "great high place." In the general understanding of popular religion, worship at the high places was not a betrayal or denial of the Lord; it was the Lord who was worshipped there, but in the Canaanite style (cf. the Assyrian officer's argument in 2 Kgs 18:22).

When Solomon died, the northern tribes threw off the yoke of the Davidic-Solomonic kingdom centered in the new capital of Jerusalem. The united kingdom had lasted less than a generation. Regarded *historically*, the reestablishment of the northern kingdom was not the breaking apart of an Israel that had been united since Mosaic times but a reversion into northern and southern tribal groups as they had existed prior to their temporary unification under David (cf. the two centuries of tribal warfare during the period of the Judges). In the history of Israelite *theology*, however, historians recognize that during this period, the concept of a united Israel developed, an Israel in which David and his descendants would play a significant role in God's purposes for Israel and the world. The theological vision of 'all Israel' (all twelve tribes) is not a historical picture of Israel in Moses's time or pre-Davidic times but an eschatological vision of the people of God. What is historical is that in the unfolding of Israel's theology, the conception of "twelve tribes" as a visionary, symbolic portrayal of the chosen people of God and their destiny in anticipation of God's plan for the salvation of all peoples now becomes an important element in Israelite theology. The "restoration of Israel" would come to mean the creation of this already / not yet, historical/ eschatological reality inherent in the promise of God, an image that will play a large role in the later theology of both Jews and Christians (cf. Matt 19:27–28; Acts 1:6; Jas 1:1; Rev 21:12).

922–721 BCE: The Northern Kingdom

The northern kingdom of Israel and the southern kingdom of Judah had long and parallel histories, mostly involving conflict between the two separate nations. We are here interested in the religious history of the divided kingdoms as reconstructed by historians. Israel—that is, the northern kingdom—could no longer consider Jerusalem, with its temple, priesthood, and ark of the covenant, as its religious center. Worship was redirected to new shrines—better, the rejuvenation of old shrines before the Davidic and Solomonic "centralization" of the cult in Jerusalem. Israelite kings regularly promoted the worship of Baal—that is, they accommodated the traditional worship of the LORD to a cultural understanding of God as "the Lord" (Baal). This adaptation of Israel's traditional faith to the religion and culture of Canaan was resisted by the teachers and preachers of the Mosaic faith preserved by the Levitical priests and teachers in the local shrines. These teachers may have promoted some kind of centralization of the cult[3] at one of the major shrines, such as Shiloh or Shechem, as a means of maintaining the traditional faith. It is historically probable that the idea of a central shrine was not invented by Josiah or the Deuteronomists in the seventh century BCE but that there had been several "central" shrines, such as Shechem, Bethel, Gilgal, and Shiloh, to which local Israelites made pilgrimage before the attempted centralization on a grand scale later attempted by the Judean kings. Encouraged by the (re)discovery of the "book of the law," Josiah's reformation was not an innovation but a recovery of an earlier vital dimension of Israel's life.

The northern kingdom lasted two centuries, 922–721. When Israel fell to the Assyrians in 721, much of the population was killed, deported, or absorbed into the surrounding countries and remaining non-Israelite sections of Canaan, thus virtually losing their identity. The image of the "ten lost tribes" does not mean that they existed somewhere and might later be "found" but that they had gradually dissolved into the non-Israelite provinces and nations, including their homeland, which became part of the province of Samaria.

922–586 BCE: The Southern Kingdom

In 2 Kings 17:18, "The Lord was very angry with Israel and removed them out of his sight; none was left but the tribe of Judah alone." Judah escaped the Assyrian devastation and remained an independent kingdom until the Babylonian exile and destruction of Jerusalem and the temple in 586 BCE—a much longer time than the United States has existed. The Judean kings tried to resist Babylon, the successor to Assyria and the major superpower in the ancient Near East. Their attempts at submission, alliance with Egypt against Babylon, and military resistance all failed. When Jehoiachin, the last king of Judea, tried to defend the city, the city fell after a terrible three-month siege. The walls of the city were broken down, the temple was destroyed, and Jehoiachin was deported to Babylon along with the Jerusalem leadership and "the elite of the land" (2 Kgs 24:10–15).

597–538 BCE: Exile

Like the exodus, the exile was deeply etched into the collective memory of Israel, and like the exodus, its historical reality was personally experienced by only a minority of Israelites. The whole population was not deported. Most remained, no longer an independent kingdom but subservient peasants in the Babylonian province of Yehud (Judah). Yet all Israel experienced the loss of the land, the loss of nationhood.

There were three deportations. The total number represents a relatively small percentage of the population. Jeremiah, who lived through the events and gives eyewitness testimony, reports a total of 4,600 Judeans sent into exile. The report in 2 Kings 24:14–17 numbers the deportees at between 8,000 and 10,000. Just as we should not think of Egyptian slavery in terms of US history, so we should not think of the exile in terms of the Nazi effort to exterminate the Jews. It was not a matter of boxcars and concentration camps, there was no racial factor, and the purpose was not extermination. Nonetheless, it was bad enough, for the deportees were still captives in a foreign land where they were forced to work for their captors, who often disdained them (Ps 137!). The stories in Esther, Ezra, Nehemiah, and Daniel recount the success of talented Jews in the country of their exile. After a while, many—probably most—heeded the advice of Jeremiah, spoken in the name of God: "Seek the welfare of the city where I have sent you into exile, and pray to the LORD on its behalf, for in its welfare you will find your welfare" (Jer 29:7). The children of the early deportees, and especially the third generation, would tend to see Babylon as their actual homeland. When the opportunity to "return home" came, many who had never seen Judea were unenthusiastic about the prospect, considered Babylon their home, and remained there—very different from the exodus story. A flourishing Judaism developed in Babylon that became a leading influence in what became the worldwide Jewish community.

While the exile literally involved the deportation of only a minority of the population, it included the leaders and tradition-bearers, such as Ezekiel. These deported scribes, priests, prophets, and teachers became the center of Israel's theology. The majority of the population that remained in Judea, now deprived of their religious leaders and instructors, tended to continue down the path of accommodation, combining the traditional faith of Israel with the surrounding cultural religion that seemed to deliver needed agricultural, economic, and political success to its adherents.

538–ca. 400 BCE: A Series of "Returns," with Most Staying in Babylon

As the superpower Assyria had been replaced by Babylon, so Babylon was replaced by Persia. The end came quickly. In 538 BCE, Cyrus and his troops overpowered a demoralized Babylon, and he was widely welcomed as a liberator. As conquerors go, Cyrus seems to have been a humane and tolerant one. He adopted a policy of restoring displaced peoples to their ancestral homes (cf. Ezra 1:2–4; 6:3–5). Judeans in Babylon could return.

In Israel's collective memory, the "conquest" (giving of the land), the "exile" (losing of the land), and the "restoration" (getting the land back) all happened to 'all Israel.' Many Bible readers have naturally thought of "the return from Babylonian captivity" as a united procession of the captives back to their homeland, which all or most of them had been forced to leave some years before. In historical reality, there were several waves of returnees stretching across at least two generations, under a variety of leaders, who journeyed to Judea to begin a new life there. The returnees and new immigrants included a broad spectrum of religious leaders with differing theologies and understandings of the nature, history, and future of the people of Israel and its role among the nations.

The canonical edition of Deuteronomy addressed a community in which the *end* of the exile was still a future hope for most people of Israelite faith—now the faith of emergent Second-Temple Judaism. Deuteronomy looks back on God's judgment not as the deportation of the whole people en masse to Babylon but as having scattered Israel "among the nations" (Deut 4:27; LXX, "among *all* the nations"). When the dust of some generations of external and internal conflict had settled, there were more Jews in various countries outside Judea than in the homeland, and so it has remained until this day. Just as the image of the gift of the land in one fell swoop to a faithful, united Israel of twelve tribes was a theological vision of Israel's origins, so the hope for restoration of the twelve tribes in the promised land became an eschatological vision, one way of portraying the ultimate purpose of God not only for Israel but for the world.

Chapter 7

The Story of the Text

The Living Voice Became a Book

We now want to trace the path that began with the Word of God that came through the living voice of Moses and the prophetic teachers of Israel to the point in our present, where the Word of God intersects our own lives—our own story. We want to hear the Word of God speaking in and through our own story, our own voices, as we teach and preach in contemporary congregations and classes. When we hold a Bible in our hands, or when it lies open before us on the pulpit or lectern, we want to hear more than the echo of our own voices and cultural "values." When we sit together in the worshipping congregation and hear the lector conclude the Scripture readings for the day with "The Word of the Lord" and we respond, "Thanks be to God," we may still occasionally ask ourselves, "What does it mean that *this* book, the words of Moses and Israel's prophets and teachers, is somehow the Word of *God*?"

Part of the answer comes from recognizing that the Bible has its own story. Just as we have come to appreciate that in conversation, counseling, and committee, to *hear* another person is sometimes possible only if we know something of their story—why they feel that way, why they speak the way they do—so with our hearing the Bible. "The Word of the Lord" was not lowered from heaven by a purple ribbon, bound in leather with gilt edges. Although conservative and fundamentalist views of the inspiration and authority of the Bible are sometimes unfairly caricatured by this cartoon, I've never met anyone who thinks *this* is what we mean by speaking of the Bible as the Word of God. If not this, then what?

Our preaching and teaching take place in a particular stream of history and tradition that shapes our own faith, theology, life, and work.

The biblical narratives present a fascinating tale filled with saints and villains alike, a complex story involving several languages; many different cultural settings; a tangled mixture of history, politics, theology, linguistics, authority—and money. The story is important in its own right, required reading for anyone interested in the history of Western civilization. There is nothing else like it in the history of literature (see bibliography). However, the following summaries and reflections on "how we got our Bible" are not for the purpose of informing or reminding us of the inspirational anecdotes included in this fascinating history that we might work into sermons and classes—though this is not necessarily to be excluded—but to reinforce our own capacity to hear and understand the Bible. Formation, not information, is the goal. This mighty flow of living and life-giving water can be seen as having four main junctions at which new tributaries transform the stream and shape our own understanding of the texts from which we preach and teach:

1. The living voice became a book.
2. The book became canonical Scripture.
3. Canonical Scripture became a translation.
4. The book becomes a living voice: preachers and teachers interpret the book in the life of the church.

In this chapter, we explore how the living voice became a book.

Moses to Josiah

The Deuteronomists considered it theologically important for their readers to have a clear understanding of how the Word of God that called Israel into being and nourished their faith through the generations was related to the book of the "law of Moses" they heard read regularly in worship and instruction. We will first sketch Deuteronomy's own delineation of the path of the Word of God from Moses's day to the readers' own.

Deuteronomy 1:1. "These are the words that Moses spoke." In the beginning was the Word, the spoken word of preaching and teaching. The narrator introduces Moses not as a writer but as a hearer who became a speaker. His words address 'all Israel' and are heard, remembered, and preserved as the living Word in the corporate memory of the whole people of God.

Deuteronomy 4:12–13. "Then the LORD spoke to you out of the fire. . . . He declared to you his covenant . . . , that is, the ten commandments;

and he wrote them on two stone tablets." God is the first writer in Deuteronomy. The whole people heard the words of the covenant as direct address from God. Then God himself wrote these words in stone, binding the spoken word to the written word. A deity who personally writes is unique in all of ancient Near East religious literature. Deuteronomy's emphasis on the *written* Torah begins with this picture of the Lord himself as the first writer of what became Israel's Scripture.

Deuteronomy 6:9. "Write them on the doorposts of your house and on your gates." The Lord, the primal speaker and writer, commands Israel to write the Torah on the doorposts of their private homes and on the city gates of their public life. In the narrative world of the text, the words to be so inscribed are not a few motto selections but the words of (the whole) Torah, which are to surround Israel's personal life at home and their civic life. The "gates" of the towns are the public places where people gather to make official political decisions and judgments (cf., e.g., Deut 17:5; 2 Sam 15:2; Prov 31:23; Isa 29:21; Zech 8:16; Amos 5:15). No specifics are given as to who is to do the writing, whether everyone can read, or how the whole of the Torah can be inscribed on the doorposts of the house—this could be done on the city gates, but hardly on the doors of private homes. The Deuteronomists are concerned not with a literal command but with creating a picture in the minds of the people of God so that every time they enter or leave their houses or town, they are surrounded by the words of the Torah, as in the opening words of the Psalter, Psalms 1:1–2. The people of God are to live in a Torah-shaped world, the real world.

Deuteronomy 17:18–19. "And when he [the future king] sits on the throne of his kingdom, he shall write for himself in a book a copy of this law, from that which is in charge of the Levitical priests; and it shall be with him, and he shall read in it all the days of his life, that he may learn to fear the Lord his God, by keeping all the words of this law and these statutes, and doing them" (RSV). God writes, the people write, the king writes. The Deuteronomists here picture the people living in the land, their life governed by the revealed will of God, represented by the king's daily study and implementation of the written Torah.

Deuteronomy 27:2–3. "On the day that you cross over the Jordan into the land that the Lord your God is giving you, you shall set up large stones and cover them with plaster. You shall write on them all the words of this law when you have crossed over." This charge is given by Moses and the elders of Israel to 'all Israel.' The entrance of the people into the land is to be celebrated by a service of worship including sacrifice and a festive meal, "rejoic[ing] before the LORD your God" (Deut 16:11), and writing the whole Torah on plastered stones, analogous to the doorposts and city gates they will build. Entering into the land is like entering their home and hometown (cf. on 6:9 above).

Deuteronomy 28:58. "Observe all the words of this law that are written in this book." The reference to *this* book, near the conclusion of Moses's speech on the plains of Moab, is the first indication that in Deuteronomy's narrative world, a *book* of the Torah was already present in Moses's time. There are several such references in this context (28:58, 61; 29:20, 21, 27; 30:10), all expressed in the passive voice: "the words of the law that are written in this book." The command included in Moses's speech is part of the prequel, picturing their future life in the land, like the reference to the book the king will have (17:18–19). What does this book contain, and who wrote it?

Deuteronomy 31:9. "Then Moses wrote down this law, and gave it to the priests, the sons of Levi, who carried the ark of the covenant of the LORD, and to all the elders of Israel." In the narrative world of Deuteronomy, the narrator quotes Moses as *speaking* throughout the text, but this is the first reference to Moses *writing* anything. He does not write until after the long speech is complete, and then neither he nor anyone else reads it. The book is not the whole Pentateuch, nor the canonical Deuteronomy per se, but the whole of Moses's instruction that is to be taught to 'all Israel,' including the Song of Moses. This Torah would be approximately the laws, ordinances, instructions, blessings, and curses now contained in Deuteronomy 12–28, concluding with the song now found in Deuteronomy 32. Both Torah and song will serve as witnesses to the Word of God given through Moses, witnesses against the people if they do not shape their lives and society by its instruction. "This book" is to be placed beside the ark, which contains the stone tablets written by God, carried by the Levites into the land at the head of the triumphal procession, taught and interpreted by "all the elders of Israel." "This book" is to be the continuing voice of God through Moses to 'all Israel,' including men, women, children, and immigrants (*gerim*), who are to gather regularly to hear the book read aloud to them (31:10–13).

Moses did not get to enter the land with the people. In the accounts in Numbers 20:10–13 and 27:12–23 taken from the Priestly tradition (P) and known to readers of the final form of Deuteronomy, God does not permit Moses to enter the promised land because of his own actions. He failed to give God the proper glory at the incident of bringing water out of the rock for the thirsty Israelites—which might seem to be a relatively minor transgression when compared with the sins of the Israelites who *do* get to enter. The narrator of Deuteronomy is aware of this tradition, does not suppress it, and even reminds the reader, in words not heard by the people in the story, that Moses, in solidarity with the rebellious generation at Horeb, participates in human sin and mortality and will not be permitted to enter the land (Deut 32:48–52). Paradoxically, the narrator consistently represents Moses as the greatest of God's prophets, the true servant of the Lord, who is denied entrance to the promised land because he vicariously bears the sins of the people. Moses dies outside the land so that they might go in (1:37–40; 3:26–28; 34:1–6). It is a matter not only of transgression but of sharing humanity and mortality—no human being can directly hear the voice of God and live. At Horeb, God spoke directly to Israel, but they could not bear the awesomeness and terror of the divine voice, and they exclaimed to Moses, "Why should we die? For this great fire will consume us; if we hear the voice of the Lord our God any longer, we shall die. For who is there of all flesh that has heard the voice of the living God speaking out of fire, as we have, and remained alive? Go near, you yourself, and hear all that the Lord our God will say. Then tell us everything that the Lord our God tells you, and we will listen and do it" (Deut 5:24–27). Moses became their mediator, heard the divine voice, spoke the Word of God to them, and wrote down the divine Torah in a book. He died for the sake of the people; *he* heard (= obeyed; cf. "The Shema Is Israel's Command" in ch. 3) the Word of God for *us*. For some early Christian teachers, the promised "prophet like Moses" (18:15–18) became one of the images used to develop the meaning of the life and death of Jesus (John 1:21, 25; 6:14; Acts 3:22; 7:37).

The readers of the canonical book of Deuteronomy have not heard God or Moses speaking directly to them. The Deuteronomists want their readers, generations and centuries later, to know that the living Word of God heard by all Israel at Horeb has a secure path through history and still resounds in the words they hear when Deuteronomy is read forth in worship and instruction.

Moses was not a fictional character. As a prophetic leader and teacher, his actions and words were formative for early Israel. He may have given memorable speeches on the plains of Moab. From the very beginning, the substance of the community's faith was transmitted to following generations by teachers and preachers in a variety of local settings, in Israel and Judah, mostly cultic. Their names and settings were, of course, known to their contemporaries, but their teaching, mostly oral, was transmitted anonymously. We should not think of the formation of the book of Deuteronomy, as did many scholars of the nineteenth and early twentieth centuries, as the composition of an "original" author progressively "expanded" by "later interpolations." This approach—in which the Pentateuch emerged through the ongoing editorial combination of four documents, traditionally designated J, E, D, and P by historical scholarship, composed from the tenth through the fifth centuries BCE—now often taken for granted, was spelled out in the older introductions and commentaries. Scholars of that period mostly thought in terms of a combination of discrete written documents composed by individual authors and combined by a somewhat cut-and-paste editorial procedure. The general JEDP model has not gone away and should not disappear completely, but the majority of contemporary Hebrew Bible / Old Testament scholars envision a more complex and dynamic process of formation and transmission involved in the worship life of the people as a whole, an interplay of oral and written material in which the final canonical form is not a patchwork but a rich compositional tapestry interweaving a variety of themes. JEDP is still a useful nomenclature, but most contemporary scholars would speak of "streams of tradition," "layers and way stations in the ongoing traditioning process," of the formation of the biblical text, or distinct "voices in the text" rather than "documents." What finally became the canonical book of Deuteronomy surfaces at more than one point in this history, with each precanonical version having its own contextual role and integrity.

The exodus group carried no Pentateuch or book of Deuteronomy into the promised land. They did carry a body of firm traditions, including some pre-exodus narratives and laws (tribal customs that had become normative). These were mostly oral, but we should not romanticize them as random folk memories told by uncouth nomads sitting around campfires repeating old stories about their ancestors, wondering what really happened in the harems of the pharaoh and the Philistine king (Gen 12:10–20; 20:1–18; 26:1–11). Like other ancient peoples, from earliest times, Israel included respected storytellers and authorized teachers of the community's oral tradition. The (questionable) notion that *written* documents always have a superior claim to reliability and truth would not come until later.

Just as David was seen as the model psalmist, then the writer of the whole Psalter, and Solomon was regarded as the archetypal wisdom teacher, then as the author of all of Proverbs and Ecclesiastes, so Moses was the figurehead leader who stood at the source of an authoritative Torah tradition, then as the author of the whole Pentateuch. But the authoritative Torah tradition was not a static tradition. Even the Decalogue, portrayed as written in stone by the finger of God, has significant variations in the two canonical forms in which it is preserved (Exod 20:1–17; Deut 5:6–21; note the rationale for the Sabbath command in each case). In Deuteronomy 27:1–9, the commanding voices of Moses, the elders, and the Levitical priests are fused into one voice; in later Israel, the voice of Moses, interpreted by the teaching of the elders and Levites, continued to be heard as the revealed Torah, the "Word of the Lord." As the tradition developed and was necessarily interpreted by later decisions of elders and Levites, this expanded and interpreted tradition was not seen as substituting their own teaching for that of Moses, but as allowing Moses to continue to speak to later situations. In the narrative world of Deuteronomy, not even Moses himself had simply repeated his own earlier pronouncements, but he had expounded/interpreted them for a new generation (Deut 1:5). As Walter Brueggemann says, "Deuteronomy is not Sinai repeated. It is Sinai interpreted."[1] When we preachers and teachers interpret the Bible for our own later and different situations, we are not imposing something new and different on the Bible but keeping in step with the Bible's own continuing reinterpretation. This requires a sound ecclesiology. Deuteronomy wants to help us form a solid theology of the continuing people of God, what it means to be a member of the church.

As new clans and tribes were incorporated into Israel, their traditions were sorted out and amalgamated. Conflicting elements were resolved or allowed to remain, with each version having its own witness to the truth of God. Though all the tribes had not been in Egypt or participated in the exodus, the Egypt-exodus-Sinai-conquest paradigm became the framework within which other traditions were incorporated. The inclusion of new groups and their traditions was not a random, informal process but—like the formation and transmission of the previous bodies of tradition—was effected in the context of worship, liturgy, and ritual associated with the making and renewal of covenants (cf. Exod 24:7–18; 34:27–28; Deut 29:1–29; Josh 8:30–35; 24:1–28). There was not yet a book of Deuteronomy.

During and after the defeat of Israel by Assyria (721 BCE), the waves of refugees who fled south to Judah included adherents of the traditional Yhwh faith and their teachers, some of whom were Levites, who now had the opportunity to associate themselves with the temple and priesthood in Jerusalem, where they seem to have been welcomed. Among these were not only those influenced by prophets such as Elijah, Elisha, and the writing prophets Amos and Hosea but also Levitical teachers who had continued to study and teach the traditional faith. Scribal types among them had likely already written texts comprising their tradition's understanding of the Mosaic Torah. It is likely that at this time the southern version of traditional Israelite theology received a vigorous religious and theological infusion from the northern teachers of the faith who had brought their traditions and texts with them. The writings of the northern prophets Amos and Hosea were updated to address Judea and the present situation there. Their versions of the stipulations in the covenant code would now be adapted to conditions in Judah in the late eighth and seventh centuries.

The developing Deuteronomic tradition not only influenced and was influenced by the prophetic tradition but was enriched by engagement with the wisdom tradition concentrated in the scribal activity in Jerusalem. The collections of Israel's prayers and praises that became the Psalter also contained a substantial element of both Wisdom and Torah. A few samples will illustrate the interrelationship between Deuteronomy and the Psalms, the tip of a very large iceberg.

The Deuteronomic teachers seem to have been active participants and leaders in community worship and instruction in which psalms were sung that were later included in the canonical Psalter. The Deuteronomists influenced and were influenced by such worship and may have composed psalms that became part of the canonical collection. Deuteronomy sometimes pictures worship as a combination of teaching and singing (31:24–26) and concludes with the Song of Moses that would readily fit into the Psalter (32:1–43). The following are a few examples.

Psalms 1–2's two poems seem to have formed a single psalm that once introduced the whole Psalter. These verses exhibit several points of contact with Deuteronomic theology. The first and last words of this introduction pronounce a blessing on those who "delight in the law [*torah*] of the LORD" (Ps 1:2) and who "take refuge [*chasah*] in him" (Ps 2:11), just as Moses in his last words pronounced his blessing on all Israel (Pss 1:1; 2:11; Deut 33:1–29). The image of those who meditate on God's Torah day and night, who are like trees planted by the water and prosper in all that they do, accords with the picture of "living in Torah" associated with the Shema (Ps 1:3; Deut 6:4–9). As elaborated in chapter 1 in this volume, the divine laughter of Psalm 2:4 resounds in the background of God's promises throughout Deuteronomy, presenting the incredible prospect that God would give little Israel and its king "the nations," "the ends of the earth" (Ps 2:8).

Psalm 19 is one of numerous "wisdom and Torah" psalms that celebrate the revelation of God not only in the created world but in God's special revelation to Israel in the Torah. This is analogous to the Deuteronomic theology of God's peoples (all humanity, God's by creation) and Israel, the people of God called by God's Word to live by God's will revealed in the Torah.

Psalm 119, the longest psalm and the longest chapter in the Bible, rhapsodizes about God's revelation in the Torah, with numerous similarities to Deuteronomy.

Psalm 82 pictures God as the Creator, the Almighty, ruler of all creation and history, but not always directly. God has parceled out the running of the world to executive assistants, divine beings that are members of the heavenly cabinet, the divine council (cf. Deut 4:19; 32:8; Dan 10:10–21). These executive assistants in the divine world are sometimes called "gods" (*elohim*), sometimes "angels," sometimes "sons of God" or "sons of the Most High." These members of the heavenly staff sometimes misuse and abuse their power, but God remains in control and will call them to account. As in Deuteronomy, the One God is passionately concerned about justice and charges those in charge of the nations of the world,

> Give justice to the weak and the orphan;
> maintain the right of the lowly and the destitute.
> Rescue the weak and the needy;
> deliver them from the hand of the wicked. (Ps 82:3–4)

As John Dominic Crossan notes, in Psalm 82, "these pagan gods and goddesses are dethroned not just because they are *pagan*, nor because they are *other*, nor because they are *competition*. They are dethroned for injustice, for divine malpractice, for transcendental malfeasance in office."[2]

Psalm 22, the most frequently quoted psalm in the New Testament and formative for New Testament theology, reflects the Deuteronomic theology of salvation history (or both Deuteronomy and the Psalter reflect this major stream of Israel's theology). The psalm begins with the lament of suffering Israel, "My God, my God, why have you forsaken me?" using the same verb found in Deuteronomy 31:6, 8 promising that God would *not* forsake Israel. The lamentation continues in verses 2–21, describing the terrors suffered by Israel at the hands of their conquerors, as in the terrible curses pronounced against disobedient Israel in Deuteronomy 28—fifty-three verses of curses.[3]

But this complaint that the LORD who delivered the ancestors does not rescue contemporary Israel is not the last word. A decisive turn takes place in Psalm 22:21b—the Holy God who is enthroned on the praises of Israel does finally save his people, and not only Israel but "all the families of the nations" (Ps 22:27; cf. Gen 12:1–3). The circle of praise for God's salvation begins in the congregation (v. 22) and then expands to all the people of Israel, including the poor, and everyone may eat as much as they want (vv. 23–26). With the salvation of Israel, the picture is not yet complete. Not only the people of God who have received the revelation through Moses and the prophets but all God's peoples who belong to the Creator will finally join in praise to the One God. "All the ends of the earth shall remember and turn to the LORD; and all the families of the nations shall worship before him. For dominion belongs to the LORD, and he rules over the nations," including even those not yet born (Ps 22:27–28, 31). The final picture of God's universal rule is not celebrated with a self-congratulatory "We did it!" History comes to a worthy conclusion, as all God's peoples praise the faithfulness of the One God, "saying that he has done it" (Ps 22:31, echoed in 1 Thess 5:24). When what became the canonical book of Deuteronomy first emerged into the light of history during Josiah's reformation, it was more than a law book. Its laws were framed in the grand narrative of the mighty acts of God the Creator, who had chosen Israel as part of God's saving plan for all peoples. The connections with blessing, festivity, carefree celebration, and joyful worship portray Deuteronomy as theology that laughs and sings.

The (Re)discovery of the "Book of the Law" in Josiah's Reformation

"I have found the book of the law in the house of the LORD" (2 Kgs 22:8). These are the words of Hilkiah, high priest in Jerusalem in 621 BCE, a declaration made during Josiah's reformation. Historians generally agree that this book was an early form of what became the canonical book of Deuteronomy. The reformation was not simply the product of Josiah's individual initiative, authority, and piety but a cooperative mission undertaken by the king and his associates at the highest level. Josiah had already begun the project of reforming Israel's religious practices somewhat along the lines of Hezekiah, his great-grandfather and predecessor, eighty or so years before. Hezekiah's reform had been squelched and reversed by his son Manasseh and grandson Amon. During his long reign, which promoted accommodation to Assyrian politics and religion, an "underground" resistance movement seems to have emerged among some scribes, priests, and sages calling for a restoration of the traditional Yhwh faith and practices, enriched and updated by Israel's experience and the demands of the present political and religious crisis. The boy-king Josiah, enthroned by the "people of the land" when he was eight years old, seems to have been under the tutelage of what became the Deuteronomic teachers (2 Kgs 21–22). When he became mature, he set in motion a reform movement in step with Hezekiah's. This included expediting repair work on the temple, which had been lagging even though funds were available. Josiah sends Shaphan, a member of his cabinet, to accelerate this project, which meant working through Hilkiah, the high priest. Hilkiah's response is a declaration that the "book of the law" had been (re)discovered in the temple. We do not know just what this means, but it does not suggest that some workmen accidentally discovered the book while moving rocks or timbers around in the course of repair work. The Bible has repeatedly been "rediscovered" by preachers and teachers such as Martin Luther, Karl Barth, and Dietrich Bonhoeffer, who did not find it hidden under church rubble, chained to a pulpit, kept from the people, or lost in a cave. The book of the law was discovered in the *temple*, during its "restoration." The book seems to have already come into the hands of the highest religious official in the land, and the deputation from the king became the occasion of its disclosure. Hilkiah sends Shaphan back to the king with book in hand. Though the king is perfectly capable of reading it for himself (23:2!), as he is charged to do daily by the Deuteronomic Torah (17:18–20!), the contents of the book—its commands, promises, and threats—are all new to Josiah, who is nonetheless the favorite king of the Deuteronomists (2 Kgs 23:20). Hilkiah reads the book to Josiah, who hears in it a devastating indictment of himself and the kingdom for which he is responsible.

The king sends the book, in the company of five officials, including the high priest, to Huldah the prophet, asking about the judgment and wrath of God the book pronounces. With an oral "Thus says the Lord," she confirms the book's written verdict and sentence. Josiah then gathers all the elders of Judah and "all the people," who go with him to the temple. Josiah reads the scroll, now called "the book of the covenant," to the assembly, and king and people covenant to obey the book's commands.

These include removing all the Baal paraphernalia from the temple and burning them, deposing the priests that previous kings had appointed to make offerings in the high places, breaking down the houses of the male prostitutes in the temple precincts, removing the Baalistic priests from the towns in Judah, and defiling the shrines where they offered sacrifices. He destroys the high places at Bethel in the north, removes the shrines in Samaria, and has the northern Baalistic priests executed (cf. Elijah, 1 Kgs 18:36–40). He banishes mediums, wizards, teraphim, and idols as commanded in Deuteronomy, which pronounced them all abhorrent (18:10–12).

The king outlaws sacrifice outside Jerusalem and arranges to keep the Passover at the central shrine in Jerusalem, the first such occasion in the history of the kingdom (23:21–23). This law of the central shrine, peculiar to Deuteronomy (12:5–8, 11–14, etc.), had never been heard of or put in practice in Israel's previous history. This is one reason the book "found" in the temple is identified as a form of Deuteronomy. Likewise, the comment in 2 Kings 23:9 that the rural YHWH priests, now unemployed, were not granted positions in the Jerusalem priesthood is an indication that the newly discovered book was an early version of (parts of) Deuteronomy, since the reference in 2 Kings specified that the law was not followed on this point, for only Deuteronomy has such a law (18:6–8).

Exile and Return: Ezra and the "Book of Moses"

Josiah's reformation was short lived, but the book that gave it direction and momentum lived on. Josiah was killed. Judea was devastated. City and temple were destroyed. Much of the leadership that could cause trouble for the conquering Babylonians was exiled. Some Deuteronomic teachers were among those deported to Babylon. Their tradition and the expanding Deuteronomic materials accompanied them into exile, where both they and those in Judea continued to interpret and expand their tradition and texts as they reflected on the past history of Israel and Judea from the perspective of the exile.

The loss of the land—the *promised* land—generated intense theological reflection, a rethinking of the past and a questioning of what could have led up to this unthinkable situation. The prophets who had spoken against nationalist religion, such as Jeremiah, were vindicated, and their writings were recovered, sorted, edited, and read with a new appreciation for their authority. Back in Judea, a group of exiled or just-returned teachers in the Deuteronomic tradition edited the final version of Deuteronomy and the Deuteronomistic History. The Deuteronomic teachers had learned the lesson the prophets of Israel and Judah had preached for generations. In Babylon, their worship of the Lord could no longer be confused with the cultural religion of their surroundings, and they were not tempted to worship the Babylonian gods as just another and more sophisticated form of their traditional worship of the Lord. If they had been implicit monotheists before, they were now clear that the Lord was the Creator, the only God. So also, for the people of Israel, belonging to the covenant could no longer mean simply belonging to the majority culture. Their goal and mission were no longer to "succeed" in cultural terms but to be faithful to their calling as the people of God, which often meant swimming against the cultural stream. The deportees had left Judea as members of a nationalist religion with its cult center in Jerusalem. Those who came (back) from Babylon to Judea had learned that their identity and mission meant living, as individuals and as a faithful community, in contrast to prevailing culture, not as a religious version of it. This is central to Deuteronomy's gospel and Torah. Its advocates had participated in a death-resurrection experience of Israel (Ezek 37!). In Babylon, Israel's self-understanding underwent a sea change from a national state to a confessional minority community within a much larger political reality, a change from "nation" (*ethnos*) to "church" (*ekklēsia*).

Most Judeans had not been taken into exile. The majority of those who had been deported did not return. Prophets such as Jeremiah who remained in Judea stayed in communication with those now in Babylon. Prophets affirming the traditional faith, such as Ezekiel, had been among the deportees. New prophets arose in Babylon, in the tradition of the classical prophets of Israel whose writings had been brought into exile with the deportees, and their contemporizing oracles were incorporated into the growing body of tradition. The anonymous prophet whose oracles appear in Isaiah 40–55 both reflected the continuing religious vitality among the deportees and contributed to its life and theology. Likewise, teachers in the Deuteronomic tradition were involved in the give and take of theological ferment during the exile. The author-editor(s) of Deuteronomy reflect this interchange.

In the *exile*, cultic assemblies and other educational opportunities where the tradition could be passed on in a controlled context were presumably difficult. In this setting, Israel discovered the value and necessity of the *written* word. In the eighth century BCE, Isaiah's call to be a prophet involved purifying his *lips* (Isa 6; cf. v. 7). Two centuries later,

Ezekiel's call was to swallow a *book* (Ezek 3:1–2). *Swallow*, not nibble. *Book*, not a verse or two. During the exile or shortly thereafter, Deuteronomy became a book that historical study can identify with some confidence as virtually the same book we have in our Bible. Was this book already Scripture, Bible, canon?

Chapter 8

The Story of the Text

The Book Became Canonical Scripture

"*The word of God for the people of God.*" "*Thanks be to God.*" We all resonate with this scene from the centuries-long liturgical tradition of the church, whether or not it is part of the worship of our particular congregation. We know the importance of hearing the Scripture read together as part of a worshipping congregation, "the people of God," even if the immediate mental image projected by the word *Bible* is that of a book on our shelf, desk, or computer. We recognize the rich symbolism firmly rooted in the traditional image. The Bible rests on the lectern or pulpit, not in the hands of the preacher or teacher—the Scripture belongs to the community of faith, not to individual clergy or laypeople. The Bible was there before we were, and apart from us, and will be there after we are gone. It is God's gift to the church, placed on the lectern in the solemn and joyful procession that begins worship, celebrated in a cloud of incense and the "Thanks be to God" of the prayers of the saints (Rev 5:8; 8:3–4). Even though the words can be repeated robotically as "just part of the ritual," they reflect the gratitude of the community of faith that God has not left us alone in the dark but has spoken to us. If God exists, and if God has spoken, this is the fundamental reality of our existence. The Deuteronomic teachers recognize this. Moses's first words in Deuteronomy are "The Lord our God spoke to us" (Deut 1:6). In regular worship, we join the whole community of faith in giving thanks to God for "the Word of God," for the divine Word mediated by Scripture and heard in the sermon and liturgy, without claiming that the words of the Bible are all directly spoken by God. This scene hovers over all our reading of Scripture, whether in worship, Bible study group, or personal

Bible study. Just as Jesus's model for personal, private prayer begins with the word "Our," always aware that we pray as part of the whole community of faith that prays with us and for us when we can hardly pray, so all our Bible reading is embraced within the church. The Bible itself is not a stand-alone book but comes to each of us through the church, as the church's *Scripture.*

This means that we can hardly read a line of Deuteronomy without the awareness that we are reading the *Bible.*[1] By binding Deuteronomy between the covers of a volume containing all the other canonical books, the church has rightly taught us that "interpreting in context" means that every verse of Scripture is to be understood in the context of the whole. But like every other book of the Bible, Deuteronomy was not originally written or understood as part of a canonical collection. Surveying the rest of Deuteronomy's story from the plains of Moab to our lectern or laptop will guard us against misunderstandings that we might not otherwise be aware of. Before we proceed to a sketch of this history, three possibly misleading impressions need to be mentioned.

First, to speak of a closed, limited canon is not a claim that all true and valuable literature is found within the covers of the Bible. The historical leaders of synagogue and church recognized that there were other documents that mediated God's truth that were valuable for the community to read. The word *canon*, of course, refers to a measuring stick. Just as a yardstick does not claim that it is the only object in the world that is thirty-six inches long, so the Jewish and Christian decision that a particular collection of texts serves as the norm for God's revealed truth by which all other such claims are measured is not a pronouncement that everything God has to say is contained in the canonical texts. Many texts outside the Bible "measure up" to the canonical measuring stick but do not become canonical themselves. The measure itself must remain constant. Martin Luther King Jr.'s "Letter from Birmingham Jail" and "I Have a Dream" speech are thus found by many preachers and teachers of the faith to express Christian truth and to mediate the call of God, just as countless sermons and booklets are used in church school and Bible study groups. But a fixed standard is necessary to adjudicate such decisions. A canon that remains continuously open and flexible cannot function as a standard.

Second, we typically read the Bible as a bound, printed volume in which the number of books and their content and arrangement are already firmly fixed. No author or reader of the biblical period could have thought in such terms. The codex, the book form in which a large number of separate pages are bound between two covers, did not exist in Old Testament times and was only beginning to be used late in the period of the formation of the New Testament. The invention of printing in the fifteenth century first made it possible to produce thousands of identical copies of the same book.

The codex and printing radically altered our perception of Scripture. The term *book* when found in the Bible always refers to a scroll, not a codex. Since finding a particular passage in a scroll meant rolling and unrolling the volume, practical considerations limited the size of a composition that could be contained in a single scroll. The Pentateuch means "five scrolls," or five volumes ("volume" = "roll"; cf. "revolve"). Genesis–Deuteronomy is a single narrative, a single lengthy "book," that can easily be contained in one codex but is too long for one scroll. Since it is one connected narrative, there can be no doubt about the order in which they are to be read, now designated Genesis–Deuteronomy. The same is true of the Deuteronomistic History, Joshua–2 Kings (minus Ruth). But Genesis–Malachi is also a grand narrative of sorts, as is Genesis–Revelation. This larger collection of books that became normative Scripture for a community would necessarily consist of a number of different scrolls stored on a shelf or in a box (ark). In the early centuries of Christianity, few congregations and far fewer individuals would possess a complete collection, and the meaning of a "complete" collection was not easily discerned prior to the invention of printed books, nor was the order in which they should be read. The number of scrolls in the "canonical" boxes of different congregations could vary, and they would be in no particular order. This means that the "book of the law" repeatedly mentioned in Deuteronomy and the Deuteronomistic History refers to a single scroll that could not have included the whole Pentateuch (e.g., Deut 17:18; 28:58; 29:21; 30:10; 31:9, 24, 26; 1 Kgs 2:3; 2 Kgs 14:6; 17:37). This "book of the law" that sparked Josiah's reformation refers not to the Pentateuch but to an early form of Deuteronomy. The anachronistic question of whether this book was "canonical" in the later sense of belonging to a fixed body of literature that serves as the rule of faith for a particular religious community cannot be answered with a simple yes or no. Any responsible answer must involve discerning the stages of an extended historical process.

Third, contemporary readers must also be wary of thinking of the canonization process in terms of simplistic caricatures. Increasing lack of information, misinformation, and misunderstandings of church history, enhanced by the popularity of novelistic treatments such as *The Da Vinci*

Code, have sometimes encouraged a widespread cultural image—a cartoon, actually—in which the biblical canon emerged on a particular day as the result of a council of rabbis or bishops with a collection of scrolls on the table, voting on each one as to whether it will be in the Bible. There never was such a day for either Judaism or Christianity. Canonization was a gradual process in which the community of faith found that some texts spoke to them in an authoritative way that nourished their faith and its authentic understanding, that others were helpful but did not become normative, and that still others were dangerous and were neglected or rejected. When catalogs of such books were occasionally made, with varying degrees of authority, boundaries of such lists of books (scrolls) were blurry, varying from congregation to congregation. This situation still existed in the time of Eusebius, who, in the fourth century CE, still described the New Testament canon in terms of four categories: (1) *homologoumena* (acknowledged), (2) *antilegomena* (disputed), (3) *notha* (spurious), and (4) books of the heretics that were dangerous to the faith (*Hist. Eccl.* 3.3.5–7 and 3.25.1–7). While a variety of criteria, such as authorship and date, were sometimes listed, the primary criterion was always whether the books in question were in fact *read*—that is, as Scripture, in the church's liturgy, by the majority of mainstream churches. We must remember that few individuals had their own Bibles; "reading" refers to the public, community reading of extensive passages in worship. This is where most people received their knowledge of the Bible. This long process culminated in a series of more-or-less official decisions by authorized leaders of the community who did not create the canon *ab ovo* but primarily made decisions that sharpened the boundary markers at the edge of the canonical lists. For what became normative Judaism, this historical process was not final until the second century CE. For what became mainline Western Christianity, the final "closing" of the canon for both Roman Catholics and the churches of the Protestant Reformation did not occur until the sixteenth century. Objective historians rightly note that political and ideological interests were inevitably at work in this history. Here as elsewhere, theological perspectives unavailable to the historian per se can affirm the Holy Spirit at work in the community of faith in this process. The canon(s) not only resulted from official decisions by a few church leaders but emerged from the life of the church as God's gift.

Can the canon be updated? The question is not new. One of the more recent proposals has emerged from the Jesus Seminar, a small group of American scholars of the last century. A "council" of nineteen members met several times in 2011 and 2012 "to determine which works from the first two centuries should be added to the traditional New Testament," deciding that the New Testament canon should now be expanded from twenty-seven to forty books, including the *Gospel of Thomas*.[2] On expanding the Old Testament canon, I think John Goldingay's response is appropriate: "Yes, it would be perfectly possible to add books to the Old Testament. You simply have to convene a meeting of an authoritative body representing all Jewish groups and all Christian groups and get them to agree on the matter. Good luck on that."[3]

For our purposes, a thumbnail sketch of how Deuteronomy and the Deuteronomistic History fits into this process can enhance our understanding.

First, the scroll discovered during Josiah's reformation was certainly accepted as authoritative by the king and the circle of prophets and religious teachers around him. It was the Word of God revealed through Moses, calling the people of God to reshape their corporate and individual life. This scroll was not, however, the only religious authority for Israel but joined the other traditions, oral and written, represented by J, E, and P, now found in Genesis–Numbers. These traditions had allowed worship and sacrifice at numerous shrines. Deuteronomy rejected this and called for a centralization of Israel's religious life focused on the temple cultus under the authority of the king and high priest in the Judean capital. The beginnings of canon formation are rooted in the time of Josiah, and Deuteronomy itself occasionally uses language that could later be understood as a somewhat "canonical" claim (e.g., Deut 4:2; 31:9–13). However, although Israel had some authoritative texts, including Deuteronomy, it did not yet have a Bible.

Second, Josiah's reformation did not establish (proto-)Deuteronomy as the sole authority. Josiah himself was killed by the Egyptian pharaoh, the Babylonians overran Judea, and Deuteronomic texts were taken into exile with their teachers. During the exile, they were reedited, interacting with other authoritative texts and traditions among the exiled Jewish scribes and teachers.

Third, with the fall of Babylon and the consolidation and expansion of the Persian Empire under Cyrus and his successors, exiles were allowed to return to their homeland, which meant, for many Jews of the generation born in Babylon, going (not going *back*) to the "old country" of their parents or grandparents. There were at least four waves of returnees and immigrants, beginning with the group led by Sheshbazzar, who set about to rebuild the temple; later groups led by Zerubbabel and Jeshua; two trips by Nehemiah and his groups; and a group led by

Ezra, which probably came after Nehemiah, in 403 BCE. Ezra was "a scribe skilled in the law of Moses that the LORD the God of Israel had given . . . the priest Ezra, the scribe, a scholar of the text of the commandments of the LORD and his statutes for Israel" (Ezra 7:6, 11). He was intent on restoring proper order and worship to Judea's religious life and was commissioned by the Persian king to do so with royal power and financial support (7:11–26). Ezra's efforts at restoration included a general assembly of all Israel at the festival of Booths, during which Ezra read to the people from "the book of the law of God" every day (Neh 8:1–18). The chronology of this period is unclear, as is the identity of the book of the law of God in Ezra's hand (Ezra 7:14). Was this book a completed Pentateuch (i.e., a collection of five scrolls), with JEDP having been edited into one grand narrative during the exile? Or did Ezra's priestly book only combine JE and P, with Deuteronomy and the Deuteronomistic History still a separate, parallel, and somewhat competing stream of tradition during the fifth century?

Fourth, we are not on historically solid ground until around 200 BCE, when the book of Sirach (Ecclesiasticus) was written in Jerusalem by Jesus ben Sirach. According to his grandson, who translated it into Greek and composed a preface for it, his grandfather had been expert in the Scriptures, identified as "the Law, the Prophets, and the others that followed them." The matter-of-fact way in which this is stated is a clear indication that at least by the late third century BCE, what became the traditional threefold division of the canon of the Hebrew Bible was already in place. Although the status and precise contents of the third division are vague, the vocabulary of "The Law and the Prophets" was firmly established, which means that by the third century BCE, Deuteronomy had long since been included in the Pentateuch. This is further confirmed by the fact that the Samaritan canon contained only the five books of the Pentateuch, including Deuteronomy as the last. The Samaritans had become a separate province politically and had separated religiously from emerging Judaism within a century or two of the completion of the present form of Deuteronomy, by which time it was deemed canonical. Likewise, "the" Scripture translated into Greek during this same general period (the LXX) included only the Pentateuch, with the Former and Latter Prophets and the writings translated later, after they, too, were accepted as canonical.

Finally, near the end of the first century CE, the Jewish historian Josephus could contrast the mass of religious books among the gentiles with the Jewish Scriptures, which comprised only twenty-two books, no more and no less. This corresponds to what became the official canon of Judaism several generations later. The twenty-two books correspond to the twenty-two letters in the Hebrew alphabet. (The *Iliad* and the *Odyssey* each have the same number of books as the Greek alphabet: twenty-four.) Just as it was assumed that the alphabet was complete and unchangeable, so with the Scripture. So also, 4 Ezra (2 Esdras) apparently refers to the same collection of Jewish Scriptures as comprising twenty-four books, divided slightly differently to accord with the Greek alphabet of twenty-four letters. About this same time, the Christian author of Luke–Acts portrays Jesus as referring to the Scriptures as "the law of Moses, the prophets, and the psalms" (Luke 24:44, with "Psalms" standing for the first and most prominent book of the third division, the [other] "writings").

These are the texts inherited by Jesus and the early church, which deeply affected their own theology and teaching. All later Christians stand in this tradition. Our understanding of Deuteronomy is radically affected by the reality that it is seen and heard from the perspective of Christian faith. Since the early church and New Testament authors thought in Greek, read their Bible in Greek, and wrote for a Greek-speaking readership, we must backtrack a bit and reflect on the significance of the translation of the Hebrew Scriptures into the Greek language, an indispensable chapter in our understanding of the English Bible.

Chapter 9

The Story of the Text

Canonical Scripture Became a Translation

The preacher's and teacher's task of *interpretation* is closely related, sometimes even identical, to the task of *translation*. There is a sense in which everyone who interprets the Bible is a translator and needs to be bilingual, not necessarily in the sense of knowing the biblical languages, but as the linguistic mediator between the world of the Bible and our own world. Understanding what translation is and how it works has great value in helping us get our minds around the task of interpretation. All the elements necessary for understanding what is involved in interpreting and translating the faith into a different language and culture were already present in the first and most important translation, the rendering of the Hebrew text into Greek, called the Septuagint (LXX): (1) history, (2) language, (3) theology, and (4) money.

History

The first translation of the Bible ever made was also the most significant in the entire history of biblical translation. By the middle of the third century BCE, Hellenistic Greek had replaced Aramaic as the lingua franca of much of the eastern Mediterranean Basin, much as English became a world language after World War II. Jews of the Diaspora, the large Jewish population of the Hellenistic world outside Palestine, had long since adopted Greek as their own language. They had mostly lost their ability to understand Hebrew, just as most Jews in the world today grow up speaking the language of their native country, perhaps know a modest amount of biblical Hebrew from synagogue worship and instruction, and need a translation in their own language if they are to understand their Scriptures. In about 250 BCE, the leaders and teachers of the large Jewish community in Alexandria responded to the needs of Diaspora Judaism by translating the Torah into *koinē* (commonly understood) Greek. This was a momentous, unheard-of decision. The Jewish community could have decided, for understandable religious reasons, that the sacred text must remain in the sacred language. Only properly educated and authorized scholars and teachers would study the Scripture; they would share its meaning with the common people. Misuse and profanation would be avoided, even considered dangerous and punished. Islam would later decide to take this direction. The medieval Roman Catholic Church had these tendencies, and Latin was the sacred language of the church for a thousand years after most people could no longer read or speak it.

We do not know the historical details of how the Greek translation came to be, but we are not completely in the dark. We can make fairly reliable inferences on the basis of the translation itself. We also have a legendary account, written perhaps two generations after the initial translation, that became widespread and respected by both Jews and Christians, the *Letter of Aristeas*.[1] This well-written short story is entertaining and edifying, apparently written to promote the social image of Hellenistic Judaism in general and to defend the validity of the LXX in particular. The narrative glorifies Judaism and pictures the Jewish people and religion as held in great respect, implicitly arguing that Jews can fit into Hellenistic culture without undue compromise or losing their distinctive identity or mission.

The story takes place in the time in which the Hellenistic king of Egypt is establishing the great library of Alexandria, with the intent that it should include every significant book of world literature. It comes to his attention that the sacred books of the Jews are not yet deposited there. The king writes to the Jewish high priest in Jerusalem, asking him to send skilled and pious scholars who are expert in the Torah and accurate texts agreed on by the majority. The high priest cooperates and, with the approval of the whole Jewish community in Judea, sends six men from each tribe with accurate Hebrew texts of the Torah. The translators are welcomed to Alexandria with royal pomp and ceremony and a weeklong banquet. The translators are then taken to a quiet and comfortable house a mile offshore. Each of the translators then makes a draft translation and reaches an agreement among themselves by comparing versions. The result of their agreement is made into a fair copy by Demetrius. The completed translation is read aloud to the large Jewish assembly, which approves it and commands that there be no revisions (*Letter of Aristeas* 308). The story was elaborated in ever more miraculous ways and was widely circulated among Jews and Christians for generations. When the LXX became the Bible of early Christianity, Greek-speaking Jews adopted other translations closer to the Hebrew text that was to become the only authorized text of the Scripture for mainline Judaism.

Language

The Jewish community represented by Aristeas realized that they needed competent linguists to translate the Scriptures. Language is a world. To translate is not merely to substitute one set of words for another but to move from one world to another. Older English still used the word in this way: "By faith *Enoch was translated* that he should not see death; and was not found, because God had translated him: for before his translation he had this testimony, that he pleased God" (Heb 11:5 KJV). God is the one "who hath delivered us from the power of darkness, and hath *translated us* into the kingdom of his dear Son" (Col 1:13 KJV). In modern English, we rarely use the word *translate* in this way, but Elizabethan English still preserved this facet of the mystery and power of language. For Enoch to be taken from the earthly world to the world of God was to be translated; for ordinary folk to be taken by God from the everyday world into the kingdom of God is to be translated.

Translation and Interpretation

Every translation is an interpretation. There can be no such thing as a completely neutral, objective translation that then, as a second step, becomes the basis for the preacher's, teacher's, or reader's interpretation. Translation is an interpretation that bridges two worlds, the *translator's own world* and the *world of the text*. We translators may know our own language and culture relatively well, but becoming interior to the ancient language and culture and the art and craft of bridge building requires a competency that an individual translator may claim, if at all, only with fear and trembling. The bridge spans depths of seventy thousand fathoms. Translation is not an individual project. It is the community of faith that spans the continents and centuries, that equips and authorizes translations and translators. The translators work together as a group whose strengths, weaknesses, blind spots, and hobbyhorses may be supplemented and corrected by their colleagues, always submitting their translation to the judgment of the people of God to whom the book belongs. This is the truth enshrined in the legendary Aristeas account of the origin of the LXX and its acceptance as Holy Scripture.

The biblical message cannot simply be repeated but must always be translated/interpreted, and such translation always involves transforming a text composed in the language, culture, and thought patterns of one world into another, "playing on a piano what was written for a violin."[2] But the music goes on. It is no accident that the authors-editors of Deuteronomy concluded the Torah not with lessons on "how to apply the Torah to our daily lives" but with a song (Deut 32) and that Christian worship includes not only explanatory instruction in the faith but hymns of praise to the One God.

"Literal" Translation?

Before leaving the discussion of translation/interpretation, it may be helpful to briefly address the question that emerges when readers of the Bible notice that some commercially produced modern translations are advertised as "literal" or "word for word."

One of the first things that most beginning students of biblical Hebrew or Greek learn on their own—by hands-on experience of their efforts to translate the biblical text into English or vice versa—is that there is no such thing as a "literal translation," that there cannot be and should not be. Students quickly come to understand that their previous interest in "literal," "word-for-word" translation may have been a legitimate theological commitment but cannot be a valid value judgment in linguistic categories. What they rightly wanted to affirm was an *accurate* translation, as close to the original meaning as possible. Linguistically, it is better to categorize translations not in terms of more or less literal but on a spectrum from *formal equivalence* to *functional equivalence*, each of which can represent the original meaning of the text more or less accurately, depending on the competence of the translators. In formal equivalence, the translation attempts to translate not only the meaning of the text but its formal structure as well. The goal of functional equivalence translation, on the other hand, is not to translate word for word, for such attempts at literal translation may in fact conceal or distort the meaning. The goal of functional translation is meaning for meaning. The unit of meaning is understood to be not the individual word but the larger semantic unit, the clause, sentence, or even paragraph or the document as a whole—all of which may need to be restructured in order to accurately convey the meaning of the original. Isolated words themselves rarely convey meaning, which occurs only in larger linguistic structures. There is no correlation between being "literal" and being accurate. In terms of transferring the meaning of the source text into the target language, a literal translation may be erroneous, misleading, or unclear, and a free translation may accurately represent the original meaning in the target language. Accuracy may in fact require a free translation to convey the original meaning, which might be obscured by a wooden, word-for-word effort to translate "what the Hebrew literally says."

Beginning Hebrew and Greek students perceive early on that even the translation of everyday language has a significance that requires a depth of knowledge and judicious decisions. Mark Twain had both composition and translation in mind when he wrote, "The difference between the right word, and almost the right word, is the difference between *lightning* and *lightning bug*."[3] Skilled and sensitive translators have learned that even the way the most common everyday words are translated communicates something important about the text. Examples abound on every page. We briefly illustrate with one example from Deuteronomy 3:27. In this pathos-filled scene, Moses asks to enter the promised land along with 'all Israel' but is denied and told not to ask again. God only grants Moses the opportunity to climb Mount Pisgah and view the land from a distance. Word for word, the Hebrew phrase is "lift up your eyes . . . and see," an ordinary expression for "look around" (as in NRSV) found more than one hundred times in the Hebrew Bible. Although understandable to speakers of both Greek and English, it is not the way people who do not live in the biblical world would express themselves. The translator's Greek could be rendered in correspondingly literal English: "Having lifted up your eyes, look." The LXX translators did not talk this way in their ordinary conversation, nor do we, unless we are nonseriously trying to sound "biblical," dropping "and it came to pass" and "behold I say unto you" into our conversation. In this case, the LXX translators were entirely serious when they intentionally decided, here and often elsewhere, to preserve something of the biblical flavor of the expression and translate with a Greek phrase that follows the Hebrew form. Their formal-equivalence translation was perfectly understandable but communicated that when we read the Scripture, we do not hear Moses and other biblical characters talking like our next-door neighbors. The LXX translators intended to communicate, even at the level of incidental expressions, that hearing the Scripture means entering the strange new world of the Bible, a world that is not the same as our everyday world and that challenges its claim to ultimate reality.

The RSV and other English translations take the same tack and translate somewhat literally (formal equivalence), "lift up your eyes," while the NRSV and others translate into everyday English, "look around." Both translations are understandable; neither is incorrect. But one speaks with the accent of a different time, place, and culture, while the other speaks to us in the idiom we normally use with one another. Should the Bible make Moses, Isaiah, Jesus, and Paul speak to us in the same English spoken by our neighbor across the back fence? The translation should be clear, but should it sound like "the Bible" or like the newspaper? This, too, is a theological decision. Such decisions require careful thought and consistent editing and may legitimately be made differently from case to case. Who is authorized to make such decisions for the Bible of the whole church?

So also, translators and those who choose and authorize them must be aware that even an everyday word such as "hand" (*yad*) may be used in significantly different ways in the Hebrew text than in the target language. The semantic fields of Hebrew *yad* and English *hand* overlap but are by no means the same. Each has meanings unacceptable in the other language. In addition to the literal anatomical meaning, the standard Hebrew lexicon lists fifteen other meanings for *yad*, some of them overlapping with English metaphorical usage (e.g., a person, a sphere of power, a spatial orientation), some of them quite strange to us (e.g., theft, memorial, monument, penis, sexual vigor, latrine). Modern English speakers are puzzled that ancient Hebrew sometimes referred to a latrine as "the hand," just as speakers of ancient Hebrew would have been bemused that in modern nautical English, the ship's toilet is called "the head."

Only through an awareness of such linguistic realities can the modern interpreter be aware of the choices every translator of a biblical text must make. Even a semester or two of such study can be an eye- and ear-opening revelatory experience, allowing one to become aware of how much there is to know and how precarious it is to entrust any one person with the task of translating the Bible. Two years of college or seminary Greek or Hebrew do not a translator make, but they do allow the student to see firsthand what is at stake in translation and the difficulty of the task. These linguistic issues need to be concretely illustrated by exploring specific theological topics, texts, and words—there are helpful books that do this (see bibliography). For purposes of illustration, we will dwell on one common three-letter word understood by everyone in every culture and language. Everyone on both sides of the linguistic bridge knows what a "son" is, right?

Theology

The Hebrew word often translated "son" is *ben*, plural *banim*. It has a wide range of meanings, some of which overlap with Greek (and English) usage, some of which seem strange to those who speak Greek or English.

1. *Son*. The most common usage is for a male child in the biological sense (e.g., Deut 1:36, "Caleb son of Jephunneh"). This, of course, corresponds to normal English usage.
2. *Children*. *Ben* in the plural is often used generically for "children," when the group includes both male and female (e.g., Deut 1:39, "your children [*banim*, sons], who today do not yet know right from wrong, . . ."; Gen 3:16, "To the woman he said, 'I will greatly increase your pangs in childbearing; in pain you shall bring forth children'" [*banim*, sons]).
3. *My son*. It is also used in the metaphorical sense as a term of kindness or endearment (e.g., 1 Sam 3:6, "The Lord called again, 'Samuel!' Samuel got up and went to Eli, and said, 'Here I am, for you called me.' But he said, 'I did not call, my son; lie down again.'").
4. *Kinfolk*. In the Israelite family, the same terms were generally used both for immediate blood relatives in the family and for wider relationships. Thus *ab*, "father," could refer to any male ancestor in the same lineage so that the children of Laban's daughters are his "sons" (Gen 31:28), and Ruth's son is the "son" of her grandmother Naomi (Ruth 4:17).
5. *Descendants*. Later generations, male and female, can be called collectively "sons" (e.g., Josh 22:27, "[in] the generations after us, . . . that your children [sons] may never say to our children [sons] in time to come, 'You have no portion in the Lord'").
6. *Belonging to a group that provides one's identity*. All of the above are related in one way or another to the biological family, and though Hebrew usage is different from Greek and English, non-Hebrews can understand the usage. But this theologically important usage of *ben* as identifying the group to which one belongs was as strange to the ancient Greek translators as it is to modern English readers. It is a matter not of metaphor but of

the "literal" meaning of the vocable *ben* in Hebrew, ancient and modern.

- Members of a nation, people, or city are called its "sons," as Israelites are "sons of Israel." Hittites are "sons of Heth," inhabitants of Jerusalem are "sons of Zion," and so on. The more than twelve hundred instances of "Israelites" in the NRSV, NIV, and other translations (KJV "children of Israel") are all *benē Yishrael* in the Hebrew text. In Hosea 1:10, "my people" is parallel to "sons of the living God" (so RSV; NRSV "children"). Thus "sons/children of Israel" means not necessarily biological descendants of Jacob/Israel but members of the people of Israel, as expressed by the modern Hebrew "Israeli." In this world of thought, the national group is there first, and individuals receive their identity by being its "sons." This is distinctively different from thinking of the primacy of the individual and that putting a number of individuals together forms a nation.
- A member of the household, slave or free, male or female, is a "son of the house" (cf. Gen 15:3).
- Members of a guild, order, or class are called its "sons." Thus when Amos denies that he is a "prophet's son," this has nothing to do with the identity of his biological father; he is denying that he is a professional prophet, stating that he does not belong to the prophetic guild (Amos 7:14).
- Members of the army are called "sons of the troop" (e.g., 2 Chr 25:13).
- Exiles are called "sons of the exile" (e.g., Ezra 4:1).
- Since the Hebrew word for "humanity," or "the human race," is *'adam* (the Adam of Genesis 1–3), members of the human race are "sons of Adam/man"; a human being is a *ben adam*, "son of Adam/man" (e.g., Gen 11:5; 2 Chr 6:30; Ps 8:4; 14:2; ninety-three times in Ezekiel as address by God to the prophet; rendered various ways in English translations: "son of man"; "children of men"; "mortal"; etc.). The phrase signifies human instead of God, not male instead of female.

7. *Part of a larger whole.* This way of thinking is extended to animals and inanimate life:
   - An individual cow or bull is a "son of the herd" (e.g., 1 Sam 14:32).

- The sparks from a campfire are "sons of the flame" (e.g., Job 5:7).
- Arrows are "sons of the quiver" (e.g., Lam 3:13).

8. *Belonging to a category.* This is defined by a particular characteristic or quality.
    - A powerful man is a *ben hayil*, a "son of power" (e.g., 1 Sam 14:52).
    - Those appointed or exposed to death are *benē tmutha*, "sons of death" (1 Sam 26:16).
    - A person convicted in court and sentenced to a flogging is a *ben ha-koth*, "son of to-be-flogged."
    - Anointed ones are *benē yitshar*, "sons of oil."
    - A hill of olive trees that produce oil—that is, a fertile hill—is an "oily hill," a *ben shemen* (Isa 5:1).
    - Age is designated as being a son of a certain number of years: "Moses was one hundred twenty years old when he died" is "son of one hundred twenty years" (Deut 34:7).

How were the LXX translators to handle this complex cluster of issues built in to the Hebrew *ben*? The Greek word for "son" overlaps with some of these usages; for others, Greek, like English, uses an entirely different way of communicating the same meaning. Most of the time, the Hebrew and Greek words for "son" were used in the same unproblematic way, and *ben* could simply be translated as the standard Greek word for "son," *huios*. Fairly often, however, Hebrew and Greek usage were so different that rendering the Hebrew word for "son" with the Greek word for "son" would result in odd or incomprehensible Greek. No Greek, for instance, would describe someone's age in the words of Joshua: "I am today a son of eighty-five years"—that is, "I belong to the category of eighty-five-year-olds" (Josh 14:10). In such cases, the LXX translator—like modern English translators—must decide whether to stay with the Hebrew idiom or use the idiom of the target language, which requires different words. We have only taken a brief look at two common words, "hand" and "son," but examples abound on every page of the sacred text. All translation requires such choices, best made by scholars who understand something about linguistics and the idioms of each language.

Money

Producing an authentic translation of the Bible is an expensive business. However legendary, the *Letter of Aristeas* illustrates that from the very beginning, it takes a lot of money to do the job right. The story pictures seventy-two highly skilled professionals, with expenses for travel, housing, meals, and royal entertainment for two and a half months, not counting travel time and breaks. Money was no problem for the project, however—the whole cost was underwritten by the royal treasury. The king who supplied the money gave no instructions, explicit or implied, as to what the final product should look like; this was left in the hands of the religious leaders, scholars, and community of faith as a whole. There was no market research, no profit motive. Ample funds were available, but no one said, "The one who pays the piper calls the tune." In later centuries, immense amounts of money could be made in the Bible business, and this could not but affect the product. Modern readers of the English Bible might well ask who the translators were, how they were chosen and on what basis, who authorized and paid for the translation, and who profits from the sales of the Bible they are reading. Within the realities of the cultural and economic pressures of the business world and in the absence of a central authority that can "authorize" legitimate translations of the Bible for all Christians, a divided church must attempt to produce and promote translations of the Bible that are not regarded as commercial products. Developing an awareness of the nature of translation is a helpful component in the toolkit of the preacher and teacher, enabling better hearing and understanding of the biblical text, an ally in the joyful and awesome responsibility of interpreting the Bible for the people of God.

Chapter 10

The Story of the Text

Preachers and Teachers Interpret the Book in the Life of the Church

A translated Bible is already an interpreted Bible. But every translation must also be continually interpreted in the preaching and teaching of the church. Modern preachers or teachers do not start at square one but always stand within a history of translation, several moves around the board. This fascinating story, covering the twenty centuries of church history, is well documented in a sizeable bibliography well worth the preacher's and teacher's investigation (see bibliography). For our purposes, the two eras of this history that illuminate and shape our own practice correspond to the two most crucial issues the church has faced in the history of biblical interpretation: (1) the reception, expansion, and interpretation of the Scripture of Israel in the earliest period of church history, 30–180 CE; and (2) the encounter of what became mainline Christian faith with the scientific worldview that emerged in the Renaissance, the Enlightenment, and the Reformation in the seventeenth to nineteenth centuries CE. For us, this confrontation of traditional theology and the modern world is focused in the beginnings of the historical study of the Bible, especially in the emergence of "higher criticism" in the nineteenth century and its later fallout in Protestant liberalism.

In the preceding chapter, we explored some of the pertinent aspects of this era of the history of biblical study. If we now backtrack to the initial period of the church's efforts to understand its Bible, it becomes clear that the earliest Jewish Christian community expanded and quickly became a predominately gentile church that found itself with the "Jewish

Scriptures" as its Bible. However, its leading preachers and teachers were not of one mind on how to understand the relation between the Scriptures of the "old" covenant inherited from Judaism and the newness of the Christian faith.

Early Christianity: The Primary Options

A bare-bones, streamlined sketch of this chapter of early Christian history illustrates three major options.

1. **Marcion, ca. 100–150.** Marcion was a talented, respected, wealthy, and devoted Christian teacher who contributed large sums of money to the Christian congregation in Rome. He was finally considered a heretic and expelled (along with his money, which was returned to him). His numerous followers continued for generations as active Christian congregations. His teachings were as follows:

- The Old Testament is not, and cannot be, a Christian book. The God of Judaism and its Scripture is a different God from the True God revealed in Jesus.
- A subordinate deity named YHWH is the Creator of this messed-up world. Jesus is the Redeemer sent by the One True God to get his followers out of it.
- The Old Testament is oriented to this-worldly, material blessings. The God of Jesus represents the spiritual world and spiritual blessings.
- The Old Testament God is a God of justice who punishes the disobedient with cruel penalties. The God revealed in Jesus is loving and merciful.
- The Christian writings that were beginning to assume canonical status along with the Jewish Scriptures are not in any way a continuation, expansion, or interpretation of the Old Testament. Marcion's list of authoritative texts consisted of ten letters of Paul (sans the Pastorals) and the Gospel of Luke, all of which had been purged of quotations from the Old Testament and positive statements about it. Marcion considered these to be later harmonizing interpolations into the original texts. What became the official canon of emerging mainline Christianity was in part a reaction to Marcion.

2. **Barnabas, ca. 125.** The document that came to be known as the Epistle of Barnabas is anonymous, but by the end of the second century

CE, it was attributed to Barnabas, the companion of Paul. Its content makes this authorship impossible. His teachings were as follows:

- The Old Testament is a Christian book and only a Christian book.
- The Jews interpreted the Scripture literally and thus never understood the divine revelation.
- The Old Testament is to be heard as the Word of God by allegorical interpretation. Allegory had been devised and long accepted in the Hellenistic world as a way of making the bawdy, violent Homeric tales not only acceptable but a means of teaching valuable spiritual and ethical lessons. Allegorical interpretation of the Old Testament allowed Barnabas to claim that none of the Old Testament laws—including the rules that distinguish clean from unclean food and the rules for sacrifice, fasting, circumcision, and the Sabbath—were ever intended to be literally obeyed. Sacrifice is spiritual, as the Old Testament already tells us in Psalm 51:16–17 and as Paul teaches in Romans 12:1; circumcision is a matter of the heart, as in Deuteronomy 10:16; 30:6, and as Paul teaches us in Romans 2:28–29. Barnabas is thus able to appeal to both the original intent of the Old Testament and its New Testament interpretation by a leading apostle for his "spiritual" understanding of the Scripture.
- The replacement of the biblical narratives with rational, spiritual meanings allowed the author to find Jesus Christ on every page of the Old Testament. In a famous example, he explains the 318 men in Abraham's band of warriors (Gen 14:14). In the Greek way of signifying numbers by letters of the alphabet, "ten" is the capital letter iota (I), and "eight" is the capital letter ēta (H). Eighteen is thus written as IH, the first two letters of the name "Jesus" (think of the IHS on our altars and pulpit cloths). Since "three hundred" in Greek is represented by the letter *T*, which resembles the cross, the Genesis text is clearly referring to Jesus on the cross. The teacher proudly concludes his lesson with "No one has ever learned from me a more reliable word, but I know that you are worthy of it," and he was likely much admired by laypeople who appreciated a teacher who "really knew the Bible and how to make it meaningful" (Barnabas 9.8–9).

3. **The core logic of the earliest Christian creed (1 Cor 15:3–5).** Our earliest reconstructable source for the teaching of Jesus, the Q teaching

document cited by both Matthew and Luke, pictures Jesus as beginning his ministry by fasting forty days and nights, like Moses in Deuteronomy, then citing three texts from Deuteronomy as he resists demonic perversions of the nature of his mission (Matt 4:1–10 / Luke 4:1–12; cf. Deut 6:13, 16; 8:3). Whether or not this is a historically exact report, there can hardly be any doubt that the historical Jesus of Nazareth was profoundly influenced by Deuteronomy both comprehensively and in detailed particulars. We do not, of course, have any writings from Jesus that present his own understanding of biblical interpretation. Our earliest extant written documentation of how his followers interpreted the Scripture in the light of the Christ event is found in 1 Corinthians 15:3–5.

> For I handed on to you as of first importance what I in turn had received:
>
> I.
>
> [That] Christ died
> for our sins
> in accordance with the scriptures
> and that he was buried
>
> II.
>
> [and that] he was . . . raised
> on the third day
> in accordance with the scriptures,
> and that he appeared to Cephas.
> (by/to Cephas, then to the twelve)

Paul cites this creedal affirmation not as his own ad hoc composition but as something he had received from the church, presumably at the time of his baptism in about 33 CE, only a brief period after the death and resurrection of Jesus and the beginnings of the church. For our purposes, it is only important to note that in this stream of earliest Christianity, the gospel was concentrated in the saving act of God in the death and resurrection of Jesus and that from the beginning, the Christ event was interpreted "in accordance with the Scriptures." This phrase does not mean that the details of Jesus's life, death, and resurrection had been predicted in the Jewish Scripture but that the biblical narrative provided the matrix for God's act in Christ. This core conviction was expressed in a number of different but overlapping ways in the New Testament, including the following:

1. Promise → fulfillment
2. Prediction → happening
3. Typology (the biblical story as a pattern for interpreting the events of Christian history and theology)
4. Symbol and allegory (not in a way that replaces the biblical narrative with ideas, ideals, and principles)
5. Use of Old Testament language, imagery, and events to tell the story of Jesus and the early church
6. "Rewritten Bible"—retelling/rewording the biblical story in the light of the Christ event
7. Use of the text of the Old Testament to mediate the Word of the preexistent Christ, who directly addresses the Christian reader of the Old Testament

The theological variety expressed in this list represents an underlying unity, illustrated below in a close reading of one key text in Deuteronomy as interpreted by Paul. None of the canonical New Testament documents adopt the approaches represented by Marcion or Barnabas. The followers of Jesus who came to confess him as the Christ neither rejected the Jewish Scriptures nor denied that they belonged to pre- and para-Christian Israel. The advent of historical study of the Bible centuries later would call the church to reevaluate some previous approaches to how the New Testament used Old Testament texts. Still, Christian understanding of "what it means" could not simply make an end run around "what it meant" in the original biblical texts but only reinterpret in the light of the definitive revelation in Christ. *All seven approaches listed above can be considered instantiations of "in accordance with the Scriptures" in the earliest Christian creed.* We will now attempt a close reading of a key New Testament text from Romans that illumines the tradition in which we stand and our own task as preachers and teachers in the church.

Paul and the "Conversion of the Imagination"[1]

Paul's interpretation of Deuteronomy 30:11–14 in Romans 10:5–9 opens an intriguing and instructive door into the world of Israel's Scripture as interpreted by New Testament preachers and teachers. At the climax of Moses's speech in Deuteronomy, Moses claims that God has plainly revealed what is right and true and that the responsibility of Israel is simply to do the revealed will of God:

> For this commandment which I command you this day is not too hard for you, neither is it far off. It is not in heaven, that you should say, "Who will go up for us to heaven, and bring it to us, that we may hear it and do it?" Neither is it beyond the sea, that you should say, "Who will go over the sea for us, and bring it to us, that we may hear it and do it?" But the word is very near you; it is in your mouth and in your heart, so that you can do it. (Deut 30:11–14 RSV)

These verses present us with a text that is preachable as is. Doing the will of God does not depend on waiting for personal experiences of divine revelation or meditating on the deep wisdom found in the ancient, exotic religions of other nations. This might seem at first to resonate with slogans from our own culture: "It's not complicated." "Just do it." It may then come as something of a jolt to read, at a key juncture in Paul's letter to the Roman church, his citation of this text from Deuteronomy with his own built-in Christian interpretation, an interpretation not intended by Moses or the Deuteronomist teachers, not immediately apparent on the surface, and never accepted by anyone outside the Christian community:

Paul's citation-interpretation	Paul's Bible
Moses writes concerning the righteousness that comes from the law, that "**the person who does these things will live by them.**" But the righteousness that comes from faith says, "**Do not say in your heart,** **'Who will ascend into heaven?'**" (that is, to bring Christ down) or "**'Who will** descend into **the abyss?'**" (that is, to bring Christ up from the dead). But what does it say? "**The word is near you, on your lips and in your heart**" (that is, the word of faith that we proclaim); because if you confess with your lips that Jesus is Lord and believe in your heart that God raised him from the dead, you will be saved. (Rom 10:5–9)	You shall keep my statutes and my ordinances; **by doing so one shall live.** (Lev 18:5) **Do not say in your heart.** (Deut 9:4 RSV; cf. 8:17) Surely, this commandment that I am commanding you today is not too hard for you, nor is it too far away. It is not in heaven, that you should say, "**Who will go up to heaven** for us, and get it for us so that we may hear it and observe it?" Neither is it beyond the sea, that you should say, "**Who will** cross to the other side of **the sea** for us, and get it for us so that we may hear it and observe it?" No, **the word is very near to you; it is in your mouth and in your heart** for you to observe. (Deut 30:11–14)

At least at first, we may find ourselves backing away from what might appear to be the hijacking of a clear call to ethical living by means of exegetical smoke and mirrors. We will return to explore the particulars of this text, but first, some general observations about "The New Testament's use of the Old Testament." The phrase has become conventional in both popular and scholarly discourse, so we will continue to employ it, though the term *use*, as either verb or noun, is not without its problems.

No one likes to be used. We like for our words to be heard, understood, and even interpreted but are usually uncomfortable when someone "uses" our words for their own purposes, especially when taken out of context: "OK, I said it, but that's not what I meant. You've got to understand it in context." What we are talking about here is how New Testament authors listened to, heard, interpreted, and understood Holy Scripture, how their and their hearers' theology and lives were shaped by it. Whether or to what extent the New Testament authors understood the role of "context" in the same way we do, *their* interpretation of the Old Testament is a matter of *our* historical context for understanding both the Old Testament and its New Testament interpretations.

Interpretation of Scripture shapes the theologies found in New Testament texts in three primary ways.

First, the narrative world projected by the Old Testament texts, in whole or in part, provides the overarching framework of New Testament theology. Every human life is lived within the framework of some narrative. Our little life stories are not independent, autonomous narratives, spun spiderlike from within our own individuality, but are and must be the segment of some larger story that gives it meaning. We are born on a moving train that was there before we boarded and will be there after we exit. This larger story is always derived from the culture and adapted to the particularities of our own situations, wants, and needs, mostly without our awareness, intention, or control. It's just there, a given dimension of human existence, like space, time, and gravity. Our perception of reality—our understanding of what's what—is always and inevitably culturally conditioned. The worldview/mindset that comes with the package of human being is the legacy of our interaction with human culture. It is crucial to realize that this cultural shaping is not done by culture in general (there is no such thing, just as there is no language in general or sports in general). We are always shaped by our give and take with a particular culture. No one lives in general. *Which* culture shapes our lives is the whole ball game. When we open ourselves to the narrative world presented by the Bible, our particular version of the "real world" confronts the narrative world projected by the Bible, which challenges our assumed lifeworld; often judges it to be false, perverse, or inadequate; and opens the door to the reality of the new world we already live in.

Paul's term for this normal, everyday reality perceived by common sense is *kata sarka*, "according to the flesh," a distinctive Pauline phrase (of the twenty occurrences in the New Testament, eighteen are found in the undisputed letters, with one each in the Deutero-Pauline Colossians and Ephesians). Leading up to our key text in Romans 10:5–9, Paul has already referred to this *kata sarka* world eight times (Rom 1:3; 4:1; 8:4, 5, 12, 13; 9:3, 5). There are no evil connotations in the way "flesh" is used here. It simply refers to the material, everyday world of human life. Like us, the New Testament authors all live in this world—it is God's good creation—but Paul and the New Testament have come to see that the present state of the world is a distortion of God's creation and to accept the world projected by their Bible as the real world, God's new creation that is already dawning.

Deuteronomy offers the Old Testament's most comprehensive and explicit projection of this narrative world and its fundamental orientation to the ethics and mission of the people of God to all God's peoples, all nations and peoples of the whole world. While this appropriation of the biblical worldview/mindset comes to expression in different ways in the work of the various New Testament writers, they share the broad outline of their Bible's narrative world that begins with the creation, proceeds through God's covenant with Israel, and looks forward to the fulfillment of the promises of the covenant-making God (see ch. 5). Earlier in his letter to Rome, Paul has already made extensive use of this pattern, intensely focused on in Deuteronomy, in which God has set slaves free, has formed them into a community, and has given them a way of life (Rom 6). In this Deuteronomic pattern, human life is never autonomous but is enslaved to some master (so also in the teaching of Jesus, e.g., Matt 6:24; Luke 6:13). The world is dominated by the power of sin, but God has unleashed the incomparably superior power of righteousness into the world. Believers are called to orient their lives by this new reality in which they actually already live to be what they are. Deuteronomy's preaching that repeatedly emphasizes God's powerful act of redemption in setting the Israelites free was not merely a matter of information but pointed to a reality in political and personal history—God let the liberating power of the resurrection loose in the world (Rom 1:4; Phil 3:10) so that those who have been delivered no longer need to serve the sinful powers of this world but are delivered in order to serve God as God's slaves. This language may at first seem repugnant to us, understood in terms of our own culture, but understood within the framework of biblical—especially Deuteronomic—theology, it portrays us as being delivered from evil, from cultural slavery, into the realm where God is Lord and Master, "in whose service is perfect freedom."[2] The fact that New Testament authors had themselves entered the strange new world of the Bible, which shaped their whole perception of reality, is clear and important, even when they make sparing or no use of direct quotation. Their conversion to faith in Christ included the transformation of their imaginations: "Do not be conformed to this world, but be transformed by the renewing of your minds, so that you may discern what is the will of God—what is good and acceptable and perfect" (Rom 12:2). Living in the reality of this biblical world was the horizon of all their thinking, however much or little they cited particular texts.

Second, not only the overarching framework but many particular elements of the thought and language of the biblical world shaped the thinking of New Testament theologians, reflected in their many indirect references to Scripture in the form of allusions, echoes, reflections, and paraphrases that give no indication to the unversed reader that they are referring to Scripture. These may be intentional and conscious or just the way the New Testament teacher-authors think, talk, and write, living in The Story. Their minds were so permeated with the language of the biblical world that they speak in its conceptuality, vocabulary, and phraseology when expressing their faith, without quoting a specific text. We may think of the language of sacrifice, atonement, resurrection, violence, election, and predestination and their talk of *God*, understood in biblical rather than cultural terms. Like the New Testament authors, our own thought and language we use in understanding and communicating the Christian faith can be profoundly influenced by this kind of encounter with biblical language and thought—learning "Bible as a second language"—even if chapter and verse are rarely cited explicitly. The last book of the New Testament is a superlative example. The twenty-two chapters, forty-eight pages of Greek text, contain around *five hundred* allusions of varying degrees of explicitness, an average of about ten references per page. The author's mind is wallpapered, top to bottom, with the language and imagery of the Bible. Yet there is not a single direct quotation! Such authors may or may not presuppose that their readers always "get it," but whether or not they recognize the specifics, readers will be aware that they are being addressed by a message that calls for transforming their own world rather than merely echoing it. A modern parallel might be Martin Luther King Jr.'s "I've Been to the Mountaintop" speech, delivered less than twenty-four hours before he was assassinated:

> Well, I don't know what will happen now. We've got some difficult days ahead. But it really doesn't matter with me now, because I've been to the mountaintop. And I don't mind. Like anybody, I would like to live—a long life; longevity has its place. But I'm not concerned about that now. I

> just want to *do God's will.* And He's allowed me to *go up to the mountain.* And I've looked over. And I've seen the Promised Land. I may not get there with you. But I want you to know tonight, that we, as a people, will get to the Promised Land. So I'm happy, tonight. I'm not worried about anything. I'm not fearing any man.[3]

King, an ordained minister who knew the Bible well, does not call attention to the biblical language embedded in the speech—all the more powerful because he doesn't—yet it both evokes the biblical world (Deut 34 in particular) and uses its language without quoting the Bible chapter and verse. Most of the hearers and readers "got it" even if they could not specify the matrix of such power-laden language. The New Testament authors typically do this, often perhaps not even aware that they are doing so but speaking unselfconsciously in the mother tongue of the biblical world, evoking a different world from what we suppose to be the "real" world, softly whispering a challenge to our view of reality and ourselves.

Finally, the New Testament does in fact contain a profusion of direct citations of the Old Testament. Each citation, however brief, is the tip of an iceberg, a tiny window through which the author's universe may be seen. Paul writes to a church, the Israel of God comprising Jews and gentiles—mostly gentiles recently converted to the faith. Paul assumes they know the biblical story of Israel and have adopted it as their own story. This is the Deuteronomic teachers' assumption in regard to their hearers as well. If they have not already done so, both Deuteronomy and Paul assume they can, should, and will learn it from their Bible and their teachers. The ambiguities involved in attempting a quantitative analysis of the New Testament's use of the Old Testament impede the effort to compile an exact list of specific citations. On any tabulation, there are more than four hundred direct quotations of the Old Testament in the New Testament (239 formally identified by an introductory formula and 197 explicit quotations not formally identified as such).

Taken together, these three ways of regarding the text clearly reveal that the New Testament, from the first verse of Matthew to the last verse of Revelation, is shaped by the narrative world of the Bible and thoroughly permeated with its world of thought, imagery, and language, both directly and indirectly.

We now return to a more focused attempt to attune our ears to Paul's interpretation of Deuteronomy 30:11–14 in Romans 10:5–9. The context of each text is important. We have seen that Paul does not casually choose the Deuteronomy text. Deuteronomy, along with Isaiah and the Psalter, is central to the formation of Paul's theology, both before and after he was called to be an apostle. In synagogue worship, he had heard the whole of Deuteronomy read dozens of times and virtually knew it by heart—as Deuteronomy has commanded. He knew it as a whole, not as a collection of usable texts. He chooses a text that occurs at a climactic point in Moses's speech to 'all Israel.' The context of Paul's citation in the Roman letter also comes at a crucial point in the argument of the letter, in the dense and difficult section Romans 9–11. Romans has two main sections: the doctrinal section 1–11 in the indicative ("who we are"), explicating the saving acts of God, and 12–16 in the imperative, setting forth the life of the believer ("what God requires of us"). We note how closely this corresponds to the theology of Deuteronomy in both content and structure: in Deuteronomy 1–11, Moses proclaims and reiterates God's saving acts that freed people from slavery and formed them into Israel, the people of God. This is followed by Deuteronomy 12–26, which spells out details of how the covenant people are to live, in terms of both ethics and mission to all nations (cf. Rom 12:1–3!).

Paul's didactic letter to the Roman church reflects Deuteronomy in both form and content. It is not always noticed, however, that the first, doctrinal section is itself composed of two sections: Romans 1–8 / 9–11. It is the second section that deals specifically with the purpose of God in universal history (*prothesis tou theou* 9:11; cf. 8:28), the role of Israel in God's saving plan, and the relation of the covenant people of God to all humanity. It is too easy and simple to understand Romans as though we can read chapters 1–8 as affirming universal sin and the need for God's grace (Rom 1:1–3:20) addressed by the good news of God's saving act for all people in Romans 3:21–8:39 and then jump from the joyous proclamation of salvation by grace in chapters 1–8 to the "therefore" of Romans 12:1 that introduces the appeal to live the Christian life as expounded in chapters 12–16. To omit careful study of Romans 9–11 from one's interpretation of Romans is to miss Paul's point and replace it with a focus on individual salvation. Romans 1–8 leads up to chapters 9–11, which explicate God's saving plan in universal history, and it is *this* affirmation that then becomes the launching pad for instruction about the character of life appropriate to the people of God. Romans is not about "how a sinful individual can still be acceptable before the holy God" but about what God is about in history. It's not about us. To understand Paul's "use" of Deuteronomy in Romans 10:5–8 and the light it may shed on our own understanding of "the New Testament's use of the Old Testament," it is necessary to attend to the theological role of its locus in Romans 9–11.

Paul begins in Romans 9:1–5 by locating his identity in Israel, the people of God, using "Israel" fifteen times in Romans 9–11 and concluding with the Deuteronomic formula 'all Israel' (Rom 11:26!). This is who Paul is, who he has always been, an identity he did not give up when he became a Christian and an apostle. Paul rings the chimes on Deuteronomic theology as he recites the blessings of belonging to the people of Israel: the sonship, the glory, the covenants, the giving of the law, the worship, the promises, the patriarchs, and the this-worldly ancestors of the Messiah.

Paul concludes the introductory paragraph of this section (Rom 9:1–5), as he will conclude this section as a whole, with an exclamation of praise that echoes the Shema, thus bracketing this crucial section of Romans 9–11 with praise to the God of all creation, the Creator who has a plan for history and will carry it through to a worthy conclusion, already guaranteed by the Christ event as actuality and pledge, already / not yet. All are guilty, all are accepted by the One God of all (9:5←→11:32–36).

In line with Deuteronomic theology in Romans 9:8–9, Paul equates Israelite identity with being both a child/descendant of Abraham and a "child of God." In this context, Paul evokes the "Sarah's laughter" scene of Genesis 18, an image embedded in biblical theology whenever one thinks comprehensively about God's plan for history and the role God has chosen for Abraham and Sarah's descendants, a matter of divine freedom, choice, and promise, not of human merit or works. On the troublesome words about God's "loving" Jacob and "hating" Esau, see chapter 16 in this volume.

Already shaped by Deuteronomic theology long before he was called by the risen Christ to be an apostle to the gentile outsiders, Paul understood this new revelation from within the framework of biblical theology projected by Deuteronomy. Now, after his conversion, not only is Deuteronomy the lens through which he sees the revelation in Christ, but the revelation in Christ is the lens through which he now sees Deuteronomy. In Romans 9:25–29, he can thus interpret the words in Hosea 1:10 and 2:23, which refer to the Lord's acceptance of sinful, excluded persons back into the people of God, as referring to God's eschatological acceptance of gentiles into Israel: "Yet the number of the people of Israel shall be like the sand of the sea, which can be neither measured nor numbered; and in the place where it was said to them, 'You are not my people,' it shall be said to them, 'Children of the living God'" (Hos 1:10). This language of Hosea interprets "the people of Israel" as becoming innumerable, corresponding to the promise to Abraham in Genesis 12:1–3, often echoed in Deuteronomy. This is not an alternative to Paul's speaking of God's wrath, judgment, and rejection of Israel, but as in Hosea and Isaiah—which seems to have already affected Deuteronomy—the final image of this dialectic is that of God's persistently outstretched hands. Both judgment and grace are proclaimed. Grace has the last word (Hos 11:8–9; Isa 65:1–2). As in Hosea, Paul identifies the innumerable people of God as "sons [=children] of God." All this is the core of Deuteronomic theology (e.g., 14:1), which Paul goes on to develop. It is this line of thought that continues in Romans 10:5–9. We will skip lightly over the familiar imagery of Romans 11, in which the gentile branches of the "wild olive tree" are grafted into Israel, the "cultivated olive tree" (Rom 11:11–24). The gentile nations, already and always God's peoples, share in God's eschatological salvation by being incorporated into the people of God so that finally all the peoples of the earth are saved. "All Israel will be saved" does not mean that everyone will finally be converted to become Israelites, but that the Israelite/non-Israelite distinction is no longer operative. The delightful variety of human history and culture is retained (cf. the startling eschatological visions of Isa 19:16–25 and Zech 9:5–8, in which Egypt, Assyria, and the Philistines all join Israel as God's people without losing their historical identities). The final victory belongs not to human nationalism but to God the Creator. Just as Jews are warned in Romans 9–10 not to boast of their favored status, the gentiles incorporated into Israel are warned in Romans 11 not to disparage Jewish "boasting" and replace it with their own. It is crucially important that in Romans 11:30–31 the contrast is not between the obedience of some people and the disobedience of others; the contrast is between the disobedience of all people (Rom 3:23!) and the mercy of God:

> And so all Israel will be saved; as it is written, "Out of Zion will come the Deliverer; he will banish ungodliness from Jacob. And this is my covenant with them, when I take away their sins" . . . for the gifts and the calling of God are irrevocable.
>
> Just as you were once disobedient to God but have now received mercy because of their disobedience, so they have now been disobedient in order that, by the mercy shown to you, they too may now receive mercy. For God has imprisoned all in disobedience so that he may be merciful to all.
>
> O the depth of the riches and wisdom and knowledge of God! How unsearchable are his judgments and how inscrutable his ways!

> "For who has known the mind of the Lord? Or who has been his counselor?"
> "Or who has given a gift to him, to receive a gift in return?"
> For from him and through him and to him are all things. To him be the glory forever. Amen. (Rom 11:26–27, 29–36)

There is no figuring this out, no making sense of it. "Who has known the mind of the Lord?" (Rom 11:34; 1 Cor 2:16, citing Isa 40:13). What God has been up to in the whole of universal history is past finding out, can only be a revealed mystery. And it has been revealed. Everything, *ta panta*, the universe, is from, through, and to God. Last word. End of Story. One can only respond in worship, praise, and self-giving (Rom 12:1!).

In the light of the coming of the Messiah and God's act in his death and resurrection, Paul sees that God's eschatological program that he had always perceived in Deuteronomy is now in the process of realization—the resurrection has already happened in Christ, "dead" Israel is being raised from the dead (Ezek 37!), and the gentiles are being included. God is the actor. God made promises to bless all peoples through the descendants of Abraham. It is not a matter of trying to imagine how the Christian mission will finally convince everyone to accept the One God of the Shema, the one Savior Jesus Christ. Paul declares that the question "*How* can this ever happen?" cannot be imagined. Even *that* it will happen is beyond our imagining. How it can happen is not our problem. Its reality is a mystery (Rom 11:25), a matter of prophetic revelation. We don't need to ascend to heaven or probe the abyss in search of divine wisdom, which is already revealed in Christ.

The Old Testament and Judaism had a stream of teaching in which a preexistent Lady Wisdom, who was with God at the creation and is manifest in Israel's history, finally came down from heaven and was embodied in the Torah—"the Word became book and dwelt among us" (John 1:14; cf. Prov 8; Sir 24:23; Bar 4:1). Paul had already identified the ultimate manifestation of divine wisdom with Jesus Christ (1 Cor 1:24, 30; 2:13; 8:6; developed in later Pauline writings, e.g., Col 1:15–20; 2:3). As in Deuteronomy 29:29, the issue is a matter not of theory or speculation but of ethics, of doing the will of God, the faithful God who has made promises and will deliver on them:

> The secret things belong to the LORD our God;
> but the things that are revealed belong to us and to our children for ever,
> that we may do all the words of this law. (Deut 29:29 RSV)

As Paul said in the last words of his earliest extant letter, again speaking in the imagery of Deuteronomy, "The one who calls you is faithful, and he will do this" (1 Thess 5:24). Those who believe and understand who they are as the people of God in terms of this narrative do not find themselves merely fascinated by theology but hear it, as in both Deuteronomy and Romans, as a call to responsible ethics. Paul goes directly from the climactic, mind-shattering praise of Romans 11:33–36 to the ethical responsibilities of the people of God, to discerning the will of God for our own times, to offering ourselves as a living sacrifice to the One True God.

If we now return to Romans 10:5–9, which occurs at the midpoint of this section in which Paul expounds the Deuteronomic Shema theology in the light of the Christ event, we will not be surprised that he rightly understands it as directed to 'all Israel,' in which he and his predominantly gentile readers are included. Paul has already emphasized that the God who has spoken definitively in Jesus Christ is the One God who has spoken through Moses in Deuteronomy (Rom 3:30). He wants all his readers in the Roman church—mostly gentile Christians, with a sizeable contingent of traditional Jewish Christians—to hear the words of Moses through which God speaks in Deuteronomy as they speak directly to later Christian readers. This simply means he has understood Deuteronomy as it wants to be understood, not distorting it or hijacking it into the service of Christian dogma (cf., e.g., Deut 5:3, and the discussion in ch. 9 of the present volume). Paul does not merely interpret Deuteronomy but continues the interpretation already found in Deuteronomy into his own preaching and teaching. It is not a matter of the interested spectator to the biblical drama inquiring what Moses once said to "them" and then asking how or whether it can be applied to "us." Paul claims that Deuteronomy speaks the Word of God, the Word of the risen Christ, directly to contemporary Christian readers. He is within the perimeter of Deuteronomy's hearing distance. We may now attend more closely to this claim with a few comments on Romans 10:1–9.

Romans 10:2. *Zeal not knowledge.* Paul claims that the Israelites *kata sarka* (according to the flesh) are sincere people, like Paul himself, with deep religious convictions. Like the rest of the world apart from faith in Christ, they literally do not know what world they are in—that is, that they now live in the world in which the Messiah sent by God has lived, has been killed by human beings, and has been raised by God from the dead. We did not invent this world. We cannot make it go away. This is the real world we live in—like it or not, know it or not.

Romans 10:4. Paul precedes his quote from Deuteronomy with a programmatic declaration about the relation of the Torah and the Messiah. The Messiah is the *telos* of the Torah. This Torah is revelatory instruction, the narrative of who God is and what God is about. It includes laws, but legal rules and regulations are not its essential nature. *Telos* can be understood merely in chronological terms to mean "end," as when a nation or state adopts a new constitution that means the end of the old one. This understanding has supported the false reading of both Paul and the Torah in terms of the individualistic question, "How can a sinful person be acceptable before God?" So understood, Paul is heard as saying that the law offers a way of salvation—just do it and God will accept you, and salvation becomes a matter of human action and merit. So understood, the coming of Christ was the end of the law: we are no longer under this system of legal merit but are accepted by God's grace or, rather, *our faith* in God's grace. In this view, common since the Reformation and inscribed in many English translations, the contrast is between two chronological periods (dispensations) in God's plan, with the Old Testament requiring human deeds specified by the Law and the New Testament requiring the one human act of faith.

But the meaning of *telos* here is not chronological, in which one system of human deeds is replaced by a different system, but purely theological, explicating the meaning of both the Torah and Christ in God's plan. Christ is not the "end" of the law in the sense of its abrogation/termination but its goal, climax, consummation, and purpose. "Righteousness" in this context does not refer to "imputed righteousness," a kind of legal fiction in which God pronounces trusting individuals as righteous but condemns those who try to live up to the requirements of the law. "God's righteousness" in this context corresponds to the typical usage of *tzedaqah* (e.g., 1 Samuel 12:7), where the word refers to God's saving deeds that redeem his people and give them life.

Paul grounds his declaration about Christ and the Torah in a seamless combination of texts assembled for this purpose. The central text from Deuteronomy 30 is prefaced by Moses's statement in Leviticus 18:5 and a phrase from Deuteronomy 8:17 repeated in Deuteronomy 9:4. Presenting such a mélange of texts as "What the Scripture says" was not unusual in first-century CE Judaism and is attributed to Jesus in Luke 4:18, which blends Isaiah 61:1–2 and Isaiah 58:16 into a single text. There were, of course, no footnotes, parentheses, chapter and verse numbers, or punctuation marks to signal such combinations.

Romans 10:5. The inferential particle *gar* (for) that begins this verse and connects it with the preceding one is unfortunately omitted by the NRSV and NIV, though it is found in several other English translations. It functions to continue the thought of Romans 10:4, not to make a new beginning in contrast to the preceding sentence. The instances of *gar* in verses 2, 3, 4, and 5 are connectors binding them together. Thus when Paul quotes Moses as saying, "The person who does these things will live by them," this is not a way of saying, "If you want to live, you must do all that the Law commands" (CEV), much less the cutesy paraphrase of *The Message*, "Moses wrote that anyone who insists on using the law code to live right before God soon discovers it's not so easy—every detail of life regulated by fine print!" Throughout Romans, Paul has affirmed the Torah as "holy and just and good" (e.g., Rom 7:12) and denied in the strongest terms that his Christian theology does away with the Torah (Rom 3:31, *mē genoito*: "By no means" [NRSV and others]; "God forbid" [KJV, ASV]; "Of course not" [NAB and others]; "Out of the question" [NJB]; "Absolutely not" [CEB and others]). The gospel he preaches reveals a righteousness on another basis than keeping the commandments of the law, but nonetheless, it is attested by the "law and the prophets" (Rom 3:21). The Christian gospel is of one piece with God's revealed Torah and in continuity with it, not its antithesis (Abraham and David in Rom 4!).

Romans 10:6a. Likewise, this reading is confirmed by Paul's beginning this sentence with the connecting particle *de*, which is very flexible but is often used to continue a line of thought, not to make a contrasting statement (contrast *alla* in v. 8, which is clear). He does not contrast what Moses writes in Leviticus with what the personified Faith Righteousness says in Deuteronomy. Verse six does not present a contrasting alternative to verse five but continues and interprets it. This interpretation is further corroborated by Paul's elimination of the reference to human *doing* from his citation of Deuteronomy, introducing it with "Do not say in your heart . . . ," words taken from Deuteronomy 8:17 and 9:4. These Deuteronomic texts warn against self-righteous pride in one's own accomplishments, whether keeping the law or believing in Christ. Paul's interpretation of the gospel in Romans has throughout emphasized the continuity—not the discontinuity or contrast—between God's revelation in the history of Israel, particularly in Deuteronomy, and the definitive revelation in Jesus Christ. Romans 10:1–9 does not contrast a supposed legalistic Judaism and the Old Testament with salvation by grace through faith in the New Testament but explicitly aligns itself with the challenge of Deuteronomy to respond to God's unwavering faithfulness with faithful obedience—that is, to "choose life," the climactic conclusion of the text he interprets here (Deut 30:19).

Romans 10:6b. Paul cites a phrase from what Faith Righteousness says: "Who will ascend into heaven?" He then inserts his parenthetical interpretation into the text, preceded by "that is," specifying what Christians now know is the ultimate meaning of the biblical text in Deuteronomy 30:12. This style of interpretation was not invented by Paul. The Qumran sect, like Paul and the early Christians, interpreted the Scripture in the light of their conviction that they were living in the times of the promised eschatological fulfillment. The Qumran scribes sometimes interpreted the Scripture by citing a phrase and then inserting *peshrō* ("It's interpretation is . . . ," "This means . . . ," or "This refers to . . .") in a manner very similar to what Paul does. For example, in Habakkuk 2:2, the Habakkuk Commentary cites the biblical text with the insertion "This refers to (*peshrō*) the Teacher of Righteousness to whom God made known all the mysterious revelations of his servants the prophets."[4] Paul was using a scholarly method of interpretation of his times used by another group of Jews who saw themselves as living in the eschatological times and who were convinced that God's eschatological Teacher was the *Moreh Tzedeq*, the "Right Teacher."

The issue that divided Paul from the Jewish teachers of his own time was not exegetical method but whether Jesus of Nazareth was the Messiah. Paul has personally encountered the risen Lord Jesus (1 Cor 15:8; Gal 2:1–16). He knows the personal reality of the faith proclaimed by the earliest Christians, to and by which he had been converted, that the biblical promises not only are a future hope but have already begun to be fulfilled. God's raising Jesus from the dead was not merely a special act God did for Jesus; the resurrection of Jesus was the firstfruits of the general resurrection, a firm part of the apocalyptic scenario of the end times (1 Cor 15:20–23). We may be pleasantly surprised to learn that, on this point at least, the author of the letter of James, that down-to-earth, practical-theologian advocate of equality and justice, shares both the ethic and theology of Paul: "In fulfillment of his own purpose he gave us birth by the word of truth, so that we would become a kind of first fruits of his creatures" (Jas 1:18). Not only is the resurrected Jesus the firstfruits of the new world coming, but the church he called into being already lives in the power of the resurrection, the preliminary sample and down payment of the full harvest to come.

The author of Deuteronomy 30 (Moses, in Paul's view) did not and could not know this, for he lived in an earlier chapter of the story of God's saving acts. Paul and his readers believe they live in the final chapter of the same story that reveals the meaning of the whole, its denouement—that all of them, Jew and gentile alike, belong to the continuing story of Israel, the people of God. This means not that Paul and early Christianity gave up on the Torah but that they now see where it was all headed and can use its language and imagery to express the *telos* of universal history. As pictured by the authors of Deuteronomy, Moses not only had the firm hope of an eschatologically renewed Israel. Moses already envisioned God's wondrous transformation of the earth and humanity in the distant future, after the judgment of exile and the scattering among the nations is over and Israel is given a new, impossible possibility: recovering the good life in the promised land (see the context in Deut 30:1–10, 19–20). The Deuteronomic teachers did not see this hope focused in a Messiah, and they resisted the apocalyptic interpretations of Israel's faith that were emerging in other streams of exilic and postexilic theology (see ch. 16 in this volume).

Paul adopted a new understanding of Deuteronomy not because he had developed a different theory of how God acts or a different hermeneutic for interpreting Scripture but because he believed the resurrection of Jesus had actually happened. In this text, Paul finds not a rational hermeneutical bridge connecting biblical text and present experience but more of a supremely powerful spark plug that leaps over Lessing's "ugly ditch" that separates the biblical world from our own. He knew he was living in the last generation of history, the goal and fulfillment of God's plan for the salvation of the world, the time to which Moses and all the prophets had looked forward. Paul's predecessors in the earliest church had already adopted and adapted the apocalyptic theology available in first-century Judaism as the symbolic world and conceptual framework for interpreting this eschatological act of God. Paul's own pre-Christian pharisaic theology facilitated the formation of his own version of this theology and shaped his rereading of the Scripture, once he was convinced that God had raised up Jesus and confirmed him as Messiah and Lord.

Romans 10:7. As Paul heard Deuteronomy's "Who shall ascend into heaven?" (Deut 30:12) in terms of his Christology of preexistence so that the biblical text speaks of the eschatological event of the incarnation, so he heard "Who will descend into the abyss?" as biblical testimony to the resurrection. Of course, there is no "abyss" in Deuteronomy 30, which refers to crossing the sea; this image can hardly be interpreted as proclaiming the resurrection. Nonetheless, Paul cannot be accused of simply rewriting his Bible so that it says what he needs to support his own theology. Here, too, he stands within a stream of Jewish interpretation that facilitates his own interpretation. The Targums were standardized Aramaic paraphrases of the Bible read out in the synagogue after Hebrew was no longer commonly understood. The Targum Neofiti paraphrased Jonah's being cast into the sea as descending into the abyss, to bring the Torah up for us, as though the Torah was inaccessible in the depths of the sea until Jonah brought it up and made it available. From the first chapter of Genesis onward, the Hebrew understanding of "sea" (*yam*) was often associated with the "abyss," the abode of Yam, the sea god, and with Tiamat/Tehom, the abyss of the sea. The unfathomable ocean depths are personified as the chaotic enemy of the God who was overcome at the creation. In Psalm 107:26, those who go down to the sea and experience its dangers are pictured as mounting up to heaven (on the dangerous waves). Paul is in step with this tradition, which had already affected Deuteronomy (cf. the influence of the Psalter on the formation of Deuteronomy discussed in chapter 7 in the present volume and the pairing of "heaven" and "abyss" in Deut 33:13). In Paul's citation of Deuteronomy, he made a traditional and biblical modulation of "sea" to "abyss," unproblematic in his situation. Here, too, the fundamental dispute would concern not exegetical method but whether the resurrection of Jesus was an event that had actually happened.

Romans 10:8–9. "But what does it say?" Here, Paul's use of the sharply disjunctive conjunction *alla* represents a clear contrast that is the actual point of the Deuteronomy passage in its own context. The generative word of the faithfulness of God that called the world into being and created, instructs, and nourishes Israel as the people of God is neither in heaven nor in the sea/abyss. The creative, transformative Word of God is the word they already have, the word "in your mouth and in your heart," the word of faith in the One God of Israel (Rom 10:8). In the narrative context of Deuteronomy, this was Moses's challenge to Israel that God's Word was already present, not merely in a book, but in the revelatory word in their memory, the word they recited every day in their family, in their mouths and in their hearts, the word inseparably bound to Israel's confession of the Shema (Deut 6:4–9). Paul unhesitatingly identifies this word with the Christian message of God's saving act in the death and resurrection of Christ. Even more, Paul goes on to declare in this very context that when Christian preachers and teachers proclaim and teach this message from the Scripture, they, too, stand in a revelatory chain that extends from God through Moses and the prophets, Jesus and the early church, and the biblical texts interpreted throughout the history of the church by faithful preachers and teachers. We must not overlook this mind-blowing declaration of what is really going on in Christian preaching and teaching. It is the risen Christ who speaks through our preaching and teaching, calling people to discipleship and nurturing them in the faith:

> But how are they to call on one in whom they have not believed? And how are they to believe in one of whom they have never heard? And how are they to hear without someone to proclaim him?
>
> And how are they to proclaim him unless they are sent? As it is written, "How beautiful are the feet of those who bring good news!"
>
> But not all have obeyed the good news; for Isaiah says, "Lord, who has believed our message?"
>
> So faith comes from what is heard, and what is heard comes through the *word of Christ*. (Rom 10:14–17)

The "word of Christ" heard in the mouth of the biblical preacher or teacher is not only the Christian message about Christ—that is, God's saving act in the Christ event. The phrase is a Greek subjective genitive represented by the preposition "of" in English translations, referring to the word *of* Christ himself. Just as "the Word of God" typically means the word God speaks, so here the "word of Christ" proclaimed and taught in the church is the word of Christ, the word Christ speaks. Paul's encouraging word is that in our biblical preaching and teaching, it is the living Christ present in the life of the church who calls people to discipleship, instructing and nourishing them for Christian mission. Paul believes that God / the risen Christ speaks not only through his apostolic preaching but in the life and message of the church (2 Cor 3:1–5; 13:3), a view he shares with and probably derived from Deuteronomy (4:5–9). According to Paul, the proclamation of the Christian gospel is not merely inspiring information about God's power but *is* the power of God (Rom 1:16).

We have chosen to study Paul as a crucial interpreter of the Scripture for the church because he is often seen as the most ardent champion of "law versus grace," with Deuteronomy on the wrong side of the ledger. We have explored Paul's interpretation of one passage in Deuteronomy in some depth. Our study reveals the "law versus grace" paradigm can be an oversimplified distortion of what both Deuteronomy and Paul want to say to us. It would be profitable to study other such texts in Paul and other New Testament books, not only to reap useful information and insights for our preaching and teaching, but to enhance our ability to hear what the Bible is saying as we listen in on early Christian teachers doing theology as they interpret the Bible for the church. Such exercises help us better understand the churchly stream of biblical interpretation in which we live every time we read the New Testament. It will never look the same.

The following are some possibilities and pump primers:

- *Matthew* emphatically begins with a genealogy focusing on descent from Abraham, important for the identity of both the Messiah and the people of God, but inserts gentiles into the genealogy (Tamar, Rahab, Ruth, and the "wife of Uriah"; Matt 1:1–18). Who belongs to the people of God, and what is their relation to gentiles? In the opening scene of Matthew's narrative, Joseph learns that his fiancée is pregnant, but not by him. Matthew has specifically designated Joseph as a "righteous man," one who is committed to God's justice as revealed in the Torah. The Torah has clear rules about such cases (Matt 1:19–25; cf. Deut 22:21–25). What does such a person do who has become a disciple of Jesus Christ? This is the problem faced by the Gospel of Matthew as a whole, addressed to a Christian community devoted both to the Torah and to Jesus. The Matthean story of Jesus reflects the Deuteronomic story of Moses and Israel: Jesus goes down to Egypt, escapes the wrath of the wicked king, goes through the Red Sea waters of baptism, is tested forty "days" in the wilderness, calls twelve disciples as the core community of a renewed Israel, ascends a mountain from which he teaches the way of life for the people of God, and declares he has come not to destroy the Torah but to fulfill it (Matt 3–7). During his testing in the wilderness, he cites Deuteronomy three times in response to the Tempter's ploys about the nature of his ministry. The story that began with Israel the people of God concludes with the inclusion of all nations at the end of the age (Matt 28:16–20). Is that Deuteronomic or what?
- *Mark*'s minimal presentation of Jesus's teaching concludes with his compression of the will of God into the Shema and the command to love God and neighbor (Mark 12:28–34).
- *Luke* reinterprets the continuing history and mission of the people of God that continues after the failure of the Messiah to return as expected. Even after the devastating destruction of Jerusalem

and the temple, history goes on. The Christ has come as the defining center of history, not at its end. The continuing history of the people of God is not a prolonged parenthesis until the end but the time of mission to all nations. As the Deuteronomic teachers had written two volumes to instruct Israel after the destruction of the holy city and exile of the people, so Luke writes two volumes. The Gospel of Luke is like Deuteronomy, narrating the life and teaching of God's prophet. The Book of Acts is analogous to the Deuteronomistic History; retelling the history of Israel after the prophet's death functions as the vehicle of Deuteronomic theology.

- Only Luke quotes God's promise to raise up a "prophet like Moses" as fulfilled in Jesus (Deut 18:15–18; Acts 7:37). Luke's adoption of the Deuteronomic prophet like Moses as a major christological category facilitates his omission of two features of the church's understanding of God's saving act in Christ important for other streams of New Testament theology, including the Christology of his hero, Paul: *preexistence* and *substitutionary* atonement. Instead of preexistence, Luke's Jesus enters the world in a marvelous way (cf. Moses!). Nor does the Lukan Jesus die for the sins of the world. The Gospel never portrays Jesus's death as an atonement for sins, nor do the early Christian missionary preachers in Acts proclaim that "Christ dies for our sins." This corresponds to Deuteronomic theology, which has no priestly doctrine of atoning sacrifice. Not just his death but Moses's whole life and teaching, including his death and "Gethsemane" plea, was given for the sake of others; 'all Israel' gets to enter the promised land, but not Moses. He gave his life for the people of God not by dying for them but by living for them, by fasting and praying for them, as intensely elaborated in Deuteronomy 9:4–29, 10:10. Based on this Deuteronomic model for understanding Christology, Luke reinterprets the meaning of discipleship in his situation, which calls for disciples no longer to die a martyr's death once and for all but to give their lives for others in loving service for them every day (compare Luke's interpretation of Mark 8:34 in Luke 9:23).
- *John* is influenced by Deuteronomic theology in many ways, including especially his interpretation of Deuteronomic "hearing" into Hellenistic "seeing" (see ch. 3 in the present volume).
- *Key Deuteronomic texts in other New Testament books* can be located in a concordance or marginal references (especially in

> the margins of the Nestle-Aland Greek New Testament or the notes of a good study Bible). Such study is eye- and ear-opening. Isaiah 50:4 is a good text to have posted on the edge of one's notebook or computer screen.

Such study reveals considerable variety in the New Testament's interpretation of the Old Testament. This does not mean that studying the rich variety of the whole Bible opens the door to anything-goes theology. It does mean that in the New Testament's interpretation of Scripture, *not just anything goes*, but *more than one thing goes*, that no one theology can capture all the mysterious dimensions of God's saving act in Christ. Beginning already in the New Testament, we stand in a great river of churchly biblical interpretation. It is a mighty river with numerous tributaries and eddies, but always a dynamic, flowing river with canonical banks that keep it from becoming a destructive flood or stagnant swamp.

IV

Israel

The People

CHAPTER 11

'All Israel'

Who Is Included?

The core theology of Deuteronomy is reaffirmed by Jesus: "Hear, O Israel: the LORD is our God, the LORD alone" (Deut 6:4). For several chapters, we have been reflecting on the first word of the Shema, asking what the command to *hear* means in the biblical sense. The command itself raises another question. It is given not to the world in general but to Israel. Who is Israel? Am I included? For Christian believers, this is a personal, existential question: "This is no trifling matter for you, but rather your very life" (Deut 32:47). The content and boundaries of the term *Israel* have shifted from its earliest documented historical occurrence in the thirteenth century BCE to the formation of the modern political state of Israel founded in 1948. A survey of this history sharpens our understanding as Christian believers of our place in this story.

The Understanding of "Israel" in Pre-Deuteronomic Traditions

1. Israel as ancestor. In the biblical story line, "Israel" is first mentioned as the new name given to trickster Jacob during his encounter with the mysterious divine figure at the Jabbok as he returned from his long sojourn in Syria (Gen 28–32; cf. 32:28). Jacob was son of Isaac, son of Abraham, to whom God gave the original covenant and promise of a people through whom all peoples would be blessed. Abraham was not an Israelite or Jew. It was through Jacob/Israel that 'all Israel' would later look back to their ancestor and mediator of the divine promise.

2. Israel as a people. Israel became a people in Egypt, as one people among the peoples of the earth. After the deaths of Abraham and Isaac, a widespread famine caused the seventy-member clan of Jacob/Israel and his sons to leave Canaan and resettle in Egypt. There they remained several generations, became a numerous people, were enslaved, and under the leadership of Moses, escaped and returned to Canaan. At this stage in the biblical story, in the early thirteenth century BCE, Israel emerges into the light of extrabiblical history as a tribal group among the other social groups in Canaan (see ch. 6 in this volume on the Merneptah Stele).

3. **Israel as the united kingdom of twelve tribes.** In the course of several centuries, the relatively independent tribes coalesced into a united kingdom under Saul, David, and Solomon, the 'all Israel' of Deuteronomy 1–1 Kings 11.

4. **Israel as the northern kingdom.** At the death of Solomon, the centuries-old division between the northern and southern groups reasserted itself, and the northern ten tribes withdrew, appropriating the ancient designation "Israel" as their national name (1 Kgs 12–2 Kgs 17). "Israel" did not include Judah but was contrasted with Judah as a non-Israelite kingdom with which Israel was often at war.

5. **Israel as the Judean placeholder for the traditions and identity of the people Israel.** The southern kingdom of Judah continued to think of Jacob/Israel as their ancestor and of themselves as Israelites. They continued to refer to God as "the LORD, the God of Israel," a faith community that now transcended national and political boundaries (e.g., 2 Kgs 18:7; 19:20; 22:18; Isa 17:6). When the Assyrian Empire demolished the northern kingdom, Israel as a political state disappeared, and the remaining kingdom of Judah became the bearers of the Israelite tradition and hope. Politically, they were Judeans; "Jews" first becomes an ethnic and political identity at this time. When the Babylonians decimated the rebellious kingdom of Judah and exiled much of the leadership, "Israel" became the religious designation for those Judeans who clung to the ancestral faith. The Babylonian Empire fell to the Persians, and some Jews returned from exile to Judea, now the Persian province of Yehud, which was populated by a mixed population, only some of whom were adherents to the traditional faith of Israel. Even among these, there were vigorous, sometimes violent debates on the identity of Israel, who counted as an Israelite, and the present obligations and future course of the people of God.

'All Israel' in Deuteronomic Perspective

The Deuteronomic teachers launched their teaching document into a world in which "Who belongs to Israel?" was a hotly disputed question, but in the narrative world projected by the text they composed, there was no ambiguity. There were no Israelites in Canaan or Egypt, none in Assyria or Babylon. 'All Israel' are those gathered on the plains of Moab, listening to Moses. In Deuteronomy, the identity of this Israel is defined theologically, not historically, geographically, politically, or biologically. Whatever the setting of their readers in actual history, the Deuteronomic teachers address them all as members of the people of Israel, descendants of Abraham, belonging to the covenant people established and promised in Genesis 12:1–3; 15:1–21. Deuteronomy does not think of the patriarch Jacob/Israel or the people of *Israel* apart from the covenant with *Abraham* that promised blessing to all the peoples of the earth through this one people. Nor does Deuteronomy think of Abraham apart from the choice of his grandson Jacob/Israel, whose twelve sons became the nucleus of the people of God. Although "Abraham" occurs over a hundred times in the Pentateuch as an independent figure, every reference in Deuteronomy to Abraham is in the combination "Abraham, Isaac, and Jacob" (Deut 1:8; 6:10; 9:5, 27; 29:13; 30:20; 34:4). *Deuteronomy is emphatic that 'all Israel' is descended from Abraham but that not everyone descended from Abraham belongs to Israel.* This is the perspective taken up by Paul and other New Testament theologians. The Edomites—direct descendants of Abraham through Esau, Jacob's twin brother—were to be respected, for the Lord was in their history too, having already given them their land. They are specifically called Israel's blood relatives (Deut 2:8). They, like the Moabites and Ammonites, whose territory Israel had passed through peacefully, were already counted among God's numerous and diverse peoples, beloved children of the Lord the One Creator God, but they had not been chosen and called to participate in the singular mission of the people of God to all peoples. They were not Israel.

In the Deuteronomic vision, 'all Israel' is ultimately to include everyone, but this ultimately inclusive people is penultimately exclusive. In the present world, Israel is called to be separate and holy as witnesses to the character and saving acts of God (see ch. 15). This does not mean that Deuteronomic theology exhibits a sectarian, narrowly rigid understanding of Israel's identity. The Deuteronomic teachers project an "ecumenical" vision that identifies all the people of God as presently belonging to 'all Israel,' including the various Israelite/Jewish groups that compete with and even condemn one another. The people of God addressed by Moses on the plains of Moab, just as they are, *all* of them, *already* belong to Israel. The Moses of Deuteronomy is not speaking as an evangelist attempting to convert nonbelievers to the faith of Israel. They already belong to Israel. Neither is he instructing them in how to engage in interreligious dialogue with people of other faiths, a task for other situations. Deuteronomy does lay the foundations for such discussions, not only considering all the peoples of the earth to be the LORD's beloved creatures and destined for ultimate inclusion in the people of God, but explicitly declaring that the LORD is presently active in their religious life (see, e.g., Deut 4:19; 29:25–26; 32:8–9). This is not a superficial "tolerance," sometimes indistinguishable from indifference, but a conviction that the One Creator God the LORD is in fact the God of all peoples, even if they do not know this. The Moses of Deuteronomy is ecumenical, speaking to the one people of God, all of them. But they have yet to learn what this means, "who we are and what God requires of us." *This* is what Deuteronomy wants to teach 'all Israel.'

In this regard, it is important to examine the meaning of the designation "people" as used in the world of biblical language and thought and to avoid reading it in terms of our cultural presuppositions. Many modern Westerners, especially Americans, often use "people" in a casual, indiscriminate sense that may simply refer to human beings in general: "that's just the way people are" or "people all over the world." Or "people" may be used to refer to an incidental group of individuals who have no particular personal bonds: "middle-income people" or "people with blue eyes." Biblical authors would never use the Hebrew or Greek words for "people" in either of these ways (Heb. *'am*; Gk. *laos*, the root of the English word *laity*). In the Bible, the planet's whole human population is not called "all people" but is typically referred to as *adam* or *benē Adam* (= "humankind," as in Gen 6:1). The world population of human beings is never expressed in the singular, "the people of the earth," but in the plural, "peoples of the earth" (e.g., Deut 14:2, contrasting the people of Israel with all the peoples of the earth) or "all flesh" (Deut 5:26, + 44× MT). The earth's human population consists of the collection of all the particular peoples. No one belongs to people in general. Just as no one can be American in general without belonging to a particular state, so in biblical thought no one can belong to humanity in general or people in general, for there is no such thing. Every human life is rooted in the particularity of belonging to a particular people, in a particular place, with a particular language. No one speaks "human"; we all speak and think in the language(s) of our people.

This means that "people of Israel" does not merely designate the inhabitants of a geographical region or political state. Unlike our situation in post-1948 modern history, Deuteronomy addressed people who lived in a time and place when there was no country called "Israel." To be sure, for the Deuteronomic teachers, "the land" was an important theological concept (see ch. 16 in this volume). The book contains 181 references to "the land," including "the land of Egypt," "the land of the Canaanites," the "land oozing with milk and honey," and "the land the LORD promised"—but there is no "land of Israel." In the experience of the reading audience, there was no longer a "land of Israel," nor a reunited, whole 'all Israel,' which existed only in memory and hope and in the present faith and life of the people of God. For Deuteronomy, 'all Israel' is a people, defined by God's purpose in history, scattered among the nations. This is, in fact, still the already / not yet life of the people of God, of the church.

In the narrative world of Deuteronomy, those Moses addressed as 'all Israel' were all descended from Abraham, but not necessarily in a biological sense. While still camped in Moab, the covenant is renewed, embracing those who had joined Israel along the way, bringing them up to date, including the east Jordan groups who had never been in Egypt (see ch. 6 in this volume):

> These are the words of the covenant that the LORD commanded Moses to make with the Israelites in the land of Moab, in addition to the covenant that he had made with them at Horeb . . . in order that he may establish you today as his people, and that he may be your God, as he promised you and as he swore to your ancestors, to Abraham, to Isaac, and to Jacob. I am making this covenant, sworn by an oath, not only with you who stand here with us today before the LORD our God, but also with those who are not here with us today. (Deut 29:1, 13–15, and commentaries thereon).

The vision of the Deuteronomic teachers also looks forward to further expansion of the one people, as the covenant is inclusively renewed with other groups who will unite with Israel. The Deuteronomists resist the theologies of their contemporaries that emphasized the necessity of having a legitimate genealogy to qualify for membership in the people of God (Ezra 1–2, 7–10; Neh 10–13). The book of Ruth seems to have been written during the period in which the final edition of Deuteronomy was composed. If so, we may be sure the Deuteronomic teachers would have resonated with a story that pictures a young Moabite widow making the decision to leave home and family to unite with the people of Israel. Her poignant words to Naomi, her Israelite mother-in-law, as she decides to give up her own people, land, and gods illustrate the Deuteronomic and biblical meaning of "people":

> Do not press me to leave you
> or to turn back from following you!
> Where you go, I will go;
> where you lodge, I will lodge;
> Your people shall be my people,
> and your God my God. (Ruth 1:16–17)[1]

Prior to the Babylonian devastation of the country, the destruction of Jerusalem and the temple, and the abolition of the kingship, Israel had been identified as a Jewish political state in which Israelites were the vast majority and had the political power. Israelites were citizens of this political state, and others, welcome or not, were outsiders. The exile had made the Jewish people a scattered Diaspora without land or state. Those who returned to Judea, now known as Yehud, a province of the Persian Empire, were a distinct religious community within the land. In the march of empire across the eastern Mediterranean, the former "land of Israel" would only occasionally and ambiguously regain a measure of national independence. Membership in the people of Israel could no longer be automatic, a matter of genealogy, nationality, and location functioning apart from human decision. To be of Jewish faith, to be an Israelite, would come to mean being distinct from the culture at large on the basis of religious heritage and commitment, in whatever national state they found themselves. This is the meaning of holiness, of being a holy people. Henceforth, the people of Israel would have two loyalties—to the LORD and the people of Israel and to the national state in which they lived, which also belonged to the peoples of the earth, created and ruled by the LORD, the God of Israel. Their life would always bear the tension of these two loyalties, especially when they were in conflict. During and after the exile, *Israel, the people of God, were no longer a nation, but they continued to be a people—a church*—scattered among the nations, its membership not necessarily identical with the surrounding culture. Deuteronomy addresses an Israel in which there was no universal agreement on what it meant to be the people of God dwelling among the nations.

The Deuteronomic teachers' ecumenical vision persisted, flourished, and was canonized as the biblical books of Deuteronomy–2 Kings. This comprehensive, formative component of Scripture profoundly influenced Jesus, the early church, and the New Testament. In the narrative world of Deuteronomy, 'all Israel' includes everyone who confesses faith in the LORD, the One God of Israel, all those who are instructed in the meaning of their faith and identity by the Torah given by God through Moses. In the generations after the promulgation of the canonical form of Deuteronomy in the sixth century BCE, the Deuteronomic vision had its ups and downs among Israel's teachers. In the succession of Persian, Greek, and Roman domination, Israel's leadership—political and religious—developed a number of competing ways to understand the nature and mission of Israel. Pharisees, Sadducees, Zealots, and Essenes struggled with themselves and one another attempting to be faithful to who they were as the people of God and what God required of them. This was the situation in the first century CE, as we continue our pursuit of the question of Israel's identity—past, present, and future—into the New Testament.

"Israel" in Jesus, the Early Church, and the New Testament

"Church" in the Old Testament? During my early childhood, neither my parents nor I had belonged to or attended a church. I was startled when, as a serious teenager only recently baptized and for the first time opening a Bible and trying to get my mind around what it meant to belong to the church, I came across a reference to "the church in the wilderness," referring to the people of Israel at the time of Moses and Sinai (Acts 7:38 KJV). I did not yet have my own copy of the 1946 RSV, used in the church we had joined, in which the KJV's "church" was translated "congregation." This translation allowed what I read in the New Testament to fit in with the theology I regularly heard in Sunday school and from the pulpit—the church began on the first Pentecost after the crucifixion and resurrection, when the Holy Spirit descended on the little band of Jesus's followers. Not only was there no church in the Old Testament, but there wasn't even a church in Jesus's time, though he had promised to build one (Matt 16:18). As everyone knew, the church began in Acts 2, but here in Acts 7, a faithful preacher of the gospel speaks of the *church* in *Moses's* time. I was mostly thinking about other things as a teenager and did not pursue the matter, which my newly acquired RSV had resolved in any case. Some decades later, even after I had read the New Testament through several times, I was again brought up short one morning by reading in the New Testament that all believers are descendants of Abraham (Gal 3:7); that "if you belong to Christ, then you are Abraham's offspring, heirs according to the promise" (Gal 3:29); that "the *churches* of Galatia" are addressed as belonging to "the *Israel* of

God" (Gal 6:16; cf. Rom 4:16). It would be a long time before I would study the Old Testament itself on this matter and recognize that Paul is echoing the language of Deuteronomy ("heirs," "promise," etc.), which in his Greek translation of the Bible designates the people of Israel ten times with the word *ekklēsia*, the word used by Stephen for "the church in the wilderness" and by New Testament authors more than a hundred times for the church of Jesus Christ. The question lingers. As a follower of Jesus, a baptized Christian, a member of the church, do I belong to Israel, the people of God? It may still come as a jolt to realize that the *Old* Testament speaks often of Israel as "church" and that the *New* Testament is permeated with the vocabulary of "Israel," "Abraham," and "people of God" as essential elements in our DNA and ID as Christian believers. We may deepen our insight by reflecting on the appropriation of this strand of Deuteronomic theology in the teaching of Jesus, the witness of the earliest church, and key texts in the New Testament.

Jesus

Although we have no texts directly from Jesus, we can be confident that his preaching and teaching were directed to people who were, like himself, already Israelites. He announced the good news of the coming kingdom of God, the hope of Israel. He did not try to persuade people to join a "Jesus movement" centered on himself and his "ideals." Nor did he preach to gentiles, trying to convert them to the Jewish faith. He limited his and his disciples' mission to "the lost sheep of the house of Israel" (Matt 10:5–6; 15:24), actually forbidding them to go to gentiles or even the Samaritans of ambiguous status (cf., e.g., Matt 9:36). Jesus calls no disciples from among his gentile neighbors and is never pictured as eating with gentiles or entering a gentile house. It is not the pre-Easter Jesus but the risen Lord of the church's faith who commands the mission to all nations, and he does so by opening his Jewish disciples' eyes to understand their Scriptures (Matt 28:16–20; Luke 24:44–49). During the time the New Testament authors were writing letters and Gospels that would compose part of the normative texts of the church, this command was being carried out under the direction of the risen Jesus / Holy Spirit as the church expanded the early mission to Israel to include all nations (Acts 1:1–16:8). Those who believed and were baptized not only became followers of Jesus; they were incorporated into the continuing life and mission of Israel to all nations.

The Earliest Church

The Jewish leaders who opposed the new Christian group cannot be dismissed as though they were intolerant bigots who should have been more open to people of other religions. Unlike many US citizens of the twenty-first century, first-century Judaism had long become accustomed to living in a multicultural society, with people of other faiths all around them. If Jesus or Paul had simply represented a new religion called "Christianity" or some such, few of their Jewish neighbors would have been convinced, but neither would they have reacted violently—let them join this new religion if they please, and we will continue being faithful members of the people of Israel. When the urbane, well-educated Jewish Pharisee Saul of Tarsus considered it his duty to track down and prosecute members of this new group that had infiltrated the synagogues, it was not because they represented another religion of which he was intolerant but because they were inviting and accepting unqualified outsiders into *Israel*, perverting and betraying Israel's identity and mission as the people of God. "Who is Israel?" and "Who belongs to Israel?" were not speculative, religion-as-hobby questions, but literally matters of life and death, questions that shook the foundations of the faith. When Paul himself came to believe that God had raised the crucified Jesus from the dead, this meant that the time Israel had looked forward to was already dawning, the eschatological time of resurrection and incorporation of all God's peoples into 'all Israel.' Paul did not invent this faith or this theology; it was the conviction of the church into which he was converted and of which he became an apostle. It is the shared conviction of the teachers who composed the New Testament.

The New Testament

It turns out that both Stephen and the KJV translation of his words in Acts 7:38 were right: there was a church in the Old Testament. The biblical authors' key terms for Israel as the people of God were *qahal* (assembly) and *'am* (a people). *Qahal* was translated in the LXX as *ekklēsia* (church), and *'am* became *laos* ("a [particular] people"; cf. "laity"). Israel's teachers had filled these ordinary words with new content and breathed new life into them—they would have said the Holy Spirit, God's own breath, had done this. Thus, for example, *people* was a common word to specify those who belonged to a certain locality or linguistic group, but it is a striking fact that nowhere in the ancient Near East or Mediterranean world was the expression "people of" used to identify the worshippers of a particular god. There was no "people of Marduk" or "people of Zeus" that corresponded to Israel as the people of the LORD. From the very beginning, the followers of Jesus applied their Bible's terminology for Israel to themselves. They did not decide to form a new community called by a new name, *church*. There was already a church. Not only the earliest Jewish Christians in Jerusalem but the new gentile Christians discovered their identity as insiders to the people of God as they heard the Scripture preached and taught by their church leaders. They understood themselves as belonging to the people of God in what had become their Scripture, and the story of Israel became their story. They belonged to the church, and whenever they heard the Scripture read, they heard the story of the church to which they belonged as extending back through the centuries of the story of Israel. This is true not only of ethnic Jews such as Paul who had become Christians but of their gentile converts, including most of the current readers of the New Testament and this book. Sometimes, early Christian addressees of New Testament texts were explicitly taught that they now belonged to the people of Israel, such as in Ephesians 2:11–14, 19–20:

> So then, remember that at one time you Gentiles by birth, called "the uncircumcision" by those who are called "the circumcision"—a physical circumcision made in the flesh by human hands—remember that you were at that time without Christ, being aliens from the commonwealth of Israel, and strangers to the covenants of promise, having no hope and without God in the world. But now in Christ Jesus you who once were far off have been brought near by the blood of Christ. For he is our peace; in his flesh he has made both groups into one and has broken down the dividing wall, that is, the hostility between us. . . . So then you are no longer strangers and aliens, but you are citizens with the saints and also members of the household of God, built upon the foundation of the apostles and prophets, with Christ Jesus himself as the cornerstone.

The early Christians did not date the beginnings of the church, the people of God, "from Jesus's birth or ministry, from his Eucharistic feast or resurrection, or even from the descent of the Spirit at Pentecost, but from the covenant-making activity of God in the times of Abraham and Moses."[2] For the most part, however, this understanding of New Testament authors is not an item of Christian doctrine to be taught but is assumed as self-evident. Ethnic gentiles who had converted to the Christian faith are simply addressed as belonging to Israel, the people of God, while "gentile" (*ta ethnē*, "the nations") came to refer to outsiders, the yet-to-be-converted. It is taken for granted that Israel's story in the biblical narrative now also belongs to gentile converts to the Christian faith. The following are a few examples.

1 Corinthians 5:1–8. Writing to a predominately gentile church, Paul castigates the kind of sexual behavior they tolerate as "a type of immorality that isn't even heard of among the Gentiles" (so CEB and other translations; NRSV and NIV here render the word usually translated "gentiles" as "pagans"). The letter simply assumes that the Corinthian Christians rightly think of themselves as belonging to Israel, the people of God, and calibrate their ethical lives by this standard. Paul then goes on to support his argument with subtle inferences that presuppose the symbolic universe of Israel, with its festivals of Unleavened Bread and Passover. Paul does not explain this thought world. He assumes that his readers have adopted the symbolic universe of the Scripture, which they, too, now assume to be the real world in which they now live.

1 Corinthians 10:1–11. Analogously, Paul addresses church members in Corinth who had been converted as adults and had learned and internalized the story of Israel from the Scripture read regularly and intensively in their congregation as *their* story. They now lived in a new narrative world that could be appealed to as the basis of a new ethic, and all this can simply be presupposed. To be Christian is to belong to the people of Israel; it's not their story or the Bible's story. It's my story.

1 Corinthians 12:2. Paul says in passing, and without explanation or argument, "You know that when you were pagans, you were enticed and led astray to idols." "Pagans" is the translation in NRSV, NIV, and others (RSV and others, "heathen"; CEB more correctly "Gentiles"). As elsewhere, the word is not intended pejoratively but is simply *ethnē*, "nations," or non-Jews. The Jewish *people* do not reckon themselves to be included among the *nations* (e.g. Num 23:9).

Galatians 3:7; 6:16; Romans 4:16. See above on these texts that affirm that all baptized Christians belong to the people of Israel.

James 1:1. James is a catholic epistle, addressed not to a single congregation but to all Christians throughout the world. It is not addressed only to Jews or Jewish Christians. No specifically Jewish issues are discussed; the addressees are all believers in Jesus Christ (2:1, 7) who await the coming of the Lord (5:7), whose leaders are "elders of the church" (5:14), who are expected to recognize specific allusions to Jesus's teaching (e.g., Matt 7:1–2 = Jas 4:11–12; Matt 7:24–27 = Jas 1:22), and who discuss the meaning of Paul's doctrine of justification by faith alone, using the same Scripture texts (Rom 3:28; 4:1–9 = Jas 2:14–26). Yet the church of

Jews and (mainly) gentiles scattered throughout the world is addressed without explanation or comment: "James, a servant of God and of the Lord Jesus Christ, To the twelve tribes in the Dispersion: Greetings" (Jas 1:1), all of whom have Abraham as their ancestor (2:21).

1 Peter 2:9–13. Perhaps the New Testament's most stunning example of this understanding of Christian identity is these words written to a gentile congregation far removed from Jerusalem in time and space: "You are a chosen race, a royal priesthood, a holy nation, God's own people, in order that you may proclaim the mighty acts of him who called you out of darkness into his marvelous light. Once you were not a people, but now you are God's people; once you had not received mercy, but now you have received mercy. . . . Conduct yourselves honorably among the Gentiles, so that, though they malign you as evildoers, they may see your honorable deeds and glorify God when he comes to judge." "Conduct yourselves honorably among the Gentiles"! Women of the churches can be addressed in passing as "[Sarah's] daughters" (1 Pet 3:6). These are startling words, not only in that they take for granted that the readers have internalized Israel's story as their own. They have accepted the author's view that the ethical life can no longer be a matter of one's individualistic conscience but that the believer's way of life must conform to that of the "holy nation, God's own people," to which they now belong and whose story they find in the Scriptures of Israel. The author himself, most likely a gentile Christian teacher in the Pauline tradition, has been shaped by Deuteronomic theology, though there is not a single explicit citation of Deuteronomy in 1 Peter.

Revelation 7:1–17. Even a cursory perusal of Revelation reveals that this thoroughly apocalyptic book's understanding of the church is not all that different from Matthew's, though expressed in a different genre. This text in Revelation fuses the same two images of the ultimate triumph of God, the people of God/church against which the gates of hell cannot hold out. Like Matthew (and James), Revelation envisions the eschatological scenario as including the restored twelve tribes of 'all Israel.' In Revelation, they number 144,000—a vast 12 × 12 × 1,000 throng offering encouragement to the little Christian congregations in first-century Asia Minor that were struggling to be faithful to the One God of Israel in what appeared to be an overwhelming un- or anti-Christian context. This is followed by a vision of the church triumphant beyond all imagining, "a great multitude that no one could count, from every nation, from all tribes and peoples and languages, standing before the throne and before the Lamb, robed in white, with palm branches in their hands. They cried out in a loud voice, saying, 'Salvation belongs to our God who is seated on the throne, and to the Lamb!'" (Rev 7:9–10). A respected exegetical tradition understands these as two distinct visions in chronological order: a very large number of Jewish Christians, the restored and fulfilled Israel, followed by the vision of an innumerable host of gentile Christians. It better fits John's own style and theology, however, to understand the visions synchronically, as two visions of the same reality. In Revelation's key chapter 4, the longed-for, conquering messianic "Lion of the Tribe of Judah" (Rev 5:5) was *announced*, but what *appeared* was the vision of the slain Lamb who conquered by self-giving suffering, ultimately worshipped by the whole universe. Correspondingly, in chapter 7, the longed-for restoration and redemption of the twelve tribes of Israel is announced, but what appears is the reality of the uncountable redeemed from all nations. The Lion *is* Lamb; Israel *is* finally all God's peoples.

Revelation 21–22. The Christian Bible ends with the grand scene that concludes The Story. It is a city—a heavenly, transcendent city—but it does not abolish or cancel out the historical this-worldly cities where people have thought, taught, toiled, and sweated to build a decent civilization and live decent lives. The city that stands at the end and goal of human striving bears a historical name, renewed Jerusalem. Its emergence at the finish line of history is not the demolition and cancelation of our historical efforts but their fulfillment and redemption. God does not start over and make all new things, but God makes all things new (Rev 21:5 insists, without becoming shrill, "These words are trustworthy and true"). In this vision, unexpectedly Deuteronomic, we humans do not finally build the City of God, nor are our individual souls taken out of the world to find eternal rest in a heavenly city. We do not build it, do not go to it. The Holy City comes down to us, to this transformed world, as a gift. This is Deuteronomic theology on steroids, reconfigured in the light of the crucified and risen Messiah of Israel.

The point of Revelation 21:12–14 is that renewed Jerusalem, as in the teaching of Jesus in Matthew 19, fuses the imagery of the historical Israel (twelve gates named for the twelve tribes) and the later Christian church (twelve foundations named for the Twelve Apostles) into one picture. Perhaps we Christians would think of the Ultimate City as having Israelite foundations, but those who enter must pass through the gates of apostolic faith. John thinks more biblically. The *apostles* are the foundation; the gates are *Israel*. Apostolic faith in the Christ who already existed at the creation and was active in the history of the world and Israel is the foundation of the city, and those who enter it are welcomed through the always-open Israelite gates into the people of God that finally embraces all God's peoples.

** ** **

From Matthew to Revelation, New Testament theologians embrace the major stream of Old Testament theology expressed in Deuteronomy and epitomized in the Shema. The church being built by the risen Jesus, in the power of the Spirit (Matt 16:18; Luke 24:44–49; Acts 1–15), is not an absolutely new beginning, but it is included in the ongoing people of the Messiah of Israel. This church does not replace Israel, nor is it a parallel community alongside Israel. The church, when it lives and acts in accordance with its own identity, is firstfruits, down payment, and guarantee of God's future when the promise of blessing for all nations is fulfilled and the present distinction between the people of God and all God's peoples in Deuteronomy's *'all Israel' includes all those who confess faith in Jesus as Lord and Christ.* Christian believers can join with all Israel in confessing their faith in the words of the Shema: "Hear, O Israel, the LORD our God, the LORD is one."

Chapter 12

Israel's Story as My Story

Ecclesial Hermeneutics

Not in the Audience but Onstage

In the preceding chapters, I have mostly spoken of the reading audience of Deuteronomy as seated in the front row, attentive to the action happening on the narrative stage. The narrator speaks, and the drama unfolds before the eyes of our imaginations. All the Israelites in the world are gathered before Moses to hear the Word of God. He speaks to 'all Israel' and to no one else. The text claims to directly address not only the Jewish people of ancient Israel but Christian readers of later centuries—including us. Without invitation or explanation, the Voice that comes through the text simply speaks to us as Israel—not "as though we were Israel" but *as* Israel. For many sincere churchgoers and readers of the Bible, this itself may be difficult enough to get their minds around. Perhaps with some tentativeness, we may have been going along with Deuteronomy's assumption about our identity as Christian believers. But while we are still pondering what may be a new perspective on who we are and what God requires of us, the text throws us another curve.

We may find ourselves more or less convinced of our Israelite identity and willing to take the risk, "OK, I'll take my place with all the other Israelites in the wilderness. I need to learn what it means to be a faithful Israelite." After all, we who reside in the twenty-first century are a lot like those Israelites in the narrative world of Deuteronomy. They were not yet born, or were only small children, during the dramatic events of the exodus from Egypt, the crossing of the Red Sea, the thunderous revelation and covenant making at Horeb, the rebellious updating of their religious heritage to include a golden calf, the fearful rejection of the

LORD's gift and offer of the promised land, and Israel's abortive attempt to take it on their own. From our front-row seat, we can identify with their situation. We weren't there either and have only heard about these fabulous events from the preachers and teachers in church and from our own reading of the Bible, a lot of which sounded like "Bible stories" for children. We might resonate with 'all Israel' as they are instructed by Moses: "Now I'm grown up, part of a new generation. I'm serious about learning Israel's story, my story. I was born in Israel or joined along the way. I belong to 'all Israel,' and now that I'm maturing, I recognize I need to learn who I am and what all this means. I get to hear the Word directly from Moses, who got it directly from God. I'm not just your ordinary church member. I'm there every Sunday, I sit in the front row, and I'm all ears." And I am told, "I don't, in fact, just sit in the audience and listen, however sincerely. I'm not in the front row; I'm on the stage, not an interested spectator, but part of the action. I'm not even requested to leave my seat and join the actors on the stage." Deuteronomy is not an *invitation* to *become* something I'm *not* but *instruction* to recognize who I already *am* and live according to this revealed Torah. I can choose how I will respond to this Torah: "I call heaven and earth to witness against you today that I have set before you life and death, blessings and curses. Choose life" (Deut 30:19). What I cannot do is choose not to belong to 'all Israel.' God has made them, and us, an offer we cannot refuse. We already belong. For those who confess faith in the One LORD God, this story cannot be about somebody else. Deuteronomy is specific about this and disturbingly repetitive and insistent.

Moses's opening speech repeatedly reproaches his hearers for their failures at Horeb and Kadesh Barnea, even though they were not yet born or not old enough to "understand for themselves" and "make responsible decisions" (see Deut 1:6, 8, 9, etc.). In Deuteronomy 4:10–14, the perspectives of the past generation of the exodus and the present generation to whom Moses speaks are fused into one:

> How you once stood before the LORD your God at Horeb, when the LORD said to me, "Assemble the people for me, and I will let them hear my words, so that they may learn to fear me as long as they live on the earth, and may teach their children so"; you approached and stood at the foot of the mountain while the mountain was blazing up to the very heavens, shrouded in dark clouds. Then the LORD spoke to you out of the fire. You heard the sound of words but saw no form; there was only a voice. He declared to you his covenant, which he charged you to observe, that is,

> the ten commandments; and he wrote them on two stone tablets. And the Lord charged me at that time to teach you statutes and ordinances for you to observe in the land that you are about to cross into and occupy.

In Deuteronomy 5:2–4, the generation gap is explicitly rejected: "The Lord our God made a covenant with us at Horeb. Not with our ancestors did the Lord make this covenant, but with us, who are all of us here alive today. The Lord spoke with you face to face at the mountain, out of the fire." Lest the reader miss it, this claim is underscored by stringing seven Hebrew words together, literally "with us, we, these ones, here, today, all of us, living." Deuteronomy insists that the whole history of Israel, from Abraham onward, belongs to each generation as their own story and that this perspective is vital for maturing in the faith, and the community's religious education passes the tradition along to every new generation, not as what once happened and is now reverently remembered, but as what happened to "us": "When your children ask you in time to come, 'What is the meaning of the decrees and the statutes and the ordinances that the Lord our God has commanded you?' then you shall say to your children, 'We were Pharaoh's slaves in Egypt, but the Lord brought us out of Egypt with a mighty hand. The Lord displayed before our eyes great and awesome signs and wonders against Egypt, against Pharaoh and all his household'" (Deut 6:20–22).

In Deuteronomy 11:1–39, it is made explicit that the address is *not to your children, who didn't see these saving events, but to you who did.* The reasonable objection has been made: "But Israel was in the wilderness only forty years. All those listening to Moses who were over forty *were* in Egypt, *did* pass through the Reed Sea, and *were* at Sinai." This stance entirely misses the rhetoric of Deuteronomy, which addresses not only the thirtysomethings and younger but specifically 'all Israel.' The objection also misses the distinction between the narrative world and the actual hearer's situation (1:34 vs. 1:39). *None* of the reading audience was "back there." *None* may say, "This doesn't apply to me; I wasn't there." It is precisely this stance that Deuteronomy wants to oppose.

In Deuteronomy 9:22–29, Moses's hearers, the wilderness generation, are charged with the sin of the golden calf, although the whole point of the earlier narratives is that the guilty ones will not inherit the land and a new generation would grow up that had *not* rebelled. Later Israel's retrospective view is fused with the experience of the saving events of the past. Long after the exodus, Israelites who had never been in Egypt are warned,

> When you have eaten your fill and have built fine houses and live in them, and when your herds and flocks have multiplied, and your silver and gold is multiplied, and all that you have is multiplied, then do not exalt yourself, forgetting the LORD your God, who brought you out of the land of Egypt, out of the house of slavery, who led you through the great and terrible wilderness, an arid wasteland with poisonous snakes and scorpions. He made water flow for you from flint rock, and fed you in the wilderness with manna that your ancestors did not know, to humble you and to test you, and in the end to do you good. (Deut 8:12–16)

The generation addressed by Moses on the plains of Moab is also regarded as participating in the sins of Israel's past, even though they were not physically present. In Deuteronomy 9:13–21, we hear one of many indictments in which "you," the reading audience, are included in the guilt and forgiveness of 'all Israel,' charged with the rebellion at Horeb: "Then I saw that you [not 'they'] had indeed sinned against the LORD your God, by casting for yourselves [not 'themselves'] an image of a calf; you [not 'they'] had been quick to turn from the way that the LORD had commanded you [not 'them']" (Deut 9:16). The Deuteronomists can distinguish the revered memory of the ancestors and how this memory functions but also collapse it into the present in one contemporizing sentence: "He [the LORD] is your praise; he is your God, who has done for you these great and awesome things that your own eyes have seen. Your ancestors went down to Egypt seventy persons; and now the LORD your God has made you as numerous as the stars in heaven" (Deut 10:21–22; cf. also, e.g., 11:2–7). This is in step with the view of tradition in Deuteronomy 11:18, which joins past, present, and future: live in the tradition and hand it on.

Deuteronomy 26:5–11 is the creedal confession recited by faithful Israelites as they make their annual thanksgiving offering. This joyful liturgical confession begins in the there-and-then past and seamlessly morphs into the here-and-now faith of the believer's grateful praise. We might remind ourselves that "thanksgiving" in the language of the New Testament is *eucharist*, which fuses past, present, and future:

> You shall make this response before the LORD your God:
>
> > *A wandering Aramean was my ancestor; he went down into Egypt and lived there as an alien, few in number, and there he became a great nation, mighty and populous.*
> >
> > *When the Egyptians treated us harshly and afflicted us, by imposing hard labor on us, we cried to the LORD, the God of our ancestors;*

> *the* LORD *heard our voice and saw our affliction, our toil, and our oppression.*
>
> *The* LORD *brought us out of Egypt with a mighty hand and an outstretched arm, with a terrifying display of power, and with signs and wonders;*
>
> *and he brought us into this place and gave us this land, a land flowing with milk and honey.*
>
> *So now I bring the first of the fruit of the ground that you, O* LORD, *have given me.*
>
> You shall set it down before the LORD your God and bow down before the LORD your God. Then you, together with the Levites and the aliens who reside among you, shall celebrate with all the bounty that the LORD your God has given to you and to your house.

The "logic" is simple but alien to modern individualism: *Israel* experienced all this. *You* belong to *Israel.* Ergo, *you* experienced it—not "as if," but in reality. This confessional identification of oneself as having been delivered from slavery is not peculiar to Deuteronomic theology. The Deuteronomists only elaborated on and made explicit the much older traditional perspective and experience of 'all Israel' when gathered for worship. Such texts as the ritual for covenant entrance and renewal in Deuteronomy 29:1–15 combine Egypt, exodus, Sinai, and later wanderings and conquest of the eastern Jordan kingdoms into the experience of the hearers as well as the experience of future generations, including the hearers in the synagogues and churches of our own time. This is not merely imaginative literary fiction. Such ritual texts used in Israel's worship represent experiential reality, just as 1 John 1:1–3 does, though we do not have adequate conceptual means to articulate it. This is the reality the worshipping community experiences in eucharistic worship, where the priest/minister/elder/celebrant does not say "Jesus once told his disciples that his body and blood was given for *them*," as though these were inspiring words said to others, now to be remembered and somehow applied to us. When we hear "given for you" as we receive the sacrament, we are not given a report of what Jesus once said to other people from which we might learn valuable lessons. The there and then of biblical narrative becomes here and now, and the eucharistic words of the biblical text are addressed by the living Christ to every generation of worshippers.

To anticipate our later discussion, all this is not just more or less interesting abstract discussion of a literary technique employed by the Deuteronomic authors, brilliant as they were. It has *ethical* implications.

In Deuteronomy 10:18–19, the LORD is the one who "executes justice for the orphan and the widow, and who loves the strangers, providing them food and clothing. You shall also love the stranger, for you were strangers in the land of Egypt." This is said to people who could have responded, "That was a long time ago. *We* were never in Egypt, never homeless aliens. We came into this land, took it by force of arms, and have built it into a great country." Deuteronomy will not allow this. Remembering that there were no chapter and verse divisions in the ancient text, Deuteronomy 10:22–11:1 is a unit that collapses "your ancestors" and "you" into one people, one reality, and then makes this the basis of how you are to treat other people. The "therefore" of Deuteronomy 11:1 is the same "therefore" of Romans 12:1. The ethic of the people of God is based on the kerygma of God's saving acts; the imperative of what we must do is based on the indicative of what God has already done. The LORD says, "*You* were an alien, without land or property, longing for a new life in a new land. I am kind to aliens. *You* be kind to them too." Should we keep objecting, "But *I* was never a slave"?

Them and Us, Exegesis and Hermeneutics

I've been arguing that authentic hearing of the Bible means engaging the story in the text with our own story. If I'm sitting in the front row, a spectator to the biblical drama, I may be curious or interested, but the two stories remain separate. Each retains its own validity, and I can apply the Bible's "lessons" to my own story in appropriate ways. We have seen that Deuteronomy considers this two-step hermeneutic inadequate, insisting that we readers belong to Israel, that Israel's story *is* our story. But many readers, including me, still see a lot of value in this two-stage approach to interpreting the Bible.

My own decades-long efforts to help serious readers of the Bible hear what the Bible wants to say have often claimed to represent a dialectical, dialogical approach. In such situations, one cannot say everything at once but must attempt to speak to people where they are, one thing at a time. Since many—perhaps the majority—of those in my classes, congregations, and conversations have tilted toward the "hermeneutical right," I have often emphasized the left column. In such situations, the preacher or teacher can begin with the clear, undialectic declaration, "*Nothing* in the Bible was written to *us*." Helping us see and acknowledge this truth is one of the contributions of a historical study of the Bible. After the validity of this point has been established, or at least clearly asserted—I'm not a first-century CE Corinthian, not a sixth-century BCE Judean, and so on—the Deuteronomic teachers insist that dialogue with Scripture be continued with an equally clear and undialectic declaration: "*Everything* in the Bible was written to *us*." One can then proceed to clarify that affirming these two undiluted propositions together is neither nonsense nor an effort at cuteness but the two poles of a dialectical hermeneutic, each of which needs the other. This tension cannot be resolved merely by saying that each side is "partly" right. Truth here is not quantitative, cannot be parceled out on a fifty-fifty or sixty-forty basis. Both sides are simply 100 percent true. Period. There is no *X* + *Y* that can be distinguished, but there is a dialectical *XY* in which past and present are inseparably fused (read Karl Barth's preface to his *Epistle to the Romans!*). While the distinction between objective historical information and existential personal address cannot be simply abandoned, in the generation after Barth, other perspectives on bridging the gap between the world of the text and the world of our daily life have opened up. Two more recent scholars whose work has been stimulating and helpful are Paul Ricoeur and Hans Georg Gadamer. Neither gives us step-by-step instructions—"follow these rules and you will understand the text"—but each provides helpful conceptual handles for grappling with the hermeneutical task as a whole.

Ricoeur and Second Naiveté

Ricoeur charts the church's hermeneutical pilgrimage, recapitulated in the experience of many individuals, as consisting of three stages: *first naiveté* through *critical distance* to *second naiveté*. The following is an oversimplified sketch.

In the "first naiveté," the reader enters into the world of the biblical story and experiences its reality and truth without being aware of any distinction between the narrative world and "what really happened." A child engrossed in hearing "Jack and the Beanstalk" or "David and Goliath" experiences the terror of facing the giant and the relief when he is killed. We need not sidetrack ourselves by pointing out the obvious, that these are two kinds of stories or that one is in the Bible and one is not. We're pondering how to read the Bible, how we in fact do read it, and how, for centuries, the church to which we belong entered into the biblical story with the prescientific naiveté of children, experiencing it as happening to themselves. One thinks of Jesus, who rebuked his disciples who hindered children from coming to him, took the children in his arms, blessed them, and said, "Truly I tell you, whoever does not receive the kingdom of God as a little child will never enter it" (Mark 10:15; Luke 18:17).

Second, with the advent of the modern world, scientific method, and historical study of the ancient literature, the Bible could no longer be read naively without asking historical and scientific questions about "what really happened." The Bible could still be heard "objectively" as written for other people in another time, place, and culture. Its claims could be heard from the "critical distance" of the analyst and spectator, and reasonable reconstructions of what "really happened" could be projected. During the several generations of church history since the rise of the modern consciousness of the world informed by scientific method, not only historical-critical studies but numerous other hermeneutical perspectives have been developed, several of which open the eyes and ears of preachers, teachers, congregations, and classes to hear what is really there in the text, voices from the text that have been silenced or distorted by our own cultural situations (cf. the sketch of the six such methods in the 1994 first volume of *The New Interpreter's Bible*, with extensive bibliographies), and hermeneutical concerns and sensitivities have been considerably expanded since then.[1] All of us have much to learn from such studies, which make our ears more sensitive to the voices of women, ethnic minorities, the physically handicapped, the economically or culturally marginal, and those whose gender identifications can no longer be considered "standard." None of these approaches should be considered alternatives to historical study of a Bible composed of historical texts.[2] Even those who resist critical perspectives and methods, or suppose they have rejected them, have in fact been affected by them. Few readers of the Bible still explain mental illness as demon possession or think of the earth as the center of the solar system. Many in the church have seen great value in these methods, but whenever the childlike reading of Scripture as embracing our own story has been simply replaced by such critical methods, the total effect has been to drive a wedge between the text and the reader, who could analyze the text but not enter into The Story and be addressed by it.

Third, in Ricoeur's model, a reading of the text in the modern and postmodern world calls for a "second naiveté," neither attempting a return to the original naiveté nor getting stuck at the level of historical, sociological, and ideological analyses. This second naiveté is not precritical unawareness, nor does it intentionally reject historical study as a threat, but it enters into the narrative world of the text as an engaged listener now equipped with the results and insights of historical study.

The common denominator and perspective of all such methods must include taking a stance within The Story. This means being instructed and challenged by its claim to be the Big Story into which my little story has been incorporated, warts and all. This means sitting together at the one table with all the saints, feasting on it, being nourished and shaped by it, not always liking its taste, sometimes choking on it and even being sickened by it, but not standing aside and nibbling while our lives are fueled at other cultural tables. This is what it means to take the Bible seriously, which may sometimes mean saying an honest "no" rather than either offering a superficial "yes, of course," or rejecting it before one has heard.

Gadamer and the Two Horizons

Gadamer thinks of the hermeneutical process as the interaction between two worlds, the overlapping and fusion of two horizons. As human beings, we have our own world, of which we are the center. We listen and look from our perspective and directly experience the reality of our lifeworld. When we encounter another person, directly or represented by a text, all communication involves a dialogue that encompasses our own self-understanding and our understanding of the world as we perceive it and the world of the other person or text. We inevitably bring our prejudices into this dialogue. In using such language, Gadamer does not mean *prejudice* only in the negative sense of, for example, race prejudice, but simply *prejudgment*, *preunderstanding*, or *presupposition*, without which we could not understand the other person or text at all. We can never totally leave our own world of presuppositions and never fully enter into the world of the text or other person, but authentic efforts to understand always involve more than observing or hearing the other from a safe distance, attempting to observe and hear the other as an object (see ch. 3 in this volume on Martin Buber's *I and Thou*). The two horizons, that of the reader and that of the narrative world of the text, can overlap and even in a certain sense be fused.

Something like this is what I have been calling the incorporation of the hearer's world into the narrative world of the text, accepting it as the real world that frames and gives meaning to our own lives. As one called into the people of God, I find myself surrounded—embraced, actually—by a host of people who are also part of the comprehensive story that stretches from creation to consummation. *But my story is not simply dissolved into theirs.* My little life is not a drop in the Great Ocean of Being but a microstory embraced and given meaning by the macrostory, the Story of Everything, which is written, produced, and directed by the One True God. I keep the story that I have and am. I am not asked to give up my individuality, my personal story that makes me *me*. My story is valued by the Creator God who treasures each individual, the God who knows our names and numbers the hairs on our heads, without whose care not a sparrow falls to the ground (Matt 10:29–31)—the incarnate God who did not merely empathize with our plight from a safe distance, who did not come among us as Humanity in General. He became incarnate in one particular life, with its own particular story. In becoming incarnate in Jesus of Nazareth, the one eternal God shared and shares our lives and models how one solitary life can join the grand narrative without losing itself (John 1:1, 14; Matt 16:24–25; Luke 9:24–25).

None of this, of course, calls into question the legitimate, real McCoy preaching and teaching that communicates the Word of God we have often heard from preachers or teachers unskilled in the technicalities of historical exegesis and theological hermeneutics—and we may thank God that this is so. There is no doubt that our saintly grandparents studied, treasured, and heard the voice of God in the Bible without all these fancy critical methods. Many people understand their own bodies and know how to diagnose their health problems without knowing much about the technicalities of medical science, and many farmers are good weather forecasters without ever having studied meteorology or learned its specialized jargon. The relation of hands-on biblical interpretation to hermeneutical theory is analogous to the relation of speaking/hearing to grammar. We learn to speak and hear, often quite well, with minimal or no knowledge of grammar. We do not first learn the rules and principles of grammar, then apply them to our tongues and brains. We learn to speak and hear by speaking and being spoken to, by living in the human story with other human beings who form our cultural context and socialize us. When in elementary and high school we study reading and writing, how our own language works, we do this as persons who can already speak and hear. It is no accident that elementary schools were once called "grammar schools," acknowledging that learning what is involved in communication is fundamental to socializing children into human society. We may not have been enthusiastic about learning grammar in elementary, middle, and high school, and the importance of knowing the grammar of our own language may not become clear until we attempt to learn a second or third language. Learning something of exegesis and hermeneutics brings what we have long been doing to the level of conscious reflection. The

Deuteronomic theologians were not Israel's first or only teachers about the meaning of the faith. But at a crucial moment in Israel's history, they reformulated the tradition into a comprehensive narrative, educating us, as the people of God, in our identity and our responsibilities, not by giving us a list of rules or principles, but by opening our eyes and ears to live in The Story we are already in.

Let us, then, accept the reality of our place on the stage. If we belong to the church, we're already there as participants in a grand drama that has been going on a long time, with no end in sight. We look *back* to what God and our ancestors have done long before we were born—not all of it pleasant and respectable, but it's part of the family story. We have Scripture and tradition to fill in the content of where we've been, but as we look *ahead*, knowing that the story won't go on forever, we have a rich variety of ways our family has taught us to picture the Ultimate Happy Ending, the Story of Everything, Where It's All Going. We look *around* to our fellow participants on the stage of the universal drama and see a lot of people making the same journey with the pilgrim people of God—some like us, many not. They may have something to say to us. We may have something to say to them. It's all in the family. We'll listen with our own ears, speak to our fellow members across the aisle, the ocean, and the denominational lines and across the many varieties of liberal-conservative gaps in the one people of God. We will speak and listen from our own perspective and utilize the methods we have learned in seminary or wherever to better understand who we are and what God requires of us.

Many of the most significant voices involve looking back, attempting to hear the voices of our fellow interpreters in the people of God from biblical times to our own. We have much to learn from this rich history in which we stand. If we now look around in our own times, attempting to resist the temptation of just cherry-picking the "easy" texts and trying to stay within hearing distance of the Bible as a whole, what do we do with the *herem* (devote to destruction) texts? For many interpreters, including myself, these texts that consign all Canaanites to destruction are among the most formidable obstacles in biblical interpretation, right up there with the New Testament's texts on the wrath of God and the fires of hell.[3] But even the texts that speak of eternal, fiery damnation do not command *us*, the people of God, to kill whole populations as an act of devotion to God. Deuteronomy's *herem* texts constitute an enormous boulder across the path of hearing to understanding to obedience. Perhaps if we work at hearing what these seemingly impenetrable texts have to say to us, we will improve our hearing in general and become more insightful and faithful interpreters not only of the difficult tests but of those we might have too quickly supposed were "easy"—like "love the LORD your God with all your heart" (Deut 6:5).

The following chapter is an exercise in the hermeneutics of hearing. Its premise is that if we enhance our competence as interpreters by struggling to hear texts that are so alien to us, we will improve our ability to listen to and understand the message of the Bible wherever we open it, and we will be less likely to read in our own assumptions without even realizing it. A new set of hearing aids may pleasantly surprise us when we experience actually those voices we once only supposed we heard and understood. Let's get on with it.

Chapter 13

A Difficult Test Case

Divine and Human Violence

The Word

In the Old Testament, *herem*, usually translated in English Bibles as "devote to destruction" or "utterly destroy," is a part of Israel's sacral vocabulary that refers to a category of things or people that have been devoted exclusively to God and are no longer at human disposal for ordinary use. The term can be applied to fields devoted to God exclusively for priestly use (Num 18:14; Ezek 44:29). Living things that have been devoted to the Lord cannot be allowed to live but must be killed as a holy sacrifice to God. Human beings condemned to capital punishment by the court cannot be ransomed but must be killed (Lev 27:26–29). The concept of devotion to God as sacrifice appears most often in a military context: the booty of war devoted to God cannot be kept by Israel but must be sacrificed to God. Such a ban could include livestock and prisoners of war, but the ban was not understood to always require the killing of animals and people (Deut 2:34–35; 3:6–7; Josh 8:2, 26–27). The *herem* in the strict sense designates the military killing of human beings and the destruction of their property as a sacrifice to God rather than as plunder for the victorious army. The issue comes into the sharpest focus in Deuteronomy and the Deuteronomistic History. While other Old Testament books report or allude to the *herem*, most references to it are found in the Deuteronomic writings, and only Deuteronomy has the *divine commands* to exterminate the Canaanites.[1]

The Texts

> The LORD said to me, "See, I have begun to give Sihon and his land over to
> you. Begin now to take possession of his land." 32 So when Sihon came out
> against us, he and all his people for battle at Jahaz, 33 the LORD our God
> gave him over to us; and we struck him down, along with his offspring
> and all his people. 34 At that time we captured all his towns, and in each
> town we utterly destroyed men, women, and children. We left not a single
> survivor. 35 Only the livestock we kept as spoil for ourselves, as well as the
> plunder of the towns that we had captured. (Deut 2:31–35)

> When we headed up the road to Bashan, King Og of Bashan came out
> against us, he and all his people, for battle at Edrei. 2 The LORD said to me,
> "Do not fear him, for I have handed him over to you, along with his people
> and his land. Do to him as you did to King Sihon of the Amorites, who
> reigned in Heshbon." 3 So the LORD our God also handed over to us King
> Og of Bashan and all his people. We struck him down until not a single
> survivor was left. 4 At that time we captured all his towns; there was no
> citadel that we did not take from them—sixty towns, the whole region of
> Argob, the kingdom of Og in Bashan. 5 All these were fortress towns with
> high walls, double gates, and bars, besides a great many villages. 6 And we
> utterly destroyed them, as we had done to King Sihon of Heshbon, in each
> city utterly destroying men, women, and children. 7 But all the livestock
> and the plunder of the towns we kept as spoil for ourselves. (Deut 3:1–7)

The texts above refer to the conquest of the east Jordan territories, in which the *herem* was not quite kosher. With Moses's approval, the Israelites killed the people but retained the property for themselves. In the promised land proper, across the Jordan, the *herem* was strictly applied.

> When the LORD your God brings you into the land that you are about to enter and occupy, and he clears away many nations before you—the Hittites, the Girgashites, the Amorites, the Canaanites, the Perizzites, the Hivites, and the Jebusites, seven nations mightier and more numerous than you—and when the LORD your God gives them over to you and you defeat them, then you must utterly destroy them. Make no covenant with them and show them no mercy. (Deut 7:1–2)

> But as for the towns of these peoples that the LORD your God is giving you as an inheritance, you must not let anything that breathes remain alive. You shall annihilate them—the Hittites and the Amorites, the Canaanites and the Perizzites, the Hivites and the Jebusites—just as the LORD your God has commanded, so that they may not teach you to do all the

> abhorrent things that they do for their gods, and you thus sin against the LORD your God. (Deut 20:16–18)

The two preceding texts refer to the *herem* strictly understood, as the laws that apply to conquest of towns in Canaan. Deuteronomy 20:12–15 specifies the rules for non-Canaanite towns: all males are to be killed, but women, children, and livestock may be taken as booty.

> If you hear it said about one of the towns that the LORD your God is giving you to live in, that scoundrels from among you have gone out and led the inhabitants of the town astray, saying, "Let us go and worship other gods," whom you have not known, then you shall inquire and make a thorough investigation. If the charge is established that such an abhorrent thing has been done among you, you shall put the inhabitants of that town to the sword, utterly destroying it and everything in it—even putting its livestock to the sword. All of its spoil you shall gather into its public square; then burn the town and all its spoil with fire, as a whole burnt offering to the LORD your God. It shall remain a perpetual ruin, never to be rebuilt. (Deut 13:12–16)

Here, the *herem* is applied to apostate Israelite towns; not just the apostate individuals but the town itself is treated as no longer belonging to Israel.

It is repeatedly stated in the Deuteronomistic History that these commands were carried out, and Israel was blamed for disobedience when these rules were compromised. Thus, except for the prostitute Rahab, who had protected the Israelite scouts and her family in Jericho (Josh 6:17–21), the *herem* was carried out against Jericho, Ai, Makkedah, Libneh, Lachish, Gezer, Hebron, and Debir and its surrounding towns (Josh 8:26; 10:28–39). The bloody conquest of the land is summarized in Joshua 10:40–42: "So Joshua defeated the whole land, the hill country and the Negeb and the lowland and the slopes, and all their kings; he left no one remaining, but utterly destroyed all that breathed, as the LORD God of Israel commanded. And Joshua defeated them from Kadesh-barnea to Gaza, and all the country of Goshen, as far as Gibeon. Joshua took all these kings and their land at one time, because the LORD God of Israel fought for Israel."

Hearing/Interpretation

We can readily agree with Deanna Thompson that "the actions God endorsed for the Israelites would today be considered war crimes."[2] We are not the first generation to be bothered by these texts. From early Christian times, serious Christian thinkers have pondered how faithful ministers of the Word should interpret these difficult texts.[3] I have found it helpful to sort out the variety of interpretations in terms of the interpreter's perspective on the historicity of the relevant biblical texts:

I. Reporter-history
II. Nonhistory
III. Secular history of religion
IV. Critical theological history

I have tried to be fair in describing each of the views summarized in the following brief paragraphs, aware that such treatment can hardly do them justice and affirming Adlai Stevenson's dictum during his political campaigns of the 1950s, "You have no right to disagree with your opponent's position until you can state it in terms satisfactory to them." Readers are encouraged to pursue alternative views represented in the bibliography at the end of this volume.

I. The Herem Texts as Reporter-History

Justifying the Herem

Many, but by no means all, interpreters who identify themselves as fundamentalists, conservatives, or evangelicals presuppose that the truth of the Bible means affirming that biblical texts report events essentially as they happened. Good reporters don't interpret or editorialize. As Sergeant Joe Friday from the classic TV series *Dragnet* would say, "Just the facts, ma'am." Readers of the Bible who revere it as Holy Scripture, especially the church's preachers and teachers, have the responsibility to interpret the meaning. Advocates of the reporter view of biblical truth have developed a number of ways of defending the *herem* commands as given by the same God definitively revealed in Jesus Christ.[4]

1. **The inspiration, authority, and truth of the Bible require it.** This argument varies from the "God said it, I believe it, that settles it" bumper sticker to sophisticated philosophical and theological reasoning. According to this view, to question whether God commanded the *herem* is to reject the Bible and to open the door to anything-goes secular humanism. This argument appears frequently within the broad spectrum of fundamentalist-conservative-moderate scholars who identify themselves as evangelicals. That even some of the more moderately critical evangelical

interpreters take such care to insist that their view does not compromise the requisite understanding of biblical authority—sometimes stated as "inerrancy" or "infallibility"—suggests that the principal issue is a doctrine about the Bible, not an understanding of God or Christ. The proliferation of "Bible churches" can suggest that the faith of the Christian community is in a book rather than in a Person, that the Word became Book and dwelt among us, and we beheld its glory.

2. Since the Bible says God commanded it, God's command is enough. God is God and does not need to explain the divine plan to mere mortals, as though we could grasp the mysterious purposes of God. Parents understand this and respond to recalcitrant three-year-olds with "Because I said so, that's why!" In this view, response to God's command is not blind obedience but trust in God. This has been argued at least since the days of Augustine in the fifth century CE. It is still repeated in defending the *herem*. At another discourse level, the ethics of a command can be defended (deontological ethics; see ch. 14), but that is a different matter from assuming God's command is identical to the biblical text. The point here is that one stream of interpretation argues that God's command can be explained as fitting in with and being supported by logical arguments appealing to human reason. Nineteenth-century American theologians such as Benjamin B. Warfield and Archibald A. Hodge of Princeton formulated a fundamentalistic conservatism as a thoroughly rationalistic system advocating verbal inspiration and biblical infallibility as the conceptual framework for understanding the authority of the Bible. This legacy was expressed in some of the following rational justifications for the *herem*.

3. The Canaanites were incorrigibly and irredeemably evil and deserved capital punishment. This theory flourished especially in the United States during the time of the Trail of Tears, when the Cherokee were displaced from their land in Appalachia and survivors of the death march were resettled in the barren Cherokee Strip of Northwest Oklahoma—also later taken away from them. This rationale was popular during the "Indian wars" on the Great Plains, when US troops were killing Native Americans and taking their land. Custer's 1876 defeat at the Little Bighorn and the 1890 massacre of the population of Wounded Knee by the US Army were lived experiences or vivid, recent memories. Their solution to the "Indian problem" was eradication. The Deuteronomic *herem* model was only slightly beneath the surface of these political decisions and was widespread among the US citizenry, including its church members. The Native Americans were the Canaanites, and the US Army was the righteous host of Israel. In this way of thinking, the Native Americans were uncivilized savages to be killed, and we were to take their land with God and good conscience. J. W. McGarvey, a frontier scholar-preacher contemporary of these horrific events, spoke for many Americans, including sincere Christian believers, when he declared, "Some tribes of men reach a point in depravity when the good of the world requires their extermination."[5]

In this aspect of their theology, such nineteenth-century preachers and teachers were thoroughly immersed in their culture, advocating a version of cultural Christianity in the name of the Bible. More recently, sometimes with more impressive academic credentials, this approach to the *herem* has morphed into another form of cultural Christianity, sometimes found in the American Religious Right and documented in sophisticated versions of some streams of evangelical theology. At least one defense of the *herem* that can have "spiritual continuity" with Christian life and action includes a justification for the killing of babies: "In conclusion, we must point out that the Bible does not understand the destruction of the men, women, and children of these cities as a slaughter of innocents. Not even the children are considered innocent. They are all part of an inherently wicked culture that, if allowed to live, would morally and theologically pollute the people of Israel."[6]

4. The Canaanites were "illegally" living in the promised land and had to be evicted or destroyed. From the time of Abraham, God had promised the land to Israel. Though the Israelites given the *herem* command had never lived in Canaan, God's promise had given Israel a title to the land. The Canaanites were only "squatters" (the word occurs fairly often in such apologetic literature) who had no right to be there. When they refused to flee, Israel had no choice but to eradicate them.

5. God's mission through the chosen people required that they have a place where they could be formed as the holy people of God. God's short-range strategy required the eradication of the Canaanites to clear out a place where Israel would not be tempted or contaminated by pagan religion in the neighborhood so that they could retain their identity as God's chosen people as a part of God's long-range plan. The *herem* was thus a one-time-only command. According to this line of thinking, it was right for God to give it and for Israel to obey it *then*, but it would be wrong for the people of God who live in the light of God's full revelation in Christ to do such things.

6. The *herem* is not a problem that needs to be solved. In this view, it is a misunderstanding to suppose that the *herem* command clashes with the will of God as revealed in Jesus Christ; the *herem* commands in fact reveal the true nature of God, and it is a false view of God and Christ that poses the problem. Neither Jesus nor God is fully described in the Gospels' accounts of the "first coming" of the Messiah. The full picture is yet to come:

> Still other pages of the New Testament present the same Jesus as the One who returns not in poverty and humility but in glory and power. He does not return as One who brings the way of salvation. Rather, he returns as the righteous Judge who speaks the final word of judgment on the living and the dead—and a fierce judgment it is for those who face it apart from him. The final judgment with its utter destruction of the heavens and the earth and all those at enmity with God makes the most bloody warfare narratives of the Old Testament seem like children's bedtime stories.[7]

Not My Problem

Some interpreters with a reporter-truth perspective on biblical texts have developed hermeneutical approaches that make it unnecessary to struggle with what these texts might have to say to believing Christians today.

1. **"It doesn't apply to us."** Various sorts of dispensationalism divide the Bible into sections, some of which once applied to "them" but no longer apply to "us." This approach became popular in early American theology while the various states were forming their constitutions and the nation was establishing its own constitution that included them all. A constitution was ratified and became effective on a certain date. Before that date, something might be legal and prescribed, but the new constitution replaced the old. It was once the law of the land but no longer applies to us. This American model was applied to biblical interpretation, with the Old Testament understood as the constitution of Israel, which was superseded by the New Testament as the constitution of the church so that Christian efforts to interpret the *herem* texts could regard them as historically important but no longer applicable. Deuteronomy, of course, explicitly rejects that view (e.g., Deut 5:2–3), as does the New Testament (e.g., Matt 5:17–20 and the hundreds of New Testament texts that cite the Old Testament as authority).

2. **It's cultural "progress."** Biblical interpreters must certainly attend to the relation of faith and culture; there is not and cannot be any Christianity or biblical interpretation that is not influenced by human culture. One way of dealing with the *herem* texts is to reduce them to a dimension of the assumed primitive civilizations of biblical times that has been

outgrown in the more advanced stage in which we presumably live. In this approach, contemporary believers need no longer attend to the kind of primitive religion expressed by texts concerned, for example, with demons, animal sacrifice, the *herem* command, and slavery, which can in all good conscience simply be ignored.

3. **"I just follow Jesus."** A wide range of different and competing approaches march under this banner, from individualistic just-me-and-Jesus standpoints that reject both the "institutional church" and its Bible to more sophisticated "historical Jesus" approaches that claim to follow Jesus as he really was but reject the traditional and editorial overlays represented by the New Testament texts that falsely claim to represent him. Since it is, of course, true that the Jesus of the New Testament never cites the *herem* texts, and it is difficult to imagine him incorporating them in his teaching, such approaches need accept no responsibility for interpreting such texts.

II. The Herem Texts as Nonhistory

Allegory to the rescue! A major hermeneutical category is represented by the interpretation of some theological heavyweights such as Origen and Augustine. Some versions of this approach regarded at least part of the biblical narrative as a literal report of what happened but evaluated such an understanding as only a preliminary step toward true understanding. However, when faced with difficult biblical stories that depict God as acting in ways unworthy of human decency, this approach tended to abandon history and devolve into a claim that the biblical narrative was not about events in history at all but entirely concerned with spiritual truths in the world of ideas. The events themselves never happened, and the biblical narratives were never intended to suggest that they did; their repulsiveness demonstrates that the biblical authors never intended them to represent actual events in history. God included such problematic passages in the inspired text to warn against literalism and inspire Christians to look for deeper spiritual meaning. The problem is not that the Bible reports actual divine commands to exterminate the population of Canaan and that Israel did it with God's blessing. These events, if they happened at all, occurred on the material level of this-worldly reality, but the Bible functions on the spiritual level. Origen explains that the problem is not within history or the Bible but within us: "Within us are the Canaanites, within us are the Perizzites; here are the Jebusites."[8] The eradication of the Canaanites really means that vices are to be so completely rooted out from the believer's heart that they cannot sprout up again. We have seen (see ch. 10 in this volume and the related bibliography) that the Bible and mainstream church history have always resisted dissolving the history-oriented biblical narratives into the more manageable world of ideas.

III. The Herem Texts as Secular History of Religion

In this approach, the *herem* texts, like other dimensions of religious life through the centuries and around the world, can be profitably studied as an aspect of ancient Near Eastern religion. For our present purpose, it is only important to know that the military-religious practice of *herem* was not unique to Israel; Israel's people and teachers did not invent it or first become aware of it by listening to Moses or Deuteronomy. The *herem* was a widespread aspect of some ancient Near Eastern military cultures, as illustrated by the ninth century BCE Mesha inscription (the "Moabite Stone," which can be seen today in the Louvre). The Moabite king recounts how he devoted an Israelite city to destruction, executing the *herem* command of the Moabite god Chemosh (Kemoš in the transliteration below). The relevant section of the inscription for our purpose reads,

> And the men of Gad lived in the land of Ataroth from ancient times, and the king of Israel built Ataroth for himself, and I fought against the city, and I captured, and I killed all the people from the city as a sacrifice for Kemoš and for Moab, and I brought back the fire-hearth of [Daudoh] from there, and I hauled it before the face of Kemoš in Kerioth, and I made the men of Sharon live there, as well as the men of Maharith.
>
> And Kemoš said to me: "Go, take Nebo from Israel!" And I went in the night, and I fought against it from the break of dawn until noon, and I took it, and I killed its whole population, seven thousand male citizens and aliens, female citizens and aliens, and servant girls; for I had put it to the ban [*herem*] of Aštar Kemoš. And from there, I took the vessels of Yhwh, and I hauled them before the face of Kemoš.[9]

Studies in the history of Israel's religion, as distinct from biblical theology, can be conducted by secular historians with the same objective honesty with which scholars who are not Latter-day Saints might study the Book of Mormon and the religious ideas and practices of the LDS church or non-Islamic scholars might study the Koran. Such studies are eminently valuable, and illuminating, but only approach the texts from the spectator stance appropriate to the historian of antiquity. The historian of Greek religion carefully examines the *Iliad* and *Odyssey* for what they have to say about their understanding of the gods and worship practices and their relation to ethics but with no responsibility to interpret their "meaning for today." Such a commitment to these texts as Scripture would obscure the historian's view.

IV. The Herem Texts as Critical Theological History

I now venture to sketch an approach to hearing the *herem* texts from a theological perspective illuminated by critical historical study.

As members of the one church of God, we belong to 'all Israel' (see chs. 11 and 16 in this volume). This means we have and are guided by Scripture, hearing and interpreting the text within the community of faith. If we accept Deuteronomy's declaration about our identity as belonging to the one people of God, "not my problem" is an option not available to members of the church facing difficult issues of biblical interpretation. The skeletons are in our own closet. It's all in the family. Every Bible is a family Bible.

All Scripture is to be understood in the light of Jesus Christ. YHWH **truth is Christ truth.** When we affirm that all Scripture is to be understood in the light of Jesus Christ, we mean not "in terms of our own reconstructions of what the 'historical Jesus' actually said and did" but in the light of the Jesus Christ event as interpreted, understood, and presented in the New Testament as the saving act of God. All Scripture must be understood in the light of the life and death of Jesus, an event in which the One God was present and active—"that is, in Christ God was reconciling the world to himself," manifesting his love for all people (2 Cor 5:19). Those who believe in the universal love of God revealed in the Jesus Christ event can never picture this same God commanding the destruction of innocent children.

All Scripture is illuminated by historical study. Historical study of the Bible and many of the texts within it means understanding it as a multilayered historical document that already contains *interpretations* and *testimonies* (interpreted testimony as truth) that must be *heard*. Many readers of this book may have had such a theological-historical approach to biblical truth for as long as they can remember, so historical study of the Bible was welcomed as filling in the outlines of a subject they had long had in mind, as in the study of world geography or US history. Others may have discovered or been force-fed "historical criticism" for the first time in college or seminary classes, saw no way of holding on to their older views (Moses wrote the first five books of the Bible, the apostle Matthew wrote the first book of the New Testament, and so on) and continuing to believe and preach the Bible with conviction, put the whole matter in parentheses for a while, received their degree and ordination, and reverted to some version of precritical first naiveté. Others may have studied historical views of the Bible in college or seminary and decided that personal integrity required that older views be abandoned and new ones be accepted—honestly but reluctantly. Still others—I have observed this in many students and colleagues and would place myself in this group—experienced such historical study as liberation. Historical study did not take the Bible from me but put it back in my hands, unburdening me from false problems that did not need to be solved and removing barriers that no longer needed to be surmounted. Among these were the vivid pictures of divine violence focused in the *herem* commands. Consider John J. Collins's summary statement on the last page of his helpful *The Bible after Babel: Historical Criticism in a Postmodern Age*: "Even within a single book, Deuteronomy, we find both a moving concern for one set of others, the widow, the orphan, and the alien, and a complete disregard for another, the Canaanites. Biblical theology, and biblical ethics, are never just a matter of telling the biblical story, whether one regards it as historical or not, but require a criterion by which different elements in the text may be evaluated."[10] Historical study of the Bible is such an illuminating criterion, allowing the text to speak and be heard in its own accents in our later time and place but with the same concerns.

Our goal is not merely to formulate a method that can be applied to difficult texts in order to make some sense of them for ourselves and the people to whom we minister. The goal is experiential, not merely conceptual—to improve our hearing whether or not we are able to articulate an abstract method that makes the process conceptually clear to others or even to ourselves. We have entered into a long and personal dialogue not only with these texts but with our fellow pilgrims among the people of God. Our ability to hear—and thus to preach and teach—has been enhanced by distinguishing the Bible's own narrative world from the story behind the text and by gaining insights from the church's story of translating and interpreting the Bible (chs. 5–11 in this volume). As we focus on the *herem* texts as an illuminating test case, I here share some of the insights achieved through historical study of the Bible in dialogue with this grand company of church teachers, past and present. I will state these insights as a series of theses, with no dogmatic overtone intended.

1. **"It never happened."** The *herem* was not commanded by God, nor did it happen in the way described by some Deuteronomic texts. We should say clearly, to ourselves and our parishioners and students, as responsible interpreters of the Bible who revere it as Holy Scripture, "It never happened." The results of historical study indicate the Deuteronomic speeches of Moses to 'all Israel' on the plains of Moab are not Moses's or God's very words, nor are they verbatim historical reports of something that actually occurred during a few days in the thirteenth century BCE. The canonical form of Deuteronomy accepted as Scripture by the people of God, Old Testament and New Testament, is the didactic rhetorical literary composition of Deuteronomic teachers in the exilic and postexilic periods. This editorial rewriting and reinterpretation of earlier traditions addressed an Israel looking back on their previous successes and failures and struggling to find their way forward as a minority community of faith returning to the promised land (cf. ch. 6 in this volume). The pictures are retrospective, though told prospectively (cf. post-Easter perspective of the Gospels). A later generation confronts the givenness of history, believes God is the Lord of history, and interprets the tradition they receive in that light. The commands to kill and dispossess are given not to the readers of the story but to the people in the story, as something already in the readers' past.

This means that the original reading audience of Deuteronomy was very much like us and other later readers. Neither they nor we are commanded by God to destroy the Canaanites. They lived centuries after the native inhabitants of Canaan had died out, and so do we. The original reading audience, the small band of Jews seeking to be faithful Israel in the Persian province of Yehud, could not have obeyed the *herem* command if they had tried. They could not have obeyed this command, and neither can we. But neither could the (post)exilic original reading audience dismiss the narratives and commands of Deuteronomy as ancient history, no longer relevant for them. They, like us, hear the command directed to 'all Israel,' and they, like us, are warned against hearing the text as once actually directed to someone else. So how should they and we hear such commands that no longer fit their or our situation? Within the narrative world of Deuteronomy, we, too, are addressed by the *herem* command and all the other commands, ordinances, laws, and testimonies that may seem irrelevant or abhorrent to us. If we can secure a better grasp on interpreting the *herem*, we might come within hearing distance of much else that Deuteronomy wants to say to us.

When we say that historical study reveals that the *herem* was never commanded and never happened, we do not mean this in the sense of unhistorical allegorical interpretation that escapes from history into the world of ideas (see "The Herem Texts as Nonhistory" earlier in this chapter). Nor do we mean that nothing happened. Deuteronomy and the Deuteronomistic History are not simply fiction. Deuteronomy, like the Bible in general, is an interpretation of events that actually happened in the space/time world of objective reality, the mighty acts of God in history, climaxed and represented by the incarnation, the act of God, the Word become flesh. And within this Big Story, numerous smaller historical events actually happened that became historical grist for Israel's theological mill. None of these stories, big or little, are simply reports, but they interpret such events theologically as testimonies to the Word and will of God.

During Israel's wars and battles, it is historically probable that Israelite warriors sometimes killed the whole population of a town or village, taking no prisoners. Israel, too, had its My Lais and Wounded Knees, but they are not definitive for the history of either Israel or the United States. The practice of the *herem* was a widespread military practice in the culture of the ancient Near East (see above). But study of the Bible itself—not just the study of "skeptical" historians—helps clarify how this difficult problem in the text is to be understood. Historical study of the story behind the text shows conclusively that there was never a command of God to annihilate the Canaanites; there was never a genocidal conquest of Canaan. It didn't happen. It is the story in the text we must hear and interpret. Historical study is helpful not only in that it lets us see "what really happened" (or didn't) more clearly but also because it redefines the hermeneutical issue. One task of preachers and teachers is to steer clear of trying to make sense of an alleged event as somehow compatible with the event of God's love revealed in Christ. Our task is to facilitate being drawn within hearing distance of a text and hearing it as the Word of God. The Christ event happened in history. The *herem* did not.

2. The church's theology, "faith seeking understanding," must always be expressed in the language and concepts of human culture. Like every sermon and Bible study lesson or conversation, all theology is a human enterprise. No theology is let down from heaven, and if it were, we wouldn't be able to understand it or find it useful. All versions of theology are conditioned by human culture—and not by culture in general but by the language, mindset, worldview, politics, economics, art, literature, sociology, history, and religions of a particular culture in a particular time and place. There are no generic humans; there are only those who are shaped by one or more human cultures. But the faith can never be identified with any particular cultural expression, and some aspects of some cultures are more appropriate than others for expressing the faith revealed by the One God (see ch. 15 in this volume). For our present concern, it is only important to know that the military-religious practice of *herem* was not unique to Israel, that Israel's people and teachers did not invent it or first become aware of it by listening to Moses or Deuteronomy. The *herem* was a widespread aspect of some ancient Near East military cultures, as illustrated by the ninth-century BCE Mesha inscription (see above).

Historical study attempts to hear every text in its historical context. The Deuteronomic commands would have been expressed and heard in this cultural context and perhaps taken for granted, just as is the cultural conventions of national boundaries, private property, and taxation are assumed by us as "just the way things are," and we are unconcerned or unaware that in centuries before and after us, some human cultures would consider these assumptions primitive, crude, uncivilized, and inhuman.

3. **"We take the Bible seriously but not literally."** Even though we can, in good conscience, acknowledge that the Deuteronomic *herem* never happened, the text of Deuteronomy itself provides pointers toward powerful, non-watered-down interpretations that facilitate the text's addressing us with the Word of God. We might point to the obvious tensions and logical historical contradictions in the text of the Deuteronomic compositions themselves. To take a clear, broad-stroke example, the conflicting pictures of the conquest in Deuteronomistic History and edited by the Deuteronomic teachers included both Joshua's and Judges' versions of the conquest: "So Joshua defeated the whole land, the hill country and the Negeb and the lowland and the slopes, and all their kings; he left no one remaining, but utterly destroyed all that breathed, as the LORD God of Israel commanded. And Joshua defeated them from Kadesh-barnea to Gaza, and all the country of Goshen, as far as Gibeon. Joshua took all these kings and their land at one time, because the LORD God of Israel fought for Israel" (Josh 10:40–42). This picture of Israel's immediate and complete possession of the land by destroying all the natives is directly followed by Judges' accounts of gradual and incomplete settlement of only part of the land, in which Israel continued to live alongside the Canaanite population: "The LORD was with Judah, and he took possession of the hill country, but could not drive out the

inhabitants of the plain, because they had chariots of iron" (Judg 1:19; cf. 1:21; 2:3; and often throughout the book). Such summary comments are not incidental. Not only is the partial and gradual settlement of the land reported, but a variety of explanations are given as to why there was no *herem* and/or why it was never implemented: Israel was unfaithful and disobedient (Judg 2:13 and often); the Lord intentionally left some native peoples, including "all the Canaanites," in the promised land to test the faithfulness of Israel (Judg 3:1–6). A different explanation had already been provided by Deuteronomy. The Lord did not immediately make a quick end of the Canaanites; otherwise, the wild animals would have multiplied and become a danger to the Israelites (Deut 7:22). Of course, the repeated warnings in Deuteronomy not to worship the Canaanite gods, not to intermarry with them, and not to be influenced by their pagan culture presuppose an Israel that had settled down among the Canaanites, not destroyed them or been commanded to do so. The same Deuteronomy that commands Israel to destroy the Canaanites gives directions about how to live among them and still remain faithful to their calling as the people of God—sometimes in the same paragraph (e.g., Deut 7:1–4). Not only that, but when Deuteronomy was combined with Israel's other traditions to form the Pentateuch, the Deuteronomic pictures of destroying the Canaanites take their place alongside other pictures in which God does not destroy the native population but drives them out of the land (e.g., Exod 23:28; 33:2; 34:11). These various sets of pictures simply cannot all be understood as accurate historical reports. The tensions and contradictions that emerge when these narratives are understood literally does not mean that all the "conquest" stories are to be ignored or rejected or that one set is to be accepted and the others dismissed. Such features in the biblical text signal that each set of pictures is to be taken with theological seriousness as part of Deuteronomy's eschatological vision (see further in the sections "The power and truth-claim of the language are manifest in myth, metaphor, and symbol" and "Deuteronomy's eschatology focuses on present fulfillment, abundant life here and now, and salvation as land and place").

In Deuteronomy's narrative world, in which 'all Israel' looks forward to the fulfillment of God's purpose in the promised land, the people of God are given the vision of a future world without evil, just as the Creator made it at the beginning. God's purpose expressed in the original creation also required more than one picture, as in Genesis 1–2. There, too, the tensions present in the two creation stories (P, Gen 1:1–2:4a; J, Gen 2:4b–25) illustrate that ultimate truths require more than one picture, no one of which can be taken literally, and both of which are profoundly theological. As with ultimate beginnings, so with ultimate endings. As the creation stories portray a world without evil, so Israel's vision of the ultimate future promises a world without evil, a world without false gods and false worship, a world in which all God's peoples will be the people of God on an earth liberated from the power of evil.

God will remove or transform evil; Israel's job is to be faithful. Such visions of the ultimate future require more than one picture. In portraying the ultimate triumph of God, evil can be pictured as banished, destroyed, or transformed. While in Deuteronomy's narrative world, Israel looks forward to the conquest and the good life in the promised land, the actual readers look back on Israel's failed history and look forward from their own exilic and postexilic situation with new hope for a new future. The Deuteronomic narrative now plays a symbolic role, with its multiple, unharmonizable pictures pointing to the unimaginable future of the fulfillment of God's purpose. The Deuteronomic teachers, by intentionally including conflicting descriptions and instructions, indicated they were entirely aware that the *herem* commands could not be carried out literally, that such an understanding did not come on the radar as an actual command to the readers they were writing for—or for anyone else. The conflicting images and commands, rather than posing a historical problem that must be harmonized or rejected, become a positive witness to God's future.

The primary content of Deuteronomy, the Torah it wants to teach the original reading audience (and us), consists of directions for living as the people of God in a world that still includes evil but is still God's world—the faithful God who will deliver on his promises. In the meantime, the world that surrounds the people of God is a world with a different culture, different ethics; different faith, religion, and values; and different presuppositions about what is important, real, and true. In the Torah that directs and nurtures the life of the people of God, even the *herem* commands and stories have a positive role to play. Deuteronomy itself gives some pointers on how to hear these commands.

4. **The power and truth-claim of the language are manifest in myth, metaphor, and symbol.** Like all creative, growing-edge literature that wants to transform its readership, Deuteronomy must create the means by which it can be understood, must build the road as it goes and not merely give information that can be fitted into the reader's previous categories. Good authors typically just do this without explaining or calling attention to it. Dante and Shakespeare, Melville and Dostoevsky,

Steinbeck and Hemingway—not to mention Seer John of Patmos and Jesus of Nazareth—just do it. "Let anyone with ears to hear listen!" (Mark 4:9, 23; Luke 8:8; 14:35). We may discern signals built into the text of Deuteronomy that point the way toward revelatory, transformative hearing.

In a speech Moses considers a matter of life and death, why include historical trivia about the "Emim," "Anakim," and "Rephaim" (Deut 2:10–11, 20–21, 23; 3:11; 9:2)? These explanatory comments about the nature of the adversary that confronts 'all Israel' as they ponder the difficult road ahead are not antiquarian tidbits for those who may be interested in such details. The obscure names, with alien overtones, conjure up images of the inhabitants of the land as more than ordinary human beings. God's good creation is peopled by God's beloved creatures, but the Anakim/Rephaim are off the screen or at the edges of God's good creation—mythical superhuman giants connected in Ugaritic texts with kings of the underworld. The adversaries faced by Israel and blocking their way into the promised land are gigantic figures; the "Emim . . .—a people, as tall as the Anakim" (Deut 2:21), also called Rephaim, Avvim, or Zamzummim by other nations, are remnants of the prehistoric giant races that lived there, of whom Og, king of Bashan, was the last. His bedstead was fourteen feet long and six feet wide by human measurement (again, suggesting a superhuman adversary; similar language is used in Rev 21:17 of the transcendent world). Og's bedstead was purportedly still on display for the ancient tourists in Rabbah of the Ammonites, just as the bones of the dinosaurs that once roamed the earth can still be seen in our museums. These adversaries that opposed 'all Israel's' possession of the promised land were like a race of Goliaths, blaspheming God's holy name, but neither David nor Israel needed to be afraid, for God would provide the victory (1 Sam 17:15–51). The heartening comments in Deuteronomy are all from the narrator to the reader, not from Moses to the people gathered on the plains of Moab.

The Deuteronomic teachers want to represent the adversary, the powers of evil that stand in the way of the fulfillment of God's promises, as superhuman. Later Jewish apocalyptic thought, already dawning in the time of the Deuteronomists (see ch. 17), would make these images much more vivid and explicit. Jesus and early Christian teachers such as Paul and John of Patmos would incorporate them into the fundamental structure of their theology. Thus, for example, Christian believers, church people, and gentiles who now belong to "the commonwealth of Israel" (Eph 2:12), as citizens with the saints (the holy people of God) and also members of the family of God, are to see themselves as engaged in a cosmic conflict. In words that echo Deuteronomy's exhortations to Israel to conquer the promised land, the church is encouraged to "put on the whole armor of God, so that you may be able to stand against the wiles of the devil. For our struggle is not against enemies of blood and flesh, but against the rulers, against the authorities, against the cosmic powers of this present darkness, against the spiritual forces of evil in the heavenly places" (Eph 6:11–12). This New Testament text is a lineal descendant of Deuteronomy's *herem* texts.

Deuteronomy itself is replete with figurative, symbolic language, explicitly calling attention to the truth and power of metaphorical language. God is like a mother eagle that stirs up the nest, pushes the eaglets over the edge, teaches them to fly on their own, and catches and nurtures them when they fall (Deut 32:10–11). God is like a parent who disciplines a child (Deut 8:5) or carries the child through the dangerous wilderness (Deut 1:31). In Deuteronomy's metaphors for God's gift of the land, the imagery is militant, the language is the language of battle, conquest, and victory. The New Testament's imagery of the people of God as the church militant, struggling against the powers of evil that are already defeated, is directly descended from the Deuteronomic vision of the mission of the people of God. There are no Canaanites to be killed, but the mission of the people of God draws its imagery from Deuteronomy. It is misguided to attempt to avoid, eliminate, or replace this problematic imagery.

The hymnody of Israel, the New Testament, and the history of the church are replete with the metaphorical language of battle, conquest, and victory—that is, the language of violence. No one suggests such imagery authorizes murder of babies or prisoners of war. But when the church continues to sing "A Mighty Fortress Is Our God" or the "Battle Hymn of the Republic," it follows the lead not only of Deuteronomy but of Jesus, and the New Testament, and the history of the church. None of this imagery is to be taken literally. All of it is to be taken seriously. Though not to be taken literally, neither is it to be filtered out, replaced, or ignored. Not even by a filter of either left- or right-wing cultural religion. The Religious Left, even the Religious Moderate/Center, is, in my humble opinion, appropriately antimilitarist. The military option is to be executed, if at all, as the last resort, and even then with repentance and without self-righteousness. But the attempt to simply eliminate militant language and associated imagery removes much of what is central to biblical faith, including the central confession of Jesus as the Messiah—the eschatological king who establishes God's kingship.

In Matthew 16:17–19, Jesus's promise to build his church—his, not ours, for he is the builder, not us—Hades and the devil are on the defensive. God's militant power, embodied in the Messiah, like Joshua leading Israel into Canaan, is on the offensive to search and destroy, rooting out the power of evil from God's good creation and storming the gates of Death, which cannot prevail against this mighty assault (cf. Gen 24:60 and already in 22:16–18). Death is the last enemy (1 Cor 15:26). As in Deuteronomy, God is the one who finally destroys the ultimate enemy (Deut 9:1–3; cf. Rev 20:11–15). The church is not called to throw Death and Hades into the lake of fire. That is God's business. God is the ultimate judge, the executioner of the divine will. The final victory is sure but still ahead of us. Even those who have died will not miss out on this eschatological victory—resurrection is an image of *that*. Mercy has the last word, already in Deuteronomy. God threatened to destroy the people of Israel, who were worse than the Canaanites, but God's mercy prevailed over all, through the one mediator who suffered for others (Deut 9:1–29). In Deuteronomy 9:12, Yhwh speaks to Moses, calling sinful Israel "your people." Moses refuses to accept the responsibility for this people and their destiny, insisting, in effect, "No, these are *your* people, your responsibility, not *mine*" (9:26), an appeal to God's faithfulness even when Israel and humanity are unfaithful—explicitly reaffirmed in Romans 3:1–4 by Paul, the interpreter of Deuteronomy. Moses appeals to the Creator, who is the Author and Director of The Story, responsible for bringing it to a worthy conclusion. This imagery is amplified in New Testament texts that appeal directly to the Shema in the light of the Christ event: "For there is one God; there is also one mediator between God and humankind, Christ Jesus, himself human, who gave himself a ransom for all—this was attested at the right time" (1 Tim 2:5–6; cf. also Rom 3–4, esp. 3:3–4, 30). This eschatological victory of the mercy of God is the worthy conclusion of the Story of Everything to which God is leading the creation. "Onward Christian Soldiers" is hardly sung in mainline churches anymore because of our aversion to militarism (though the violence of "A Mighty Fortress Is Our God" from Luther and Ps 46 is still sung with gusto in both Protestant and Roman Catholic churches).

Martin Luther King Jr., opponent of all violence, filled his preaching and teaching with the Bible's powerful imagery of conquest and victory. His 1964 acceptance speech for the Nobel Peace Prize reverberated with the language of Revelation: "We shall overcome." This is a vision of God and the people of God at the eschatological celebration including all God's people, celebrating God's victory in the promised land. God has defeated the threatening powers of evil and conquered—not by violence but by suffering love that is finally victorious over the whole restored/new creation. Texts such as Romans 8:37—"We are more than conquerors through him who loved us"—translate the verb *nikaō* and the cognate noun *nikē* (of sportswear fame) not only as "conquer" but as "overcome" or "overpower." This vocabulary and imagery is found in Jesus's words for God's eschatological victory (e.g., Luke 11:20–22; John 16:33) and especially in Revelation's promises to the faithful people of God who share in this victory—those who *overcome* (KJV), those who *conquer* (NRSV cf., e.g., Rev 2:7, 11, 17, 26; 3:5, 12, 21). "We Shall Overcome" is sung not only as an expression of gritty determination to resist the structural injustices of this world but in the calm confidence that the power of God's love revealed and activated in the Christ event will finally prevail. In the grand tradition of Christian hymnody, theology sings when it does not, and cannot, know how to conceptualize its faith within its own this-worldly rational categories. Dr. King's last public address was filled with the images of conquest and victory. He concluded with the words of the "Battle Hymn of the Republic," his last words spoken in public: "Mine eyes have seen the glory of the coming of the Lord."

We perhaps need to remind ourselves that Deuteronomy is a worship book that concludes with a song. At God's command, Moses not only taught 'all Israel' the Torah but taught them and us a song to be sung through the centuries as a testimony to the faith, even as a witness against those who sing it when they forget to hear and live by the way of life revealed in the Torah (Deut 32; see ch. 16 in this volume). Deuteronomy is theology that laughs and sings.

5. **Discipleship means living in the story-shaped world.**[11] Accepting Deuteronomy's claim that as Christian believers, we belong to 'all Israel,' that Israel's story is our story, we realize that we belong to a community of faith that has a long history of struggling with difficult texts in its Bible. Knowing something of this history does not mean merely acquiring pieces of more or less interesting information. Realizing that one stands in this history is itself an aid to interpretation. Such study is a matter not of information but of formation, transformation. This does not necessarily mean that studying how Christian theologians of the past, Bibles in hand, have interpreted such texts for their time will show us how to hear God's message through these texts for our own time. This happens only occasionally. Reading the history of interpretation of the Bible as a whole,

and especially of particular texts, places our struggle not only within the life of our congregations and denominations but in the larger family story (Deut 4:32–40). Dialogue with this story helps shape us into interpreters who are better able to discern the will of God for our own times. Only rarely in learning our story will we find a ready-made solution to the problems faced by our own generation. This is not the practical value of studying the history of interpretation. Rather, without looking for a specific, usable answer, as preachers or teachers equipped with the insights of past generations of 'all Israel,' we are better prepared to hear the Word of God that comes through the Bible—even the *herem* texts—and to discern the will of God for our time and place. There is no system, no method, that solves and prescribes this. But we now engage in the hermeneutical process, making concrete decisions neither dictated nor forbidden by biblical texts, guided by hearing a number of voices from within the Bible and the history of 'all Israel' to be faithful to the God who speaks through it. This is what Deuteronomy insists on—providing structures and instruction for ongoing reinterpretation of the revealed will of God, not supposing that all future issues can be settled merely by quoting the authoritative text (e.g., 1:9–18; see below on Levitical scribes as Israel's teachers). This is what the New Testament insists on—discerning the will of God in ever-new situations, which calls for informed and transformed "renewed" minds (Rom 12:1–2; "discern" in NRSV, REB, NAB, ESV, HCSB; "test and approve" in NIV; "figure out what God's will is" in CEB).

6. Discernment means improvising. As a way of understanding our place in the people of God, I have used the metaphor of the front-row spectator versus the onstage actor. I think it's a helpful metaphor, but here it breaks down. In real life, we Christian believers find ourselves onstage as participants in the ongoing drama of which the One God of Israel is Author, Producer, and Director, but the Author has not written out the details of the action and speech of every scene. The beginning, end, and major turns of the plot are clear. We participants are not responsible for the story as a whole, but we find ourselves called upon to decide much of the action and dialogue of each scene. We may sometimes feel we have forgotten our lines or consider the ones we have read and memorized as no longer appropriate. But "the show must go on." What should we do? At this point the metaphor limps, especially if we think in terms of ad-libbing. Some preachers and teachers of the faith are better than others at ad-libbing, having the "gift of gab" and the ability to think on their feet. But we are not called to make up the story as we go along. *Improvising* is very different from ad-libbing. First Thessalonians, probably the earliest

New Testament book, presents the preacher-teacher of a new congregation describing himself as having been "approved by God to be entrusted with the message of the gospel, even so we speak, not to please mortals, but to please God who tests our hearts" (1 Thess 2:4). We have been "entrusted with the message of the gospel." Ad-libbing the sermon or lesson can be an irresponsible rejection of the role we are called to play.

A better metaphor than ad-libbing, used by several contemporary interpreters, is *improvising*, in the musical sense of the term—a highfalutin word for "jamming," as in "We once were thrilled to hear two local guys jamming with the Preservation Hall Jazz Band from New Orleans."

- To be sure, improvisation is a *musical* term, not the usual way of talking about the conceptual, discursive speech of the good sermon, lesson, or conversation. Still, we rightly say that good music "speaks to us," or "speaks to the heart," and can generate thoughts and words appropriate to the occasion. Music shares with poetry and visual art a kind of truth that often cannot be expressed in prosaic speech that strives for logical clarity.
- Improvising is done in *community*. No one can "jam" alone. Improvisation involves listening and sensitivity to where the other players are coming from and where they are going. Good soloists are not always good at improvising.
- Improvising presupposes that one *knows a lot of scripts and scores from the past* but is not the repetition of any of them. Each performance is generated just for that occasion, which might never be repeated again.
- Improvising must be done by *skilled, disciplined artists* who know and can reappropriate and respond to the music of the past, including its written scores and the ways they have been performed, so shaped by past works of art that one plays intuitively, almost instinctively, with no thought of a "method" that is being "applied." Improvisation is musical art, not spontaneous speaking—when we've forgotten our lines, or never knew them, or don't even know there are lines—where we all just say what we think.
- Improvisation represents a hermeneutic in step with Deuteronomy, which ends with a *song* to be learned and sung by 'all Israel.' Our worship services frame the lesson and the sermon with music. Deuteronomy concludes with the Song of Moses that Israel is to be taught and to sing for all generations to come, which does not

tell them what to do in every situation but helps form them into the kind of community that can discern and live out the will of God. As in the Preservation Hall Jazz Band, such music is worship, celebration, joy.

- This is the point where regular, *disciplined Bible reading and study* play their proper role. Deuteronomy expects the people of God, led by Israel's preachers and teachers, to regularly read the revealed Word of God, to think and talk about it among themselves all the time (Deut 6, etc., in relation to confessing the Shema). For preachers, teachers, and laypeople in our own time, this might mean developing a daily discipline of Bible reading, not just looking things up for one reason or another, not just reading a devotional verse or two, but engaging in a daily practice of living in The Story. The concert musician's adage is appropriate to such Bible reading: "If I miss one day's practice, I can tell it. If I miss two days, the critics notice it. If I miss three days, everyone notices it." Such disciplined study of the Bible is not an exercise in personal piety, a spiritual discipline that is "good for me." It allows me to join in the song; to play with others who are skilled musicians; to participate in the conversation, hearing and speaking with all the saints and discerning the will of God for my time and place. It's part of what it means to say, "I belong to the church."

V

The Lord Our God

The Torah

Chapter 14

The Torah for All Israel

"It's about God"

In fear and trembling, addressed by the Word of God, we now ask more directly, What does the Bible want us to hear? Answer: the Torah, the theological message of Deuteronomy. Actually, we might have started with this question and answer on the first page of this book. But this approach runs the same risk as jumping to the answers at the back in our high school algebra textbook—we might be able to repeat the right answer but not understand it—we might even know that we don't understand it and might not even know or understand the question. This is what we have been doing in the preceding chapters: perhaps repeating the Shema every day, trying to get a better handle on what it means to *hear* and to be addressed as belonging to *all Israel.*

The Deuteronomic teachers of Israel ask us to believe that the faith of all Israel can be confessed twice every day in one sentence. Of course, it takes them thirty-four chapters of Deuteronomy and six more books of the Deuteronomistic History to unpack what they—and we—are saying when we confess our faith, but it is all already there in the Shema, four Hebrew words, six in English translation (Deut 6:4b).

The faith of Israel is "the Lord is our God, the Lord alone" (Deut 6:4). It's about God. I remember hearing Woody Allen report his experience with speed reading. He had been impressed by claims that with discipline and practice, he could increase his reading speed by ten times or more. He knew that presidents John Kennedy and Jimmy Carter had benefitted from speed reading courses. Though still somewhat skeptical, Mr. Allen gave it a try and reported that after working at it for a while, he became convinced that it actually worked: "I read *War and Peace* in twenty minutes. It's about Russia."

"It's about God." I doubt that the Deuteronomic teachers, not to mention Moses or Jesus, would commend speed reading the Bible. But if we are looking for a three-word summary of its 1,800 pages, "It's about God" would be on target. The Bible is not about us, not about our search for happiness, our quest for meaning—not even about our efforts to establish a just society or our search for God. This would be the story of human religion, including Canaanite cultural religion and the whole spectrum of US cultural religion—Right, Middle, Left. This is what Deuteronomy wants to warn 'all Israel' against, and it claims to provide the alternative.

"It's about God." I also remember our three-year-old Bonnie coming home from Sunday school in the small rural church I was serving, beaming about how she liked her teacher and the half-dozen children that sat with her in a circle on little red wood chairs.

"What was today's lesson about?" I asked, making conversation at lunch.

"God," she said.

I have since thought of that little scene when I read Matthew 18:3: "Truly I tell you, unless you change and become like children, you will never enter the kingdom."

The Bible is about God. Deuteronomy is about God. Not God in general. Not that "There is a God," not checking "yes" on a questionnaire in the slot after "Do you believe in God?" In the Shema, the confessional core of all faith and theology, Deuteronomy does not celebrate diversity and antidogmatic individualism—"Believing in God, however you think of God." Like every person, God has a story, a face, and a name. It is *this* God, YHWH, the LORD, who is the one God. It turns out that we cannot believe in this God without understanding ourselves as the people of God. Israel's confession is not "There is a Supreme Being called 'the LORD'" but "the LORD is *our* God." "Our" means not "Ours but not yours" but "We belong to that community of 'all Israel' that confesses that the One God we believe in is YHWH, the LORD God of Israel."

As preachers and teachers trying to get our minds around the theological message of Deuteronomy, we find help in the books on systematic and biblical theology arranged according to the traditional rubrics: God the Creator, Christology, soteriology, ecclesiology, and so on, typically concluding with eschatology. Such topical approaches to theology have their value for helping us sort out biblical teaching into specific topics.

It's not a bad idea, for instance, to make a notebook, paper or digital, with a page for each of the dozen or so traditional topics, then to work carefully through a book of the Bible listing texts, ideas, and notes under these manageable rubrics. We could read carefully through Deuteronomy, make a list of themes that emerge from the text—such as "God," "Worship," "World," "Torah," "Sin," "Salvation," and so on—and record texts under each heading with our comments and cross references. We would end up with helpful lists and a commentary of our own making, our own summary of the "Theology of Deuteronomy" derived from our study of the text itself. We would see what's there and what's not there. Does Deuteronomy have a messianic hope? Does Deuteronomy understand animal sacrifice as atonement for sins? Does the repeated presence of a topic indicate a lack in Israel that needs to be remedied? Does the absence of a topic mean it is unimportant or that it is simply assumed by all concerned? After completing the exercise, the list could be kept for future reference and modification, perhaps for comparison with similar lists related to study of other biblical books. Even if the list is thrown away or never looked at again, the exercise itself is valuable to refocus the eyes and ears, minds and hearts, with which we approach the biblical text.

But this is not the Bible's own way of doing theology. Deuteronomy, especially, insists that all theology is the doctrine of God, "theology proper." "Eschatology," "soteriology," and so on have no independent standing as topics but only receive biblical Christian meaning when they are filled with the content of the meaning of God, who defines himself and is confessed by 'all Israel' as the One God whose name is the LORD and who in the incarnation receives a human face.

Rather than arrange Deuteronomy's theology topically, we will work with the narrative-rhetorical flow of the text, attempting to discern the Deuteronomic teachers' own way of structuring their theology. The story line moves from creation through the call and mission of Israel to the consummation of God's purpose for the world. God calls the universe into being. When humanity rebels and planet earth goes awry, God calls a particular people into being as God's witnesses and agents in God's reconciliation of the world to himself. This will be a world of justice—the will of God done on earth and in heaven. For the theocentric theology of the Deuteronomists, "God" is not one topic among others but the only question in town. But how can we readers get a better grasp of Deuteronomy's "doctrine of God"? It seems to me that if we asked the Deuteronomic teachers, "What do we need to know about God, and what does the LORD want to teach us about 'God'?" their response would be both clear and surprising: the LORD wants us to know, and reveals to us, what it means to be the *people* of God, to say that the One God is the God of *Israel*, *our* God. Their teaching book includes 'all Israel' fourteen times, framing the whole text with its occurrence in the first verse and concluding with 'all Israel' as the last words of the book (Deut 1:1; 34:12). Just as the early church teachers affirmed that what Christian believers mean by "God" cannot be expressed without talking about Jesus Christ, the Son of God, so Israel's Deuteronomic teachers affirmed that the essential character and acts of the LORD could not be communicated without talking about Israel, the people of God, whom they called "sons of the LORD your God" (Deut 14:1 RSV; NRSV, "children"). Central to God's own identity and character is the identity and character of the people of God. More succinctly and technically, for the Deuteronomic teachers, just as all theology is essentially the doctrine of God, the doctrine of God is essentially ecclesiology. "Understanding God" means understanding Israel, who we are and what God requires of us. We will develop this central aspect of Deuteronomic theology under three headings that focus on Deuteronomy's doctrine of the church:

Chapter 15—Where We Are: Between the Times, between Two Cultures
Chapter 16—Who We Are: 'All Israel'
Chapter 17—What God Requires of Us: "Do Justice, Love Mercy, Walk Humbly"

Chapter 15

Where We Are

Between the Times, between Two Cultures

The Story in the Text

The theological brilliance of the Deuteronomic teachers is that their narrative portrays all Israelites in the world as a single large community, a homeless people gathered in the desert between Egypt and Canaan, the promised land. The parents and grandparents were liberated from Egyptian slavery, but they have no personal memory of the experience; their whole life has been lived in the setting of the barren desert. No Israelite in the world had ever lived in a house, raised crops on a farm, been to school, been inside a temple, participated in a festive gathering of sacrificial worship. Before entering into the multicultural, civilized world of Canaan, they listen to the Word of God, the Torah taught by Moses, the greatest of God's prophets. Moses speaks of the dangers that lie ahead of them. These threats to the good life are not physical or economic—the Lord has promised to destroy or drive out their enemies and give them a healthy and prosperous life. The danger is that in this new life, their understanding of themselves and the faith by which they live will be shaped by the Canaanite cultural religion that lies before them. The whole purpose and message of Deuteronomy could be summed up as equipping the people of God to recognize and resist the seductions of cultural religion by hearing and obeying the revealed Word of God. Walter Brueggemann assesses the life-situation of Deuteronomy's hearers, then and now. We are at the boundary:

> More than at any other moment in Israel's history, here there is a long reflective pause. It is as though Israel's traditionalists had intuitively known

> that this is the hour of destiny; as though Israel knows that hard, disciplined reflection is never more needed than at this moment, when the new situation of land requires a new Israel with a new faith. Deuteronomy more than anything else in the tradition provides the most radical and bold articulation of faith.
>
> . . . And so at the boundary is the place of Torah. Torah, according to tradition, is from Sinai. But it is freshly presented, interpreted, and urged at the boundary.[1]

We might pause briefly to remind ourselves of the ways such phrases as "faith and culture" and "religion and culture" are used and try to bring them into sharper focus for understanding what is going on in Deuteronomic theology. For two generations, H. Richard Niebuhr's classic *Christ and Culture* has provided the handle by which many of the church's preachers and teachers have attempted to come to terms with this issue. The titles of the book's main sections spell out the options as Niebuhr sees them:

> "Christ against Culture"
> "Christ of Culture"
> "Christ above Culture"
> "Christ and Culture in Paradox"
> "Christ the Transformer of Culture"

While seeing some value in each perspective, Niebuhr leads the reader through the various approaches, culminating in "Christ the Transformer of Culture," clearly his own emphasis. Quite against Niebuhr's intent, however, the book has sometimes encouraged a false dualistic understanding, as though readers could stand with the Christ of the Bible, tradition, and the church's faith as they face the cultures of this world, confronted with the decision of how to relate "Christ" and "culture." The reality, however, is that the Christ we have, the faith we already have as members of the people of God, and the ways we understand the Bible are already thoroughly permeated by human culture, which stands on both sides of the equation.

To be human requires a human community that transmits human culture to us and nurtures us in its appropriation. This socialization occurs in interaction with virtually everyone around us, beginning with parents, family, friends, neighbors, and schoolteachers, and continues throughout our lives. All human beings participate in culture as an essential element of being human, shaped by the forces studied in the humanities and social sciences, whether or not we have taken courses in language, art, music, history, philosophy, anthropology, literature, law, politics, economics, sociology, psychology, and religion. This means that our understandings of God, Christ, and church are inevitably conceptualized, thought and spoken about, in terms of various cultural understandings. Even for the Deuteronomic teachers, the reality of our situation must not be pictured as the choice between God and the world, church and human culture. The LORD, the God of Israel, is the Creator of the whole world—secular and sacred, Israel and "the nations," the people of God and all God's people, the church and the world. It was not only Israel that God loved, "for God so loved the world. . . ."

We have spoken of 'all Israel' in the narrative world of Deuteronomy as "blank hard drives" being filled in with Mosaic content, as though they did not already have a religion and culture of their own. There is some truth in this image, though the metaphor needs to be adjusted. In the Deuteronomic narrative, Moses and the people received only the Ten Commandments at Horeb, and the rest of the Torah was put on hold. Actual instruction for Israel's religious, social, and political life in the land is not given until the new generation, encamped on the plains of Moab, receives it from Moses shortly before they will put it into practice in the promised land. In the narrative world of Deuteronomy, Israel faces the clear choice between the Word of God they hear from Moses and the cultural religion they will confront in Canaan (Deut 30:15–20; cf. Josh 24:15). Nonetheless, even in the narrative world, the Israelites are already involved in human culture. They speak, read, write, cook, shepherd flocks, marry, and found new families in the ways they have been socialized to consider normal. In the real world of the first readers, the reading audience also already inevitably shares many of the cultural assumptions that directly affect the way they understand theology and ethics. These religious beliefs are not first taught to them by Moses; they have been instilled in them by the culture they share with many of their neighbors in the ancient Near East. They already know about prayer, sacrifice, altars, temples, festivals, priests, prophets. Most importantly, they already have ideas about the gods—specifically about *Baal* "the Lord"—that have been deeply significant for how they have lived their lives. Israel's choice is not a simplistic "cultural god" or "the true God" but how to adapt the inevitable culturally conditioned imagery and language used for God so that it expresses Israel's faith in YHWH. In Canaan, the Lord who supplied rain and made life possible was *Baal*, often described in Canaanite mythology as the "rider on the clouds." In the name of keeping the faith pure from pagan influence, Israel's teachers could have rejected all such language (which could only have meant that they would have borrowed language from some other stream of human culture). But in the Old Testament, YHWH, the God of Israel, the One True God, is often described as being in charge of rain and clouds and specifically as the one who "rides upon the clouds" (Ps 68:4; cf., e.g., Ps 104:3; Jer 4:13; Nah 1:3). The language of human religious culture was adopted and adapted by Israel's prophets and teachers, who struggled to fill it with the content of their own religious tradition. YHWH was not merely the desert tribal God. Nor was YHWH to be identified as "the Lord" in the Canaanite sense, a nature fertility god. As in the anonymous Jesuit "Crusader's Hymn" from the seventeenth century, YHWH was ruler of all nature and Lord of history and all nations who makes the woeful heart to sing. This is no cultural god but the LORD God who commandeers all nature, culture, and history for his purpose!

The following are some fixtures of the cultural world shared by Israel and most of their neighbors:

- *Slavery*. Modern Western culture simply assumes that slavery is wrong, period. But the Deuteronomic teachers and all the people they portray in their writings do not decide to be slaves or slave owners, whether they will be for or against slavery. They raise no question about their standard of living being supported by what they simply assume to be a given element of society. In this they are in step with virtually everyone in the ancient world, including Moses, Jesus, and the authors of all the books of the canonical Old and New Testaments. Centuries later, many people of various cultures and faiths—some of them on the basis of their understanding of the Bible and Christian faith—would oppose and finally eradicate slavery as an assumed and necessary component of the social structure. In the biblical story, however, the LORD God of Israel does not abolish slavery. Israel gives thanks to the LORD who heard their cries and liberated *them* from the misery and degradation of slavery, but the same LORD never condemns the Egyptian social system built on slavery, nor did he liberate the other Egyptian slaves. In Deuteronomy, in fact, the LORD assumes that the Israelites, now liberated, will have their own slaves and gives commands through Moses for how they should be treated (Deut 5:14–21; 12:12, 18; 15:13–17; 16:11; 21:14; 23:15). In the New Testament, Paul simply assumes the existence of slavery, even among Christian congregations (e.g., 1 Cor 7:21–23; Phlm 1–16). So also, the stories Jesus told, and the ethical instruction he gave his disciples, assume the existence of slavery without ever saying a word against it (e.g., Matt 6:24; 8:9; 10:24–25; 13:27; 18:23–33). The only biblical text that even comes close to an explicit condemnation of slavery as an institution is the lamentation of the early Christian prophet John (Rev 18:13). To be sure, in biblical theology, such references to slavery always assume the shared humanity of master and servant, that both are beloved creatures of the one Creator, and biblical instruction to both masters and slaves always mitigates the usual cultural understanding. In Deuteronomy, in contrast to all other ancient Near East law codes, slaves are to be included in the Sabbath rest and holiday festivals and protected from physical abuse by their masters.[2]

- *Circumcision.* Ritual circumcision of male newborns or pubescent boys was not invented by Israel or Israel's God. Archaeological evidence indicates that when the LORD gave Israel commands and instruction about circumcision, the practice had been in the culture of the ancient Near East since at least 3000 BCE (cf. Jer 9:25–26). Israel adopted the cultural practice and gave it a religious interpretation as the command of the LORD. In the Torah and Judaism, circumcision became the mark of God's covenant with Israel and was extended symbolically into the church's understanding of the incorporation of Christian believers into the people of God. Deuteronomy assumes this understanding of circumcision but mentions it only twice (Deut 10:16; 30:6), in each case with a symbolic interpretation.
- *Animal sacrifice.* From time immemorial, people had worshipped the gods by sacrificing animals to them. Not only did the "primitive" peoples assume the cultural practice as a religious given, but so did classical Greece, including Plato and Aristotle, and Judaism and the Greco-Roman world of New Testament times, including Jesus and Paul.
- *Covenant.* We discussed the nature of God's covenant with Israel earlier, in chapter 5. Here we need only to point out that the book of Deuteronomy itself represents an adoption and adaptation of human political culture. It is almost universally agreed that the conception, form, and content of Deuteronomy's understanding of "covenant" (*berit*) is influenced by the Assyrian suzerainty treaties that claimed sovereignty over another state that remained in charge of much of its own affairs. Such a *berit*

was not a bilateral contract between peers, agreed to in advance, but a unilateral imposition from above. The king, and sometimes subjects, understood the covenant as the "gift" of protection, which required loyalty, obedience, and tribute in return. The following elements of Esarhaddon's vassal treaties correspond to Deuteronomy, sometimes using the same exact language:[3]

1. Titulary ("titular summary")
2. Historical introduction, the basis and motivation for the vassal's loyalty
3. Stipulations of the treaty
4. List of divine witnesses
5. Blessings and curses
6. Recital of the covenant
7. Deposit of the tablets

We have already discussed the military practice of the *herem* as illustrating Israel's adoption of a widespread cultural practice and interpreting it as God's command (ch. 13). But numerous other cultural mores taken for granted in the civilizations of the ancient Near East were already woven into the fabric of the world in which ancient Israel was born—for example, the nature of personal and social justice and the necessity of capital punishment to ensure a just society; monarchy as the assumed form of government; prophecy, priesthood, and prayer as inherent in legitimate and inspiring worship; and the patriarchal family as essential for a stable society and good life for everyone.

The practice of prayer provides an example deeply embedded in our own religious experience. We should not assume that prayer is a particularly biblical, Jewish, or Christian practice, as though Israel and the church prayed but the pagans did not. Some form of prayer is virtually universal in human religious experience. Worshippers of Baal prayed fervently and sincerely (1 Kgs 18:20–40). Prayer is part of human culture. *How* to pray, the content and meaning of prayer, and the character of the God to whom one prays—this shaping of human religion by the revelation of the LORD is what biblical faith, Old Testament and New Testament, is about.

** ** **

The Israelites listening to Moses in Deuteronomy were not "blank hard drives" waiting to be filled with Deuteronomic content. Their choice was not between the "pure Word of God" delivered by Moses and the "human cultural religion" of the Canaanites they were warned against. We have seen that the Bible itself teaches us that this apparently clear choice in fact muddles the actual situation. The story in the text must be heard in dialogue with the reader's own story.

The Reader's Story

The narrative-world Israelites on the plains of Moab all had the same story, but the actual listening audience of canonical Deuteronomy was dispersed in a variety of cultural settings and already involved in the cultural religion around and within them. 'All Israel' was scattered among the Israelite population that lived in the Persian province of Yehud and its Palestinian environs, or in what had become their native land in Babylon, Egypt, or elsewhere. These readers were certainly not blank slates waiting to be filled but were already acculturated, to some extent socialized and assimilated into a variety of cultural settings. God's revelation does not write on a tabula rasa but *overwrites* the contents of cultural religion already there.

The Lord who speaks through Deuteronomy is no tribal God, and Israel's faith is no henotheism. The God of Israel is the One God who called both world and church into being by his almighty Word. Neither world nor church got started somehow on its own. The creative, transforming Word of God is the power that generates and sustains both world and church (Gen 1:1–3; 12:1–3). The Lord God of Israel is not a creation of human cultural religion but the One Creator God who affirms and celebrates human creativity, human culture. The central problem addressed by Deuteronomy and faced by 'all Israel' is not how to relate an uncontaminated Bible, gospel, or tradition to a world that threatens to adulterate it. Deuteronomy wants to instruct the people of God, who also belong to this world, about how to be faithful to their mission to all of God's world and its peoples, how the good news of the saving acts of God are to be related to human culture. This culture includes the meaningful profundities of human religion.

If Moses were invited to address a conference of preachers and teachers gathered in a desert retreat setting today on "How to Be a Successful Church in a Multicultural World," he would accept without hesitation. The full text of his speeches is still available, and he is still open to invitations. Canaanization is no longer a danger. *He would speak about the McDonaldization of the church.*[4] What topics might he have chosen for his sermons, lectures, workshops, and seminars? The following are among his possible options:

1. *"McDonaldization as a Strategy for the Successful Church: Plusses and Minuses."* As the church faces an uncertain future in a new world, the people of God can learn from institutions and movements that have a proven track record of succeeding in a complex world.
2. *"Stay in the Wilderness."* We are safe, fruitful, and happy where we are. The new world across the Jordan is filled with unknown dangers, physical and theological. We know how to live in the desert, but Canaan is an agricultural land. Egypt was dry, watered by the Nile. We've lived forty years in the desert and have never seen it rain. Rain will be a new thing for us in Canaan. YHWH is a desert God, for people on the move. Baal is the god who knows agriculture and supplies rain. If we cross the Jordan, we're sure to be corrupted. People will want to know how to worship the rain gods. We know how to shepherd flocks but not how to farm. In learning how to survive and flourish in the new world, our own faith might even be compromised. Better to stay where we are.
3. *"Learn from the Past."* We have a glorious past, starting out as seventy people who went down to Egypt, and are now vast multitudes. Since the actual authors of Deuteronomy are looking back on Israel's history in the land, the Deuteronomic Moses could not only look ahead to Israel's future but point back to the time of David and Solomon, when we had a magnificent temple and were growing by leaps and bounds. Those were the days. We need to find out what we've been doing wrong and get back to the golden age of our origins.
4. *"Get up to Date."* God has called us to become a great, innumerable people, a megapeople. We are now the smallest of all the peoples (Deut 7:1, 7, 17). We need to learn how to grow, for God has promised to bless us. If we stay like we are, we will continue to shrink. We need to stop sticking our heads in the sand. We need to get in there and look around, see what works, and adjust to the changing world so that we, too, can be a growing church.
5. *"Destroy Them!"* The promised land is occupied by pagan squatters who have no right to be there and who would contaminate the faith and practice of Israel revealed by God. The God who will finally destroy all evil calls us to join the battle now. Onward, Christian soldiers! Recover the Holy Land from the infidel!
6. *"Convert Them!"* God has promised a transformed humanity living according to God's will in a transformed world. By the grace

of God, we have already heard this message and been converted. Our job is to convert others. When we get across the Jordan, we will be the LORD's witnesses, going door-to-door, winning others to God.

7. *"Live and Let Live."* God wants us to live, to have a good life. "Choose life" (Deut 30:19–20). We have a happy, secure life that works for us. We know we will be living in a multicultural context where people do not share our way of thinking, with its values, politics, and religion. We need to respect their way of life and live so they will respect us. We don't want them to impose their religion on us, and we don't need to try to impose our religion on them. Tolerance. Openness. Accept others just as they are. A lot of people are looking for that kind of church.

McDonaldization as a Strategy for the "Successful Church"

We would hardly be surprised if the Deuteronomic teachers had chosen this catchy title as Moses's theme for his desert workshop on the future of the church. If "god" or "religion" can be defined as that which gives meaning and purpose to our lives, then global capitalism, the generation of societies based on consumerism, plays the cultural role of God and religion, the assumed mythological framework within which we live our lives. By definition, such mythologies are barely at the level of conscious choice. They are the assumed framework of a worthwhile and meaningful life. Such consumerism must necessarily be supported by nationalism and militarism, as each nation strives to keep its own economy strong. The index to success and riches is numbers. Successful businesses placard to the public not how much money they are making—that's for investors—but how many hamburgers or Hondas they have sold. A 1955 sign registers "More than 15 Million Sold," increasing to "More than 6 Billion" in a 1970s sign, and "99+ Billion" on the latest sign I have noticed. Our son, a regional manager for an international chain of fast-food restaurants, sums up his monthly meeting with top brass in the corporation this way: "It's all about numbers." Across the denominational and cultural spectrums, "successful" ministers are those whose attendance and budget numbers are good and getting better. A successful church is a growing church.

Numerical growth is not to be sneezed at. The move from small beginnings to impossible, mind-blowing numbers is a story that might have reminded Moses of Abraham and Sarah. The "More than 99 Billion" reverberates with the uncountable stars of the heavens and sands of the sea (Gen 15:4–6). Abraham and Sarah, like the McDonald brothers, Colonel Sanders, and Steve Jobs, followed their dream, never gave up, and succeeded beyond all they could have imagined; lived happy and productive lives; and made a contribution to society while becoming admired—not to say idolized—by the world at large.

Moses, like us, could think of other helpful parallels. McDonald's is a happy place to go. Children are served Happy Meals. Get the children to come, and you get the adults. All McDonald's' PR and advertising are upbeat. Nothing negative is said after we get there. "I'm lovin' it" is a simple, warm, folksy, inviting image. And there are no surprises. Go to any McDonald's the world over, and you know what you are going to get. International McDonald's leadership does their market research, determines what people like, and tries to deliver it in a more attractive way than the competition. And people don't like surprises. People know what their kind of church is supposed to be and what their preachers and teachers are expected to say, and if they don't find those things, they get a new preacher or switch churches. That's the way the business world works. And when I go to McDonald's, I'm the center of attention. I go there because *they* serve *me* (cf. Mark 10:45). I'm not asked to do anything except be there and give them my money, and I hardly notice that I'm expected to clear my own table. If I don't clear my table, no McDonald's manager will make me feel guilty or do or say anything else that might hinder my return or—God forbid!—encourage me to take my business to another restaurant down the street. The service is prompt, efficient, and predictable. When I come back home, the family may ask, "How was the service?"—the same question I hear when I come back from church.

The Moses of Deuteronomy considers the McDonaldization of the church to be its major THREAT. Moses warns against adopting the attractive, reasonable goals and methods of Canaanite cultural religion as the recipe for a successful church. We preachers and teachers may think of strategies the church can learn from a successful business. There are books and motivational speakers along that line. Next time, we won't ask Moses. Maybe we can get one of the McDonald's executives to speak to our fellowship dinner on something like "Ten Tips on Becoming a Successful Church."

Moses wants to tell us who we already are.

Chapter 16

Who We Are

'All Israel'

All theology is essentially the doctrine of God; in Deuteronomic theology, the doctrine of God is essentially ecclesiology, the doctrine of the church (see ch. 14). For the Deuteronomic teachers, a solitary Israelite is inconceivable, an oxymoron. Those who confess their faith in the words of the Shema cannot speak of God except as "*our* God," just as those who pray the Lord's Prayer can only address God as "*Our* Father." No believer in Yhwh, the Lord God of Israel, could check "None" on the religious affiliation questionnaire. One cannot share Israel's faith without being *in* Israel. Just as "the point of Christology" is not about Jesus but about God,[1] so the point of talking about the church is not to talk about ourselves but to talk about God (see ch. 13)—though to speak of either is to speak of the other. Deuteronomy's pointers toward a deeper understanding of who we are emerge as a series of confessional declarations—who *we* are.

We Are the Saved Community

Karl Barth could say without hesitation, "I have been saved."[2] Much of "mainline" Christianity is still tentative or awkward in talking about salvation. When I began reading the Bible on my own in high school, I discovered that the language of salvation permeates the Bible. It was refreshing and liberating some years later to learn that Barth and other significant theologians spoke readily of the saving acts of God and spoke of the church and themselves as "saved." In a pivotal, defining declaration, the conclusion of Moses's final blessing on 'all Israel,' we hear, "Blessed are you, O Israel! Who is like you, a people saved by the Lord?"

(Deut 33:29; author's translation). Coming within hearing distance of Deuteronomic theology can help mainliners reappropriate this fundamental aspect of what it means to say, "I belong to the church." For the Deuteronomists, the church is the saved people of God. Salvation is personal and corporate. God saved, is saving, and will save the people Israel. Individuals are saved because they belong to the people of Israel; they do not first "get saved" and then join the people of Israel as an optional second step. To say "I belong to the church" means "I have been saved, I am being saved, and I will be saved."

Salvation is the act of God—past, present, and future. To speak of Israel as the saved people is to speak of God as the Savior. Such language is not a claim about who we are but a confession of what God has done. Church members can learn from Deuteronomy to confess their faith with a declaration of what God has done in the past that modulates from past to present and from them to us, as modeled by the creedal declaration of Deuteronomy 26:5–10. God saved them/us from slavery and gave us *life*. While the Deuteronomists are sparing in their explicit talk of salvation, they speak freely of *life*, the Deuteronomic synonym for "being saved." To live the one and only life I have under the taskmaster's lash, used up in the 24/7 weariness of making bricks for someone else's house or temple, is hardly to have a life at all. To be liberated from such slavery, to be given life, is salvation. Jeremiah, the prophet most influenced by the Deuteronomic teachers at one stage of their history, defines being saved as "liv[ing] in safety" (Jer 33:16). Neither he nor they thought in terms of going to heaven; they were concerned with abundant life in God's good creation:

- to lie down at night in the security of my family with no fear of invading armies,
- to enjoy carefree good health and festive meals and reap the fruits of my own labor instead of seeing them go into the king's or corporation's coffers, and
- to have my new husband receive an honorable discharge from the military so I can welcome him back home before the battle even begins instead of having him give his one and only life by dying in battle for our country (Deut 20:3–7; 24:5);
- to be delivered from the anxiety and depression of frantically trying to be happy ("Are we having fun yet?") while being unable to keep from wondering what my life is for anyway but trusting

that the way of life has been revealed in the Torah of the one and only God,

- to live each day not with my hollow claim of innocence but with the assurance of God's forgiveness for my failings (Deut 9:8–29), and
- to live in the glad confidence that the LORD God of Israel is running the universe, and I'm not responsible for fixing all the world's troubles but set free to live responsibly in God's world;
- this is the "joy of your salvation," life in the here and now (Ps 51:12).

The lives of the saved people of God include both liberation *from* threats to life and freedom *for* service to others—being set free from the slavery that conditions me to think only of myself. The same Jesus who quotes Deuteronomy in response to the friendly Jewish teacher's question also responds to the inquiry of another Jewish leader in a way that speaks of "being saved," "entering the kingdom of God," and "entering life" as all referring to the same reality (Mark 10:17–31; cf. 9:42–46). Salvation is the gift of life in the here and now. Even when characterized as "eternal life," this refers not only to what happens to us when we die but to a quality of life—life lived in the trusting community of Israel, the saved people of God.

We Are the Elect, Chosen Community

To belong to Israel is to be saved. To be saved is to be chosen. Every word of Deuteronomy is addressed to Israel, the saved and chosen people of God. In the narrative world of Deuteronomy, everyone addressed by Moses was an Israelite by birth. Without being consulted, they have already been included. Before any Israelite had ever done anything, good or bad, they had already belonged to the chosen people (see ch. 10 in this volume on Paul's exposition of Deuteronomy in Rom 9–11). The exclusive basis for God's choice of Israel from all the peoples of the earth is God's love for his "treasured possession," on whom God had "set his heart" (Deut 4:37; 7:6, 7; 10:15; 14:2). We have already reminded ourselves that this language is continued in the New Testament, in which Jesus, Paul, and others take up Deuteronomy's language of election and apply it to the church (e.g., Matt 22:14; 24:24–31; Luke 18:7; John 13:18; 15:16, 19; Rom 8:33; 9:11, 18; 11:5, 28; Col 3:12; 1 Thess 1:4; 2 Tim 2:10; Titus 1:1; 1 Pet 1:2; 2:9; 2 Pet 1:10; 2 John 1, 13; Rev 17:14). The church is incorporated into Israel, the ongoing people of God—it does not "replace Israel"!

Paul famously elaborates this common New Testament perspective in Romans 9:10–13, where he quotes Malachi 1:2–3: "I have loved Jacob but I have hated Esau." It is important to understand that "Jacob" and "Esau" do not refer primarily to the individual twin boys, the sons of Isaac and Rebekah. "Jacob" is the Israelite people (Gen 32:24–28; Deut 32:9, 15; 33:4, 10), and "Esau" is Edom, the people of the Edomites (e.g., Gen 36:1, 8, 19; Deut 2:4, 5, 8, 12). These texts are talking about the sovereign God's choice of Israel for a special mission among the peoples of the earth.

Likewise, the binary declaration of YHWH's "love" and "hate" must be an instance of the common idiom in the Hebrew Bible, in which "love" means "choose" and "hate" means "not choose"—that is, "reject" in this neutral sense. This Hebrew linguistic usage is illustrated in, for example, John 12:25, the one loving/hating his life in this world, and in Matthew 6:24, where Jesus declares that no one can serve two masters but must love one and hate the other—that is, choose one with no emotional overtones of either affection or hostility. So also, in Luke 14:26–27, those who choose to follow Jesus must "hate" their family. The typical English translations do not express the biblical meaning: to choose / be chosen by Christ means no other loyalty may take priority over the God whose first commandment is "no other gods before me" (Exod 20:3). Discipleship is a matter of priorities. In regard to God's choosing the people of Israel but not choosing the Edomites, Deuteronomy specifically emphasizes not only that God loved both Jacob/Israel and Esau/Edom, as God loves all peoples, but that God was active in the history of the Edomites and gave their land to them, just as he did for Israel (Deut 2:4–8, 12, 22, 29). But God did not choose Esau and his descendants for the special role in the universal history of God's reconciliation of the world to himself. They were among God's peoples; they did not (yet) belong to the people of God. This is the meaning of "election." It has nothing to do with God arbitrarily selecting some individuals for salvation and others for damnation; it's a matter of choosing one people as the bearer and witness of God's purpose for all peoples.

God's election is no violation of human responsibility and freedom of choice. God's choice of us and our choice of God function on different planes. We are free and responsible, but as human beings, we cannot decide who our parents are, what family we are born into, or who our siblings and fellow citizens are. When, in Romans 9:18, God chooses whom he wills, it is an affirmation that God is God, not bound by the human scene. God is the Creator; the creature cannot argue with God as though Creator and creature are peers. This is the point of the potter analogy in

Romans 9:19–24 so problematic to modern and postmodern individualistic humans who think of themselves as autonomous. When Paul declares that from the same lump, the potter can make one pot for special and another for ordinary use, we may naturally object, "But I'm not a pot!" True enough, but Paul wants us to know that we are all nonetheless creatures, created by the One God; we did not decide to be born, cannot decide not to die, and cannot choose some other world in which to live our one and only life. Paul does not answer the question or respond to the objection; he does not allow the question in the first place. It is an honest question, but whether asked in anguish or disdain, it is not a question with which the *creature* can challenge the Creator. Whoever supposes that we humans are dealing with some Great Mystery of Being and that this possibly real Entity can be called to account by human beings with our own values, common sense, or sophisticated philosophical reason is thinking in terms of a god, idol, or spiritual world we have constructed, not the God revealed in the narrative world of Scripture. Especially as articulated in the sermons of Deuteronomy, God the Creator chooses whom he wills. This is a matter of the will of God, the *prothesis* (purpose) of God already represented in Romans 8:28, and those who are *called*, the covenant community of the people of God: "We know that in everything God works for good with those who love him, who are called according to his purpose" (RSV). Such language is the confessional language of those who speak from within the community of faith, not the objective language of the observer who claims to stand outside the different worlds projected by the culture and the Bible and judges between them by the canons of human reason. Such confessional language expresses gratitude for what God has done for "us" and is not making judgments about what God has not done for "them."

We Are a Covenant Community

We have discussed the nature of Israel as a covenant community in chapters 5 and 15 in this volume. Here we only need to remember that the concept of a "new covenant" was not devised by the Christian church but was already found in Jeremiah 31:31–34 as one of the images of the hope of Israel, the eschatologically renewed covenant. Believers in Jesus as the Messiah of Israel saw themselves as members of the covenant community of Israel, living in the time when God's promises are already dawning.

We Are a Holy Community

Holy means other, different, set apart for a sacred purpose. To refer to someone or to a group of people as holy has nothing to do with pretentious superpiety or hyperreligiosity; it means being *different* from the ordinary. When God is called "the Holy One of Israel" and when the worshipping congregation sings the praise of God in Reginald Heber's early nineteenth-century hymn "Holy, Holy, Holy," we are joining the eternal praise sung by the heavenly chorus of seraphim and cherubim: "Holy, holy, holy is the LORD of hosts; the whole earth is full of his glory" (Isa 6:3). God is worshipped not as the Great Goodie-Goodie but as the Transcendent One, the Creator who is enthroned beyond the creation, the One who is not a part of our world but the Wholly *Other*.

The Deuteronomic tradition assumes throughout that God is the Holy One (Deut 32:51; Josh 24:19; 1 Sam 2:2; 6:20), whose dwelling is not in a tent or temple in this world but a throne in heaven (Deut 26:15), whose thousands of heavenly attendants can be called his "holy ones" (Deut 33:2–3). The "holy ones" do not belong to this world, its culture, and its values; they are other, separate, and different, not fitting in. The first occurrence of "holy" in Deuteronomy is in the Decalogue: "Observe the sabbath day and keep it holy" (Deut 5:12). The Sabbath is identified not as morally superior but as *different*, a special day different from ordinary days and not to be confused with them. When the Deuteronomic teachers repeatedly refer to 'all Israel' as "the holy people of God," Israel is instructed to understand themselves as called and chosen for a special purpose, not to number themselves as simply one of the peoples of the earth. This is not, first, a matter of morality or ethics. To be the holy people of God is to be chosen, different, consecrated, set apart (Deut 7:6; 14:2, 21; 26:19; 28:9).

The Deuteronomic teachers designate '*all* Israel,' the people as a whole, as holy. This probably represents the more "democratic" E tradition transplanted from the north and incorporated into the developing D tradition (see ch. 6 in this volume) and contrasts with the understanding being advocated by their contemporary theological competitors, represented by P, the priestly tradition, in which it was primarily the Jerusalem priests who were set apart as holy. This explicit perspective of the E tradition, affirmed by the Deuteronomic teachers, is now found separately in Exodus 19:5–6: "Now therefore, if you obey my voice and keep my covenant, you shall be my treasured possession out of all the peoples. Indeed, the whole earth is mine, but you shall be for me a priestly kingdom and a holy nation. These are the words that you shall speak to the Israelites." In Deuteronomy's view, the holiness of the priesthood belongs not only to the official priests in Jerusalem and the whole tribe of Levi but to the people as a whole. It is this view of the E and D traditions that is taken up in the New Testament, where "saints" (*hagioi*, or holy ones) is applied not to hyperreligious people but to the church as a whole (cf., e.g., the discussion of 1 Pet 2:9–13 in ch. 11 in this volume). This affirmation of the "priesthood of all believers," found already in the Old Testament, is a claim not that individual believers "don't need a priest to pray for us, since we can go directly to God," but that we need, have, and are priests. The whole people of God is God's chosen and consecrated community that mediates between God and God's peoples, the non-Israelites, the nonchurch, the outsiders destined to finally all become insiders. 'All Israel,' including the Christian church, is the holy, priestly community entrusted with this mystery of the kingdom of God, witnessing to all the peoples of the earth, blessing them in God's name, interceding for them, and even sacrificing and suffering for them, as did the Messiah, the Great High Priest who is model and mentor for them (Heb 4–10). There are three things to note about Deuteronomy's understanding of the priestly ministry of the holy people of God, each of which is developed below:

- The "priesthood of all believers" by no means obviates the need for an order of specialized priests and Levites, about which Deuteronomy is particularly concerned to give instructions (see below in this chapter).
- Defining holiness in cultic terms does not deny its ethical importance but in fact enhances it (see ch. 17 in this volume).
- The holiness of the people of God is both gift and demand, both indicative and imperative, both the work of God in and among us and our own work in response to God's grace. Holiness is not an ideal or goal toward which Israel should strive but a reality already given by God. Holiness is not an effort to become something we are not but to recognize who we are as church members and to set our priorities and live consistently with our true identity. Ethics means not "Try a little harder to be a little better" but "Be who you are with grateful praise." When the author of Hebrews charges his readers, "Pursue peace with everyone, and the holiness without which no one will see the Lord" (Heb 12:14), church members are addressed as those who already belong to the holy people of God. This identity includes a job description.

We Are the Ecumenical Community

The 'all Israel' addressed by Moses is essentially an ecumenical, catholic community. *Oikoumenikos* refers to the whole inhabited earth; *katholikos* means to be universal, all-inclusive. The people listening to Moses do not think of themselves as individuals with their own personal faith who have decided to join up with Israel as a way of nourishing their private spirituality, nor do they think of independent congregations who may or may not develop formal or informal connections with other such congregations. Moses speaks to them as already one people. Israel was there first, before any of the tribes, before any individual Israelite. Israel did not come into being by having a group of individual Israelites get together and decide to form a "people of Israel." To share the faith of Israel confessed in the Shema—that the One God of the whole world is the LORD revealed in the history of Israel—means they already belong to the one people of God. They are not asked to *join* anything. They have already *been* joined to all those throughout the world who share their faith. The Deuteronomic teachers address 'all Israel' as gathered in one ecumenical council, composed, to be sure, of twelve different and sometimes warring tribes—those from eastern Jordan and those from western Jordan; those from North Israel and those from Judea; those biologically descended from Abraham, Isaac, and Jacob; and those who have been incorporated within Israel in the course of their long and varied journey through history. 'All Israel' was one but not homogenized—a tossed salad, not a melting pot.

In the history behind the text, the 'all Israel' addressed by Deuteronomy was in reality already a diaspora, scattered among the nations. Yet local customs and traditions were incorporated into the grand vision of 'all Israel,' and they were one people, neither a scattered group of struggling independent congregations trying to make it on their own nor a large congregation who might say, "We're doing quite well on our own, thank you." Both the story in the text and the story behind the text gave them an ecumenical self-understanding. According to Acts 2, devout Jews from every nation under heaven, coming from different cultures and speaking a variety of languages, respond in unison to the first proclamation of the gospel. Their response begins with the signature "we" of the whole people of God: "In our own languages we hear them speaking about God's deeds of power" (Acts 2:11). Awareness of this unity in variety, with heavy emphasis on the *unity* side of the phrase, became increasingly important for Israel's self-understanding and ethos/ethic.

We Are a Structured, Hierarchical Community

We are not a democracy. Deuteronomy presents the people of God as a hierarchical, monarchical community. Direction for the life of 'all Israel' proceeds from the Lord through Moses to the whole people as the Torah is taught, interpreted, and enforced by Levites, priests, judges, and other officers.

Deuteronomy conveys no sense of the church as a collection of individuals seeking a little companionship in their own "journey of faith," their own "search for God." Their identity is not as individuals seeking fellowship and a support group who work out their identity in a fellowship group of other seeking individuals. They are first God's creatures, and all other human beings are already their companions on life's journey. Those called into the people of God are members of the chosen, covenant community, confessing faith in the Lord in the words of the Shema, hearing the Word of God spoken through Moses on the plains of Moab, and finding the meaning of their individual lives in belonging to this missionary, priestly people. Listening to Deuteronomy, we hear ourselves addressed as all belonging to one people, with one book and one authoritative tradition (one ecumenical Tradition; several distinct, lowercase traditions). Loyalty to the One God, whose Torah is mediated by one book (with some variety in content and structure) and one authoritative tradition (with considerable variety held together in one history and one community), was then, through local community leadership, manifesting the unity in variety already modeled in canon and tradition. Moses's first words established a structured leadership that both assumed and insisted that to belong to 'all Israel' involved structural lines of authority and rejected an understanding in which each Israelite and each congregation "did what was right in their own eyes" (Judg 17:6; 21:25). To belong to the church means to belong to a structured, governed community.

To be sure, there is a place for individuality, democracy, and majority-rules governance in the life of the church, but the church as a whole, the one people of God, is not a democracy. Our bad experiences with this-worldly kings and queens should not make us hesitant or suspicious in speaking of the kingdom of God. We are a hierarchical, monarchical community that appropriately thinks of governance in top-down terms, not a grassroots discussion group, with everyone doing as they think best. The One God is the Creator, the Ancient of Days, the Almighty King who may be thought of as enthroned at a round table to discourage arguments over precedence among his subordinates but whose own chair is inscribed "The Buck Stops Here." The chair of the board owns at least

51 percent of the stock. The universe is not governed by a representative committee or plurality of minor deities and powers that share or compete for rulership. The LORD our God is One. To confess faith in the LORD, the God of Israel, is to declare that all things are ultimately in one hand, that the world and life are not a matter of negotiation with and among a variety of forces and powers. Israel's faith, honed to razor sharpness in Deuteronomy, is radical monotheism—in social and political terms, monarchy.

It is only because in this human world that there is no individual good enough, wise enough, and strong enough to be trusted with absolute power that democratic governments divide power into a system of checks and balances, in theory ultimately dependent on the will of the people. The Deuteronomic teachers are very aware of the problems involved in the concentration of human power in the hands of kings and priests. The extensive teaching in Deuteronomy 17–18 on the role of kings, priests, prophets, and judges in the life of Israel presents the people of God, seen from the human side, as a "constitutional monarchy" in which "power does not flow downward from a hierarchy; rather, governing elements operate alongside one another in parallel fashion."[3] Prophets and judges have priority over kings and priests in mediating the will of God. The people establish an independent judiciary answerable only to YHWH's revelation in the Torah (Deut 16:18–20; 17:8–13, which includes an appeals system and the first of Moses's acts in 1:9–18). Deuteronomy is insistent that the revelatory "chain of command" goes directly from God through the prophet Moses to 'all Israel.' The king has no special place; priests are included among the lay judges. All take their place among the people of God, to whom the revealed Torah is given.

Deuteronomy and the Deuteronomistic History preserve and report the historical reality that from the beginning, there had been more than one view of kingship in Israel (e.g., 1 Sam 7–12). Nonetheless, an individualism in which everyone "did what was right in their own eyes" is steadfastly rejected (Judg 17:6; 21:25). The thrust of the Deuteronomic teachers' whole theology is that the One God is not one power among the powers of this world but transcendent "above all earthly powers" (Martin Luther, in "A Mighty Fortress Is Our God"). Thus while God is the one true king of Israel (1 Sam 8, the "early source") who reluctantly permits Israel to have human kings, the retrospective Deuteronomic view, shaped by bitter experience, regards this king as only the imperfect agent of God's rule, a temporary subordinate whose power must be carefully restricted and who neither makes, interprets, nor enforces the law—a matter of the people's courts—but is to be constantly engaged in the study of God's revealed Torah, which is the final authority for him as for 'all Israel' (Deut 7:14–20). And so with all human and churchly claims to authority and power.

Deuteronomic theology thus joins with 'all Israel,' celebrated in the Psalms, praising the one true king of the universe and all its peoples, who is enthroned upon the praises of Israel (cf., e.g., Pss 10:16; 22:28; 24:10; 29:10; 44:4; 47:2, 6–8; 68:24; 74:12; 84:3; 93:1, 3; 96:10; 97:1, 6; 99:1; 103:19; 145:1, 13). This theology of the kingdom of God reaches its climax in the message of Jesus, who made the present-and-coming kingdom the core of his proclamation and who taught his followers to pray "Thy kingdom come, thy will be done on earth. . . ."

'All Israel' affirms that we live in a hierarchical monarchy, a world and a church ruled by the One God. The whole church accepts the commission of the risen Lord in the final words of the Gospel of Matthew, prefaced by "All authority in heaven and on earth has been given to me" (Matt 28:18). The question, of course, is how this authority is mediated to the people of God and functions so that they can hear, understand, and obey their Lord in personal, family, church, social, and political life. In Deuteronomy, Moses does not back away from this task of the preacher and teacher; he grapples with it head-on. The following are the results of the Deuteronomic teachers' reflections:

1. The people of God are called to live according to the will of God, the LORD of Israel and the One True God of all the world, as a witness to all peoples.
2. The will of God is not discovered by human searching but is revealed through God's prophet Moses. Israel is contrasted with the gamut of mediums, soothsayers, spiritual advisers, mediums, and wizards who claim—mostly with unpretending sincerity—to help people discover the spiritual powers at work in the world and in their own lives. For the Deuteronomic teachers, God communicates his will by sending prophets to Israel who reveal the meaning of the history they are living through. Like the king and priest of these two chapters devoted to Israel's leadership (Deut 17–18), "the prophet" refers not to an individual but to the "institution" of prophecy, the succession of prophets God sends to Israel. Even in Israel, some are sincere but false prophets

(1 Kgs 22; Jer 23). True prophets are "like Moses" (Deut 18:15), and none has arisen greater than Moses (Deut 34:10).

3. The Deuteronomic teachers already perceive, and encourage us to recognize, that the will of the One God of point 1 above is absolute; there is already an element of ambiguity and relativity at point 2. Only the Decalogue was heard by 'all Israel' at Horeb and written by God himself (4:10–13; 5:22; 9:9–10:5); all the rest was given by God through the prophet Moses. But from the very beginning, these prophetic words of the supreme prophet of the One True God given to 'all Israel' were fused with the words of human preachers and teachers:

> Then *Moses and the elders of Israel* charged all the people as follows: Keep the entire commandment that I am commanding you today. . . .
>
> Then *Moses and the Levitical priests* spoke to all Israel, saying: Keep silence and hear, O Israel! This very day you have become the people of the LORD your God. (Deut 27:1, 9)

It is not clear how we later hearers of the text of Deuteronomy are to picture this. Did Moses, the elders, and the Levitical priests speak in unison? Antiphonally? Did Moses deliver the Word of God, which the elders and/or Levites then interpreted to the people, on the model of Nehemiah 8:9? In any case, this is a symbolic, not literal, picture. What is clear is that the Deuteronomic teachers want their contemporaries and following generations to know that the faithful preachers and teachers they hear in worship and instruction mediate the Word of God to them. They should not conceptualize the event of the church's preaching and teaching as merely explaining what God once said and "how it applies to us." Worshipping hearers and engaged students in 'all Israel' are themselves addressed in their own present by the revelatory Word of God, and this has been the case from the very beginning. The church is a hierarchical community ruled by the Word of God, which is always heard in the present as the words of the church itself, spoken by its authorized leaders and evaluated and discerned by the whole community. For Christians, this paradigm finds its ultimate fulfillment in the incarnation. The Absolute Word enters and is manifest in the relativities of human flesh (John 1:1, 14).

In all this, the Deuteronomic teachers do not provide a schematic process and structure for practical implementation of their theology, as though the hermeneutical methods used by local interpreters were instructions and patterns revealed directly from heaven. Within the overall hierarchical structure that begins with the will of the One God mediated by prophetic revelation, the community knows itself to be the one ecumenical community of the people of God. It knows its identity not in terms of tribes, congregations, or denominations but as 'all Israel.' This self-understanding includes an awareness of itself as a community structured, authorized, and empowered to discern and enact the will of God for every culture and changing situation in which it is called to be the people of God.

We Are a Worshipping Community

Neither Deuteronomy nor any biblical text contains the simple positive command "Thou shalt worship." Biblical authors share the assumption of the ancient world in general that all human beings worship. It is inconceivable that anyone should suppose they are self-sufficient, in charge of the world and their own life. So also Paul, presenting the fundamental basis of the Christian gospel, does not depict the essential human problem as a secularized society that no longer worshipped but assumes a human race that had "exchanged the truth about God for a lie and worshiped and served the creature rather than the Creator, who is blessed forever! Amen" (Rom 1:25). Deuteronomy is not so much a list of laws but a series of three sermons in a worship setting, passionately urging Israel to worship YHWH and instructing them in what it means to worship the One True God.

Even the "laws" (i.e., Torah, or instruction) often deal with worship, and *all* the legal instruction is preceded by the foundational command forbidding the worship of self-made idols and commanding worship of the LORD alone (Deut 5:6–9). Deuteronomy is a worship book that includes laws, not a law book with rules about worship. Deuteronomy is not a worship book in the sense that it specifies all the details of authentic worship. It is not comparable to the instructions for early Christian worship represented by the second-century CE *Didache* and book 5 of the fourth-century CE *Apostolic Constitutions*, nor is it an ancient Jewish version of later Christian liturgical manuals, such as the Anglican Book of Common Prayer. Nonetheless, Deuteronomy is permeated by the concern that the whole life of Israel be framed by and filled with worship of the LORD. If we mentally walk through the narrative world projected by Deuteronomy, we recognize that Moses's three sermons are replete with reverberations of a worship service:

Chapters 4–11

This proclamation and exhortation rehearses the hearer's participation in saving history, inviting worshippers to hear and obey.

Chapters 12–26

These instructions for the life of such a people focus on their worship life, such as the pilgrimage festivals and maintenance of the holiness of the community.

Chapter 28

In this chapter, by far the longest in Deuteronomy, the reading audience hears pronouncements of the LORD's blessing on those who hear and obey and "fifty-three verses of curses" on the unfaithful and disobedient. We are accustomed to thinking of blessings in a worship setting; Deuteronomy supplies the corresponding curses, like the Lukan Jesus (Luke 6:20–26).

Chapters 29–30

The covenant is renewed; the people of God make a renewed commitment to the covenant stipulations and make provision for accepting new members into the covenant community.

Chapter 31

The whole Scripture is read repeatedly to 'all Israel.'

Chapter 32

The service concludes with a song to be learned and sung by future generations as testimony against them if they fail to live by the covenant stipulations.

Chapter 33

Moses pronounces a concluding blessing on each of the tribes of 'all Israel.'

Chapter 34

The preacher dies, having given his life for the people, who have entered to worship and now depart to serve, accompanied by the Word of the LORD they have heard and interiorized.

We may be stunned by the prominence of worship and empowered to hear by the fact that no law book has any of these features. There are no law books that laugh and sing. Deuteronomy is a worship book.

Daily Worship, 24/7

To worship is to honor and serve someone as lord. By pointing to YHWH as the One LORD, Deuteronomy insists that there is only one who can be served in this absolute way. Worship is not simply an attitude but action; worship is *service* in the everyday world and in particular acts that praise and honor the Lord as God. In Romans 12:1–2, Paul begins his explication of the Christian life that proceeds from the faith he has expounded in the first eleven chapters of the letter: "I appeal to you therefore, brothers and sisters, by the mercies of God, to present your bodies as a living sacrifice, holy and acceptable to God, which is your spiritual worship." This was already the Old Testament understanding of worship. Jesus, Paul, and early Christianity did not "spiritualize" the sacrificial worship of ancient Israel; worship was already a matter of everyday life and work in the Old Testament.[4]

Weekly Worship: The Sabbath

We who think of worship as a Sunday activity, "going to church," might suppose that in ancient Israel, too, faithful Israelites went to worship every Sabbath in the synagogue. In the Second-Temple Judaism that emerged after Deuteronomy's time, each Sabbath, faithful Jews regularly attended the synagogue as a place of nonsacrificial prayer and teaching, the practice adopted and adapted by early Christianity as pictured in the New Testament (e.g., Luke 4, Acts 13). In the time of Deuteronomy, Israel celebrated the weekly Sabbath in the context of the family, but there would not be weekly community worship until centuries later.

In Deuteronomy, every day is regarded as worship in the sense of service and devotion to God, but the Sabbath is to be observed as a distinctive, holy day. In the comprehensive biblical narrative, the Creator himself ceased from work on the seventh day, but the Sabbath command is not given to humans until the time of the exodus. Even then, the command is given not to humanity in general but exclusively to Israel. While other peoples can be condemned for acts of killing and stealing, no non-Israelite is ever reproached for not keeping the Sabbath. In Deuteronomy, Israel's weekly Sabbath worship is a witness to the historical saving act of God that created the saved people (Deut 5:15). It so happens that on the day I write this, the *New York Times* has an article about Elie Kligman, a talented Jewish baseball player who must decide whether to sign a fat major league contract that requires him to play on the Sabbath. The *Times* article mostly revolves around personal religion—as though such religious convictions may be admired and respected, a good thing, but there's no need to be fanatical about it. But Mr. Kligman's choice is not about his personal religious commitments in the sense of what good they do for him. He belongs to a religious community called to worship (and observe dietary rules) in a certain way that calls attention to the separateness of Israel. Observance of Sabbath rules is more important than six-figure salaries. Such lives function as a testimony to the rest of the world of the truth of their faith in what God is up to in the world.

In all Israel's traditions, the Sabbath is a day when ordinary work ceases. It is a day of rest, refreshment, and family time—a gift from God and a testimony to God's grace. It is not cheap grace but a gift *to* God. Refraining from work for one day every week decreases one's productivity and profit by 14 percent, a "tithe plus" of time Israel gives back to God, cutting into their disposable income and giving an advantage to their commercial and military competitors. Later Israelites were sometimes reluctant to worship God in a way that affected their bank account (cf., e.g., Neh 13:15–21), but worship was not only for the benefit of the worshipper; Sabbath observance was an essential practice in Israel's mission to the nations.

Sabbath observance is worship also in the sense that it is a witness to the holiness of the people of God, a foretaste of the quality of saved life in the here and now, an anticipation of the goal of life and history. In the Deuteronomic version of the Decalogue, the commentary on the Sabbath command is the longest of all, specifying that Israel is to observe the Sabbath because they are freed slaves, redeemed by the LORD from the nonlife of slavery in Egypt. Slaves must work all day, every day, seven days a week, fifty-two weeks a year, with no life of their own. Liberation meant that they could catch their breath, relax, and *live.* This Sabbath rest (*noakh*) not only means restoration and refreshment of bodily, mental, and emotional vigor and release from constant, life-draining physical labor. Sabbath rest means more than survival. Sabbath meals are feasts—not gluttonous but good meals shared at Israel's pilgrim festivals in the promised land oozing with milk and honey, where one no longer must frugally ration the available food but can "eat and be satisfied," enjoying the festivity of a good dinner party. Our eyes and ears may skip easily over such details in the biblical narrative as Ruth 2:14: "At mealtime Boaz said to her, 'Come here, and eat some of this bread, and dip your morsel in the sour wine.' So she sat beside the reapers, and he heaped up for her some parched grain. *She ate until she was satisfied*, and she *had some left over*." Most of the world, for most of its history, has never seen a billboard proclaiming, "All you can eat, $12.95." Being satisfied, having some left over to share, is reserved for rare, festival occasions (remember, "festival" = "feast"). This is the kind of life celebrated weekly by Israel as a testimony to and in anticipation of the good life the faithful God promises to everyone.

This dimension of the biblical meaning of rest points to a trusting dependence on the faithful God who continues to run the universe even if I take a day off. In the Sermon on the Mount, Jesus proclaims this relaxed, trusting freedom from anxiety as the disciples' heritage (Matt 6:19–34). Sabbath rest is taken by an early Christian teacher as a one-syllable summary of salvation, the *rest* promised to the people of God (Heb 4:1–9). Such rest is not mere inactivity but the low-key, exuberant joy of those who confidently live in the glorious freedom of the children of God (Rom 8:21), the down payment on the Sabbath freedom God will grant to the whole creation (Rom 8:18–25; cf. v. 21). In Deuteronomy, those who know themselves to be ex-slaves liberated by God share this liberty. In Deuteronomy, Sabbath rest is to include male and female slaves, and the farm animals likewise must not be forced to work unceasingly. Although Sabbath observance did not involve sacrifice or "going to church," the Sabbath rest epitomized central aspects of Israel's worship: family celebration, thanksgiving, feasting, experiential instruction in the meaning of belonging to the people of God, and inclusive openness and acceptance of the outsider resident alien (*gēr*) and the slave. The full experience of 'all Israel's' worship was actualized three times each year in weeklong pilgrimage festivals.

Every Year: Sacrifice and Pilgrimage Festivals

In the life the Deuteronomic teachers envisioned for Israel in the promised land, Israel's community worship orbited around three pilgrimage festivals to be celebrated by 'all Israel.' Since each of these festivals involves sacrificial killing of animals (unlike the worship implicit in everyday life and faithful observance of the Sabbath), we first note a few characteristics of sacrificial worship in the ancient world in general:

- The practice was understood by various groups and individuals in widely different ways. The sacrifice on the altar could represent a bribe or payment to the deity or the feeding of a hungry god who enjoyed the taste and smell of burning meat. Sacrifice was sometimes made to appease an angry God or to avert potential or coming catastrophe; to ensure productive fields, herds, flocks, and wives; or to secure victory in battle; in extreme cases, it even involved the sacrifice of one's own children for "the good of the country." Sacrificial worship was mostly done without reflection or question, as a cultural tradition that they continued just because they were religious, and that's the way their religion worked.

- Somewhere buried in many of these intertwined explanations or assumptions was the unarticulated human need to acknowledge one's dependence on the divine powers that give us life and to express gratitude. Studies of the history of religion, reflected in the earliest descriptions of human religion in the biblical narrative, point to gratitude, the gift nature of sacrifice, as its central meaning—not obedience to a command, payment of a debt, or atonement for sins but *gratitude*. Both Cain and Abel, different as they were, testify to the fundamental human need to bring a gift to God (Gen 4:1–7). Without any biblical command about sacrifice, the act of sacrificial giving actualizes our human need to give something *back*, even to enter into and maintain a personal relationship to the deity who does in some sense need us, just as we need God. In the words of Martin Buber,

> You know always in your heart that you need God more than everything; but do you not know too that God needs you—in the fullness of His eternity needs you? . . .
>
> Two great servants pace through the ages, prayer and sacrifice. The man who prays pours himself out in unrestrained dependence, and knows that he has—in an incomprehensible way—an effect upon God, even though he obtains nothing from God; for when he no longer desires anything for himself he sees the flame of his effect burning at its highest.—And the man who makes sacrifice?—I cannot despise him, this upright servant of former times, who believed that God yearned for the scent of his burnt-offering. In a foolish but powerful way he knew that we can and ought to give to God. This is known by him, too, who offers up his little will to God and meets Him in the grand will. "Thy will be done," he says, and says no more; but truth adds for him, "through me whom Thou needest."[5]

Although neither Buber nor Deuteronomy encourages us to define the faith of Israel in cultural terms, the warmth of Buber's affirmation of human, reverential longing also radiates from Deuteronomy's instruction about sacrificial worship—worship of the God who chose Israel because of his own love and grace and part of the response of loving God with all our heart and soul and might (Deut 6:4–6).

The following observations are intended to enhance our hearing of Deuteronomy's particular interpretation of sacrificial worship:

1. In accordance with God's command, Israel's worship necessarily involved the sacrifice of animals, for which the divinely revealed Torah gave specific instructions. Throughout the ancient Near East, virtually all animal slaughter was as such a religious act, ritually performed by authorized persons (including the patriarch, or pater familias). All meat that appeared on the dinner table had been killed in worship to some god or another. In early Israel, ritual sacrificial slaughter was performed in the household or at the local shrine staffed by Levitical priests.
2. In Josiah's 621 BCE, reformation sparked by the (re)discovery of the book of the Torah, ritual animal sacrifice, and therefore legitimate community worship was limited to the three pilgrimage festivals to the central shrine in Jerusalem: Passover / Unleavened Bread, Weeks (Pentecost), and Booths (Tabernacles). The centralization of legitimate worship in Jerusalem was a radical and controversial decision. Intended to curb the Canaanization of local worship, it meant not only that the local shrines could no longer serve as community worship centers but also that all animal slaughter outside Jerusalem was now no longer part of a specific religious ritual (Deut 12:1–28; 2 Kings 22–23). Animals could be killed for food, but sacrifice of animals as a special act of worship required a pilgrimage to Jerusalem, where the sacrifice could be supervised by properly ordained priests and safeguarded from (further) accommodation to Canaanite culture.
3. We know from the Old Testament itself and from extracanonical materials from Ugarit that each of Israel's major religious festivals had been celebrated in Canaan centuries before the emergence of Israel in the land. The common denominator of the varieties of Canaanite religion was the celebration of the powers of nature that gave fertility to fields, flocks, and family under the aegis of the Baals worshipped in the Canaanite cults. Each of the major religious festivals of Canaanite culture was associated with a week of harvest in spring, summer, and fall.
4. Israel adopted and adapted the religious festivals of Canaan in ways that expressed their own faith. The principal, fundamental difference between Canaanite religion and Israelite faith is often expressed in one word: historicization. One could also say that in Israel's worship, Baal, lord of nature and himself a part of nature, was replaced by YHWH, the Creator who is Lord of the universe and its history. Israel's faith was the response to the

> revelation of God's mighty saving acts in history, not the discovery of the spiritual realities in nature and in ourselves. Thus while the *Passover / Unleavened Bread* festival may involve the same ritual acts in Canaanite religion and in Israel's worship, in Israel the Passover is done "for the LORD your God," not for the lord of nature. Here, it is helpful to remember the fundamental distinction proclaimed in the Shema between the personal God who has a personal name (pronounced "the LORD" out of reverence) and "the Lord" of the Baal cult, where "Lord" is a title, not a personal name (see ch. 3 in this volume).

In Israel's story, the blood smeared on the doorway is not to protect Israel from evil spirits that are part of the annual cycle of nature and the pattern of nomadic life year in and year out. The sacrifice of *Passover* lambs bears witness to the story of the once-and-for-all act of God when Egypt was judged and Israel was delivered. Israel ate unleavened bread not as an annual ritual of the agricultural calendar but because they left hurriedly in the night, fleeing their Egyptian overlords, before the dough had time to rise. So also the rough shelters they lived in during the festival of *Booths* (Tabernacles) were not part of the customs of the agricultural year. Booths was understood historically as recalling Israel's exodus experience of living in the wilderness. In the Old Testament itself, the feast of *Weeks* (Pentecost) manifests only the rudiments of historical reinterpretation. The cultic calendars associate the festival with the Sinai events. Later Jewish tradition, which influenced the New Testament interpretation of Pentecost, specifically identified Weeks as the festival celebrating God's gift of the Torah. This understanding was in the background of the Pentecost story in Acts 2, where the Torah merges with the Christian gospel.

Like earlier Israel and Judaism, the Christian church has also adopted and adapted cultural elements into its theology and worship. From the beginning, the annual Christmas and Easter celebrations incorporated aspects of the surrounding culture in order to express and communicate its faith. While neither Christmas nor Easter originated simply as early Christianity's adoption of pagan religious festivals, these key events in the liturgical year can easily be so obscured by layers of cultural veneer that the Christian gospel represented by the birth, death, and resurrection of Jesus can hardly shine through. Christmas imagery and sermons can appropriately and powerfully utilize the turn from darkness to light inherent in the good news of the birth of the Messiah that happens in the natural world at the time of the winter solstice, but this must not become simply a Christian adaptation of the annual victory of light over darkness celebrated in many of the world's religions, ancient and modern. Christian faith celebrates the once-and-for-all Christ event, the advent of the Light of the World in the historical event of the birth of Jesus, the incarnation of "the true light, which enlightens everyone, [that] was coming into the world" (John 1:9). All Christian preachers and teachers are aware of the danger of the "commercialization of Christmas," when businesses look forward to a "good Christmas" to redeem lagging sales of previous months and both gift givers and gift receivers become depressed and wearied by advertising hype and manipulation of must-have gifts. But Christians need bear no malice against Santa (still faintly Christian), the little drummer boy or girl, or Rudolf, for even amid these trappings, the light of God's saving event in sending the Messiah still shines through, and the Deuteronomic teachers might well join in the Christmas pageant and parties.

The Easter celebration—when the spring festivals of nature religions of the Northern Hemisphere, ancient and modern, celebrate the annual "birth of new life"—might be another matter. The Christian celebration of Easter is not a spring festival worshipping the fertility powers of nature; it proclaims and rejoices in the once-and-for-all event of the resurrection of Jesus. This does not necessarily mean that Christian preachers must inveigh against eggs and bunnies, cultural fertility symbols long associated with spring festivals by peoples of all religions and none (again, only in the northern half of the planet). Here, the Deuteronomists (and the New Testament!) might have more to teach us. The scandal of the cross cannot be allowed to disappear (Gal 5:11); neither can the centrality of the cross and the resurrection as actual events in the core of the gospel (1 Cor 15:3–5) be replaced by inspirational chirpiness (web pages such as "150 Inspirational Spring Quotes for a New Life" are easy enough to find). Here the Deuteronomic teachers insist that the worshipping community stand with the traditional historical faith in God's saving acts, even though they, too, might join in the gleeful laughter of children at the annual Sunday school Easter Egg Hunt.

Noting some of the specifics of Deuteronomy's interpretation of sacrificial worship helps us avoid hearing all biblical texts about sacrifice through one cultural filter, ancient or modern:

- In Deuteronomy, sacrificial worship is praise and thanksgiving. A part of the sacrificed animal is offered on the altar, but most of it is consumed in a feast by the worshippers themselves, a special thanksgiving dinner that celebrates the goodness of life.

- In Deuteronomy, sacrificial worship is a time of inclusive fellowship. The worship celebration includes everyone—the whole family, the servants and slaves, the resident alien. They are not just given survival rations, but they join with 'all Israel' in the extravagance provided by God and celebrated in worship (see "Weekly Worship: The Sabbath" in this chapter).
- In Deuteronomy, sacrificial worship is part of the community's provision for the needy—the poor, the widow, the orphan—who are included in the celebration of the larger family of 'all Israel.' There is enough for all.
- In Deuteronomy, sacrifice was not an atonement for sins. This priestly interpretation, found in the detailed instructions of Leviticus 1–7, has its own validity, is incorporated in some streams of New Testament theology, and requires its own hermeneutical approach. This understanding of sacrifice, however, is entirely absent from Deuteronomy, which has nothing to say about Yom Kippur (Day of Atonement) and has no daily sacrifice in the tabernacle or temple, no sin offerings, and no guilt offerings. Though the vocabulary of sin, sinfulness, and God's grace and forgiveness is common in Deuteronomy and the Deuteronomistic History, acceptance before God is mediated not by atoning sacrifice but by repentance and prayer (cf., e.g., Deut 9:18–20, 27; 20:18; 1 Sam 12:23; 2 Sam 12:13; repeatedly in 1 Kgs 8:30–50). God's people do sin. Sin is taken seriously. God does forgive, and God's forgiveness is not cheap grace. Grace is always amazing grace. But in Deuteronomy, Israel does not come to worship with accumulated sins to be atoned for or covered by the act of sacrifice. Israel lives each day not with the assumption that they are innocent but in the glad confidence that they are forgiven sinners. Sacrifice is the celebration of a good thanksgiving dinner, not lamentation or bargaining with God about our sins.
- In Deuteronomy, sacrificial worship includes Israel's obligation to support the priestly and teaching ministry (Deut 18:13). It turns out that Deuteronomy's instruction not to muzzle the ox treading out the grain, interpreted by Paul as God's command for the Christian community to provide for the livelihood of Christian ministers, does in fact grasp a Deuteronomic concern (Deut 25:4; 1 Cor 9:8–12; see ch. 17 in this volume). For the Deuteronomic

teachers, sacrificial giving is right because it helps give needy people a decent life and pays the salary of the church's teaching ministry. This, too, is worship.

We Are a Formative, Nurturing Community

Dennis T. Olson makes a compelling argument that the appropriate genre niche for Deuteronomy is not law but *catechesis*: "Deuteronomy understands the law and the commandments primarily in the context not of a courtroom but a classroom."[6] Deuteronomy does not distinguish sharply between worship and religious education, preacher and teacher, sanctuary and classroom. The class is in a worship context; worship includes teaching. The rituals of worship have an inherent, sacramental meaning but also exercise a pedagogical function. Part of the reason we perform these rituals is so that worshippers—and not only the children among them—can ask, "What is the meaning of the decrees and the statutes and the ordinances?" (Deut 6:20). The worship service—liturgy and sermon—functions not only to raise such questions but to provide nourishing substance, teaching the content of the faith by which the community lives.

Deuteronomy thus has a penetrating concentration on the church's task to nurture the faith of its members and hand on this faith to the next and succeeding generations:

> Take to heart all the words that I am giving in witness against you today; give them as a command to your children, so that they may diligently observe all the words of this law.
>
> This is no trifling matter for you, but rather your very life. (Deut 32:46–47)

Moses had received the transforming, nurturing, and guiding Word directly from God. Moses is *the* prophet. None greater had appeared in Israel's history (Deut 34:10). Those who appear after him are measured by the Mosaic standard; they must be "like Moses" (Deut 18:15–22). But Moses is also the *teacher* par excellence. Moses is never called a teacher in Genesis–Numbers, but Deuteronomy emphasizes that at Israel's beginnings, there stood not only a prophet but a teacher, a role assigned to Moses by God at Sinai (Deut 4:14; 5:28). Moses's words were handed down not as prophecy but as Torah, the teaching. Preaching and teaching are inseparable; teaching is a component of the preaching ministry. The prophetic Word is to accompany Israel through all generations, under the care of Israel's teachers. In his last words to 'all Israel,' Moses not only speaks to the assembled multitudes himself but joins his voice with that of *Joshua* (Deut 32:44). The Word of God that Israel is to hear for all coming generations is the direct voice mediated by Moses, but Moses's voice is itself mediated by Joshua, who is equipped and authorized for that role: "Joshua son of Nun was full of the spirit of wisdom, because Moses had laid his hands on him; and the Israelites obeyed him, doing as the LORD had commanded Moses" (Deut 34:9). It is important for future generations of Israel to know that their faith is not second- or thirdhand, that they themselves continue to be addressed by the original revelation of the Word of God that continues in the life of the community of faith. But as is the case with the worship life of the community, the educational responsibility cannot be delegated to religious specialists but rests on the community as a whole, which emerges especially in the family, the festivals, and the roles of priests, Levites, and elders.

The family is central in the religious education of the present and coming generations. This formative communication of the faith happens in everyday family conversation, not as a separate category of "church talk." Families did not have their own copies of the Bible, a possibility that would not emerge in anyone's imagination until the invention of printing in the fifteenth century CE. The Word was passed on and around orally, formally in cultic settings and informally in the life of the family. We recall that the Shema is immediately followed by

> Keep these words that I am commanding you today in your heart.
> Recite them to your children and talk about them when you are at home and when you are away, when you lie down and when you rise.
> Bind them as a sign on your hand, fix them as an emblem on your forehead,
> and write them on the doorposts of your house and on your gates. (Deut 6:6)

"Keep these words . . . in your heart" means simply to keep them in your mind, in your memory, to *know them by heart.* Personal copies of Scripture and libraries of multiple scrolls were the prerogatives of very wealthy individuals and communities. The words of Scripture are not necessarily to be intentionally memorized and their recitation drilled into children, but the words and images of the Bible are to permeate everyday family talk in such a way that children grow up within the world of the biblical narrative and precepts, which they absorb into mind, heart, and life

(Deut 6:7–9; Ps 1:1–2). A few choice verses are symbolically attached to the doorposts of the house; every time anyone goes in or out of the house, it is through a portal framed by the faith of Israel. However, "doorposts of your . . . gates" refers not to the family home—houses did not have lawns with gates—but to the town or city gates. The public life had not only the Ten Commandments placarded publicly but the whole of the Torah, available to be read and pondered by all who could read or be read to. This is already a visionary picture, difficult to imagine literally, but it communicates the significance of the Torah for Israel's public life as well as family and personal life, which were all of one piece.

Israel's worship festivals, held three times each year, provided settings for intensive education in the Scripture and traditions of Israel. Though adopted from the Canaanite religious year, they were historicized by Israel's teachers to become teaching occasions. During the festivals, Israel's story and Torah were dramatized, taught, and rehearsed. Think of a family church camp held three times each year, totaling more than two weeks, in contrast with an occasional (or even regular) half-hour Sunday school lesson![7]

Local priests, Levites, and elders were charged with giving guidance and instruction to 'all Israel.' Deuteronomy does not provide logistical procedures and details for implementing this vision, which is left to the particular communities of later generations, but the grand vision is clear: the responsibilities of parents and the function of festivals are not left to haphazard individual or congregational initiatives but involve the execution of a comprehensive program of educating each Israelite generation in the faith for their own good, the good of generations to come, and the facilitation of Israel's mission in the world.

The final, canonical form of Deuteronomy was composed and promulgated during a time when the status and role of Israel's priests was hotly debated. Deuteronomy comes down on the side of full clergy status for all Levites. All Levites are priests, not laymen or "staff" as opposed to "ministers." Their primary job is to teach the faith. The Levites in Deuteronomy are authorized, qualified, and paid teachers of Israel, charged to hand on the faith and guard Israel against becoming victims of the local cultural religion (Deut 33:8–10). The Deuteronomic teachers want to instruct 'all Israel' that they have authorized and qualified ministers and that all bear the same title on their office door: "Minister of Education."

The Deuteronomic teachers feature such local minister-teachers in the grand vision they want to impress on our collective memory and imaginations. The time for Moses's death draws near. He will not be permitted to enter the promised land with Israel; he will depart to die alone and be buried by the LORD in an unmarked grave. He commits the theological nurture and pastoral care of Israel to their future leaders (31:9–13).

The whole Torah is to be read to all Israel in the context of the fall festival, the "camp meeting" in which Israel dwells in "booths." It's the annual family church camp; intensive instruction to all Israel in the whole Torah is given every seven years in a rustic worship setting. The implementation of this scene envisioned for the future life of Israel in the land is left to the reading audience. But the grand vision itself must not be lost: God has revealed the way of life for the church. This revealed Word of God continues to be available in the Scripture. The Israelite teachers do not urge their listening audience to "read their Bibles" privately, piecemeal, at their own discretion. They *hear, together* (including men, women, children, and *gerim*), *the whole of God's revealed Word* every seven years. In an average lifetime, each member of the people of God hears "the whole Bible" seven or eight times in the festive context of the celebrating, worshipping community. Israel's preachers and teachers, themselves called to live in The Story, are charged to keep the whole Torah ever before the community of faith. If this Torah is true, it is the meaning of their lives and ours (32:47).

We Are the Evangelistic Community, Entrusted with the Gospel

Deuteronomy is for insiders, to ripen/mature/enable/empower/equip them to live in the land as the people of God. But the revelation is not for themselves alone. They are entrusted with the gospel (1 Thess 2:4). Paul was challenged, "If God loves everyone equally, and if both Jews and gentiles have all been unfaithful to God's will, what difference does it make whether or not I belong to Israel, the chosen people of God?" His response, developed at length in Romans, is this: "In the first place the Jews were entrusted with the oracles of God" (Rom 3:2). The revelation of God entrusted to the people of God does not belong to the church; it is God's gift to all humanity, entrusted to the church. The church's religious gaze is not turned inward on their individual spirituality or congregational success but turned outward to all people, all humanity, all God's peoples. Individuals may decide whether they can get excited about "evangelism" and "missions," but Deuteronomy wants us to know that the 'all Israel' to which we belong has been a missionary, evangelistic community from the very beginning. Israel exists not for itself but as part of God's plan for the ultimate blessing of all peoples (Gen 12:1–3). To belong to the church is to belong to an evangelistic, missionary community that participates in God's mission to the world.

To be sure, Moses does not charge the Israelites to go door-to-door when they get to the promised land, inviting Canaanite neighbors to attend Israel's festivals or trying to convince the Canaanites to transfer their membership to Israel. Nonetheless, Israel is to live its life before God with the awareness that the whole world is watching, that non-Israelite nations will recognize true wisdom and justice when they see it and will be attracted to it (Deut 4:5–8). Human beings, as such, want to *belong*. Moses does not send Israel across the Jordan to convert Canaanites to Judaism. But as the holy people of God among God's peoples in the whole world, Israel is to manifest this divine lure in their personal, social, and political lives.

During the exile, prophets such as the anonymous disciple of Isaiah who composed Isaiah 40–55 had taught exiled Israel to see themselves, in their situation as a tiny minority community in a strange land, as witnesses to the Creator God's purpose for the whole world (Isa 43:10, 12; 44:8). Seen in a global context, this, of course, has always been the situation of the people of God. Like all God's peoples, Israel has the light of the Creator God, whose first words in the Bible were "let there be light" (Gen 1:3; Isa 45:7). But as the people of God, Israel has been entrusted with the revelatory light of God's purpose in history, the light that reveals God's character and purpose. In this sense, Israel has the evangelistic and missionary task of being a "light to the nations" (Isa 42:6; 49:6; 51:4; cf. Matt 5:14–16). This mission cannot be entered into lightly or unadvisedly; it may call for particular acts of service, even suffering, and possibly death. Israel, the same servant of God that is to be the bearer of God's revelatory light to all the other peoples of God, also suffers on behalf of the nations not yet included in 'all Israel' (Isa 42:6; 52:13–53:12; cf. Matt 16:16–18). The Deuteronomic teachers seem to have been influenced by this exilic prophet in their understanding of the identity and mission of the people of God. It is easy to imagine Israel's response to Moses on the plains of Moab: "Whoa! I didn't know I was getting into something like this. Sounds highly theoretical, theological, speculative. I just wanted to get out of the slavery of making bricks for pharaoh's big hotels, the rat race of trying to make a living, to be free to do my own thing in the land of the free and the home of the brave. Now you're not just trying to get me to join some mission project but telling me I already belong to a group that's supposed to be concerned about the whole world?" Yet this evangelistic, missionary vision is indeed what Moses proclaims, and not just as his own do-gooder ideal, his own take on "the meaning of church membership," but as the revealed Word of God, the purpose of the exodus and the calling and formation of the covenant people.

We ourselves might ask, "Even if this is true, is it right and fair?" Shouldn't we tell people what they're signing on for when they leave Egypt and join the church? Before we answer too quickly, we might study the Gospels more closely with this question in mind. All four Gospels, in their different ways, adopt the God → Moses → exodus → Israel pattern for their understanding of the meaning of Jesus Christ and his call to discipleship.

Matthew begins the story with Abraham and then pictures the birth of Jesus like the birth of Moses, with the evil king trying to kill him. Like Israel, Jesus goes down to Egypt and returns, passing through the waters of baptism as Moses and Israel passed through the waters of the Reed Sea. Jesus's forty days of testing in the wilderness correspond to Moses's and Israel's forty years of testing in the wilderness (they failed; Jesus was victorious). As Moses delivered God's Torah to all Israel at Mount Sinai, so Jesus's inaugural Sermon on the Mount interprets the law of God.

As Jesus begins his ministry—*before* he delivers the Sermon on the Mount about the nature of discipleship, *before* he sends the disciples out on a preaching mission that finally is to embrace the whole world, and *before* he says that he is going to his cross and that anyone who follows him must take up their cross—he calls twelve disciples.

They don't ask, "Where are you going?" Nor do they look over their options, examine the teaching of other religious leaders, and decide Jesus's teaching is the best. His Word, his call to discipleship, creates disciples. Wouldn't it have been more honest, fairer, to lay this out in advance, before asking people not only to sign on to the project but to give their lives for it?

Like Israel on the plains of Moab, like the fishermen beside the Sea of Galilee, we first learn what it means to belong to the people of God along the road, after we have been on the journey for a while.

We Are a Trusting, Confident, Hopeful Community

The heading for this section reflects Leander Keck's 1992 Beecher Lectures at Yale Divinity School, published the next year as *The Church Confident*. Keck points not to the swaggering self-confidence of a "growing church" but to confidence in God, confidence in the gospel. This section could have been appropriately labeled "The Church as a Community of Hope," but the biblical understanding of hope—represented by Paul's "in hope we were saved" (Rom 8:24, see the whole context)—has been culturally diluted so that "We hope so" often means "It would be nice, but probably not." In the Bible, "hope" means leaning on and trusting in a verity that is true, real, and sure—but not yet. It is in this glad confidence in God's ultimate future that the Deuteronomic teachers call the people of God to live, celebrating the goodness of life in the present.

Eschatology is thus not a theoretical topic, not speculative, not a matter of human curiosity about "the end of the world," but closely related to ethics. The community of faith has been given the mystery of the kingdom of God and knows what the Story of Everything is all about and where the whole world is going (Mark 4:10–11). This shapes their understanding of what is true, good, and right. As the people of God, we are called to be witnesses to God's justice to the world, to do what is good and right in our personal lives and to promote and establish God's justice in the social and political world. The issue is this: Is God's justice to be worked out, by God and by us, within the confines of the present world? Or does the reality of God's justice have an ultimate future dimension? Deuteronomy's eschatology can be presented as a series of six affirmations. That they do not readily fit into a single logical system is not necessarily a detriment to their witness to the truth of God.

I. Deuteronomy's eschatology focuses on present fulfillment, abundant life here and now, and salvation as land and place.

Deuteronomy certainly pictures realized eschatology, the fulfillment of God's promise of abundant life in the present. The hope-filled people of God, chastened by their testing in the desert and instructed by the Word of God directly from Moses, are ready to march into the promised land and enjoy the good life. The longings of a displaced people for a place and a home are about to be fulfilled. Prosperous middle- and upper-class North Americans, themselves mostly descendants of immigrants, can too easily forget the life-robbing anxiety of not having a place, a land:

> Breathes there the man, with soul so dead,
> Who never to himself hath said,
> This is my own, my native land!

Walter Scott's eighteenth-century poem recited by American immigrants need not be jingoistic "patriotism" but can represent the heartache of people looking for a place, a land, a home where they can work, raise a family, and live with dignity, self-respect, and the respect of others. Careful readers of the Bible can note the abundance of Deuteronomy's vocabulary expressing the deep meaning of having land, an inheritance, a place in the sun.[8] Landowners, even of a half-acre plot, speak of "my place." We urbanized modern Westerners, even those of us who live in the country rather than the city, may have difficulty perceiving the depth of feeling associated with having land, a piece of this good earth to call our own, or even a homesite with a vegetable garden. In serving rural pastorates, I have often noticed the tendency among good, loving, sensitive people to assume that no matter how much money one has, in order to *be somebody*, one needs land. Otherwise, one is something of a drifter, even if a wealthy drifter—with no roots in the earth, a lot of things belonging to them but not belonging anywhere themselves. The Matthean Jesus echoes the words of Deuteronomy and Psalm 37 when he pronounces the blessing of God on those who are meek: "Blessed are the meek, for they shall inherit the earth" (Matt 5:5). Jesus blesses the "poor in spirit," who are not doormats but know their identity as the oppressed people of God in the world who have renounced the violent methods of this-worldly power (Matt 5:3). *And what is their blessedness?* They shall inherit the earth/land. Both the Hebrew *'eretz* and Greek *gē* mean the whole "earth," as in "the heavens and the earth" of Genesis 1:1 and "heaven and earth" of Matthew 5:18. Both words also mean "land," as in "land of Israel" (e.g., 1 Sam 13:19; Matt 2:21). Throughout the Bible, the phrase "the land" is resonant with both "the earth" in the sense of God's creation and "the land" in the sense of Israel, the promised land. Both "inherit" and "land/earth" are steeped in the language and imagery of Deuteronomy. The enslaved laborers in Egypt were promised a land, and in Deuteronomy, the word has overtones not only of the land oozing with milk and honey west of the Jordan but of the earth itself and all its peoples, all of whom are chosen to have a place in the kingdom of God. Not having a place, being out of place, not finding one's name on a place card at the banquet, or not "knowing your place" means being lost. To be given a place is salvation. One of the early Jewish names for God, used to avoid pronouncing the sacred name of YHWH, is *Ha-Maqom*, meaning "the Place." Psalm 90 (attributed to *Moses*) begins, "LORD, you have been our dwelling place in all generations."

Near the end of the Civil War, Union general William T. Sherman issued Special Field Order 15 on January 16, 1865, which promised freed slaves "forty acres and a mule" along the South Carolina and Georgia coasts. The more than four hundred thousand acres had previously been owned by their slave-owning masters. *Receiving the land was salvation.* They could say, "Now I'm not owned; I'm an owner, with my own *place*." There is something deep inside us as human beings, something ultimate about having a place. The land Israel will enter when they cross the Jordan is not just real estate. It is the promised land. God is the Promiser. God has been faithful, and we have a land. We're home. In Jewish and Christian theology, preaching, hymnody, and art, this imagery has represented the promised fulfillment of life. When the departing Johannine Jesus promised his disciples, "I go to prepare a place for you," he plugged into this Deuteronomic hope of Israel and gave it an eternal dimension.

This is the primary picture of eschatological salvation in Deuteronomy. It is here and now. It calls us to ethical living and social justice. Now.

One reason Deuteronomy is attractive to some streams of Christian faith is that it deals with the love and justice of God as imperatives for the present. The prophet Moses delivers God's ethical instruction, dies with the dream unfulfilled, and leaves it for us to do. Ethics is not motivated by hope of heaven or fear of hell. There is no second coming of Moses. Just do it (Deut 30:11–14).

This is a major thrust of what Deuteronomy has to say. Indispensable. Is it all and enough?

II. Deuteronomy also has a significant future eschatology.

The Deuteronomic teachers do not insert a few glimmers of the ultimate future as an optional supplement to their dominant present eschatology. The creation-to-consummation framework of the Story of Everything gives the present its meaning, legitimacy, and quiet confidence that allows present life not only to go on but to be celebrated (see ch. 5 in this volume). The concentration of Deuteronomic theology and ethics on the present world neither serves as justification for the modern "prosperity gospel" nor illustrates how unrealistic the do-good-because-it-pays theology is. Psalm 37, influenced by Deuteronomy and cited by the

Matthean Jesus, contains the lines "The meek shall inherit the land, and delight themselves in abundant prosperity," and "Those blessed by the LORD shall inherit the land" (vv. 11, 22). The author goes on to confirm his theology with his own observation: "I have been young, and now am old, yet I have not seen the righteous forsaken or their children begging bread" (v. 25), to which biblical theologian John Barton responded, "You obviously don't get out enough."[9] I was present when a gentle, saintly faculty colleague once erupted, splattering lava on the sacred text, "Well, by God, *I* have."

The Deuteronomic teachers do not relax or modify their ethical rigor because it is "just an ideal that doesn't always work out in practice." All that Moses says in the sermon on the plains of Moab is set within the framework of universal history ruled by the Creator God who will bring history to a worthy conclusion. All that Jesus says in the Sermon on the Mount is likewise said within the framework of universal history. Jesus and the New Testament authors spoke within a context already deeply influenced by this eschatological substructure. New Testament theology presupposes elements of the detailed apocalypticism that had developed since the Deuteronomists' time, including the descent of the Son of Man from heaven, the resurrection of the dead, and the final judgment. This apocalypticism was just beginning to dawn when the final edition of Deuteronomy was promulgated. The Deuteronomic teachers accepted the fundamentals of eschatology as represented, for example, by Deutero-Isaiah but were hesitant about some aspects of the new apocalyptic views emerging in some currents of exilic and postexilic theology. The Deuteronomic teachers resisted anything that could be interpreted in otherworldly ways that detract from the responsibility of the people of God in this world.

III. Deuteronomy's future eschatology can be easily summarized.

'All Israel' looks forward
- —to a transformed humanity
- —in a transformed world in which there is no evil.

God will bring this new world into being
- —in continuity with the present world
- —without revoking or overriding human responsibility.

The Deuteronomic teachers did incorporate some facets of emerging apocalypticism into their own theology. All are to be understood dialectically.

IV. God is sovereign, but human beings are responsible.
The Deuteronomists joyfully affirm the sovereignty of God, who has a plan for the world that requires the transformation of both the earth and its inhabitants—the faithful God who takes the responsibility and has the power to finish what he has begun (Ps 22:31; Deut 9:4–5; 1 Thess 5:24; Phil 1:28). God will circumcise human hearts so that they can truly love and obey: "Moreover, the Lord your God will circumcise your heart and the heart of your descendants, so that you will love the Lord your God with all your heart and with all your soul, in order that you may live" (Deut 30:6). In this symbolic surgical imagery, the transfiguration of the people of God already underway does not happen by divine force (2 Cor 3:15–18). The Almighty does not bully. This transformation of human hearts is both gift and command. We are commanded to love God with all our hearts (Deut 6:5), but with the Shema in mind, Paul declares that God's love is a gift, poured out in human hearts by the Holy Spirit (Rom 5:5). The spirit of God changes human hearts; individual human beings are called to repentance; they must change their own hearts, and they can do so:

> So now, O Israel, what does the Lord your God require of you?
>
> Only to fear the Lord your God, to walk in all his ways, to love him, to serve the Lord your God with all your heart and with all your soul, and to keep the commandments of the Lord your God and his decrees that I am commanding you today, for your own well-being. Although heaven and the heaven of heavens belong to the Lord your God, the earth with all that is in it, yet the Lord set his heart in love on your ancestors alone and chose you, their descendants after them, out of all the peoples, as it is today.
>
> *Circumcise, then, the foreskin of your heart, and do not be stubborn any longer.* For the Lord your God is God of gods and Lord of lords, the great God, mighty and awesome, who is not partial and takes no bribe, who executes justice for the orphan and the widow, and who loves the strangers, providing them food and clothing. You shall also love the stranger, for you were strangers in the land of Egypt. (Deut 10:12–19)

> Surely, this commandment that I am commanding you today is not too hard for you, nor is it too far away. It is not in heaven, that you should say, "Who will go up to heaven for us, and get it for us so that we may hear it and observe it?" Neither is it beyond the sea, that you should say, "Who will cross to the other side of the sea for us, and get it for us so that we may

> hear it and observe it?" No, the word is very near to you; it is in your mouth and in your heart for you to observe. (Deut 30:11–14)

This dialectic is not to be parceled out as though God is partly sovereign and we are partly responsible, with God doing God's part and us doing ours. No. Rather, God is truly sovereign, and we are truly responsible. This can be grasped by a community that, after some struggle, decided its understanding of God's saving action must be expressed in the truly human / truly divine christological terms of Bible and creed (cf. Mark 15:39, and the 451 CE Definition of Chalcedon). This community then can intentionally instruct us, "Work out your own salvation with fear and trembling; for it is God who is at work in you, enabling you both to will and to work for his good pleasure" (Phil 2:12–13). We can joyfully and confidently affirm this and live by it without reducing it to human math and logic.

V. The fulfillment of God's plan means the elimination of evil.

Evil is not coeternal with God, not a given aspect of the universe that may be held at bay, though continuing forever as a constant threat that God and the world must always struggle to overcome. In biblical theology, evil is an aberration, not an essential part of God's good creation. The consummation of God's purpose includes the elimination of evil. Biblical theology pictures this beyond-our-imagining transcendent event in two contrasting ways, neither of which is dispensable, though they are not conceptually harmonizable.

In the first picture, the evil powers of this world will be overcome and destroyed; the universe must be cleared of evil to make way for the final coming of the kingdom of God. The conquest stories of Israel's early history picture the divine solution in this way. God destroys evil; Israel need only be faithful. Variations of this imagery were taken up by New Testament theologians who portray the ultimate victory of God as destruction of the cosmic evil powers represented by Satan and his demons. This solution is pictured in the New Testament exorcism stories in which Jesus expels or destroys local demons and in the cosmic versions of God's eschatological victory to which these stories point (Matt 8:28; Rev 19:17–21; 20:7–15). The final result? Evil is gone, and God's universe and God's people can live in peace.

The second picture of the final victory of God portrays evil people and beings, including the devil himself, as finally transformed and incorporated into the eschatological kingdom of God. In this set of images, the ultimate power of the universe is not divine violence but the transforming love of God, which no power in the universe can resist forever (Col 1:15–20; Eph 1:9–10). In Deuteronomy 32, as elsewhere in biblical theology, the restored ultimate dominion of the One God will include even the transcendent powers of evil.

VI. Likewise, the course from the "present evil age" to the "age to come" can be pictured in two contrasting ways.

The ultimate future is continuous with the present. In this-worldly "eschatology from below," the beginnings of God's kingdom in the present world expand like leaven in the lump and flow without interruption into the ultimate kingdom of God for which we pray. The gentile nations are converted and form an eschatological parade to Zion to worship the One True God, or a final messianic king, equipped with God's power and wisdom, who finally extends God's rule throughout the earth (cf., e.g., Isa 2:2–4; 11:1–9).

The ultimate future is discontinuous with the present. In transcendent "eschatology from above," developed by Israel's apocalyptic thinkers such as Daniel, the world is so evil, and the forces of good so weak, that no way can be seen from the here-and-now of the present evil age to the there-and-then of God's coming kingdom, which must come crashing in from the heavenly world (cf., e.g., Dan 2:1–45; 7:1–27).

Though these two visions of ultimate reality are dialectically combined in biblical theology, it is clear that the Deuteronomic teachers clearly emphasize the former. In step with the theology of Isaiah 40–55, they see the people of God as already entering into the final phase of God's plan for history, as repentant 'all Israel' is regathered in the promised land in a world no longer threatened by evil, with divinely transformed hearts living in joyful obedience to God for all their days, with God's will done on earth as it is in heaven.

The *Aleinu* prayer comes at the conclusion of each of the three daily Jewish prayer services. The two paragraphs combine the particularistic and universalistic themes of Israel's faith and praise. The first paragraph speaks in terms of Israel as the one people of God in contrast to the nations who worship other gods. The second paragraph calls for universal recognition of God by all people, in the confident hope that "all humanity will call upon your name," citing Zechariah 14:9: "And the LORD will become king over all the earth; on that day the LORD will be one and his name one." Extending the vision of the Shema and Deuteronomy, the vision of the future unity of all humanity joining in worship and praise to the One God became part of the daily service and life of the people of God.

As the people of God among all God's peoples, we preachers, teachers, and other church folk are called to be God's witnesses and do God's will in the present world. This includes grateful praise for the good world in which we live and enjoyment of its delights. The future belongs to God. Though unmapped, it is secure. And it has profound implications for ethics.

Chapter 17

What God Requires of Us

"Do Justice, Love Mercy, Walk Humbly"

What does God require of us? The Deuteronomic teachers have a clear, one-verse answer: "*Justice, and only justice, you shall pursue*, so that you may live and occupy the land that the Lord your God is giving you" (Deut 16:20).

What is justice? "Everybody *knows* what justice is. Getting people to *do* what's right, that's what we've got to work on." This was the response of a candidate for a position in Christian ethics during an interview with the seminary's search committee. I thought the general thrust of her answer was in the right direction. Justice does indeed require action, not just discussion. But is it true that "everybody already knows what justice is"? The Deuteronomic teachers did not think so, and they asked 'all Israel' to sit still for thirty-four chapters on who we are and what God requires of us. There is no substitute for repeated immersion in the narrative world of the biblical text itself, which shapes the reading audience to better hear the Word of God that comes through it and to discern what it calls us to do and be as we face the personal, social, and political decisions of our own time and place. Before charging out to right the world's wrongs, we must sit still, listen, and think through what we hear. The following reflections on the nature of Deuteronomy's ethics are intended as hearing aids. They claim to be neither a summary of Deuteronomy's ethics nor a commentary on the book's specific texts dealing with personal and social ethics. There are several instructive commentaries along that line that set Deuteronomy's laws in their historical-cultural context and interpret them in the light of Christian faith (see bibliography).

Deuteronomy's Ethic Is for Insiders, for the People of the Covenant, 'All Israel'

The foundation for Israel's ethic is Israel's gospel. The Deuteronomic teachers have no ethics in general but speak only to those who confess their faith in the words of the Shema, that the One God is YHWH, the God of Israel, "our God." These insiders to the people of God know they have been delivered and accepted and are willing to be instructed in what this faith requires. They accept the supreme commandment of love as basic to all else, the commandment that is bound to the Shema itself (Deut 6:4–5). They accept the Ten Commandments as declaring the will of God and know that the first commandment, to worship only the LORD, is basic to the other nine, which cannot stand on their own.

All Deuteronomy's ethical teaching presupposes that the hearers belong to 'all Israel,' and does not presume to give legislation that should be imposed on the world at large. Deuteronomy's Torah is for the covenant people. When they transgress, they are charged not merely with violating a law but with abandoning the covenant that binds them to God and one another (e.g., Deut 4:13; 5:2–3; 17:2; 29:1, 25). The ethical instruction of Deuteronomy makes little sense to those who do not share its faith and theological perspective. The God of the Deuteronomic teachers wants not forced or robotic obedience but an ethic that makes sense to those whose sense of right and wrong is shaped by their faith in the LORD God. This does not mean that members of the people of God can ignore the ethical issues of the wider world to which they too belong, just as it does not mean that outsiders must first be converted to Israel's theology before they can receive any help from Deuteronomy's ethical instruction. Israel's ethic is not sectarian, as though Deuteronomy were a manual of conduct concerned only for the purity and righteousness of the members of their own group (contrast the Community Rule of Qumran [1QS]). The ethic of Deuteronomy, while directed only to insiders, has a universal perspective. Like prophets such as Amos and Isaiah, Deuteronomy assumes there are universal norms that apply to all peoples (Amos 1:3–2:3; Isa 1:23; 3:9; 5:8–9, 23; 10:1–2). The Deuteronomic teachers justify the annihilation of the Canaanites partly on the basis that even though they do not have the revelation from Sinai, they have violated fundamental norms of right and wrong they should have known (Deut 18:9–12; 25:17–19; cf. Gen 15:12–16; Rom 1:18–32). They are condemned not because they worship false gods instead of the LORD but because they disregarded these universal norms. (There is a variation of this in

Rom 1:18–32: all people should have known the Creator from the creation, but they are not condemned for not having known Yhwh, the Lord revealed to Israel.) Nonetheless, the Deuteronomic teachers have no direct interest in an ethics-in-general that attempts to proclaim and justify a universal ethic on philosophical or commonsense grounds. Their concern is exclusively directed to instructing the people of God in how they should live to carry out their special calling. There is no smugness in Israel's insider/outsider language. From the beginning, Israel knows it is called to be the people of God for the blessing of all nations (Gen 12:1–3) and always has the nations of the world on its ultimate horizon. Like the Jesus of the Gospels, the Deuteronomists know themselves to be sent to the lost sheep of the house of Israel to teach Israel the way of life. They speak within the historical reality of the separate existence and mission of Israel (Mark 3, Matt 10, etc.).

The Deuteronomic teachers' strategy of communication is reflected in Matthew's presentation of the Sermon on the Mount. The Matthean Jesus has called a community of disciples into being by his powerful Word and, with the gentiles in his peripheral vision, ascends a mountain to instruct his disciples (Matt 4:1–25; cf. v. 15). The great crowds that follow him include people from the Decapolis and "beyond the Jordan"—the location, of course, of Moses's sermons in Deuteronomy. When Jesus ascends the mountain, his disciples follow him, and his teaching is directly addressed only to them (Matt 5:1). Matthew and the Matthean Jesus have a universal perspective that includes nondisciples, who will be happily surprised to learn at the Last Judgment that their deeds of compassion for the least and lowly have actually been done for Christ himself and in the service of God (Matt 25:31–46). The ethic of the Sermon on the Mount, however has been directly spoken to disciples of Jesus Christ. This ethic is an ethic of discipleship that makes no sense to those outside the community of faith and discipleship. And yet the careful reader is surprised, *pleasantly* surprised, to learn at the conclusion of the Great Sermon that "when Jesus had finished saying these things, the crowds were astounded at his teaching, for he taught them as one having authority, and not as their scribes" (Matt 7:28–29). That is, his ethic was an ethic of command, from one who would claim that God had given him all authority in heaven and on earth (Matt 28:18). The crowds, who had not been called as disciples and had made no profession of faith, had been there all along. They had listened in, and some of them would later respond to the invitation to discipleship. Deuteronomy's ethic begins with the command to hear but still welcomes those not registered in the community of faith to *over*hear, to listen *in* on what was said to someone else. Sincere seekers devoted to truth and justice who attend church but do not count themselves among those affiliated with "institutionalized religion" might be addressed by the God who speaks to and through 'all Israel.'

Israel does not formulate its faith and life in marketable terms "relevant" for the culture. The people of God must teach and live by their own faith, spoken to one another and confessed in worship of YHWH, the One God of Israel, but with the world in which they live always within view. The whole world is watching.

Deuteronomy's Ethic Identifies Justice with the Will of God

Everyone claims to be against injustice and in favor of justice. This only restates the question at the beginning of this book: What is right and fair, how should we live our one and only life, who gets to say, and how do *they* know?

What is the foundation, grounding, and warrant for believing/saying some things are right and others are wrong? On what basis can we say, "I should"; more particularly "we should"; or most difficult, "you should" or "they should"? Should anyone try to tell anyone else what to do? *Note:* Either a yes or no to *this* existential question still leaves the "should" question hanging in the air. The question cannot even be posed without presupposing this primal, universal "should." The *should* question is inescapable for human beings. Animals don't ask it. Not only the Bible but also our culture do not assume we all already know what is right. One dimension of the culture wars revolves around precisely this issue. Some of the following options are on the table.

1. Individual Conscience (Individual, Psychological). The conviction that issues of what is right and what is wrong are settled by the individual's internal judgment comes to expression in a variety of ways, from Ernest Hemingway's and Woodstock's "If it feels good, do it" to sensitive, serious philosophical and theological arguments that each person's conscience is the Supreme Court where all ethical issues are decided. Neither the concept nor the vocabulary for "conscience" occurs in the Old Testament, the teaching of Jesus, or the Gospels, where ethics is an internal issue among the people of God. The relative frequency of the word in Acts and the Epistles represents the dialogue of the church with the Greek world ("conscience" [*syneidēsis*], twenty-nine times). We modern Westerners mostly stand in this Greek tradition and are often unaware of where our presuppositions come from. The Deuteronomists, and biblical theology in general, encourage what we would call a sensitive conscience—that is, a heartfelt concern to do what is right. What they object to is that in deciding what *is* right, human judgment takes the place of the will of God.

2. Rational Ethical Idealism (Philosophical, "Common Sense"). Individualistic hedonism's "If it feels good, do it" is replaced by "If it fits with ultimate reality as defined by science and reason, do it." At least from Plato to our own time, philosophers have debated whether there is a stand-alone ethic based on universal rational principles, which can and should (!) be tapped into by human reason. If so, the good is that which is reasonable, and reasonable people who can follow a logical argument will know what is good and that the prescribed action is in step with the nature of the universe. Evil people are either not smart enough or not honest enough to do this. For theists, the will of God was identified with what is rational. Jesus's teaching is valid because it is rational, and rational people can be persuaded to follow it if they think clearly (so, e.g., John Locke).

3. Ethos (Sociological, Political, Chronological, Geographical, Multicultural). All of the above are mostly individualistic—my feelings, convictions, ideals, and rationality. But *ethics*, in and out of the Bible, is a relational term. If I were the only person in the world, would I ever have need or occasion to ask if whatever I decide to do or not do is "right"? There would be no issues of social ethics, but we still could not be the masters of our fates, the captains of our souls. We would still belong to God, still be God's creatures, "not self-contained at all, even when we think we're all by our lonesome."[1]

It is the presence of others that complicates the question and that gives rise to the term *ethics*. The term is derived from Greek *ethos*, the characteristic spirit of a community or era manifested in the customs it takes for granted as true and right. An ethical transgression involves doing something that "is just not done," a violation of community standards neither receiving nor requiring further grounding. Such conventions are necessary for community life. Without them, no group or society can endure. Right is what supports the life of the community, and wrong is that which calls it into question. The community itself is threatened by conduct that does not fit within the rules and cannot tolerate such conduct. The good life for the individual is bound up with the good of the social group or political state. I am a good, ethical citizen if I abide by the laws of the city, state, and nation to which I belong, including its unwritten cultural expectations and/or those of my peer group or social setting that sets the norms for "what's done." These are represented in the overlapping force fields of family, street gang, social club, sorority/fraternity, football team, military unit, political party, business or professional peers, or neighborhood that is high or low on the socioeconomic scale.

In this model of settling the question of right and wrong, the community I belong to and that gives me my identity sets the moral and ethical standards, often without my giving any conscious thought to the matter—until I come up against someone who belongs to a different community shaped by different assumptions, with each of us claiming to do "what's right." Paraphrasing Tip O'Neill, such an ethic claims "All ethics is local" or "When in Rome. . . ." What a culturally conditioned community in a particular time and place says is right *is* right for them. Period.

4. **Deontological Ethics and the Revealed Will of God.** The basic stance of biblical ethics, taken as somehow normative by all who regard the Bible as Holy Scripture, is that justice, what is right and good, is determined by the will of God. The foundational law for the people of God begins not with "We the people" but with "I am the LORD your God, who brought you out of the land of Egypt, out of the house of slavery" (Deut 5:6). The will of God has been revealed in the historical dialogue between YHWH and Israel, is preserved in Scripture and tradition, and is embodied in the life and teaching of Jesus, who taught his disciples to pray, "Thy will be done on earth as it is in heaven."

In Jewish, Christian, and Islamic faith, justice is right because the One God commands it. God commands it not because there is a superior ideal or principle that God follows but because God is God. This God is YHWH, the God of Israel and Jesus, revealed as the God of justice and love. Because God is the Holy One, God the One and Only, God can say what no creature can say: "Because I said so; that's why." Those who believe in this God respond in gratitude that God has not left us to go our own way in ethical blindness or darkness (Ps 1, 119, and often).

Israel's and the Bible's ethic is an ethic of command, *deontological* in the technical vocabulary of ethical discussion (from the Greek impersonal verb *dei*, meaning "what must be," "what is commanded"). Deontological ethics can have a simple, even simplistic form: "Just do it." Command ethics has a more sophisticated, philosophical form. It is well argued that society and the safety of nation, town, and community depend on it. It is the military ethic, drummed into the psyche of every police officer and soldier of every nation. The safety of the whole unit depends on unquestioning obedience. Someone up the chain of command is responsible, has thought it through, knows what they are doing, and has chosen the best option. "Theirs not to reason why, / Theirs but to do and die": Tennyson's mentality in "The Charge of the Light Brigade" has been repeated often, with many variations and nuances. For example, my job is to obey orders, not have a discussion group pondering the justice of the command. Especially after the Holocaust and the attempts of Nazi officers to defend their actions by the military ethic—"I was just following orders"—many thoughtful people have developed a legitimate suspicion of the command ethic. But the biblical ethic of obedience is not robotic or Pavlovian, not a slave mentality in the cultural sense. Deuteronomy and the prophets of Israel, like Jesus and Christian authors of the New Testament, address us as responsible, thinking persons—"response-able," acting in response to the call and command of God. The issue is whether one believes there is one Commander, whether he has a name, whether his own being is self-giving love. The Christian community claims that "God is love" (1 John 4:8, 16). The claim is not that God is "loving," an adjective that may be applied to others, but that God's very being, the ultimate power at the center of all that is, is love. The Christian community claims that this One has lived among us and suffered the definitive miscarriage of human justice, all perpetrated by people who believed they were doing *right*.

The Deuteronomic teachers are concerned with human justice. Israel, the people of God, are given God's revealed Torah not only as the norm for what is good and right for the chosen people in the promised land but as a mediator of God's justice to the whole world. For Deuteronomy, human justice, inside and outside Israel, is not a matter of our own best human judgment; neither is it the product of "might makes right" or its denial by some versions of secular humanism.

Israel's teachers do not understand the source, basis, and norm of justice as internal to Israel, not even as of, by, and for the people of Israel. There are no royal or legal decrees in Deuteronomy or the Deuteronomistic History. The king does not make the laws. Kings, prophets, priests, courts, Levites—are all subject to something already *given*, which must be *interpreted*. The revelation of God's will was a given, revealed from God through Moses, *outside* the land, *prior* to the founding of the kingship and temple and the appearance of Israel's prophets. Israel, under the guidance of prophet and priest, must interpret God's Torah and live by it in the midst of an alien culture in which Israel participates as responsible citizens.

It is God's command that is interpreted in the ongoing life of Israel. But the God of Deuteronomy not only speaks but listens, and without ceasing to be Commander in Chief or settling disputed issues by majority vote, the LORD is affected by what he hears. The Deuteronomic teachers invite us to ponder the divine-human dialogues that continue to shape and reshape both Israel's life and the life of God (cf., e.g., Deut 5:22–33; 9:6–10:11; but also 3:23–28). The ethic of God's command is not absolutely unilateral but dialogical. The continuing reinterpretation of God's command participates in this dialogue, as interpreters not only listen to the text but hear The Story in dialogue with their own stories.

Deuteronomy's Ethic Is Expressed in Its Vocabulary of God's Command

God's commands are not all created equal. "You shall love the LORD your God with all your heart" (Deut 6:5), "You shall not murder" (Deut 5:17), and "You shall not boil a kid in its mother's milk" (Deut 14:21) function at different levels and in different ways in shaping the believer's ethic. Every reader of the whole book notices that Deuteronomy is filled with distinct but overlapping words expressing God's command, drummed repetitively into the hearers' ears. Torah/law, command, ordinance, statute, and decree/testimony are not redundant synonyms but intended to be understood in a somewhat hierarchical manner.

The Commandment, the Torah. The terms *mitzvah* (commandment) and *torah* (instruction, often translated "law") are used in the singular as overarching, comprehensive terms that designate God's revealed will as a whole. We are familiar with the initiation ceremony of bar mitzvah or bat mitzvah, literally "son of the commandment" or "daughter of the commandment," in which a Jewish boy or girl enters the realm of the commandment, understood as a comprehensive, singular entity. *Mitzvah* is often found in Deuteronomy in this sense (e.g., Deut 6:1; 8:1; 15:15; 26:13). There are no Bar Mitzv*oth* (pl.) celebrations.

In Deuteronomy, the term *torah* is used in the same comprehensive way as *mitzvah*. *Torah* basically means "instruction," not "law" in the sense of a legal code. The Deuteronomic teachers use *torah* only in the singular, designating YHWH's all-inclusive body of instructions for the life of Israel, the people of God. Israel is first called to keep the commandment, or keep the torah, as though this were a yes-or-no, all-or-nothing decision, as in the "I do" of the traditional marriage ceremony. The three letters, two syllables of the Hebrew text say it all. Particulars are not specified; there are no footnotes or fine print.

Worship, Justice, Love. The terms *avad* (worship, serve), *tzedeq* (justice, righteousness, what is right), and *ahav/ahavah* (love, loyalty, commitment) form the next rank of Deuteronomy's ethical vocabulary. Just as *commandment* and *torah* constitute the formal norm of Israel's ethic as the command of God, so *worship, justice*, and *love* constitute the material norm:

> You shall fear [= reverence, worship] the Lord your God; him alone you shall **worship**. (Deut 10:20; cf. 5:7–9, the first command of the Decalogue)

> You shall **love** the Lord your God with all your heart, and with all your soul, and with all your might. (Deut 6:5, fused directly with the Shema)

> **Justice**, and only justice, you shall pursue. (Deut 16:20)

These are primal commands from which flow the particulars of Israel's life. In Israel's theology, there is a hierarchy of truths that includes ethical truth. All God's commands flow from and are dependent on the primal commands of worship, love, and justice. They are fixed beginning points for the moral life. For the Deuteronomic teachers, egocentric people do not truly worship and therefore cannot hear or obey the other commands in Deuteronomy, including the other commands of the Decalogue. They may decide not to steal, murder, or commit adultery, but they do not regard such actions as worship and obedience to God. Unlike, for instance, Deuteronomy's commands dealing with agriculture and economics, the command to worship God is a world changer. When one decides to obey this command, the axis of one's world shifts. The people of God are an eccentric people—that is, they have a different center for their world than people who worship at other altars or claim not to worship at all. The first commandment—to worship only Yhwh—involves a radically different understanding of ethics. The commands to *love* and to *do justice* are likewise not particular commands in a long list of laws but their source, norm, and context for interpretation and implementation.

Ordinances, Statutes, Testimonies. This cluster of terms, often found together, refers to the corpus of detailed rules that flow from the primal commands. The will of God summed up in the Torah, even when oriented to the primal commands of worship, love, and justice, cannot be obeyed in general. Thus Moses delivers the particular laws that constitute the nitty-gritty of life to the people of God listening patiently on the plains of Moab. How should Christian believers respond to this long list of laws that not only include being gracious to the stranger (Deut 10:19) and not muzzling the ox that treads out the grain (Deut 25:4) but command the severance of the hand of a woman who violates community standards of modesty when defending her husband in a fight (Deut 25:11)[2] and prescribe that beef may be eaten but not pork, trout but not catfish (Deut 14:3–10)?

Serious Jewish and Christian scholar-theologians have proposed several handles by which the detailed rules of Deuteronomy's torah may be grasped, documenting their detailed research in the plethora of journal and dictionary articles, monographs, and commentaries. I here attempt only to sketch a few approaches that have turned out to be less useful and to point out some helpful directions for the path ahead:

1. Some scholars have considered the laws to be simply a historical hodgepodge resulting from the centuries-long process of adopting and adapting various rules from the culture and reshaping them to fit Israelite faith.
2. A respectable number of scholars have been positively impressed by the thesis that Deuteronomy's laws are structured according to the Decalogue, a view that goes back at least as far as the Reformation and John Calvin. While there is general agreement that the Decalogue functions as a primal command that is basic to all the detailed laws, most scholars have regarded efforts to fit Deuteronomy's two-hundred-plus laws into a ten-point outline corresponding to the Ten Commandments as forced and unconvincing.
3. Beginning in the early history of the church, numerous approaches to interpreting Deuteronomy's laws (and Old Testament laws in general) divide them into two categories, sometimes contrasting the "ritual law" with the "moral law." The first category, dealing with the particularities of Israel's religion, such as circumcision, the food laws, and festivals are considered as abolished by the coming of Christ. The moral laws, represented by the Decalogue and the elements that correspond to the interpreter's understanding of ethics, are regarded as eternally valid. However, the contrast between ritual and moral laws was never made by the Israelites and their teachers, who did not distinguish religious

rules from the law of the land. The whole of life was regarded as a sacred unity under the command of the Creator. Likewise, neither the Deuteronomic teachers nor other streams of Old Testament theology regarded the Torah as temporary; rather, they saw it as representing the command of God that will endure "forever"—that is, ages long, as long as the sun is over the earth (Deut 5:29; 12:28; 28:45; 29:29).

4. A fairly common approach is acknowledging that the laws of Deuteronomy represent another time and culture and need not necessarily be obeyed literally; instead, they express "principles" or "ideals" that can be "applied to today." This approach is out of step with Deuteronomy's own understanding. Neither *ideal* nor *principle* is found in Deuteronomy or elsewhere in the Old Testament. The danger is that this approach simply opens the door to reading in the interpreter's personal ideals and principles instilled by the stream of cultural religion in which the interpreter operates.

It appears, however, that the vocabulary of the Deuteronomic teachers themselves provides helpful pointers for understanding and living by the Torah. Israel's way of life is a response to the Torah and the primal commands of worship, love, and justice. None of Deuteronomy's two-hundred-plus commands should be understood or implemented in a way that violates these primal commands. The words *ordinances*, *statutes*, and *testimonies* are often used together without emphasizing their differences, like the phrase "rules and regulations" in English. They can be understood as simply a rhetorical repetition of synonyms, but each of them also gives the Torah a distinctive stamp, characterizing the corpus of rules that give insight from case to case.

Ordinances, Judgments (*Mishpatim*). An ordinance designates something that has been ordained—that is, decided upon and promulgated as right. The common Old Testament noun *mishpat* (sg.) is derived from the verb *shapat*, "to judge"—the activity of the official who sits behind the bench in the courtroom and is called a *shophet*, or "judge." His or her decisions are called *mishpatim* and become the law for that particular case, the justice rendered by the court. By using this term to designate what is just and right, Israel's teachers signal that *every ethical decision is a judgment call.* Every judge is an umpire who decides what is right in that particular case. What is right depends on who the judge is. In biblical thought, "right" is not an ideal or abstraction. It is the judge's decision that *creates* right. The universe is run not by ideals, principles, or natural laws but by a Person. The character and purpose of this Person have been revealed in the Torah. This is the faith communicated by Deuteronomy.

Precepts, Statutes (*Hoqim*). These decisions that ultimately derive from God, the just Judge, and are mediated by the human courts of prophets, priests, Levites, judges, and the lived experience of Israel, enter into Israel's tradition. Those go through an informal, long-term sifting process, and those that endure are written down and become part of Israel's normative tradition. Israel's Torah/Commandment is not to be changed, nor are the primal commands *worship*, *love*, and *justice* to be modified or outgrown. But at the precept level, Israel's corpus receives additions, modifications, and deletions in the course of generations and different streams of Israelite law.

Testimonies, Decrees (*'Ēdōt*). The third term for particular Israelite laws is *'ēdōt*, sometimes translated "decrees" as a synonym of "statutes." The basic meaning, however, is "witness, testimony," and when used of Israel's Torah, it can carry this overtone. Israel's laws are not only to regulate Israel's own life according to the will of God, but when the people of God live in the distinctive way instructed by the Torah, these laws function as testimony to the world of who YHWH is. Israel is called to be God's witness to the world by living as the "peculiar" people who treasure this law as their identity. This is particularly true of the "ritual" laws (e.g., circumcision, food laws, the Sabbath) that have no particular moral or ethical significance and are not given to the nations but serve as identity markers of the people of God and their mission to the world.

Deuteronomy's Ethic Means Living in The Story

Rather than proceeding through the long lists of laws in Deuteronomy and attempting to derive instant relevance or "applications for our life today," the interpreter gets a sense of the Deuteronomic Torah by repeatedly reading, studying, and living in the Deuteronomic *narrative* (cf. Ps 1). Deuteronomy is concerned not with inculcating ideals and general principles but with specifics—fourteen chapters of concrete instruction/rules/laws. Such instruction corresponds to life, which is always life in particular. The Deuteronomic teachers want to instruct us in an ethic that is a matter of hearing and seeing before it is ever concerned with doing—they want to teach us how to hear and see. This means that living in the story-shaped world that frames our own story has a formative effect that we cannot reduce to ideals and principles to be "applied." For example, "You shall not watch your neighbor's ox or sheep straying away and ignore them; you shall take them back to their owner" (Deut 22:1). We may be able to find in this text a "principle" that can be "applied," though this hermeneutic misfires in many Deuteronomic statutes. It is better just to enter into the Bible's narrative world and look through the eyes of our ancestor in the faith who looks out the kitchen window while doing the dishes and sees a stray animal. They don't recognize the ox. No one sees them looking. Getting involved is only asking for trouble. In any case, it's not really the *law*. There is no "Section IX, Paragraph 3, Article 11: *Oxen, strayed*. Citizens who observe strayed oxen must provide for them in the following ways (11a, 11b, etc.). A warning will be issued for the first offense. Subsequent violations are punishable by a fine not to exceed twenty-five shekels." This is not the way biblical "law" works. It typically does not define terms or specify procedures for implementing the law or penalties. In the crucial rules for the central sanctuary, those who live "far" from the chosen place are permitted to slaughter animals for food but not for sacrifice—but the rule does not define how far "far" is (Deut 12:21). Even the crucial command for Sabbath observance does not specify when the "Sabbath day" begins and ends, which are crucial matters for keeping the law. Examples abound. The Torah does not function as a legal document and is misrepresented when interpreted legalistically. But whoever has been shaped by living in The Story that includes Deuteronomy 22:1 cannot look out the kitchen window, see the stray animal, and say, "Not my problem."

As I write this in April 2021, the TV news is filled with images of a large, muscular man knocking an Asian woman, age sixty-five, to the sidewalk and repeatedly kicking her in the face. Some stopped and looked. Some made videos. Most passed by on the other side, perhaps on their way to synagogue or church. When the good scribe asked Jesus about how to *apply* the love command, Jesus did not specify more rules but told a story (Luke 10:25–37). You either get it or you don't.

> I'm sitting in my car in the parking lot on a nice day, car window down, while my teenage daughter does a little shopping. I'm listening to the car radio, but two empty parking spaces away, I can't help noticing an SUV with a mom in front and a four-year-old in the back seat complaining and talking back to his mother. "Just wait 'till your daddy gets here," she says. Out of the hardware store two doors away comes a large, muscular man carrying some plumbing supplies, and she reports what their son has said. Without a word, he turns toward the back seat, leans over, and hits the

> child with his fist, hard. I hear three or four thuds, a whimper. As they drive off, I see their license tag, a local number. I go to church and want to "go by the Bible." Nothing in Deuteronomy tells me what to do.

Deuteronomy does not represent YHWH's command as specifying what must be done or not done for every situation (see "Discernment means improvising," pp. 211–12 above). To faithfully obey the commandment, Israel must discern from case to case what being faithful in that situation requires. God's Torah gives direction for the whole of life by calling for loving God with all the heart, soul, and might. It is not a law in which we may search for loopholes, for areas not covered in which we can do our own thing. This is not an individualistic discernment; for the Deuteronomic teachers, one's personal (not private) decisions are to be made as one who belongs within the people of God and shares their faith and mission, an Israel that has traditions and teachers to help discern the will of God. God's command does not lift responsibility for discernment and decisions from the shoulders of either the individual Israelite or the community as a whole. Living in The Story helps shape us to make appropriate decisions and act on them without either assuring us that we have kept the law or condemning us because we haven't. Israel is shaped by the Torah to do justice and love mercy, knowing that it lives as a people forgiven by the grace of God even when they fail to recognize or do the will of God.

Israel's statutes, ordinances, and testimonies are not only, or even primarily, guidelines for personal ethical decisions but intended to shape a society in accord with God's justice revealed in the Torah. On Sunday morning, December 29, 2019, a gunman entered the sanctuary of a church not far from our home. He killed two people in the worshipping congregation with shotgun blasts before he was fatally shot by seventy-one-year-old Jack Wilson, a member of the church's volunteer security team. The *Fort Worth Star Telegram* reported on January 13, 2020,

> Jack Wilson reflects on those six seconds and knows if he hadn't shot the gunman, more lives would have been taken that day his two friends were killed during a service at a White Settlement church.
>
> "I did what God would want me to do—would have me do—in that situation," Wilson said Monday after he received the Governor's Medal of Courage in Austin. "And understanding that had I not done what I did, the situation would have been extremely much more chaotic."
>
> "When you put that weapon on, even though you're not law enforcement, you are supposed to be your brother's keeper."[3]

Wilson's sincerity and heroism are unquestionable, and we can be grateful that he acted to save the lives of other people. We can join in the affirmation and praise of police, military, and even private citizens who, in all good conscience, sometimes use deadly force to protect others. We can affirm "What God would want me to do—would have me do—in that situation" as the norm of Christian ethics. "Thy will be done . . ."

The newspaper, often a defender of the cause of justice in our city, neglected to publish a parallel column that might have read,

> The city council, state legislature, and US Congress reflect on those six seconds and know that if they had acted to make and implement more responsible gun laws and if they had acted to discourage a culture of me-first violence that includes the proliferation of guns, many more lives would have been saved.
>
> When you are elected and take office, you are supposed to be your brother's keeper.

What it means to live in The Story can be illustrated by an extended look at the struggle of a missionary teacher in the first generation of the people of God after the death and resurrection of the Messiah to interpret the biblical faith to a new Christian congregation asking how their new faith informs their everyday lives. Looking over the apostle's shoulder, we see a preacher at work interpreting the Bible centuries after it was written, in another culture and language, for practical problems in the life of the church. With Scripture in hand and heart and the traditions of the new Christian community already guiding his interpretation, the apostle Paul responds to the questions of the new congregation in Corinth. The task is the same as that of the Deuteronomic teachers who face the task of instructing 'all Israel' on how to live as the people of God in their own country, now a multicultural society ruled by a foreign government.

This is the same task of Christian ministers in any country in the world in the twenty-first century CE. In 1 Corinthians 7–11, Paul addresses two questions that arise for all Christian believers, their preachers, and their teachers—questions inborn and culturally conditioned in every human being:

> With whom may I sleep? (1 Cor 7)
> With whom may I eat? (1 Cor 8–11)

The two clusters of personal and social issues are related to cultural understandings of sexuality (marriage, divorce, remarriage, homosexuality, pre- and extramarital sex) and dietary and social taboos related to what we eat and with whom. Firm laws and customs regarding what decent people do in both areas of life are already present in the Greco-Roman culture and religion of Corinth in which the Christian congregation is deeply embedded. Most members of the church are gentiles who only a few months before had worshipped Zeus and the "many gods and many lords" (1 Cor 8:5) of what had been their world. Now they belong to the church and have accepted its Scripture and tradition as norms for their new life. Both issues they inquire about are addressed by the Scripture, with Deuteronomy in particular providing specific rules on both sexuality and diet. However, when Paul gives instructions to the new Christian congregation in Corinth, he does not begin by quoting the Bible at them. He begins where the people are, with the current live issues of the Corinthian church. He does not need to look up the "Bible teaching" on these topics. As an Israelite, a Pharisee, a faithful Jew, he has always, daily (Deut 6:4–9), lived in The Story. He has instructed the new Corinthian converts who have only recently been incorporated into 'all Israel' and adopted The Story as their own. Paul looks to the Bible for instruction and wants the Corinthians to do the same. Though Paul makes few specific quotations in this section, as he responds to the Corinthians' questions, the words of Scripture reverberate only slightly beneath the surface of Paul's letter, which oozes with biblical allusions and quotations—forty-eight instances in these five chapters, including at least eight from Deuteronomy. We look over his shoulder as he dips into these resources and interprets their meaning to those who are maturing in the faith (1 Cor 3:1–23).

1 Corinthians 7:1—"Now concerning the matters about which you wrote. . . ." A new section of the letter is signaled by the initial *peri de* (now concerning . . .), repeated at 1 Corinthians 7:25; 8:1; 12:1; and 16:1, 12 to indicate a new topic. Paul had received a letter from the church asking for his instruction on these particular issues of ethics and church life, but only now, several pages into the letter, does he turn to their current problems. He begins the letter not with responses to their questions but with six chapters about the real problems they had not recognized to be problems, as they continued to see the world through the lenses and mindset of contemporary cultural religion. Instant relevance, letting the present culture set the agenda, was not Paul's understanding of ministry. He first reminds them that the basis for decisions about what God requires of us is our new identity—as the people of God who belong to 'all Israel' the ecumenical church in "every place," called into being by the Word of the risen Christ just as Paul had been called as an apostle (1 Cor 1:1–8). Paul then reminds them that the basis for ethical living is not human wisdom, whether common sense or impressive philosophy, but God's revelation in the Christ-event, focused on the scandalous event of the cross and God's act in raising *this* man from the dead as the model of what a truly human life must and will be (1 Cor 1:18–3:23). Nor can one's life be based on a favorite preacher, some of whom have charming personalities and charismatic power, some of whom manifest the weakness and vulnerability of the Crucified One (1 Cor 4:1–21).

Paul then focuses the ethical spotlight and resources of Scripture and Christian tradition on three situations in church life that are out of step with the new identity of the Corinthian Christians. Paul challenges the superior attitude of those church members who believe that their newfound freedom in Christ allows them to ignore the conventions of popular morality—in other words, "I no longer care what people think; Christ has set me free from all that" (1 Cor 5:1–13). Paul rebukes church members who take one another to court to have differences settled by city and state laws rather than by their new identity within the people of God (1 Cor 6:1–11). Paul rejects the claims of an ethic liberated from law observance—"All things are lawful for me"—when this motto is cited to justify casual sex (1 Cor 6:12–20). He also rejects the sexual ethics represented by the motto "It is well for a man not to touch a woman." This Corinthian group seems to have understood human sexuality as sinful in itself, a part of this evil, fleshly, material world that truly spiritual beings must avoid. Couples already married were encouraged to abstain from sex, live separately, or divorce. This was the practice of some Hellenistic religious groups and was later advocated by some streams of heretical gnostic Christianity. Paul, though unmarried himself, will have none of this and instructs married couples to stay together. All these ethical stances, argued by the Corinthian groups on religious grounds, Paul considers to be built on the sandy foundation of cultural religion—whether the religion of the cultural Right or Left—rather than the church's one foundation, Jesus Christ our Lord (1 Cor 3:10–23).

1 Corinthians 7:7—"Each has a particular gift from God." Paul's ethical instructions are not one-size-fits-all. As he will explain in a later response to the Corinthians' question about how to evaluate the charismatic gifts of the Spirit that were both blessings and disturbances in the life of the congregation, obedience to the will of God is conditioned by each individual's aptitude and personal situation. Though Paul is quite aware of the Deuteronomic and other laws of the Torah concerning issues of sexuality, marriage, and divorce and will indeed quote texts from Deuteronomy, he does not claim to resolve the Corinthians' issue by quoting Bible verses.

1 Corinthians 7:8–16—"I give this command—not I but the Lord; . . . to the rest I say—and not the Lord. . . ." Paul makes distinctions between what is directly from the Lord (pronouncements of the Lord Jesus, whether pre- or post-Easter, earthly or heavenly) and his own instructions, just as Deuteronomy distinguishes what was said directly by the LORD at Horeb and what was mediated by the prophet Moses (Deut 5:1–32). Moses's commands, however, also represented the Word of God, and Paul insists, with a bit of sarcasm directed to the Corinthian prophets who claimed to speak the Word of the Lord Jesus directly from heaven, in the power and authority of the Spirit, "I think that I too have the Spirit of God" (1 Cor 7:40; cf. 1 Cor 14:1–38, especially 37–38). Paul recognizes that his instructions, to be heeded as the Word of God, are provisional, are conditioned by the situation, and may need further interpretation. This is thoroughly in step with the way the Torah functions in Deuteronomy's address to 'all Israel.'

1 Corinthians 7:12–14—"For the unbelieving husband is made holy through his wife, and the unbelieving wife is made holy through her husband. Otherwise, your children would be unclean, but as it is, they are holy." These words reflect the Deuteronomic understanding of 'all Israel' as the *holy* people of God, understanding holiness not only as personal piety but as the sacred power of God that blows like the wind or breathes like the breath that energizes a living body, mysterious and possibly dangerous. Moderns may have difficulty sharing this conception of divine holiness, but we may nonetheless grasp the import of Paul's instructions to those Corinthians wondering if "mixed marriages" should be dissolved. Paul instructs such couples to stay together, though it is no sin if they divorce, in line with Deuteronomy rather than Ezra and Nehemiah (cf. Ezra 1–2, 7–10; Neh 10–13). The believing partner communicates God's holiness to the whole family rather than the unbelieving partner obstructing it.

The significant point here, as in all the Bible's ethical instruction, is that for Christian believers, all ethical decisions are made in the context of belonging to the church, the holy people of God. Sex, marriage, separation, divorce, and remarriage are not simply matters of my private life, which no politician, preacher, church, or Bible has a right to meddle with. If I bring God into the discussion at all, it is just between me and

God. But those who join 'all Israel' in confessing faith in "the Lord our God," those who make the church's confession, "Jesus is Lord," have given their lives (back) to the One whose will determines all ethics. Christians and Jews of various theological and ethical traditions may legitimately discern / argue about *what* this confession calls for and how it is communicated and implemented, but the fact that ethics is a matter of the revealed will of God is no longer up for grabs. Precisely in this context, Paul asks, "Do you not know that your body is a temple of the Holy Spirit within you, which you have from God, and that you are not your own? For you were bought with a price; therefore glorify God in your body" (1 Cor 6:19–20). *You are not your own . . .*

1 Corinthians 7:17—"Let each of you lead the life that the Lord has assigned, to which God called you. This is my rule in all the churches." Paul does not say how this rule is to be implemented. In this connection, Paul's further instruction of appropriate headgear in congregational worship, likewise not to be taken literally in our different situation, concludes, "If anyone is disposed to be contentious—we have no such custom, nor do the churches of God" (1 Cor 11:16). Individual Christians may decide many ethical issues for themselves—but not by themselves. We are not our own. We were bought with a price. We belong to the church.

1 Corinthians 7:19—"Obeying the commandments of God is everything." This startling statement is the conclusion of a paragraph dealing with the variety of social positions and strata represented in the one church, now composed of Jews and gentiles. The church includes married, separated, divorced, single, slave, free, master, servant, and people who understand biblical commands differently. Even circumcision, the significant mark of the covenant for Jewish people and the clear biblical command of God is still a matter of heated debate in Paul's time. In this situation, and still in our own, the command of God can be interpreted in different ways, but understanding one's life as obedience to God's command is the heart of the matter. Paul does not quote the Bible here, but this, too, is thoroughly Deuteronomic.

1 Corinthians 7:26—"In view of the impending crisis. . . ." Paul makes clear that even his premarital counseling and instructions to married couples are given in view of his perception of the nearness of the end. Deuteronomy has a different eschatology, and most modern Christians have still another, but the point remains firm: exactly what one does in obedience to God's command is conditioned by perception of God's eschatological calendar. If Paul had thought the world would endure for generations after his time, he would have had different commands about whether to marry and have children. The *schema* (present form) of this world is always passing away, and God's command must always be interpreted anew, without ceasing to be God's command.

1 Corinthians 7:32–33—"Anxious about the affairs of the world. . . ." In accord with Jesus's teaching in the Sermon on the Mount, people of faith continue to live in this world, the world of God the Creator, without whose knowledge not a sparrow falls. Paul, like Jesus, verifies that adoption of apocalyptic categories as the best means for expressing some aspects of the faith need not mean otherworldliness or frantic calculation of the end-time calendar. This is the strength of Deuteronomy's this-worldly ethic. Believers do not live detached lives, unconcerned with what "they" are doing in the world of politics and economics. They are involved but go about their work with quiet confidence. Harvey Cox once said something like "Revolutionaries are so grim. Every now and then they should celebrate as though all the things they struggle for were already realized." Sharing the robust this-worldliness of Deuteronomic theology, Paul agrees exactly. Even though he believes that the Messiah will return in the near future and that the world as we know it will soon end, the followers of Jesus can go about their work serenely, enjoying the delights of this world (1 Cor 7:29–31).

1 Corinthians 8:1—"Now concerning food sacrificed to idols. . . ." With this phrase, repeating the *peri de* of 1 Corinthians 7:1, a new subsection begins that continues through chapter 10. It is not a random collection of off-the-cuff instructions but a rhetorically thought-through response to the second of the Corinthians' questions. The issue is whether Christians may eat meat that has been ritually sacrificed to an idol, especially if this involves attending a banquet in a local temple.

1 Corinthians 8:1–11—"All of us possess knowledge." This is the slogan of the liberal group, now freed from their pagan past, that now shares the Christian confession of 'all Israel' that there is no God but the One. In responding to Paul's preaching that Jesus is the Messiah, their conversion included confession of their faith as expressed in the Shema and their acceptance of the story of Israel, along with Israel's Scripture, as their own. Paul, of course, shares their liberated monotheistic knowledge but shifts immediately to the command inseparably bound to the Shema, the command to love God. In Paul's view, their question deals with their relationship to their neighbors, inside and outside the church, but—like Jesus in Mark 12:29–31—he speaks of the love of neighbor as inseparable from the love of God. Paul speaks from within the theological perspective of Deuteronomy, in which individual precepts must be understood as expressions of the primal commands of worship, love, and justice. The love command cuts both ways: worship toward God and justice that does right by the neighbor.

As Paul will make clear later in this section (1 Cor 10:26, citing Ps 24:1), he shares the conviction of the liberal group that if there is only one God, the Creator of all, then the whole earth and everything in it is the Lord's, and "we all have this knowledge." But their conduct as liberated Christians, delivered not only from Egyptian slavery but from the cultural conventions of religion, must keep in mind the effect of what they do on their "less-enlightened" brothers and sisters in the church, for whom Christ also gave his life (1 Cor 8:11). Liberal Christians have a responsibility not shared by the more conservative, traditional members of the church. Without condescension, liberals are charged to conduct themselves in a way that does not mislead their brothers and sisters in the church to act against their own conscience, naive and tradition-bound though it may be. *I* know that idolburgers served in the cafeteria of the temple annex are uncontaminated by idolatrous rites, but "weak" church members might not understand and follow my example, though for them it would be compromising disobedience to the One True God. *This* is the reason Paul appears to change the subject in the next paragraph (no chapter divisions in the ancient text!).

1 Corinthians 9:1–27—"Am I not free? Am I not an apostle?" Paul does not shift away from the Corinthians' question, "As a believing Christian, what can I eat and with whom?" Paul is not changing the subject. Paul's apostleship was in fact challenged in the Corinthian church, but in this long section, his assertions about his apostolic authority and freedom serve to illustrate how all Christians are to *use* their Christian freedom. The topic is still eating and drinking, as well as marriage (1 Cor 9:4–5)—all Deuteronomic topics (cf., e.g., Deut 20:6; 24:1–4). This becomes his handle on teaching about support for traveling missionary teachers—also an issue in the Corinthian congregation. In this context, Paul cites Deuteronomy 25:4: "You shall not muzzle an ox while it is treading out the grain." Paul knows, of course, that Deuteronomy *was* talking about oxen and that God the Creator cares about all animal life. But he also knows that Deuteronomic statutes repeatedly deal with adequate support for Israel's Levitical teaching ministry (Deut 12:19; 14:27; 18:1; 24:8; 26:12). And he is thoroughly convinced, as he says at the conclusion of his last extant letter, that "whatever was written in former days was written for our instruction, so that by steadfastness and by the encouragement of the scriptures we might have hope" (Rom 15:4).

1 Corinthians 10:1–5—"Our ancestors . . . all passed through the sea, and all were baptized into Moses . . . and all ate the same spiritual food." The subject is still "What may I as a believing Christian eat and with whom?" but the striking thing about this statement is that Paul confidently bases his argument on the presupposition he assumes is shared by his gentile Christian readers, that the Israelites of the exodus are also *their* ancestors. *The* Story has now become the story of gentile converts who were still worshipping Zeus a few months previously. Paul assumes without explanation or argument that they know this and interprets the biblical story in Christian terms and without allegory. The ancestors in the faith, 'all Israel,' were baptized, and they *ate "spiritual food" together.*

1 Corinthians 10:6—"Now these things occurred as examples [*tupoi*, 'types'] for us. . . ." Namely, they were to eat but not become idolaters.

1 Corinthians 10:9—"We must not put Christ to the test, as some of them did." Paul interprets the whole exodus story as an example for contemporary Christians. He does not mean merely object lessons or sermon illustrations of what we should do and not do, but he understands the biblical story as including "types," accounts of historical events in the story of our own spiritual ancestors that were prefigurations of our own present Christian experience in the church. They/we were delivered, were baptized, were fed by bread from heaven, and received the water of life in the parched desert when Moses struck the rock. Paul says the rock was Christ. For Paul, this does not mean that somehow the rock was a symbol or parable of the Christ event. He adopts a fragment of Jewish tradition in which the rock followed Israel through the wilderness, constantly providing life-giving drink just as the manna gave the daily bread of life. Thus when Paul, referring to the rebellious conduct of some of the Corinthian Christians, says, "We must not put Christ to the test, as some of them did," he affirms that in some real sense, Christ was present with pre-Christian, Old Testament Israel, our ancestors in the community of faith. Paul does not deny that the rebellious acts of Israel during the wilderness period were against YHWH, but he identifies the presence of God with Israel as the presence of Christ and vice versa. There is an important christological point here, even a proto-Trinitarian point. Paul, in line with biblical theology as such, thinks of the grand narrative, the Story of Everything, from creation to consummation. The Christian version of this, most explicit in the New Testament in the theology of Luke–Acts, projects universal history as a drama of five acts: Creation, Covenant, Christ, Church, and Consummation. This is Paul's perspective too, but his preexistence Christology and proto-Trinitarianism understand the Holy Spirit as the spirit of God, identical to the spirit of Christ and with Christ himself. This means that to say God is present throughout the whole drama, beginning to end, is to say that Christ was present throughout the whole of universal history. Christ was not only present incarnationally in the midst of history, but as the whole of history is the story of God, so the whole of history is the story of Christ. Paul is not "teaching" this "doctrine" to the Corinthians but *assuming* it as he gives them instructions on practical issues of church life.

I elaborate this point here because it helps us grasp another key element of Pauline theology: his concept that Christian life is lived not merely as an attempt to follow the teachings of Jesus; it is lived *in Christ.* This expression is not to be confined to some sort of Christ mysticism. Christ spans all history, creation to consummation. These words address a practical issue in church life faced by one who has lived his whole life in obedience to the revelation of God's will in the Torah. Paul did not abandon this view when he came to faith in Jesus as the Christ. Paul will later write to the Romans, "For the law [Torah] of the Spirit of life in Christ Jesus has set you free from the law of sin and of death" (Rom 8:2). Allowing one's thought to be guided and shaped by the Spirit instead of the flesh (Rom 8:4–5) is a matter not so much of individual "spirituality" but of which world one is living in. The Spirit's Torah is effective in the world already dawning "in Christ," the realm of the believer's life. The apostle here reminds the Corinthians that the people of God still live by the Torah, the Christ-Torah, now experienced and lived out in the context of the life-giving Breath that breathes through the body of Christ. All baptized believers have been baptized into the one body and the one Spirit, shaped, illuminated, and empowered by this dawning new world (1 Cor 12:1–13; Gal 3:27). To live "in Christ" means to live by Christ's Torah, to live in The Story of which God's act in Christ is beginning, middle, and end (1 Cor 15:20–28; Rom 11:36). And just as Christian ethics is a matter not of following a list of rules but of living our lives as incorporated into the church, the body of Christ, so Christian ethics means living in The Story, being shaped by it, and making our ethical decisions as those who belong to 'all Israel,' those who are "in Christ."

1 Corinthians 11:21—"For when the time comes to eat, each of you goes ahead with your own supper, and one goes hungry and another becomes drunk." In all this, Paul has not lost the thread. He has been asked about what Christians may eat and with whom. He concludes this long section with instructions about the Eucharist, which in Corinth was part of a fellowship meal for nourishment and friendship, the joy of a good dinner party. The Corinthian eucharistic fellowship dinner had degenerated into a boisterous banquet that emphasized the social stratification of Hellenistic culture. As on a jetliner, where our own culture has become accustomed to such inequality, there was a first-class section for those who could afford it and business and economy classes for people lower down the social scale. Such distinctions were important, especially for insecure people and those who saw the church as only a religious version of ordinary life. The one body, one table, one loaf, one cup had degenerated into their pre-Christian frame of reference.

1 Corinthians 11:23–26—"'This cup is the new covenant in my blood. Do this, as often as you drink it, in remembrance of me.' For as often as you eat this bread and drink the cup, you proclaim the Lord's death until he comes." Paul is no longer merely giving instructions on whether or not to eat idolburgers. The whole discussion has been shifted to a new framework.

- Paul cites the Words of Institution *received* from the Lord. The church did not invent this ritual. It was received from the Lord in the past, was handed on in the church's tradition, is renewed in the living present, and is "delivered to you" by the apostle and prophet who speaks in the name of the Lord. It came from the Lord in the past, as surely as did the Ten Commandments. The church's Lord commands, "Do this." The command comes from the Lord who continues to speak in the present (1 Cor 11:23a).
- The Lord is not one of the many lords of cultural religion but the One Lord *Jesus*, the One LORD *YHWH* (1 Cor 8:5–6; 11:23b). Paul does not identify the Lord Jesus with YHWH of the Old Testament. But in ways that cannot be reduced to conceptual neatness, he uses the biblical language of the lordship of the One God when speaking of the transcendent Christ, affirming a "christological monotheism" or "monotheistic Christology."
- The Lord calls the church to look *back*, to remember the saving acts of God in the past, "in remembrance of me" (1 Cor 11:24, 25). For both Jesus and Paul, "remember" reverberates with the Deuteronomic command, present thirteen times in Deuteronomy, plus seven warnings not to forget.
- The Lord calls the church to look *out* to the whole congregation and the ecumenical church, for there is one loaf, one cup, and

one table and all are welcome; they are to wait until everyone is there, exactly as in Deuteronomy (1 Cor 10:16–18; 11:21 vs. 11:33; cf. Deut 16:11). Corinthian Christians gather about the one table with 'all Israel.'

- The Lord calls the church to *look out beyond itself* to the whole world, for the eucharistic celebration, like the Torah of Deuteronomy, is a testimony, a proclamation to outsiders, God's peoples who do not yet belong to the people of God (1 Cor 11:26; cf. Matt 7:28).
- Like the festivals of 'all Israel' in Deuteronomy 16, the Eucharist is a feast to be celebrated, not a fast expressing hunger. Biblical theology has considerable space for fasting and lamentation, the Psalms are filled with laments, and Jesus pronounced blessings on those who mourn—not just those whose sorrow is for personal troubles but those who lament a world of injustice and pray for the coming kingdom of God, when the will of God will be done on earth (Matt 5:4; 6:10). But not at the Eucharist, not at the feasts in Deuteronomy 16. The people of God sometimes fast and lament, but not in Deuteronomy, not at the Eucharist.
- The Eucharist celebrates the worshipping congregation's participation in the *renewed covenant* (1 Cor 11:25). The tradition Paul quotes is resonant with the overtones of Deuteronomy. The Eucharist is a covenant meal. The covenant was made with 'all Israel' at Sinai. None of Moses's hearers on the plains of Moab were there. Yet they are commanded *not* to say that the covenant was only made with their ancestors. Participation in God's gracious covenant is not only a remembered event of the past but a present reality in which the little congregation in Corinth or Waxahachie experiences in the living present. They, too, received it at Horeb (Deut 5:2–3). It was renewed with 'all Israel' on the plains of Moab. Moses promises it is open to the future and will include later generations who will be incorporated into the people of God (Deut 29:14–15).
- The Eucharist looks forward. It is to be celebrated "until [I] come" (1 Cor 11:26). For most of the human population of this planet throughout history, scarcity and hunger have been the daily experienced reality or the constant threat. Every Eucharist is an anticipation of the messianic banquet, the grand eschatological homecoming thanksgiving dinner, for the whole family, when the time of scarcity and zero-sum competition is over

and there is plenty of food and drink for all. Not just survival but extravagant plenty. It will happen. The community of faith anticipates and celebrates it every time we gather at the Lord's Table. Our ethical conduct is to be shaped by the reality of this future celebration. Everybody will be there.

Concluding Unparabolic Postscript

Places in the Heart—*Sally Field and the Promised Land*

I could picture a congregation, church school class, or Bible study group having a good potluck dinner and watching *Places in the Heart*—an oldie, still available on DVD—and talking about what is involved in hearing what a text that was written in another time, place, and culture—whether Waxahachie, Moab, or Jerusalem—has to say. I suggest reading Deuteronomy five times, then watching the movie. Or watching the movie, then reading Deuteronomy five times.

** ** **

Act 1

The movie begins with a long-distance shot, from a helicopter, of the whole town: Waxahachie, Texas, 1935. It's the Great Depression in a racist, segregated world. That's just the way the world is, and people hardly notice. It is Sunday morning in a peaceful, happy, prosperous, church-going land. People worship God; crops are good. There are nice homes and stores; it's a good place to raise a family. From our transcendent perch outside the narrative, we hear the sound of singing, praises, and thanksgiving to God.

The camera zooms in on one house, the home of a happy family: a couple in their early thirties, Royce and Edna Spalding, and their two children, Frank and Possum. They've been to church and are enjoying Sunday dinner. Royce is a police officer, responsible for keeping the peace. Theirs is a loving family, happy and healthy, with plenty to eat and drink—a family gathered around a table, enjoying life, and giving thanks to God.

What phrase could you use to describe that scene? Perhaps *Shalom Elohim*, the "Peace of God." Not just the absence of war, though war is unimaginable in such a scene. It was, in fact, 1935, and the United States was not engaged in any international conflict. It is the peace of Romans 5:1, the peace of John 20:19: it was the first day of the week, the third day after Jesus had been killed. Fearful disciples who had failed him huddled behind locked doors. Christ can't be there. The impossible happens, and Christ is there and speaks: "Peace be with you." Jesus is with them, blesses them with the peace of God, and sends them forth to continue his mission. As we gather regularly around the Lord's Table on Sunday morning, we share the peace of God with one another, speaking the same words: "Peace be with you." This peace of God, which surpasses all understanding, will guard our hearts and minds in Christ Jesus (Phil 4:7). The word of the Lord endures forever. That word is the good news that was announced to you (1 Pet 1:25).

Act 2

Gunfire in the background.

Someone is at the door: "Willie has gone and got drunk again and is down by the tracks shooting his pistol. Better go get him before he hurts somebody."

Willie is a young Black man, a known and accepted figure in town. Royce knows him and leaves Sunday dinner on the table.

He has arrested Willie before for his own good and that of the town and approaches him in a friendly, nonthreatening way to get the gun. Willie accidentally shoots and kills Royce.

While Edna and her sister are preparing Royce's body for burial, a group of vigilantes comes by dragging Willie's body behind their truck. They hang his body on a tree, and most of the town considers that justice has been done.

The vulnerable young widow and her two children are about to lose their land.

The banker comes by to tell her that a payment on the land is coming due; if she can't make the payment, she loses the land.

Many struggles and hardships ensue. The banker brings his blind brother-in-law, Mr. Will, and forces Edna to take him as a boarder. Mr. Will is an unfortunate person without much of a life, but he is distinguished from Willie by being called "Mr."

In the course of the story and the struggle to keep the land, Edna, her family, and the community experience many troubles. A tornado devastates part of town. The Depression makes life hard for most people, though the wealthy survive better by foreclosing on the poor. Nothing personal, but business is business. Through many toils and troubles, social and personal, the community endures, and Edna and her children strive to save the land. All seems lost when another Black man shows up, hungry and looking for work. Edna feeds him but sends him away. He returns—is brought back by a law officer who accuses him of stealing, but Edna defends him and hires him, and with his skill, leadership, and hard work, they raise a large cotton crop that brings in enough money to save the land. It appears the story will have a happy ending, but some local members of the KKK, incensed by the Black man's success, beat him terribly. He flees for his life and doesn't get to share in the good life of the land he had made possible.

The man's name is Moses.

Act 3

The story ends as it began, with the church at worship.

It's Sunday, and people are going to church.

This time, the vista is not the spectator's view from the helicopter, not even from the front row of the narrative theater. The scene is inside the church, and we are there with the people of God. Only a few people are there, the faithful few. The minister reads the text from 1 Corinthians 13, and communion is served as in most Disciples of Christ churches by passing the bread and cup down the pews. The camera zooms in, and an adulterous husband is now seen to be reconciled to his wife; they hold hands and share the bread and the cup. As the camera follows the eucharistic bread and wine down the pews, it comes into focus that what had been only the faithful few is now a large crowd. Everybody in the story is there. Moses is there, as are the KKK people who beat him up. The banker and those on whom he had foreclosed are there. Royce Spalding is there with his whole family, and seated by Royce is Willie, who had killed him. The vigilantes who had killed Willie are also there.

The closing scene is like the opening scene: a happy family, and everyone is there, gathered around a table. When Willie serves the communion to Royce, he says the last words in the story: "Peace of God."

** ** **

Karen and I saw the movie in Enid, Oklahoma, in 1985. We talked it over on the way home and for a while thereafter—especially the responses of people in the theater lobby and parking lot.

There were a few tears. Some thoughtful silence.

Some were serious: "Well, it was a good story, but the real world is like most of the movie; it's not like the happy ending."

Some just didn't get it: "Pretty good story, but I thought the Black guy had killed the sheriff."

And there was some laughter, changing the subject, telling other stories. Sarah's laughter.

Some talked and laughed the relaxed, confident laughter that already echoes in the peace of God, of people who trust that the prayer Jesus taught his disciples will actually be answered, that the will of God will be done on earth as it is in heaven, and that all God's peoples will join in the joyful laughter that will finally resonate throughout the whole creation.

Notes

Preface

1 In this book, 'all Israel' in single quotation marks represents the quasi-technical term used fourteen times in Deuteronomy for the whole people of God.

Chapter 1

1 The Hebrew name of God, יהוה, the Tetragrammaton, is transliterated YHWH, printed in the text in small capital letters without vowels. Following synagogue practice, the sacred name is not spoken but pronounced *Adonai*, the Hebrew word for "Lord." Throughout this book, when translating or referring to YHWH in the texts of Jewish Scripture, I will usually follow the English-language convention found in the JPS, NRSV, and many other translations of the Bible that respect the sacred name of God by rendering it as "the LORD," printing LORD in small capital letters. When "Lord" is simply a polite term of address or means "ruler" or "sovereign," even when referring to the God of Israel, the word will be printed in normal font. In New Testament citations, I follow the NRSV and other translations by printing "Lord" in normal font throughout, including citations from the Old Testament. Likewise, New Testament references to Jesus as Lord follow the Greek text and standard English translations by printing "Lord" in normal font. See the full discussion in chapter 3.

2 Adapted from Reinhard Feldmeier and Hermann Spieckermann, *God Becoming Human: Incarnation in the Christian Bible*, trans. Brian McNeil (Waco, TX: Baylor University Press, 2021), 367.

3 Henceforth, "God's peoples," in the plural, is used for all the human beings in the world, with "people" in the singular (people of God, people of Israel, people of Egypt) designating a particular people. See chapter 11.

4 The phrase is from C. Kavin Rowe, *Christianity's Surprise: A Sure and Certain Hope* (Nashville: Abingdon, 2020), 11–33 passim.
5 Deanna A. Thompson, *Deuteronomy, Belief: A Theological Commentary* (Louisville: Westminster John Knox, 2014), 80.
6 Walter Brueggemann, *Genesis, Interpretation: A Bible Commentary for Teaching and Preaching* (Louisville: Westminster John Knox, 1982), 116.
7 Rowe, *Christianity's Surprise*, 91.

Chapter 2

1 Strictly speaking, since Israel had been in the wilderness "only" forty years, everyone forty years or older *had* been in Egypt and experienced the Exodus and revelation on Sinai / Horeb. The rhetoric of Deuteronomy works on another level, addressing 'all Israel' as post-Egypt, pre-Canaan.
2 In an earlier edition of Deuteronomy, the whole seems to take place on one day (1:3; 8:1; 9:1; 32:48); in the edited final edition that became canonical, Deuteronomy comprises three speeches, apparently on three different days separated by breaks of unspecified length.
3 On Deuteronomy as catechesis rather than law, see especially Dennis T. Olson, *Deuteronomy and the Death of Moses: A Theological Reading*, Overtures to Biblical Theology (Minneapolis: Fortress, 1994), 7–14.

Chapter 3

1 Patrick D. Miller, *Deuteronomy*, Interpretation: A Bible Commentary for Teaching and Preaching (Louisville: Westminster, 1990), 97.
2 Miller, 97. Cf. Thompson, *Deuteronomy*, 223–24: "What we have here is not easy, relativistic pluralism . . . at the same time, however, Deuteronomy does not advocate a narrow exclusivism."
3 Leander Keck, *The Church Confident* (Nashville: Abingdon, 1993), 49.
4 Cited in Keck, 50, from Daniel Liechty, *Theology in Postliberal Perspective* (Philadelphia: Trinity Press International, 1990).
5 Martin Buber, *I and Thou*, 2nd ed. (Edinburgh: T&T Clark, 1958), 39. See Russell Pregeant's helpful chapter, "Learning to Treat the Text as Subject," in his *Knowing Truth, Doing Good: Engaging New Testament Ethics* (Minneapolis: Fortress, 2008).
6 Martin Buber, *Moses: The Revelation and the Covenant* (New York: Harper, 1958; repr., Amherst, NJ: Humanity Books [Prometheus Books], 1998), with introduction by Michael Fishbane, 51–53. *HaShem*, the-Name, is a traditional Hebrew way of avoiding pronouncing the sacred name of God.
7 Buber, *I and Thou*, 80.
8 For a powerful treatment of Johannine theology based on the key scene in John 9:1–41, see J. Louis Martyn, *History and Theology in the Fourth Gospel*, 3rd ed., New Testament Library (Louisville: Westminster John Knox, 2003).

Chapter 4

1 The vocabulary and conceptuality of biblical theologians have been enriched by the seminal works of Peter L. Berger and Thomas Luckmann, *The Social Construction of Reality: A Treatise in the Sociology of Knowledge* (New York: Random House, 1966); and Alfred Schutz and Thomas Luckmann, *The Structures of the Life-World*, trans. Richard M. Zaner and H. Tristram Engelhardt Jr., 2 vols., Northwestern University Studies in Phenomenology and Existential Philosophy (Evanston: Northwestern University Press, 1973, 1983).

2 "The Story" (with a capital *T* and *S*) to indicate the Bible's grand narrative is adopted from Charlotte Coyle, *Living in The Story: A Year to Read the Bible and Ponder God's Story of Love and Grace* (Eugene, OR: Wipf & Stock, 2021).

Chapter 5

1 James A. Michener, *The Source* (New York: Random House, 1965), 157–58.

2 My understanding of Deuteronomy's structure reflects an adoption and adaptation of Duane L. Christensen, "Deuteronomy in Modern Research: Sources and Issues," in *A Song of Power and the Power of Song: Essays on the Book of Deuteronomy*, ed. Duane L. Christensen, Sources for Biblical and Theological Study (Winona Lake, IN: Eisenbrauns, 1993), 9.

3 For convenience, avoiding constant repetition of "the narrator" or "she or he," I refer to the narrator as "he." In the culture of the biblical world, most, but not necessarily all, of the actual authors of books regarded as canonical by the Jewish and Christian traditions were male.

4 The phrase is from Karl Barth, "The Strange New World within the Bible," in *The Word of God and the Word of Man*, ed. Karl Barth (New York: Harper & Brothers, 1957), 28–50.

Chapter 6

1 John Goldingay, *Old Testament Theology*, vol. 1, *Israel's Gospel* (Downers Grove, IL: InterVarsity, 2003), 863. Cf. John Goldingay, *An Introduction to the Old Testament: Exploring Text, Approaches and Issues* (Downers Grove, IL: InterVarsity, 2015), 3: All Old Testament books were composed between the eighth and second centuries BCE. "I use the methods of biblical criticism, not to criticize the text, but to understand it" (Goldingay, 5).

2 See details and explanation in Michael Carasik, *The Bible's Many Voices* (Philadelphia: Jewish Publication Society, 2014), 79–80.

3 In religious studies, "cult" does not have the pejorative connotations it has acquired in contemporary culture but refers to the system of organized worship, with its personnel and practices. For pre-Josiah central cult centers, see the evidence, argumentation, and bibliography in Hans-Joachim Kraus, *Worship in Israel: A Cultic History of the Old Testament*, trans. Geoffrey Buswell (Richmond: John Knox, 1966), 125–78.

Chapter 7

1 Walter Brueggemann, *Old Testament Theology: Essays on Structure, Theme, and Text* (Minneapolis: Fortress, 1992), 586.

2 John Dominic Crossan, *Birth of Christianity: Discovering What Happened in the Years Immediately after the Execution of Jesus* (San Francisco: HarperSan-Francisco, 1998), 575.

3 The phrase is from Thompson, *Deuteronomy*, 201, who offers helpful suggestions for interpreting such overwhelmingly horrific pronouncements.

Chapter 8

1 In some academic discussions, a careful distinction is made between *scripture* and *canon*, with *scripture* applying to a text that functions authoritatively in a religious community and *canon* used only in a more restricted sense of a specific list of such writings. Thus not all scripture is canonical, but all books in the canon are Scripture. In such discussions, to refer to a text as scripture recognizes its authoritative claim but does not bring up the issue of how many such texts there may be, how they received this status, and what is implied by calling a document "canonical." *Scripture* can be used in the singular or plural, capitalized or not, but *canon* specifies an explicit, limited collection. In more popular discussions, these terms are used more or less interchangeably, in overlapping ways, with *Bible* and *biblical* used generally to refer to a community's authoritative texts. This is the way these terms are used in this book.

2 See Hal Taussig, *A New New Testament: A Bible for the Twenty-First Century, Combining Traditional and Newly Discovered Texts* (Boston: Houghton Mifflin Harcourt, 2013), 555–58.

3 Goldingay, *Introduction*, 50.

Chapter 9

1 English translations of the story are available in reliable critical editions such as R. J. H. Shutt, "Letter of Aristeas," in *The Old Testament Pseudepigrapha*, ed. James H. Charlesworth (Garden City, NY: Doubleday, 1985), 7–34.

2 J. H. Skilton, "The Translation of the New Testament into English 1881–1950" (PhD diss., University of Pennsylvania, 1961), 381, cited in Harry Meyer Orlinsky and Robert G. Bratcher, *A History of Bible Translation and the North American Contribution*, Biblical Scholarship in North America (Atlanta: Scholars Press, 1991), 90.

3 Letter to George Bainton, October 15, 1888.

Chapter 10

1 The phrase is from the title of Richard B. Hays, ed. *The Conversion of the Imagination: Paul as Interpreter of Israel's Scripture* (Grand Rapids, MI: Eerdmans, 2005).

2 These words that reflect Saint Augustine's prayer are found throughout all branches of the church and are part of the Collect for Peace in *The Book of Common Prayer.*

3 Martin Luther King Jr., "I've Been to the Mountaintop," transcript, Memphis, Tennessee, April 3, 1968, American Rhetoric, https://www.americanrhetoric.com/speeches/mlkivebeentothemountaintop.htm. Like his speeches in general, his "I Have a Dream" speech (August 28, 1963, at the Lincoln Memorial, Washington, DC) is also permeated with unidentified biblical language.

4 Michael O. Wise, Martin G. Abegg Jr., and Edward M. Cook, eds., *The Dead Sea Scrolls: A New English Translation* (New York: HarperCollins, 1996), 119.

Chapter 11

1 Deuteronomy includes conflicting traditions on relations to surrounding nations, as on other points. For details, see the critical commentaries, especially Excursus 21, "The Background and Development of the Regulations about Admission to the Assembly of the Lord," in *Deuteronomy*, by Jeffrey H. Tigay, JPS Torah Commentary (Philadelphia: Jewish Publication Society, 1996), 477–80. In any case, there is no silencing Deuteronomy's ecumenical understanding of 'all Israel' and its call for acceptance and justice for the immigrant.

2 Paul S. Minear, *Images of the Church in the New Testament* (Philadelphia: Westminster, 1960), 70.

Chapter 12

1 See James Earl Massey, "Reading the Bible from Particular Social Locations: An Introduction" (150–53) and "Reading the Bible as African Americans" (154–60); Chan-Hie Kim, "Reading the Bible as Asian Americans" (161–66); Fernando F. Segovia, "Reading the Bible as Hispanic Americans" (167–73); George E. Tinker, "Reading the Bible as Native Americans" (174–80); and Carolyn Osiek, "Reading the Bible as Women" (181–87), all in *The New Interpreter's Bible* (Nashville: Abingdon, 1994).

2 Cf. John J. Collins, *The Bible after Babel: Historical Criticism in a Postmodern Age* (Grand Rapids, MI: Eerdmans, 2005), and the bibliography he lists.

3 For my own efforts to hear what the New Testament's hell and damnation texts have to say to us, see M. Eugene Boring, *Hearing John's Voice: Insights for Teaching and Preaching* (Grand Rapids, MI: Eerdmans, 2019), 107–19.

Chapter 13

1 Of the seventy-nine occurrences of the term (verb or noun) in the Hebrew Bible, fifty-one are found in Deuteronomy or the Deuteronomic History (eleven in Deuteronomy, forty-one in the Deuteronomic History).

2 Thompson, *Deuteronomy*, 32.

3 The most thorough history of interpretation of which I am aware is Christian Hofreiter, *Making Sense of Old Testament Genocide: Christian Interpretation of Herem Passages* (Oxford: Oxford University Press, 2018), an Oxford dissertation supervised by John Barton.

4 An extensive literature reflects this internal debate among interpreters who stand within the fundamentalist-traditionalist-conservative-evangelical spectrum, an instructive sample of which can be read in C. S. Cowles, ed., *God and Canaanite Genocide: Show Them No Mercy*, Four Views On (Grand Rapids, MI: Zondervan, 2003); and Gregory A. Boyd, *Cross Vision: How the Crucifixion of Jesus Makes Sense of Old Testament Violence* (Minneapolis: Fortress, 2017).

5 McGarvey also wrote a long book defending the Mosaic authorship of Deuteronomy. The quotation in the text is from "Biblical Criticism," *The Christian Standard*, September 24, 1898.

6 Tremper Longman III, "The Case for Spiritual Continuity," in *God and Canaanite Genocide: Show Them No Mercy*, ed. Stanley N. Gundry, Counterpoints (Grand Rapids, MI: Zondervan, 2003), 173–74.

7 Daniel L. Gard, "A Response to C. S. Cowles," in Cowles, *God and Canaanite Genocide*, 56.

8 *HomJos* 1.7, cited from Hofreiter, *Old Testament Genocide*, 67. See Hofreiter's thorough and documented report of the allegorical approach to dealing with *herem* texts, 58–108.

9 Images of the Moabite Stone may be readily seen on the internet, where various translations are also available. The text is from "The Stela of Mesha," Livius.org, accessed August 12, 2021, https://tinyurl.com/m854ewmp.

10 Collins, *Bible after Babel*, 161.

11 The phrase is from Brian Wicker, *The Story-Shaped World: Fiction and Metaphysics: Some Variations on a Theme* (Notre Dame, IN: University of Notre Dame Press, 1975).

Chapter 15

1 Walter Brueggemann, *The Land: Place as Gift, Promise, and Challenge in Biblical Faith*, Overtures to Biblical Theology (Minneapolis: Fortress, 2002), 44.

2 See further information and bibliography in Tigay, *Deuteronomy*, 148.

3 See Moshe Weinfeld, *Deuteronomy 1–12: A New Translation with Introduction and Commentary*, vol. 1, Anchor Bible (New York: Doubleday, 1991), 7; and numerous other commentaries and studies.

4 So far as I know, the phrase was created and popularized by sociologist George Ritzer's 1993 book *The McDonaldization of Society*, since revised and reprinted several times. The relation of the concept to church growth was explored in John Drane, *The McDonaldization of the Church: Consumer Culture and the Church's Future* (Macon, GA: Smyth & Helwys, 2001).

Chapter 16

1 Schubert M. Ogden, *The Point of Christology* (San Francisco: Harper & Row, 1982).
2 Karl Barth, *The Epistle to the Romans*, trans. Edwyn C. Hoskyns (London: Oxford University Press, 1933), 311. Barth's exposition of Romans 12 points out that the believer's salvation is not expressed in chirpy talk about going to heaven but leads to mourning, sharing the travail of the cosmos, and *mission* and *ethics*.
3 Richard D. Nelson, *Deuteronomy: A Commentary*, Old Testament Library (Louisville: Westminster John Knox, 2002), 214. Nelson presents a thorough discussion of the Deuteronomic "constitutional proposal," in which human authorities are instituted as a "democratic" system of checks and balances through which the sovereignty of YHWH is exercised in the life of Israel (213–15).
4 See the powerful exposition by Ernst Käsemann, "Worship in Everyday Life: A Note on Romans 12," in *New Testament Questions of Today*, New Testament Library (London: SCM Press, 1969), 188–95.
5 Buber, *I and Thou*, 82–83.
6 Olson, *Deuteronomy and the Death of Moses*, 7–14, 44.
7 Passover / Unleavened Bread and Booths lasted one week each. The duration of the Pentecost festival is not specified, perhaps there was only one day of official ritual (Deut 16:1–15).
8 See Brueggemann, *Land*.
9 John Barton, *Ethics and the Old Testament* (Harrisburg, PA: Trinity Press International, 1998), 87.

Chapter 17

1 Russell Pregeant, email of April 10, 2021.
2 For the Deuteronomic teachers and their hearers, endangering the organs of procreation was more than a violation of "community standards." Cf., e.g., Genesis 24:2–3, 9 where placing the hand under the thigh is a solemn oath, like placing the hand on the Bible. Such swearing is a matter of community order that makes life possible, like our court system in which witnesses are sworn. For ancient Israel, violating the genitals was a matter of the first commandment to be fruitful and multiply (cf. on Gen 1:28 below and Gen 38:9–10; 47:29) and a matter of participation in God's purpose to multiply Israel for the salvation of the world (cf. on Gen 12:1–3). *Listening* to the Bible requires attention to the overtones of its own meaning, not immediately reading our own cultural understanding into the biblical text. *This* is what Deuteronomy warns against.
3 "Man Who Stopped Church Shooter Receives Texas' Highest Honor," *Fort Worth Star-Telegram*, reported on January 13, 2020, https://www.star-telegram.com/news/politics-government/article239237733.html.

For Further Reading

Incidental items documented in the notes are not included here. The following selection includes books, chapters, and articles by respected academic scholars who have a concern for preaching and teaching the Bible in the church or synagogue. The list includes a broad theological spectrum, from fundamentalist and conservative scholars such as Edward J. Young, to a range of evangelical scholars who accept historical-critical methods and results in various degrees, to rigorous historical critics with a more liberal theological orientation such as Walter Brueggemann.

Exegesis, Translation, and Interpretation

Barth, Karl. *The Epistle to the Romans*. Translated by Edwyn C. Hoskyns. London: Oxford University Press, 1933.

———. "The Strange New World within the Bible." Translated by Douglas Horton. In *The Word of God and the Word of Man*, edited by Karl Barth, 28–50. New York: Harper & Brothers, 1957.

Bryan, Christopher. *Listening to the Bible: The Art of Faithful Biblical Interpretation*. Oxford: Oxford University Press, 2014.

Collins, John J. *The Bible after Babel: Historical Criticism in a Postmodern Age*. Grand Rapids, MI: Eerdmans, 2005.

Crim, Keith R. "Modern English Versions of the Bible." In *The New Interpreter's Bible*, 1:22–32. Nashville: Abingdon, 1994.

Daniell, David. *The Bible in English: Its History and Influence*. New Haven, CT: Yale University Press, 2003.

Goldingay, John. *Models for Interpretation of Scripture*. Grand Rapids, MI: Eerdmans, 1994.

González, Justo L. "How the Bible Has Been Interpreted in Christian Tradition." In *The New Interpreter's Bible*, vol. 1, edited by Leander Keck, 83–106. Nashville: Abingdon, 1994.

Jobes, Karen H., and Moises Silva. *Invitation to the Septuagint*. 2nd ed. Grand Rapids, MI: Baker Academic, 2015.

Juel, Donald H. *Shaping the Scriptural Imagination: Truth, Meaning, and the Theological Interpretation of the Bible*. Edited by Shane Berg and Matthew Skinner. Waco, TX: Baylor University Press, 2011.

Metzger, Bruce. *The Bible in Translation: Ancient and English Versions*. Grand Rapids, MI: Baker, 2001.

Smart, James D. *The Strange Silence of the Bible in the Church*. Philadelphia: Westminster, 1970.

Strawn, Brent A. *Lies My Preacher Told Me: An Honest Look at the Old Testament*. Louisville: Westminster John Knox, 2021.

The Old Testament (Introductions and General)

Alter, Robert. *The Hebrew Bible: A Translation with Commentary*. New York: W. W. Norton, 2018.

Brueggemann, Walter. *An Introduction to the Old Testament: The Canon and Christian Imagination*. Louisville: Westminster John Knox, 2003.

Carasik, Michael. *The Bible's Many Voices*. Philadelphia: Jewish Publication Society, 2014.

Childs, Brevard S. *Introduction to the Old Testament as Scripture*. Philadelphia: Fortress Press, 1979.

Collins, John J. *Introduction to the Hebrew Bible*. Minneapolis: Fortress Press, 2004.

Goldingay, John. *An Introduction to the Old Testament: Exploring Text, Approaches and Issues*. Downers Grove, IL: InterVarsity, 2015.

Hamilton, Mark W. *A Theological Introduction to the Old Testament*. Oxford: Oxford University Press, 2018.

Harrison, R. K. *Introduction to the Old Testament*. Grand Rapids, MI: Eerdmans, 1969.

Longman, Tremper, III, and Raymond B. Dillard. *An Introduction to the Old Testament*. Grand Rapids, MI: Zondervan, 1994; 2nd ed., 2006.

Young, Edward J. *An Introduction to the Old Testament*. Grand Rapids, MI: Wm. B. Eerdmans, 1953.

History of Israel

Ackroyd, Peter R. *Exile and Restoration: A Study of Hebrew Thought in the Sixth Century B.C.* Old Testament Library. Philadelphia: Westminster, 1968.

Bright, John. *A History of Israel.* 4th ed., with an introduction and appendix by William P. Brown. Louisville: Westminster John Knox, 2000.

Fretheim, Terence E. *Deuteronomic History.* Interpreting Biblical Texts. Nashville: Abingdon, 1983.

Gottwald, Norman K. *The Tribes of Yahweh.* Maryknoll, NY: Orbis Books, 1979.

Miller, J. Maxwell. "Introduction to the History of Ancient Israel." In *The New Interpreter's Bible*, 1:244–271. Nashville: Abingdon, 1994.

Miller, J. Maxwell, and John H. Hayes. *A History of Ancient Israel and Judah.* Philadelphia: Westminster, 1986.

Noth, Martin. *The History of Israel.* New York: Harper & Brothers, 1958.

Commentaries and Studies on Deuteronomy

Brueggemann, Walter. *Deuteronomy.* Abingdon Old Testament Commentary. Nashville: Abingdon, 2001.

Christensen, Duane L. "Deuteronomy in Modern Research: Approaches and Issues." In *A Song of Power and the Power of Song: Essays on the Book of Deuteronomy*, edited by Duane L. Christensen, 3–20. Sources for Biblical and Theological Study. Winona Lake, IN: Eisenbrauns, 1993.

Clements, Ronald E. "The Book of Deuteronomy." In *The New Interpreter's Bible*, vol. 2:269–538. Nashville: Abingdon, 1998.

Driver, S. R. *A Critical and Exegetical Commentary on the Bible. Deuteronomy.* 3rd ed., reprinted. London: T&T Clark, 1895/1978.

Lincicum, David. *Paul and the Early Jewish Encounter with Deuteronomy.* Grand Rapids, MI: Baker Academic, 2010.

Millar, J. Gary. *Now Choose Life: Theology and Ethics in Deuteronomy.* NSBT 6. Downers Grove, IL: InterVarsity, 1998.

Miller, Patrick D. *Deuteronomy.* Interpretation: A Bible Commentary for Teaching and Preaching. Louisville: Westminster, 1990.

Nelson, Richard D. *Deuteronomy: A Commentary.* Old Testament Library. Louisville: Westminster John Knox, 2002.

Olson, Dennis T. *Deuteronomy and the Death of Moses: A Theological Reading.* Overtures to Biblical Theology. Minneapolis: Fortress, 1994.

Person, Raymond F., Jr. *The Deuteronomic School: History, Social Setting, and Literature.* Studies in Biblical Literature 2. Atlanta: Society of Biblical Literature, 2002.

Rad, Gerhard von. *Deuteronomy: A Commentary.* Old Testament Library. Philadelphia: Westminster, 1966.

Sonnet, Jean-Pierre. *The Book within the Book: Writing in Deuteronomy.* Biblical Interpretation Series. Leiden: Brill, 1997.

Thompson, Deanna. *Deuteronomy.* Belief: A Theological Commentary on the Bible. Louisville: Westminster John Knox, 2014.

Tigay, Jeffrey H. *Deuteronomy*. JPS Torah Commentary. Philadelphia: Jewish Publication Society, 1996.

Weinfeld, Moshe. *Deuteronomy and the Deuteronomic School*. Oxford: Oxford University Press, 1972. Reprint, Winona Lake, IN: Eisenbrauns, 1992.

———. *Deuteronomy 1–12: A New Translation with Introduction and Commentary*. Anchor Bible. Vol. 1. New York: Doubleday, 1991.

Wright, G. Ernest. "Introduction and Exegesis of Deuteronomy." In *The Interpreter's Bible*, edited by George Author Buttrick, 2:311–331. Nashville: Abingdon, 1953.

Biblical Ethics

Barton, John. *Ethics and the Old Testament*. Harrisburg, PA: Trinity Press International, 1998.

Hays, Richard B. *The Moral Vision of the New Testament: A Contemporary Vision of New Testament Ethics*. San Francisco: HarperSanFrancisco, 1996.

Niebuhr, H. Richard. *Christ and Culture*. New York: Harper & Brothers, 1951. Expanded edition with foreword by Martin Marty and a preface by James M. Gustafson. New York: Harper & Brothers, 2001.

Pregeant, Russell. *Knowing Truth, Doing Good: Engaging New Testament Ethics*. Minneapolis: Fortress, 2008.

Herem

Boyd, Gregory A. *Cross Vision: How the Crucifixion of Jesus Makes Sense of Old Testament Violence*. Minneapolis: Fortress, 2017.

Gundry, Stanley N., ed. *God and Canaanite Genocide: Show Them No Mercy*. Counterpoints. Grand Rapids, MI: Zondervan, 2003.

Hawk, J. Daniel. *The Violence of the Biblical God: Canonical Narrative and Christian Faith*. Grand Rapids, MI: Eerdmans, 2019.

Hofreiter, Christian. *Making Sense of Old Testament Genocide: Christian Interpretation of Herem Passages*. Oxford: Oxford University Press, 2018.

Lamb, David T. *God Behaving Badly: Is the God of the Old Testament Angry, Sexist, and Racist?* Downers Grove, IL: InterVarsity, 2011.

Nidisch, Susan. *War in the Hebrew Bible*. Oxford: Oxford University Press, 1993.

Rad, Gerhard von. *Holy War in Ancient Israel*. Grand Rapids, MI: Eerdmans, 1991.

Seibert, Eric A. *Disturbing Divine Behavior: Troubling Old Testament Images of God*. Minneapolis: Fortress, 2009.

Smith, Martyn John. *Divine Violence and the* Christus Victor *Atonement Model*. Eugene, OR: Pickwick, 2016 (a 2014 doctoral dissertation directed by David Hilborn at the London School of Theology).

Sparks, Kenton L. *God's Word in Human Words*. Grand Rapids, MI: Baker, 2008.

Thomas, Heath, Jeremy Evans, and Paul Copan, eds. *Holy War in the Bible: Christian Morality and an Old Testament Problem*. Downers Grove, IL: IVP Academic, 2013.

Williams, James G. *The Bible, Violence, and the Sacred: Liberation from the Myth of Sanctioned Violence*. New York: HarperCollins, 1991.

Biblical Theology

Brueggemann, Walter. *The Land: Place as Gift, Promise, and Challenge in Biblical Faith*. Overtures to Biblical Theology. Minneapolis: Fortress, 2002.

———. *Old Testament Theology: Essays on Structure, Theme, and Text*. Minneapolis: Fortress, 1992.

Buber, Martin. *I and Thou*. 2nd ed. Edinburgh: T&T Clark, 1958.

———. *Moses: The Revelation and the Covenant*. New York: Harper, 1958. Reprinted with an introduction by Michael Fishbane. Amherst, NJ: Humanity Books (Prometheus Books), 1998.

Childs, Brevard S. *Biblical Theology of the Old and New Testaments: Theological Reflection on the Christian Bible*. Minneapolis: Fortress, 1992.

Feldmeier, Reinhard, and Hermann Spieckermann. *God Becoming Human: Incarnation in the Christian Bible*. Translated by Brian McNeil. Waco, TX: Baylor University Press, 2021.

———. *God of the Living: A Biblical Theology*. Waco, TX: Baylor University Press, 2011.

Goldingay, John. *Old Testament Theology*. Vol. 1, *Israel's Gospel*. Downers Grove, IL: InterVarsity, 2003.

Hurtado, Larry W. *Lord Jesus Christ: Devotion to Jesus in Earliest Christianity*. Grand Rapids, MI: Eerdmans, 2003.

Keck, Leander. *The Church Confident*. Nashville: Abingdon, 1993.

Martyn, J. Louis. *History and Theology in the Fourth Gospel*. 3rd ed. New Testament Library. Louisville: Westminster John Knox, 2003.

Minear, Paul S. *Images of the Church in the New Testament*. Philadelphia: Westminster, 1960.

Rad, Gerhard von. *Old Testament Theology*, Vol. 1. New York: Harper & Brothers, 1962.

Rowe, C. Kavin. *Christianity's Surprise: A Sure and Certain Hope*. Nashville: Abingdon, 2020.

Author Index

Scripture Index